The
Hindutva
Paradigm

RAM MADHAV

The Hindutva Paradigm

INTEGRAL HUMANISM AND THE QUEST FOR A NON-WESTERN WORLDVIEW

WESTLAND
NON-FICTION

First published by Westland Non-Fiction, an imprint of Westland Publications Private Limited, in 2021

1st Floor, A Block, East Wing, Plot No. 40, SP Infocity, Dr MGR Salai, Perungudi, Kandanchavadi, Chennai 600096

Westland, the Westland logo, Westland Non-Fiction and the Westland Non-Fiction logo are the trademarks of Westland Publications Private Limited, or its affiliates.

ISBN: 9789391234089

10 9 8 7 6 5 4 3 2 1

Typeset in Adobe Garamond Pro by SÜRYA, New Delhi
Printed at Thomson Press (India) Ltd.

Contents

Preface

'All ideologies are idiotic, whether religious or political, for, it is conceptual thinking, the conceptual world, which has so unfortunately divided man,' bemoaned renowned philosopher Master Jiddu Krishnamurti.[1] Europe was the mother of ideologies—from the capitalism of Adam Smith to the social conservatism of Thomas Hobbes and John Locke; the liberalism of John Stuart Mill to the communism of Karl Marx. All these ideologies have finally led to the creation of schisms and confusion in the world, as Master JK pointed out. That's why American historian and social thinker Morris Berman had warned, 'An idea is something you have. An ideology is something that has you.'[2]

India has historically been the land of ideas. From Vedic times through to those of Mahavira, Buddha, Shankara, Aurobindo, Vivekananda and Gandhi, the great men of India have been philosophers, articulating profound ideas for the welfare of mankind. India has not produced any ideologues like Marx or Mill, neither did it articulate any ideologies. Yet, the deeply philosophical ideas of its sages and savants have continuously inspired and influenced mankind across history and geography.

Deen Dayal Upadhyay was one such philosopher. He had articulated the refreshingly stimulating Integral Humanist philosophy. It was not a closed ideology but an open and inclusive idea. More than five decades have passed since its philosophical precis has seen the light of day. The golden jubilee of the Integral Humanism lectures was celebrated in a big way in 2015, and it was followed by the birth centenary of Deen Dayal Upadhyay in 2016– 17. However, both the philosophy and the philosopher continue to remain an enigma, not only to the outside world but even to their own followers.

Very few can really comprehend Deen Dayal's philosophy and there are even fewer of those who can coherently articulate it. There are a couple of reasons for it. Firstly, Deen Dayal presented his thesis on Integral Humanism through a series of four lectures in 1965 at Bombay (now Mumbai). The thoughts that he presented in those lectures needed further reflection and deliberation to be developed into a comprehensive philosophy. Unfortunately, he did not get enough time to complete that task. He lived for less than three years after he first voiced this philosophy. Secondly, Deen Dayal's followers did not make the effort needed to take forward his core thoughts and give them the shape of a complete political philosophy. Instead, they were preoccupied by vague theories like Gandhian Socialism for several years, and subsequently settled for the relatively easier formulation of Cultural Nationalism.

Some individuals had attempted to explain Integral Humanism through academic theses or political writings. A think tank called Deendayal Research Institute (DRI) was established in the 1980s in Delhi. It encouraged several scholars to work on his thesis. Several publications in the form of books and journal articles followed. When Deen Dayal's birth centenary came up in 2016, some serious-minded scholar-politicians, like the former member of parliament (MP) Dr Mahesh Chandra Sharma, devoted long hours to compiling the leader's writings and speeches. A fourteen-volume *Complete Works of Deen Dayal Upadhyay* was published as the centenary project. All of these efforts are praiseworthy.

*

My association with Deen Dayal's ideas goes back to my childhood. My father was a senior Jana Sangh leader in Andhra Pradesh and had several interactions with Deen Dayal Upadhyay in that capacity. I saw old pictures of Upadhyay visiting my home. After his demise, one of the first things that my father did, like many other party workers of that period, was to hang a portrait of Deen Dayal in our drawing room. Until the infamous Emergency in 1975, no Jana Sangh function was conducted without garlanding Deen Dayal's portrait.

As an RSS functionary from the early 1980s, I had several opportunities to listen to lectures by eminent Sangh leaders on Integral Humanism. Dattopant Thengdi, a senior Sangh leader, had insisted on not using the phrase Integral Humanism, since Hindu philosophy cannot be equated with other 'isms'. Thereafter, the phrase 'Ekatm Manav Darshan' came into vogue. 'Integral humanist thought' or 'integral humanist philosophy' became its English equivalent.

Deen Dayal Upadhyay's birth centenary year gave me the opportunity to deliver a few lectures on his philosophy at different places to different sets of audience. In the process, I was able to refresh my knowledge about the very profound ideas that Deen Dayal had articulated in his treatise five decades ago.

Sometime in 2017, my colleague Rajat Sethi came to me with a proposal. Amazon had acquired Chennai-based Westland Publications that year and made it into its Indian publishing arm. Rajat mentioned to me that they were open to the idea of publishing a book on Deen Dayal Upadhyay and his Integral Humanist philosophy as there was no book on the subject in the mainstream. Moreover, with the rise of Hindutva to the centre stage of Indian national politics, its relevance too has increased.

When I signed the contract with Westland in 2018, I assumed that it would be an easy job for someone like me to complete the book in a year's time. But my commitments as the General Secretary of the Bharatiya Janata Party (BJP) and other engagements with the India Foundation did not allow me to pursue this writing project. Moreover, as I began penning my thoughts, I realised that I had ventured into an arena that required a lot of further reading to justify my adventure. Finally, I could complete the first draft of the book in March 2020. When I re-read it, I realised that it needed further embellishment. Two things helped me. The COVID-19 pandemic brought the entire country to a grinding halt in early 2020. Moreover, the Party relieved me from the post of General Secretary after October that year. Consequently, I made use of the subsequent six months to make necessary edits to my first draft and submitted the final version to the publishers.

I must thank Karthika and her team at Westland for their patience with my delay and for their perseverance in pushing hard on printing deadlines to bring the book into the market in a record time. They not only tolerated the delay on my part, but also sought to encourage me by publishing an anthology of my other writings in October 2020, *Because India Comes First: Reflections on Nationalism, Identity and Culture*. Rajat continued with his gentle prodding that helped me finish work on the manuscript by May 2021. A senior Research Fellow at the India Foundation, Deeksha, who is like my daughter, took enormous pains to locate and compile all the references from various books in my library and also from sources on the internet. Without the support of these two, the book would not have taken shape.

This book has fifteen chapters and a concluding essay. The first three chapters deal with the life of Deen Dayal, the political situation in the country during that period and a summary of Deen Dayal's four lectures on Integral Humanism. The remaining twelve chapters deal with various aspects of the Integral Humanist philosophy. I have tried to look at his ideas from the prism of Western philosophical doctrines and contested many contemporary Western ideas in its light.

This book is my humble attempt to give a twenty-first century interpretation to Integral Humanism. I have no claims nor credentials to scholarship. I am not trying to present this book as the ultimate comprehensive exposition on Deen Dayal's thoughts either. As I said earlier, many have attempted it before, and many more may continue to take forward the churning. This book is a modest offering by one such seeker of the wisdom that Integral Humanism radiates. If readers find any useful ideas in the book, the credit should go to Deen Dayal and the many elders with whom I have had the good fortune to interact personally or through their writings. If there is anything unworthy in it, please consider it as my own ignorance.

∾

1

Deen Dayal Upadhyay: The Man

The Rashtriya Swayamsevak Sangh (RSS) is difficult to understand, but easy to misunderstand. When the organisation was founded in September 1925 at Nagpur in central India, it did not have a name nor a constitution or statement of objectives. It began as an activist movement. The name followed months later. The founder of the organisation, Dr Keshav Baliram Hedgewar, popularly and reverentially known as Doctorji by RSS cadres, was a non-practising medical doctor, an activist social reformer and a politician. He started the RSS with the avowed objective of uniting Hindus, not just on any theoretical or ideological basis but on the simple premise that Hindustan, or India, is Hindu Rashtra, a nation of Hindus. That was his core conviction.

There is a popular anecdote that is often narrated in RSS shakhas (units). Once, while addressing a gathering of eminent citizens, Doctorji had insisted that Hindustan was Hindu Rashtra. A lawyer from the audience got up to challenge him. 'Who said Hindustan was Hindu Rashtra?' the lawyer questioned Doctorji. 'I, Dr Hedgewar, say that Hindustan is Hindu Rashtra. Hence it is,' Doctorji is believed to have confidently retorted.

The RSS began to take root across the country as an activist movement based on a strong organisational edifice, incorporating all the nobler aspects of popular Hinduism, including its festivals and literature. The intellectual scaffolding for the institution was developed by Hedgewar's successor, Madhav Sadashiv Golwalkar, the second and the longest serving Sarsanghachalak. Fondly called Guruji by RSS members, it was Golwalkar who presented academic and intellectual arguments that formed the organisation's worldview. Golwalkar was an ascetic, profoundly seeped in Hindu spirituality and religion. He turned to ancient Hindu civilisational wisdom to develop the philosophical locus for the organisation he was spearheading. But Golwalkar too, during his stewardship of the organisation for over 33 years, did not attempt to propound a separate ideology for the organisation.

The initial years of the organisation were dedicated to mobilising cadres for the immediate twin objectives of unification of Hindus and freedom from British rule. By the time India gained independence in 1947, the RSS had grown into a major mainstream movement in the country. This background of the RSS has prompted some scholars to dismiss the organisation as anti-intellectual. But, while the core of the organisation remained activism-centric, right after independence, the RSS also slowly started nurturing intellectual pursuits with the publication of periodicals and other literature.

Deen Dayal Upadhyay, who grew up under the tutelage of Guruji, was one of the first leaders who attempted to develop a structured ideological framework for the RSS movement. As per available historical records, he became a Pracharak—a dedicated full-time functionary—of the RSS sometime in the early 1940s. Pracharaks in the RSS, many of whom are highly talented and educated, remain unmarried and lead unassuming lives, totally dedicated to the cause of the organisation. Swami Chinmayananda, the founder of the Chinmaya Mission, described Pracharaks as 'white-clad *sanyasis*'. Dr Hedgewar was a medical doctor while his successor Guruji Golwalkar, besides being an ordained ascetic of the Ramakrishna Mission, was an academic with post-graduate credentials in chemistry. The third chief, Madhukar Dattatraya Deoras, popularly known as Balasaheb, was a graduate in law while Rajendra Singh, the fourth chief, was a professor of nuclear physics. In fact, Singh was highly regarded by eminent contemporary nuclear scientists, like Homi Bhabha. His decision to quit academics to head the RSS was regarded by many as a loss to the nuclear fraternity and a gain to the RSS fraternity. Similarly, the later chiefs of the RSS, too, had good academic credentials: K.S. Sudarshan was an engineer and Mohan Bhagwat practiced as a veterinarian.

Upadhyay too belonged to the same pantheon. Like his contemporaries in the RSS, he had remained unknown to the outside world until certain events catapulted him into public life in the early 1950s.

DEEN DAYAL: THE STUDENT

Deen Dayal was born into a lower-middle class Brahmin family on 25 September 1916 in a village called Nagala Chandrabhan near Mathura in Uttar Pradesh. It was a sleepy village with over three thousand people, largely farmers and daily wage earners. By the time he turned eight, Deen Dayal had lost both his parents—Bhagwati Prasad and Ram Pyari. He was forced to lead a nomadic life in the initial years of his life, as he had to move from place to place looking for shelter and support from relatives. By the age of 15, he had lived at more than 10 places. This constant migration came as a blessing for the curious and studious child that Deen Dayal was. But it also resulted in delays in his early education as he was forced to remain at the mercy of relatives. After moving around for about two decades, Deen Dayal found a home in the RSS in 1937.

Children who face such upheavals and unpredictability so early in life are likely to end up as vagabonds. But Deen Dayal took the personal travails in his life in his stride and carried on with his education and other activities with utmost fastidiousness. He was an intelligent and hard-working student. The frequent transfers of his guardians took him to different places. He went to schools in Alwar and Pilani in Rajasthan. But wherever he went, he always excelled in studies and secured top ranks, gold medals and scholarships.

Deen Dayal grew up to become a caring and service-minded young man. While he himself had been less-privileged, Deen Dayal took keen interest in helping other students with limited opportunities. He started an association called Zero Club. True to its name, it was a club of students who would secure very low grades at school. He would take time out to tutor these students. This virtue of service remained a lifelong quality that he demonstrated as a public activist in the RSS and later in his political career as well. In fact, a large part of his philosophical thesis of *Ekatm Manav Darshan*—integral humanism—focuses on the concept of service as a sacred obligation of mankind.

The RSS is a unique organisation. Its strength lies not at the top, but at the grassroots. The Shakha, a grassroots programme, is the core activity of the RSS. It is designed in such a way that every participating member is trained to mentally and physically devote at least one hour every day to society and social good. The RSS describes it as Samskar—a higher life-virtue. Deendayal's views in this regard can be summed up as: To eat one's own is *Prakriti* (natural); to steal from others and eat is *Vikriti* (unnatural); and to feed one's own food to others is *Sanskriti* (culture).

This hour-long Shakha is the recruiting ground for the RSS. Trained in the Shakha in values like patriotism, honesty, sense of service and discipline, thousands of RSS volunteers enter into public life and continue to serve the community and the country through organised and individual efforts. In over more than nine decades of its existence, the RSS has produced millions of such volunteers, who are called Swayamsevaks—those who serve the country and community voluntarily. Shakhas are omnipresent in the country today. There is hardly a block in the country that doesn't have RSS Shakhas. Tens of thousands of voluntary functionaries, who run countless activities of the RSS, are present across the country today.

It is in one such Shakha of the RSS in Kanpur that Deen Dayal's initiation into public life began sometime in 1937. He was pursuing his college education at that time and was introduced to the RSS by a classmate, Baluji Mahashabde. It was an association that lasted for the rest of his life. Deen Dayal also got the opportunity to meet and interact with Dr Hedgewar during one of the latter's visits to Kanpur.

In 1940, Dr Hedgewar passed away. He was succeeded by a 35-year-old spiritually inclined academic, Madhav Sadashiv Golwalkar. The Indian independence movement had entered the penultimate phase. On the one hand, Congress had launched the Quit India movement in 1942 in the country; on the other hand, Netaji Subhash Chandra Bose had launched an armed struggle for freedom through the Azad Hind Fauj—Indian National Army—from outside India. The new Sarsanghachalak of the RSS, Guruji Golwalkar, had raised a call for youngsters to join the organisation in large numbers as full-time Pracharaks to serve the country. In this charged atmosphere of patriotism, that call had attracted a large number of youth to the RSS. Deen Dayal was one among them. Attracted by the RSS's vision, he too became a Pracharak in 1942 after graduating from Allahabad in Teacher Education.

DEEN DAYAL: THE PRACHARAK

As described earlier, the Pracharak system is a unique dimension of the RSS organisation. A Pracharak is a celibate, who has voluntarily decided not to have a personal life. There is no salary offered, no bank account and no personal income. The RSS takes care of the basic needs of the Pracharak by way of monthly allocation of meagre funds. Food is taken care of by the households of Shakha participants. Pracharaks have to be perpetually at the disposal of the organisation, accepting any function assigned to them, anywhere in the country. They can't have any personal choices, much less any ambition, and certainly no urge for name and fame. They have to remain an invisible lifeline of the organisation. It is a tough life, filled with a lot of uncertainty. In a way, it is more challenging than the life of an ascetic. Unlike an ascetic or a saint, the Pracharaks remain well within the periphery of the civic life of society, yet they are expected to remain uninfluenced by its mundane attractions. The Pracharaks are expected to be role models for RSS functionaries. Unlike saints and ascetics, the Pracharaks cannot just remain objects of reverence; they must become living examples for others to emulate. Due to the phenomenal growth of the organisation, the life of a Pracharak has certainly become less daunting today; yet it remains challenging, especially in this time and age.

In spite of the hardships involved and the lack of incentives, the Pracharak system has always attracted the best of young and brilliant minds in large numbers due to its appeal to the innate idealism of youth. While it is voluntary in the sense that one can opt out of it anytime, a large number of Pracharaks remain lifetime RSS functionaries. Deen Dayal too joined the ranks of those Pracharaks and remained one until his demise. Anecdotes about his humility, commitment, idealism and resoluteness towards ethics in public and personal life abound. True to RSS tradition, he was a man of values. It is difficult to maintain values in politics. But Deen Dayal was an exception.

FORAY INTO POLITICS

India became independent on 15 August 1947. It was not a peaceful and pleasant moment for India. The country was partitioned along religious lines, causing immense bloodshed and mayhem. While independence was the common objective of all Indians, partition was not. And yet, it happened. The movement for independence, the partition of the motherland and the bloodletting that followed led to an intense ideological churning in the country.

At the root of the partition was the infamous two-nation theory propounded by Mohammad Ali Jinnah, the leader of the Muslim League. Jinnah became the 'Father of Pakistan' and its first Secretary General after partition. In the middle of an intense struggle for independence, India came face-to-face with a crude new challenge when Jinnah and the Muslim League suddenly upped the ante and insisted that Hindus and Muslims were two different nations that could never live together as one. For the first time in history, the Indian nation was faced with a big question about its core identity. Until then, every Indian would proudly describe the country as a multi-religious mosaic with the motto: *Anekta mein ekta*, meaning unity in diversity. For millennia, people professing different faiths had lived congenially as one society and one nation. Yet, when Muslim League threw the gauntlet, challenging this age-old belief in the innate unity in outward diversity, the Indian leadership had dithered and displayed a general lack of conviction to stand up to that divisive challenge. The result was the Partition.

For RSS youth like Deen Dayal, the nation was the Goddess Mother. Partitioning her was an unbearable and unacceptable reality for them.

The post-Independence Congress leadership under Jawaharlal Nehru was willing to reconcile with the aftermath of the two-nation theory and was preparing to build a new, secular nation. In the years immediately following independence, destiny had been cruel to India; it snatched away two stalwarts of the freedom movement—Mahatma Gandhi and Sardar Patel—in a span of just two years. In the process, it was kind to Jawaharlal Nehru. He became the sole and dominant inheritor of the Congress legacy. Gandhi had declared him his political heir. But Nehru's ideological moorings and motivations lay elsewhere. Gandhi would always describe himself as a Sanatani Hindu. But Nehru was different. 'You realise, Galbraith,' Nehru once told his friend, the author John Kenneth Galbraith, 'I am the last Englishman to rule India.'[1] Historian and biographer B.R. Nanda quotes Hindu Mahasabha leader N.B. Khare describing

Nehru as 'English by education; Muslim by culture and Hindu by an accident of birth.'[2] Interestingly, author and politician Shashi Tharoor, in his book *Nehru: The Invention of India*, calls Khare's comment a tribute to Nehru, not an insult. He writes, '… in fact it was a tribute to the eclecticism that had made Jawaharlal Nehru the product of the syncretic traditions to which a twentieth century Indian was heir.'[3]

Nehru wanted independent India to emulate European ideas and institutions. Many other leaders in the country, some of whom were his fellow-travellers in the freedom movement, had different ideas about the future of India. They included leaders like Dr B.R. Ambedkar, Dr Ram Manohar Lohia and Dr Syama Prasad Mukherjee. After independence, all three walked out of the Congress, charted their own political course and subsequently emerged as challengers to Nehruvian thought in the Indian political firmament.

Dr Syama Prasad Mukherjee, a Hindu Mahasabhaite-turned-Congressman, was one of the first to walk out of Nehru's government to start his own political party in 1950—the Bharatiya Jana Sangh. He approached the RSS leadership for support for his fledgling political outfit. Smarting under the untruthful allegations of conspiring in Gandhi's murder and a subsequent 18-month-long ban on the organisation, the RSS leadership was looking for an opportunity to cultivate political support for its mission. Although the leadership was clear about the future of RSS as a non-political socio-cultural outfit, it was not averse to the idea of some of its members entering politics and creating political space for its thought process.

Thus, when Syama Prasad approached the RSS for support, the organisation's leadership decided to seize the opportunity. Some of the important Pracharaks, like Atal Bihari Vajpayee, Lal Krishna Advani, Sundar Singh Bhandari, Nanaji Deshmukh, etc., were encouraged to work in Syama Prasad's new political outfit, the

Bharatiya Jana Sangh. Deen Dayal Upadhyay, a young functionary of the RSS at that time, was also among those assigned to work for the political outfit. Thus began the political career of this young Pracharak, which lasted 17 years.

At the time of deputing some senior functionaries to the Jana Sangh, RSS chief Guruji Golwalkar is believed to have issued an important guideline about the relationship between the two organisations—the RSS and Jana Sangh would function like parallel rail tracks that would never separate, but also never merge. This 'never to become one, yet never to separate' formula guides the relationship between the two organisations even to this day.

Deen Dayal's rise in the new political party's leadership hierarchy was rapid. Syama Prasad was so impressed by the dedication, intelligence and hard work of the young man that he once commented that had he been lucky to have a few more Deen Dayals in Jana Sangh, he would have transformed Indian politics. Deen Dayal became the General Secretary of the Jana Sangh in its very first session in December 1951 when the party was formally launched. He continued to serve in that capacity for a full 16 years until the Calicut session of the party in December 1967. It shows the love and confidence that he enjoyed from successive presidents of the party as also the leaders and cadres alike.

BIRTH OF BHARATIYA JANA SANGH

The emergence of Bharatiya Jana Sangh on the political horizon of the country was a historic development. It was not just another political party—it was one with a distinct philosophy and programme. The dominant political philosophy at that time was led by Jawaharlal Nehru. Whatever he said, did or wrote became the new philosophy of the ruling Congress party. Existing opposition parties like the Hindu Mahasabha, Ram Rajya Parishad and Swatantra Party were no match for the power and influence of the ruling establishment. The communists and socialists did have a say in certain pockets of the country, but they too lacked national appeal or a charismatic leadership to challenge Congress and Nehru. Moreover, while Nehru inherited his political ideas from Europe and the West, the communists borrowed their political philosophy from the Soviet Union—in effect, both were cut off from Indian grassroots realities. Jana Sangh was established to fill this gap and offer a quintessential Indian alternative to the Nehruvian political philosophy.

It was an arduous challenge. Congress didn't just come with a political philosophy; it was also the party that had led India to independence. A majority of Indians were so overawed by the historical aura of the Congress party that the merits or otherwise of the political philosophy that leaders like Nehru were espousing hardly mattered to them. Gandhi understood this. That was why he had insisted that the Congress be disbanded as a political party and reconstituted into the Lok Sewak Sangh, a non-political organisation.

'Though split into two, India having attained political independence through means provided by the Indian National Congress, the Congress in its present shape and form, i.e., as a propaganda vehicle and parliamentary machine, has outlived its use. India has still to attain social, moral and economic independence in terms of its seven hundred thousand villages as distinguished from its cities and towns. The struggle for the ascendancy of civil over military power is bound to take place in India's progress towards its democratic goal. It must be kept out of unhealthy competition with political parties and communal bodies. For these and other similar reasons, the A. I. C .C. resolves to disband the existing Congress organization and flower into a Lok Sevak Sangh....', Gandhi wrote in *Harijan*, a few days before his assassination. In fact, this became famous as his 'Last Will and Testament'.[4]

But the trappings of power were so intense that the Congress leadership was not willing to abide by Gandhi's 'last will' of disbanding the party. Gandhi's suggestion appeared most logical and rational. The Indian National Congress of the independence movement was a common platform for people professing disparate ideologies to come together with the common objective of securing independence. Independence was the result of the combined efforts of all those groups and ideologies. After independence, many of those leaders charted different courses to start their own movements and initiatives guided by their own principles and ideologies. Had Congress not turned itself into a political party using undue credit of independence, a better level-playing field would have been available for all those groups and ideologies to flourish. People would have had an opportunity to judge the parties not on their past glory but on their vision for the future of the country.

For example, leaders like Deen Dayal Upadhyay were much in tandem with Gandhi's thinking than perhaps Nehru himself. 'A comparative study of the teachings of Gandhiji and Deen Dayalji indicates that both the thinkers agreed on the primacy of man, the paramountcy of Dharma (or truth), *Gram Swaraj*, decentralisation, *swadeshi*, holding of wealth in trust for society, *sarvodaya, antyodaya*. Integral humanism is the further scientific evolution—an updated, revised and enlarged version of Gandhiji's thought endowed with a firm philosophical base,' Kandarpa Ramachandra Rao, an erudite scholar, writes in his book on *Integral Humanism*.[5]

Nehru, on the other hand, had held most of these ideals in contempt. He was more influenced by European or Western thinking than the quintessential Indian ideals of Gandhi. He used to stoutly defend Western civilisation as superior when compared to others in the world. Yet, after the Congress had donned the avatar of a political party after independence, people automatically assumed that Nehru was not only the political heir but also the ideological heir of Gandhi.

The tag of 'party of independence' gave a distinct advantage to Congress, and became a daunting challenge for the newly formed Bharatiya Jana Sangh.

Deen Dayal became the General Secretary of the newly created Bharatiya Jana Sangh in 1951 and steered it through the rough and tumble of the initial 17 years. It was not an easy task. Nor was it smooth sailing. The founder and mentor of the largely non-political motley assembly of leaders from the RSS, Dr Syama Prasad Mukherjee, passed away while in detention in Srinagar, under suspicious circumstances. This took place in 1953, just 18 months after the founding of the party. He was leading an agitation launched by the Jammu Kashmir Praja Parishad for complete integration of the state of Jammu and Kashmir into the Indian Republic. It came as a bolt from the blue for the party in general and Deen Dayal in particular. Deen Dayal was just 37 years old at that time and practically without any political experience. The responsibility of building up and guiding the nascent political party fell on his shoulders. Nehru and the other Congress leaders were already fiercely attacking the Jana Sangh. Nehru had even declared publicly that he would not allow 'an inch of space for the saffron flag to fly'.[6] The Jana Sangh flag in those days was saffron in colour with a traditional lamp as its symbol. Even under such trying circumstances, Deen Dayal persevered and diligently led the party, which was soon catapulted into the position of the principal ideological opposition to the grand old party of India, the Indian National Congress.

Deen Dayal, like many other leaders of the nationalist movement, had strong antipathy for the communist ideology of class hatred. Hence, for him and for the Jana Sangh, the communists were as important political adversaries as the misguided leaders of the Congress. Both had to be defeated. It is this political approach that had dominated the thinking of the RSS-inspired leaders and cadres of the Jana Sangh in the initial years and had led to its emergence as a non-Congress and non-Leftist ideological fulcrum.

TURBULENT YEARS

Even as Deen Dayal worked towards building the Jana Sangh, he had to face intense pressures from within and without. The sudden demise of Syama Prasad had left a void as there was no leader of national stature to lead the party. The issue of Jana Sangh's future became a big subject of discussion after the demise of its founder. After the demise of Dr Syama Prasad, senior leaders from parties like Hindu Mahasabha and Ram Rajya Parishad had argued that the three outfits be merged into one party. Ram Rajya Parishad was a party founded by a Hindu religious leader, Swami Karpatri. It toed an orthodox Hindu line in politics and was unabashedly anti-Dalit and did not open its doors to those sections. The Hindu Mahasabha, on the other hand, was a pan-Hindu party, but expressly anti-minority. It refused admission to Muslims and Christians in the party. The Bharatiya Jana Sangh was to be a party for all Indians irrespective of caste and religion. The efforts towards the merger of the three parties did not fructify on this fundamental contradiction itself. Later, Karpatri would harshly blame the Jana Sangh leadership for its 'irreligious' behaviour and cite that as the reason for the failure of the merger.

In a way it came as a boon for Jana Sangh. The relentless hard work by the RSS-inspired young leaders in Jana Sangh, under the guidance of Deen Dayal Upadhyay, had resulted in firmly establishing the party in a few years' time. The first general elections in 1952 did not yield encouraging results for the party. It ended up winning only three seats in the country, one of which was Syama Prasad's from Kolkata.[7] But that the Party had secured more than 3 per cent of the popular vote, thus fulfilling the mandatory guideline of the Election Commission of India (ECI) to be recognised as a national party, was a source of solace.[8] By the time the second general elections came along in 1957, the party had grown in size and strength.

Describing the mood in the party during those challenging years, Deen Dayal would say: 'There was a general belief in political circles that the Bharatiya Jana Sangh will not continue after the death of its founder Dr Syama Prasad Mukherjee. We have spent the last five years fighting this apprehension. The results of the second general elections have proved that the Bharatiya Jana Sangh has not only survived, but is progressing as well. We could not have been true to our leader if this had not happened.'[9]

Jana Sangh's growth in the initial years was slow and steady. It did not register any spectacular electoral victories in the first decade of its existence. In the second general election in 1957 too, although the Party had 127 candidates contesting, mainly in the Hindi heartland, it could win just four Lok Sabha seats. Of the 650 candidates who contested for state legislatures, 57 romped home victorious. Although Jana Sangh's vote share had doubled to more than 6 per cent, it was not a big prospect for a party wanting to challenge the Congress. In fact, the Swatantra Party, a much later entrant into Indian politics in 1959, started attracting more dissident leaders from different parties and was thus more visible and active. The communists had already occupied the Opposition and their strength was continuously on the rise in the first decade of electoral politics in independent India. But the fact remained that under Deen Dayal's leadership, the Jana Sangh was laying firm foundations for its long-term growth.

DEEN DAYAL: THE IDEALIST

One of the reasons for the slow and steady growth of Jana Sangh was the attitude and conviction of Deen Dayal Upadhyay that politics should not be seen just as a means for capturing power. He would always insist on practising value-based and principled politics, and he was not one to endorse shortcuts. The central thrust of his politics was national interest. For securing that, he wanted politics to be healthy and principled. Deen Dayal, in fact, was a reluctant politician. His mentor and guru, Golwalkar, had said this at a condolence meeting at Jaunpur in Uttar Pradesh after his demise. 'Deen Dayalji was the most reluctant politician, and had many times expressed his distress at the kind of work he has been entrusted with. He would rather prefer to go back to his previous work as a Sangh Pracharak. I told him that I could see nobody else who would do the work as well as he could. It needed an unshakable faith and complete dedication for a man to remain in this mess and yet be untouched by it,' he said.[10]

Deen Dayal used the initial years to lay strong moral and ethical foundations for the new party. He was more like a mentor and teacher in the party than a leader. He would educate the cadres about democracy, value-based politics, national interest and threats from alien ideologies like Communism. It was his belief that the path of principled politics may be long-winding, but it is long-lasting and good for the nation. Hence, the cadre were encouraged to work with dedication and devotion, not for any short-term gains for the party but for securing the long-term interests of the country.

Speaking at the Mumbai session of the party in 1954, at a time when the party was facing serious challenges like electoral defeats, the death of their founder and talks of merger with Hindu Mahasabha and Ram Rajya Parishad, Deen Dayal chose to enthuse party cadres by placing before them the hoary ideal of the bright future of the nation. 'Adult franchise is a big step towards educating the electorate politically. We will have to educate the public appropriately for the success of democracy. Our attitude has been vitiated as a result of over a thousand years of slavery. Narrowmindedness and obscurantism have harmed our progress. Discriminations on the basis of caste and untouchability have shaken the foundations of our society. English education has given us wrong values of life. There is lack of discipline and self-restraint. We no longer believe in the dignity of labour. We must establish the right values for educating our countrymen. We must make them aware of the oneness of this country, extending from Kashmir to Kanyakumari. Enlightened public opinion is the guarantee of a bright future of our nation. There is lack of wealth everywhere but this cannot be addressed from outside. We must put together all our resources, save and spend less. We must focus our attention on our ultimate objective and march ahead with self-confidence and dedication.'[11] Hardly a political speech.

Besides educating cadres about virtuous behaviour in public life, Deen Dayal also started framing a code of conduct for elected members of his party. By 1957, the Jana Sangh had started winning in good numbers in local elections in north Indian states, especially in Uttar Pradesh. Party leaders had entered a couple of state legislatures besides Uttar Pradesh by 1957. Deen Dayal felt the need for proper training of legislators, and the first such training class was held in 1960 at Pune. It was indeed a new thing in Indian politics in those days.

As part of the legislators' code of conduct, Deen Dayal would exhort: 'Walking out of the House and a tendency to create chaos through shouting and sloganeering, which are always aimed at capturing newspaper space, are not to be considered proper by Jana Sangh. We have advised our members to stay away from such a conduct; they should not protest in this unbecoming manner during the address of the Governor or President to the House in the name of registering protest. Dedication to democracy means that we must respect the parliamentary form of government scrupulously. Democracy cannot function without such conventions.'[12]

As a leader committed to principled politics, Deen Dayal was categorically opposed to party hopping and defections. The Swatantra Party, a new entrant in 1959, was solely dependent on disgruntled leaders defecting from various political parties. Deen Dayal viewed it as an unethical method for short-term interests. He would not allow Jana Sangh to tread such a path. 'We must be more disciplined and organised as a party. A single instance of indiscipline would weaken our party and people would lose faith in us. If we are self-disciplined, we can train the people to be disciplined. People must identify themselves with principles of the party. Party hopping and defections would weaken the faith in democracy. For the defectors, it is their personal interest, not the party's, that is paramount. Society has been shocked by such betrayal. We must re-establish people's faith in democracy through hard work and sacrifice,' he advised Jana Sangh cadres.[13]

Discipline, dignity and decorum are the hallmarks of democracy, according to Deen Dayal. When a Jana Sangh member of the Madhya Pradesh Legislative Assembly, Pandarirao Kridhant, threw a shoe at the Deputy Speaker of the House, Deen Dayal was greatly pained. During a subsequent address, he referred to this incident and disapproved of the action of the member. 'Whatever may be the reasons for the Member's frustration and anger, his conduct was against all parliamentary conventions. It is also against the Jana Sangh's code of conduct. None of our workers should resort to this kind of behaviour. We must exercise self-discipline,' he cautioned.

The parliamentary elections in 1962 were an important milestone in Indian politics in general and Jana Sangh's politics in particular. The Congress under Jawaharlal Nehru was a waning force. The Opposition was occupied by hordes of parties. Sensing an opportunity in the sliding popularity of the Congress, the non-Congress and non-Jana Sangh parties had formed alliances purely on the basis of short-term electoral interests. The Hindu Mahasabha and Ram Rajya Parishad decided to contest elections together. The communists were having a field day clinching alliances with whosoever was available. The so-called right-wing Swatantra Party became their partner in Andhra Pradesh, the Akali Dal in Punjab and Republican Party in Maharashtra. They had even proposed an alliance with Congress in Kerala on the pretext of halting Jana Sangh. On the other hand, the Swatantra Party too was on an alliance spree. They had entered into alliances with the Akali Dal,

DMK and the communists. The Republican Party had an alliance with Praja Socialist Party (PSP) in Vidarbha and with the remnants of the Muslim League in Uttar Pradesh.

For the idealist in Deen Dayal, it was a great learning experience. 'There are no permanent friends or foes in diplomacy; there are only permanent interests,' Henry Kissinger has said. It applies as much to politics. That parties could so easily and uninhibitedly form alliances without any commitment to principles and programmes, came as a rude awakening to the idealist in Deen Dayal. The changing contours of the Indian political landscape were still unacceptable to him. He refused any such alliance for Jana Sangh. In those days, there used to be a lot of gossip in political corridors about his close friendship with socialist patriarch Dr Ram Manohar Lohia. The Jana Sangh and the Lohia faction of the Socialist Party had worked together in the 1963 elections of the Uttar Pradesh legislature. There were speculations about the possibility of the two parties forming an anti-Congress front together.

But Deen Dayal was not convinced. 'Different parties have different viewpoints. People don't take them into account. Out of goodwill they sometimes feel that certain political parties should get together. But there are certain fundamental issues that justify separate existence of the parties. Only goodwill is not enough. That is why we have decided that we won't live in any imaginary world and enter into an alliance whose success is doubtful. It would be good to work together on issues where a consensus is possible; otherwise we should operate from our respective platforms,' Deen Dayal insisted.[14]

IDEALIST-TURNED-PRAGMATIST

However, this steadfastness of Deen Dayal's idealism had to finally give way to pragmatism in the later years. He realised shortly afterwards that while some parties hobnob with each other only for the sake of power, larger national interest can also become a catalyst for ideologically disparate parties to come together. He would himself experiment with such alliances later, in the larger interest of promoting a non-Congress alternative in the country. The 1960s witnessed massive popular activism on different issues. The Indo-China War of 1962 had brought various non-Congress parties together and the subsequent years witnessed massive political activity across the country. Nehru's demise in 1964 had led to an internal power struggle within the Congress party. By the time of the 1967 general elections, the Jana Sangh had emerged as a major political opposition to the Congress. The party secured 35 seats in these elections and it stood second in another 75 seats.[15] The party's vote share too had grown considerably.

Deen Dayal had analysed the results in his own way: 'It is clear that the Jana Sangh is not only ahead of all other non-Congress parties but also secured more votes than both the Communist parties, Socialist Party and Praja Socialist Party put together.'

The general elections in 1967 also saw a massive decline in the strength of the Congress in a number of state legislatures. Several states witnessed hung verdicts, and in many of them, no single party could come anywhere near the majority mark. That created a peculiar situation in which a coming together of all the different non-Congress parties to form governments became not just a possibility but also an inevitability. It was an unprecedented scenario. The Jana Sangh was within striking distance of gaining power. Finally, Deen Dayal's idealism had to give way to realpolitik. The result was the birth of the first ever non-Congress alliance, the Samyukt Vidhayak Dal (SVD).

The SVD included parties like Bharatiya Jana Sangh, PSP, Samyukt Socialist Party (SSP), Jan Congress, Republican Party of India (RPI), Jan Kranti Dal (JKD), Congress (O), Bharatiya Kranti Dal (BKD), Lok Tantrik Congress (LTC), Swatantra Party, DMK, Communist Party of India (CPI), Communist Party of India (Marxist) (CPM) and the Akali Dal. While several of these parties had very little in common, they had joined hands with the objective of forming governments in states. For the first time, ideologically opposite poles like the Jana Sangh, Swatantra Party and the communist parties had come together under one umbrella. These parties, together with a couple of other smaller regional ones, had succeeded in forming and running SVD governments in as many as eight states—Bihar, Haryana, Kerala, Tamil Nadu, Orissa, Punjab, Uttar Pradesh and West Bengal—between 1967 and 1971.

The SVD experiment had provided an opportunity for the Jana Sangh to come to power but it had also raised the hackles of many a party worker, as the arrangement was seen as a compromise with party ideology and beliefs, especially in those states where the Jana Sangh had to rub shoulders with its ideological foes, the communists.

Naturally, the responsibility of convincing agitated party colleagues fell on the idealist-turned-pragmatist-realpolitik Deen Dayal. He had to refine his own earlier aversion for coalitions for the sake of forming governments in order to justify Jana Sangh's decision to join SVD governments in various states. In his autobiography, veteran leader L.K. Advani, a long-time colleague of Deen Dayal, recalls the animated discussion that took place at the Calicut party conference in December 1967 over this issue.

Vishwanathan, a Tamilian settled in Punjab, delivered a powerful speech criticising Deen Dayal's decision. An articulate and compelling speaker, he forcefully put across his viewpoint stating, 'Let not the Jana Sangh delude itself that by cohabiting with Communists, we will be able to change them.' He used a vivid metaphor to drive home his point: '*Kharbooja chakkoo par gire, ya chakkoo kharbooja par; katega to kharbooja hi* (whether the melon falls on the knife or the knife falls on the melon, it is the melon that gets cut).'

Deen Dayal had to use a combination of wisdom and realpolitik to convince the cadres about the efficacy of the SVD experiment. 'It is an irony of the country's political situation that while untouchability in the social field is considered to be evil, it is sometimes extolled as a virtue in the political field. If a party does not wish to practise untouchability towards its rival in the political establishment, it is supposed to be doing something wrong. We, in Jana Sangh, certainly do not agree with the communists' strategy, tactics and their political culture. But that does not justify an attitude of untouchability towards them. If they are willing to work with us on the basis of issues, or as part of a government committed to an agreed programme, I see nothing wrong in it. The SVD governments are a step towards ending political untouchability. The spirit of accommodation shown by all parties, despite their sharp differences, is a good omen for democracy,' he argued with the recalcitrant members of his own party.

By 1967, the party had grown in stature and strength. It secured close to 10 per cent of the popular vote and emerged as the second-largest party after the Congress in terms of its vote share. But all was not going well within the Jana Sangh. A party born out of the womb of the RSS school of thought had to endure a period of internecine squabbles at the highest levels. Balraj Madhok, a senior leader of the party who was one of the founder members since 1951, and a Member of Parliament from Delhi in 1961 and 1967, became the party president in 1966. The party went to polls in 1967 under his leadership and secured good victories. However, Madhok's relationship with his colleagues in the party, including Deen Dayal, Vajpayee, Nanaji Deshmukh, etc. had soured beyond repair. He had rubbed the RSS leadership the wrong way by insisting on limiting its role in party affairs. The party leadership was in a big bind over the prospect of groupism in the ranks.

For a leadership steeped in the RSS culture of discipline, the prospect of internal discord, that too at a time when the party was rising as an alternative to the Congress, was simply unacceptable. This led to a change of guard towards the end of 1967. Deen Dayal

Upadhyay became the party's choice in taking over as the president, replacing Madhok. The change formally took place at the party conclave at Calicut in December 1967.[16]

Deen Dayal's elevation was heartily welcomed by cadres across the country. It couldn't have happened without the approval of the RSS leadership. In the RSS's scheme of things, the Pracharaks are expected only to work as the organisation's backbone, never to come in the forefront. However, in Deen Dayal's case, an exception was made because of the peculiar situation that had developed in the party at that juncture. Several years later, Guruji would throw some light on the thinking of the RSS leadership at that time. 'He [Deen Dayal] really never wanted this high honour, nor did I wish to burden him with it. But circumstances so contrived that I had to ask him to accept the president post. He obeyed it like a true *Swayamsevak*, which he was,' Guruji said.

In his inspiring presidential address, Deen Dayal laid out his forward-looking vision. 'We are energised by the glory of India's past, but we do not regard it as the pinnacle of our national life. We have a realistic understanding of the present, but we are not tied to the present. Our eyes are entranced by the golden dreams about India's future, but we are not given to sleep and sloth; we are *karmayogis* who are determined to translate those dreams into reality. We are worshippers of India's timeless past, dynamic present and eternal future. Confident of victory, let us pledge to endeavour in this direction,' he exhorted the cadres present.[17]

But this arrangement was to remain short-lived. Destiny seemed to have had other plans for Jana Sangh. In just a couple of months after becoming the president, at a time when he was all set to lead the party to newer heights, Deen Dayal was removed from the scene by a quirk of fate. He was found dead by the side of the railway track near Mughal Sarai station in Uttar Pradesh on 11 February 1968.

A pall of gloom descended over the rank and file of the party.

Deen Dayal preferred to travel by rail most of the time, stating that it provided him with the opportunity to interact with workers who came to meet him at several stations, and also offered him ample time to read and write. The Justice Chandrachud committee, appointed to look into the circumstances of his death, concluded that there was no political angle to it. However, it failed to identify the reason or the culprits, thus leaving more questions than answers.

Deen Dayal was just 52 at the time of his death. He was the second top Jana Sangh leader to die under mysterious circumstances, the first being the founder, Dr Syama Prasad Mukherjee. Incidentally, Syama Prasad too was just 52 at the time of his demise.

2

Twentieth Century:
100 Years of Political Tumult

The last couple of centuries have been witness to a variety of political ideas being experimented with across the world. Several among them were developed into governance models during the nineteenth and twentieth centuries. Interestingly, some of those ideas have had shorter shelf lives and met their sticky end within the same period. Empires collapsed, monarchs were defeated, and freedom, liberty and democracy became flavours of the season in large parts of the world by the end of the last century. The twentieth century, especially, had become so tumultuous that it prompted the Soviet Communist ideologue Leon Trotsky to observe, 'Anyone desiring a quiet life has done badly to be born in the twentieth century'[1].

CHURNING OF IDEAS IN THE WEST

It was the Enlightenment phase in European history that had given birth to nationalism in many countries, romance with which lasted till the end of the Second World War. Nationalism of the nineteenth century was a liberal idea encompassing Enlightenment ideals like freedom, rule of law, human rights, etc. A lot had been

written in that century about the virtues of liberal nationalism that
was seen as essential for modern states to become nation-states. In
America, the discourse largely centred on national patriotism versus
sectoral patriotism, or illiberal or ethnic nationalism versus liberal
or civic nationalism. It was euphemistically called 'Americanism'.

In Europe, the romance began with Otto von Bismarck, a
German statesman, in the late nineteenth century. Bismarck was the
mastermind behind the unification of Germany in 1871. It took six
decades of wars, revolutions and, ultimately, the skilful manoeuvring
by this Prussian minister-president for German political unity to be
achieved. The Franco-Prussian War of 1870 had acted as a catalyst
in forcing the 38 German states to forge the union of 'blood and
iron', as Bismarck described it. The 'Iron Chancellor', as Bismarck
was referred to later, had created Europe's largest nation matching
in prestige and strength with Britain and France. He became its first
chancellor and ruled until 1890. Bismarck ran a government that
was liberal in terms of material needs of the people, but it did not
grant them any political liberty. The rise of Germany as a united
nation had led to greater attraction towards nationalism in the
West. Many nation-states had emerged around the world by then.
Interestingly, some, like America, became states first and tried to
build a national identity later. Historian David Armitage described
them as 'state-nations'.

By the early decades of the twentieth century, liberal democratic
nationalism started dithering. Together with the two world wars,
the devastating impact of the Great Depression of the 1930s had
turned liberal nationalism into a bankrupt idea. Its place was taken
over by fascism in Western Europe and communism in Eastern
Europe. 'As democratic republics dithered and stumbled during
1920s and 1930s, Fascist and Communist regimes seized control
of their own destinies and appeared to offer compelling alternative
models of modern political, economic and social organisation,'
wrote Gideon Rose, editor of the prestigious journal *Foreign Affairs*.[2]

Unfortunately, the two alternatives that emerged in response to capitalist liberal nationalism proved more draconian and dangerous. It did not take long for both fascism and communism to descend into 'organised barbarism'.

Nationalism was not a bad thing until mid-twentieth century. But the two world wars changed that narrative. Nationalism had suddenly become a cuss word. Multilateralism emerged as the new term in vogue. It got institutionalised at the beginning of the twentieth century when the League of Nations came into existence, immediately after the First World War. When the League of Nations failed to prevent the more expansive Second World War, it had to give way to a more robust multilateral institution—the United Nations (UN). The birth of the UN in 1945 was seen by many as mankind's answer to war and conflict in the world. Ideas like internationalism, multilateralism and globalisation replaced the discourse on nationalism.

The twentieth century also witnessed the rise of mass politics instead of politics by a few. Elitism gave way to populism. The age of demagogy had arrived. Italy and Germany became frontrunners in championing mass politics under authoritarian demagogues like Benito Mussolini and Adolf Hitler, and a new form of illiberal nationalism, based on race and national superiority, surfaced. On the other hand, the Communist Revolution of 1917 brought Lenin onto the centre-stage in Russia. In America, it started taking the form of economic and trade protectionism, isolationism, antipathy for immigration, etc. The Fascist regime theories of perverted and illiberal nationalism championed by elected dictators like Hitler and Mussolini had threatened the reign of liberal nationalism, albeit temporarily. Scholars, who were singing paeans of nationalism until a few decades ago, started writing its obituary. 'Nations and nation-states are anachronisms in the atomic age,' declared Harvard political scientist Rupert Emerson.[3] Leaders like Franklin Roosevelt, the president of America during the Second World War, started talking about a 'liberal international order.' Creation of international multilateral institutions, starting with the UN, began in earnest. It all had culminated in the emergence of 'globalisation' towards the end of the twentieth century.

The last two decades of the twentieth century saw the world being swept away by globalisation. It had helped narrow the gulf between the developed and the developing world; made nations more technology-driven and had captivated every democratic and open nation. Although it had its fair share of naysayers, globalisation, after all, wasn't all that bad. It helped many countries rise faster. The new 'Asian Tigers' had emerged in the last decades of the twentieth century as strong global economic players. The global power axis had started shifting away from the Pacific-Atlantic region towards the Asia-Pacific region. Despite opposition from some sections internally, countries like India too benefitted significantly from globalisation. The windfall of benefits from globalisation is conspicuous in its presence in the developing countries in the last few decades. Average per capita income grew three-fold in India in the last three decades of the last century.

The USA was known for its skyscrapers until the last century. Until the 1970s and 1980s, close to 90 per cent of the world's tallest buildings were in the US, with a few others in Latin America and Europe. But by the early twenty-first century, things had drastically changed. With their economies booming, countries in Asia and the Middle East became home to a large number of skyscrapers. 'Today about 50% of the world's tallest buildings are in Asia, another 30% are in the Middle East, a meagre 16% are in the US, and a handful are in Europe. In 2015, three quarter of all skyscraper completions were located in Asia (China and Indonesia principally), followed by the UAE and Russia. As of 2018, the US only had three (Hartsfield-Jackson International Airport in Atlanta, Georgia; Los Angeles International Airport; and O'Hare International Airport in Chicago) of the eleven busiest airports in the world, a number of which (Beijing Capital International Airport, Dubai International Airport, and Shanghai Pudong International Airport) were fledgling airports twenty years ago,' writes Michael O' Sullivan in *The Levelling*.[4]

The advent of the era of multilateralism had coincided with a significant geopolitical development in the world. American scholars had always nurtured the idea of global supremacy of the 'American Way'. The renowned American intellectual and abolitionist of the nineteenth century, Frederick Douglass had echoed that way back in 1869, when he declared in front of a big audience, 'We shall spread the network of our science and civilisation over all who seek their shelter, whether from Asia, Africa, or the isles of the sea. All shall here bow to the same law, speak the same language, support the same government, enjoy the same liberty, vibrate with the same national enthusiasm, and seek the same national ends'.[5] This idea of pan Americanism had come to be interpreted as the 'liberal international order' in the aftermath of the Second World War by President Roosevelt. By the end of the twentieth century, however, scholars like Francis Fukuyama started talking about the creation of a new world order.

Communism came as a response to liberal democratic nationalism, which had propagated capitalism and market-centrism. The state was a secondary institution in nationalist Europe where free market capitalism had ruled the roost. Lenin's Bolshevik Revolution of 1917 had challenged the supremacy of the market and the man. As British economist Harold Laski pointed out, unlike the French Revolution of 1789, the Bolshevik Revolution was inspired by a 'body of coherent principles'.[6] Lenin loathed democracy and described it as 'a machine for the suppression of the working class'.[7] Like his master, Karl Marx, he too believed that capitalism would produce its own gravediggers. Communist regimes had been notoriously brutal with their masses. Lenin and subsequent leaders of communism had run their countries with an iron hand. For them ideas like freedom, equality and democratic governance were bourgeois myths. Once he had full control over the Soviet Union, Lenin started arguing that revolutionary communism could not be halted at its frontiers. Like American liberal thinkers, he too had nurtured an ambition of global domination. The Communist International (Comintern) had been created in 1919 to spread communism globally. The world by then had been split into two major blocs—the democratic capitalist countries of the West on one side, led by the US, and communist dictatorships on the other, led by the USSR. An era of Cold War had endured for decades bringing the world to the brink of the Third World War on a couple of occasions.

In the mid-1980s, fissures started erupting in the USSR body politic, ultimately leading to its dismemberment and collapse in the early 1990s. The West's aggressive globalisation push had started around the same time. Sceptics believe that the West had seen the collapse of the USSR and the end of bipolarity in global politics as an opportunity to once again attempt a West-centric global standardisation. Several scholars in the West were gung-ho over this prospect. Francis Fukuyama's famous article in 1989, in the reputed *The National Interest* journal, was provocatively titled 'The End of History?' Later, in 1992, he expanded his thesis into a book titled *The End of History and the Last Man*. Fukuyama's argument was that with the collapse of the Soviet Union, humanity had reached 'not just ... the passing of a particular period of post-war history, but the end of history as such: that is, the end point of mankind's ideological evolution and the universalisation of Western liberal democracy as the final form of human government'.[8]

The unipolar world that Fukuyama had pompously propagated in his article was the dominant thought in the West at the time of the unfolding of globalisation in the last decades of the twentieth century. Many scholars in the world were sceptical about the validity of Fukuyama's arguments regarding the dominance of the Western liberal ideology over mankind. History proved them right and Fukuyama wrong.

In over three decades since its conception, globalisation too appears to have reached the end of its tether since the dawn of the twenty-first century with more and more countries increasingly turning inwards. Global institutions like the UN are losing their relevance and influence. Nationalism is making a grand comeback, albeit in a modified and mellowed down form. Countries are looking for a new meaning for their identity and existence. They are realising that in the cacophony of globalisation and the international order, they have lost their traditional cultural moorings and a civilisational anchor. A new awakening is set to sweep the world. The world of the twenty-first century is going to be different from that of the last couple of centuries in many ways.

INDEPENDENT INDIA'S GLOBAL PURPOSE

At the time when the world was passing through these ideological and political churnings in the mid-twentieth century, India was being reborn. India took its place on the stage of the world theatre as an independent nation in 1947. Eminent Indians witnessing global developments had envisioned a new role for independent India in steering the world through confusion and conflict. Indians, too, have historically nurtured the ambition of spreading the influence of their cultural, religious and civilisational values throughout the world. '*Krinvanto Viswamaryam*—Let us Ennoble the World' has been the motto of Hindu scriptures from time immemorial. For many, it is verily the raison d'etre of India's existence. Independence and the creation of a unified political entity of India after almost a millennium of subjugation and slavery, first by the invading hordes from West Asia and later by the colonist British, considerably enthused large sections of Indic scholars. Many saw in India's independence, not just a release from British colonial rule but a virtual rebirth of the ancient civilisational nation of Bharat. Sri

Aurobindo, an erudite revolutionary-turned-sage and a profound scholar-thinker, was one such leader who saw India's place in the global order.

'Indian renaissance is arising. The sun of India's destiny would rise and fill India with its light and overflow India and overflow Asia and overflow the world. The function of India is to supply the world with a perennial source of light and renovation. Whenever the first play of energy is exhausted and earth grows old and weary, full of materialism, racked with problems she cannot solve, the function of India is to restore the youth to mankind and assure it of immortality. Such a time is now at hand,'[9] exhorted Sri Aurobindo, at the dawn of India's independence. Talking of India's nationalism, he said, 'To recover Indian thought, Indian character, Indian energy, Indian greatness and to solve problems that perplex the world in an Indian spirit and from an Indian stand-point—this is the mission of nationalism.'[10] Renowned Hindu saint Vivekananda had declared decades earlier that India was *'Jagat Janani'*—the Universal Mother.

It was this sense and sentiment of a global purpose of India that had motivated countless men and women to plunge into the independence movement and sacrifice their time, family, career and even life towards its cause. Swaraj, for them, was not just a political goal to be achieved but a moral and spiritual obligation to be performed, and a mission to be accomplished. Gandhi, who entered India's independence movement in the 1920s, was one leader who had appreciated this innate national sentiment of Indians for a grand revival of their ancient civilisational nation to fulfill a global destiny. In the era of competing political ideologies of the twentieth century, Gandhi was the only leader from the southern hemisphere to come up with a distinctly political programme to offer to the world. His Ahimsa (non-violence) and Satyagraha (truthful resistance) were original political ideas that had become catalysts for countless social and political revolutions in the world in the last century. Following in his footsteps, at least four eminent persons, from four different countries—Dominique Pire, a priest in Belgium; Adolfo Perez Esquivel, a teacher in Argentina; Martin Luther King, Jr, a black civil rights activist in the US; and Nelson Mandela, a black political leader in South Africa—who were all Gandhians, won the prestigious Nobel Peace Prize. Gandhi though never got the honour.

Gandhi introduced a lot of religious and spiritual symbolism into the independence movement that he was leading in India. His discourses would contain chants and songs like *Raghupati Raghava Raja Ram* with a nationalistic interpolation such as in *Isvar Allah Tere Naam*.

Many Westerners who studied India's independence movement closely also came to similar conclusions about its ambition. Describing renowned freedom fighter Lokmanya Bal Gangadhar Tilak's political philosophy, Theodore L. Shay wrote in his book *The Legacy of Lokmanya*, 'There is no doubt as to which course Tilak and the nationalists would choose for free India. These men foresaw a great destiny which was not alone political. First they saw free India as a bastion of freedom and justice in the world, as a source of strength, material and moral, in the affairs of the world. Tilak believed that "from the point of view of the peace of Asia and the world, it is absolutely necessary that India should be self-governed internally and made a bulwark of liberty in the East". But more than this, Tilak foresaw India's role in the world as a messenger of a world re-awakening, or a world re-discovery of spiritual values ... he knew the *Sanatana* Dharma was not solely India's possession but that it belonged to the world, that it was eternal, and that which is eternal is universal; and he saw in it the answer to the progress of mankind for guidance, for peace and for justice.'[11]

Eminent historian Arnold Toynbee would also mirror a similar sentiment in one of his writings. 'My first point is that India occupies a key position in the world, and has always done so. My second point is that India is an epitome of the present day world. My third point is that in India there is an attitude towards life, and an approach to the handling of human affairs that answers to the needs of the present situation—and this not only inside India, but in the world as a whole,'[12] he wrote.

EUROPEAN INFLUENCE ON NEHRU

Independent India, during the initial years, had witnessed enormous churning over fundamental questions about its future, role and mission. There clearly emerged two distinct schools, one led by the country's first prime minister, Jawaharlal Nehru, and the other by Mahatma Gandhi. As discussed in the previous chapter, there arose serious differences of opinion between the two stalwarts of India's freedom movement. Gandhi wanted the quintessential Indian civilisational idea to guide its future whereas Nehru was inspired by European ideas like socialism, etc.

Their disagreements had begun much before Independence, in the late 1920s. Although essentially about the development model for free India, these differences were much deeper in nature and displayed the divergent worldviews that each subscribed to. Gandhi believed that India had enough wisdom to guide its own destiny whereas Nehru believed that Indian wisdom was outdated and outmoded. Gandhi turned to religion and spirituality every time he needed answers, whereas Nehru was an agnostic. Gandhi was always open to new ideas but generally disapproved of elements of Western civilisation, whereas Nehru was an ardent admirer of the West.

On 12 January 1928, Nehru wrote a letter to Gandhi in which he communicated his opinion rather bluntly. 'You have stated it somewhere that India has nothing to learn from the West and that she had reached a pinnacle of wisdom in the past. I certainly disagree with this viewpoint. I think that Western or rather industrial civilisation is bound to conquer India, may be with many changes and adaptations, but none-the-less, in the main, based on industrialism. You have criticised strongly the many obvious defects of industrialisation and hardly paid any attention to its merits,' he wrote.[13]

Nehru let go of a great opportunity for experimenting with a wholly indigenous utopia immediately after Independence, Bryan Teixeira wrote in his book *A Gandhian Futurology*. 'Gandhi and Sri Aurobindo were two revolutionary leaders who had the most highly evolved community development models, based on years of experiment and practice. Both offered educational systems that provided for the holistic development of the individual in terms of intellectual, spiritual and craft skills; both offered small-industry community development that could serve India's economic needs without denying the advantage of modern technology. Furthermore, both offered experience with village panchayats, or village councils, and their participatory mechanisms,' Bryan wrote, wryly adding, 'The first prime minister was Nehru, a Gandhi associate although NOT a disciple. Yet the policy that India chose was one of intensive urban-based industrialisation. The government rejected a unique indigenous development model in favour of following the Western path. It simply ignored the panchayat system and Hindu traditional methods of education. Education continued to be based on British model.'[14]

Gandhi was rooted in Indian genius, while Nehru never fully appreciated it although he wrote extensively about the history and culture of India. Nehru was a romantic. His romance with Western ideas like socialism began very early in life. He was invited by leaders of the Soviet Union to Moscow in 1927 on the occasion of the decennial celebrations of the Communist Revolution in Russia. Upon returning from Moscow after a three-day visit, Nehru declared himself to be a socialist. On 29 December 1929, on the banks of River Ravi, while addressing a massive gathering as the President of the Indian National Congress, Nehru had categorically declared: 'India will have to go the Socialistic way, if she seeks to end her poverty and inequality.'[15]

Nehru's romance with socialism continued after independence, much more freely, as the main ideological challengers to socialism, like Gandhi and Patel, had ceased to exist by 1950. In fact, it was these two personalities that had stood rock-like in the way of a communist takeover of the Indian independence movement, especially after the communists seemed to have won over Nehru to their side by the late 1920s. The Congress Socialist Party was started within the Congress in 1934 as a Left caucus, led by Acharya Narendra Dev and with others who viewed Gandhi as an anti-rational mystic. The All India Trade Union Congress (AITUC), which was originally the trade union wing of the Congress, was taken over by the caucus in the mid-1930s. The growing influence of the communists in the Congress did not escape Gandhi's attention. He was never greatly impressed by communism because of its class hatred and use of violent means to achieve its objective of a classless society. 'I do not know,' he told some Indian communists who tried to convert him as far back as 1924, 'whether Bolshevism is for the good of Russia in the long run. But I do know that insofar as it is based on violence and denial of God, it repels me. I am an uncompromising opponent of violent methods even to serve the noblest of causes.'[16] 'Socialism and Communism of the West are based on certain conceptions, which are fundamentally different from ours. One such conception is their belief in the essential selfishness of human nature. I do not subscribe to it, for I know that the essential difference between man and the brute is that the former can respond to the call of the spirit in him, can rise superior to the passions that he owns in common with the brute and, therefore, superior to selfishness and violence, which belong to the brute nature and not to the immortal spirit of man. That is the fundamental conception of Hinduism, which has years of penance and austerity at the back of the discovery of this truth,' said Gandhi.[17]

Sardar Patel's antipathy for the communists is also well-known. He never trusted them. He told M.O. Mathai, Nehru's Special Assistant, '...if we have to build up the nation, Communists would have no place there'.[18]

But Nehru became a diehard socialist by the early 1930s, a halfway journey to the Left. The Soviet Union was his ideal. He would repeatedly talk about the Soviet model and its lessons for India and mankind. It is another matter that while Nehru was under an intense spell of the Soviet Communist model, Lenin was dying a broken man in Russia. 'Marx himself would have been horrified to have the Russian Socialist experiment called utopian,' commented Elise Boulding, Professor Emeritus of Sociology at Dartmouth College in her pathbreaking work, *Cultures of Peace: The Hidden Side of History*. She cited Moshe Lewin's *Lenin's Last Struggle* that documented how 'the overwhelming scale of the problems that faced Lenin at the close of World War I repeatedly drove him into the arms of hardened army professionals and bureaucrats from Czarist times who were least likely to implement revolutionary goals. According to some scholars he realized too late that he had made the wrong alliances, and his final months were a tragedy of realized failures.'[19]

None of this, not even the fact that both Marx and Lenin had stated that no one can really know what a fully socialist society would look like, ever mattered to Nehru. He would relentlessly talk about Socialism in different ways and in different phrases, sometimes as 'socialistic society' and some other times as 'socialist pattern of society'. He hardly explained to the people as to what he really meant by all those words and phrases.

Whether India had really turned socialist and whether this borrowed idea of socialism or socialist pattern of society did any good to the country can be easily understood by looking at the India of the early 1960s. When Punjab needed a new capital city, what came up was the exotic and lavishly built city of Chandigarh. Built along class lines, the city stands out as a shining example of Nehru's hollowness of socialism, which essentially stood for creation of a classless society.

For all his grandiloquence about socialism, Nehru left India

more poverty-stricken, more hunger-ridden and more backward by
the time he hung up his boots.[20] India was the only country in the
world to have continued with food rationing nineteen years after
the Second World War. Its agricultural productivity remained one
of the lowest in the world. Dr Ram Manohar Lohia, the real and
eminent socialist leader, had created a flutter in Indian Parliament
in 1963 when he asserted that '...270 million Indians were living
on a horribly meagre income of three annas a day (roughly $0.01)
while Nehru's pet dog had spent nearly three rupees a day (roughly
$0.5)'.[21]

INDIAN PHILOSOPHICAL ALTERNATIVE

It was in these circumstances that the need for an original Indian
idea to guide the destiny of its people was felt by some people in
the country. In fact, just around the time that Nehru was turning
to socialism in the late 1920s, the country had also witnessed
the silent rise of an alternative school of thought in the form of
the RSS in 1925. The RSS school of thought grew parallel to the
Nehruvian-socialist thought in Indian polity. Nehru championed
the socialist thought whereas the responsibility for articulating an
alternative philosophy based on Indian wisdom and genius fell on
the shoulders of leaders like Golwalkar and Deen Dayal Upadhyay.

Nehru, for all his democratic credentials, was intolerant to
the 'other' viewpoint. On occasions, he would even snub Gandhi,
using a harsh rhetoric. His unilateralism and authoritarian approach
had forced many of his colleagues to part ways and become his
ideological adversaries. The founder of Bharatiya Jana Sangh,
Dr Syama Prasad Mukherjee was one such leader who had resigned
from Nehru's cabinet in 1950 owing to differences on policies.
Others like Acharya Kriplani too became bitter critics. Already,
there were quite a few leaders like Dr Ram Manohar Lohia, Piloo
Modi and Minu Masani who were sworn ideological enemies
of Nehruvian policies and programmes. On the whole, a united

opposition had emerged by the early 1960s that would challenge the ruling Nehruvian dispensation on ideological and political grounds.

Bharatiya Jana Sangh was also a part of that opposition. It had become a major source of irritation for Nehru in Parliament and outside. He was so infuriated by its resistance to his policies that on one occasion he lost his cool and stated that he would crush the Jana Sangh. Syama Prasad responded by saying that he would 'crush the crushing mentality.'[22]

The RSS-inspired school of thought that guided the Jana Sangh's policies and programmes had more fundamental differences with Nehruvian thinking than merely economic differences. Jana Sangh had an issue with the very politics and political ideology of Nehru. Western-style modernity, European brand of secularism, contemporary European ideas about nation and people's rights, and romantic internationalism were the hallmarks of Nehruvian thought. Nehru generally abhorred religion and tradition. In a letter dated 22 May 1944 to his sister, Vijayalakshmi Pandit, he wrote from Ahmednagar: 'I do not take to religion; I resent its ways and outlook. I see no escape from any conflict of the mind in that fashion. Nor do I approve of allowing my mind to sink into a sentimental morass, which is soothing no doubt and often helps in a small way, but which is not good enough. It is a kind of self-intoxication which dulls the mind and prevents clear thinking. The relief it gives may be compared to the relief obtained from some intoxicating drug or alcoholic drink.'[23]

Nehru's views on nationalism too were of strong dissent. He believed that Socialism was a more significant and progressive idea than nationalism. 'My outlook was wider, and nationalism by itself seemed to me definitely a narrow and insufficient creed. Political freedom, independence, were no doubt essential, but they were steps only in the right direction; without social freedom and a socialistic structure of society and the state, neither the country nor the individual could develop much,' he declared, after his visit to Moscow in 1927.[24]

JANA SANGH: THE ANTIDOTE TO NEHRUVIANISM

Nehruvian discourse became the dominant national discourse of post-Independence India. The Jana Sangh and its thought-parent, the RSS, were the principal antidotes to this discourse. The issues, symbols and idioms that the duo had used consistently in the post-Independence era were a direct challenge to Nehruvian thought. As a result, the two sides had got locked into a no-holds-barred ideological battle right from the beginning.

The assassination of Mahatma Gandhi on 30 January 1948 had become the first flashpoint between Nehru and the RSS. Nehru blamed the RSS for the murder and imposed a ban on it. Although the judiciary and investigating agencies had categorically absolved the RSS leadership of any involvement in that ghastly incident, daggers had already been drawn. The rivalry that began in 1948 was to last until the Sino-Indian war of 1962. The Chinese aggression, that was viewed by many Indians as downright deceit by China, had helped in rallying people of disparate persuasions together under the banner of patriotism and national interest. The services rendered by RSS cadres during the 1962 war left a positive impression on Nehru, and the RSS was invited to take part in the Republic Day Parade on 26 January 1963, marching shoulder-to-shoulder with the Indian armed forces.

However, this outward bonhomie was not to mitigate the ideological and philosophical gulf that had existed between the two sides from the beginning. While the Nehruvian camp was led single-handedly by Nehru himself, the political response came from leaders like Deen Dayal Upadhyay and Atal Behari Vajpayee. Balraj Madhok, an effervescent leader of the Jana Sangh, too had chipped in with his 'Indianisation' discourse.

Addressing the first meeting of the Bharatiya Jana Sangh, as its newly-elected president, Syama Prasad laid out his vision for the role of the new party.

'One of the chief reasons for the manifestation of dictatorship in Congress rule is the absence of well-organized opposition parties. Bharatiya Jan[a] Sangh emerges today as an all India political party which will function as the principal party in opposition. Opposition doesn't mean senseless or destructive approach to all problems that confront responsible government. While, therefore, we may have to attack or criticize official measures or acts, our aim will be to approach all problems in constructive spirit so that we may keep the public vigilant and make humble contribution in developing a real democratic structure for the sound administration of the country.'[25]

Although a large number of cadres and leaders including Syama Prasad were inspired by the core RSS vision of 'Hindu Rashtra', and partly Savarkar's Hindutva, the Jana Sangh, from its very inception, presented and articulated a pan-Indian vision using contemporary vocabulary. Its leaders took care to use words like Indian and Bharatiya in place of Hindu in their public parlance. People of different religions were invited to join not only the party organisation, but were also nominated to contest elections at various levels.

Right in his first address, Syama Prasad had exhorted: 'We have thrown our party open to all citizens of India irrespective of caste, creed or community. The people must be united by a bond of fellowship and understanding inspired by deep devotion to the spirit of a common motherland. It is obviously for the vast majority of Bharat's population to assure all classes of people who are truly loyal to their motherland, that they will be entitled to full protection under the law and to complete equality of treatment in all matters, social, economic and political. Our party gives assurance unreservedly.'[26]

The party manifesto had unequivocally stated its objective as '... the building of Bharat on the basis of *Bharatiya Sanskriti* and

Maryada as a political, social and economic democracy granting equal opportunity and liberty to all individuals so as to make her a prosperous, powerful and united nation, progressive, modern and enlightened.'[27]

There were attempts from the very beginning, by Nehru and the communists, to brand Bharatiya Jana Sangh as an upper-caste, Hindu communal party of the Hindi-speaking states. Even people like Dr Ram Manohar Lohia occasionally attacked the Jana Sangh as a communal party. Deen Dayal took up cudgels against such unwarranted criticism. In responding to those critics, he articulated his party's vision on various occasions.

Refuting allegations that Jana Sangh was anti-Muslim and anti-Pakistan, Deen Dayal explained his conception of Akhand Bharat and communalism. 'Referring to the establishment of *Akhand* Bharat, Dr Lohia proposed in the course of his speech that if the people of India wanted to attract their Muslim brethren in Pakistan there must be an amendment in the Constitution making it obligatory that either the President or the Prime Minister of India should be a Muslim. This proposal betrays a lack of appreciation of the intrinsic unity of Bharat and its people. *Akhand* Bharat is more a cultural concept than territorial. It is true that the achievement of this ideal is only possible through the unity of hearts of the people of India. But unity is never created or promoted by political patchwork. Unity manifests itself in equality. No section of the society can demand a price for unity and if it degenerates into such an attitude, no price can inculcate a feeling of oneness in that section. The moment you think in terms of winning communities on the basis of paying them [a] price in the form of political power, you sow the seeds of separation. History of the last forty years bears ample testimony to the fact. In order to induce the Muslims into identifying themselves with the nation and its goal of freedom, all sorts of 'cheques' were offered, but we did not succeed. The motive of the Congress leaders was not bad. But they fell into the trap of the Britishers; while to the Hindu they appealed purely in the name of national independence, they qualified their appeal to the Muslim with a number of guarantees and conditions, which did not discriminate against, but for the Muslims,' he wrote in an article.[28]

Explaining the Jana Sangh's concept of nationalism, he wrote: 'There is also a difference in the concept of nationalism avowed by Jana Sangh, and as conceived by others. All except Jana Sangh believe in territorial nationalism. Jana Sangh believes in cultural nationalism. Others feel that in India, a nation has to be made. Jana Sangh believes that Bharat is a nation from times immemorial. It can therefore seek inspiration and guidance from the current of national life while others, except for occasional impulses, fail to tap the nation's vast sources of strength and inspiration. Thus, they look to the West not only for guidance in modern science and technology but also for all ideas of economy, polity and society. Jana Sangh is, of all parties, the most Bharat-based.'[29]

Deen Dayal was a strong advocate for a complete ban on cow slaughter and in fact equated the fight against cow slaughter with a fight for preserving democracy itself. When prominent saints and social organisations got together under the banner of Gohatya Nirodh Samiti and launched a nationwide agitation for achieving that objective in the mid-1950s, the Bharatiya Jana Sangh extended its support to the movement. Deen Dayal equated the demand for a comprehensive ban on cow slaughter with Swarajya and democracy. 'The *Gohatya Nirodh Samiti* has always regarded the issue of the cow as one concerned with fundamental rights of the Bharatiyas. The acceptance or denial of this fundamental right will itself determine the nature of *Bharatiya* independence. Those who have meant *"Swaraj"* as a mere transfer of power, have failed to appreciate the distinction and disparity between *"Swaraj"* and *"Parraj"* (slavery). The concept of *"Swaraj"* presupposes the resuscitation of "our" values of life and points of honour. And the cow, by far, constitutes the centre of all our points of honour. Hence, whenever foreigners have invaded our land they made the cow a special target of repression. Similarly, the urge for our independence always flowed from our sentiment for cow–protection. The conflict in our life essentially owes its origin to the type of Government obtaining in our country [sic]. Those who want to establish foreign values of life in Bharat, who want to base the future of Bharat on a new foundation borrowed from abroad, having wiped out our ancient way of life entirely, they raise their eyebrows and twist their nose on the problem of cow protection. But the teeming millions of *Bharatiyas* do revere their points of honour even today. And for this very reason our rulers studiously refrain from categorically refusing to ban cow-slaughter and want only to beguile the people in return. But this may be called a fool-hardy attempt at imposing foreign rule over the local populace. Hence the battle for cow-protection amounts not only to a battle for freedom but to that of democracy too,' he insisted.[30]

While the Kashmir question brought Nehru and Jana Sangh face-to-face in the early 1950s, Nehru's handling of issues like the merger of Goa and other territories under the occupation of certain European powers raised serious hackles from the Jana Sangh leadership. Nehru, influenced as he was by Western political ideas, believed that like in Kashmir, a plebiscite would be the way forward to decide the future of regions like Goa, Dadra and Nagar Haveli, etc. The Bharatiya Jana Sangh, however, took serious objection to this view. It not only opposed Nehru's stand but openly supported the popular agitation for merger of Goa in the Indian Union.

Jana Sangh's rejection of the proposal for conducting a referendum in Goa and holding a plebiscite in Kashmir was not merely on political grounds. It also reflected its ideological moorings. While opposing the referendum in Goa, Deen Dayal declared: 'This is wrong. National unity is our Dharma. Elections and majority can decide as to who will form the government.... What the government will do will be decided by Dharma.'[31] He referred to Abraham Lincoln's rejection of the proposal of a few American states to secede on the slavery issue. When the civil war broke out between the Confederate forces and the forces of the American Union led by Gen. Robert E. Lee on 17 September 1862, Lincoln responded by issuing the Emancipation Order, which gave all Confederate states hundred days to rejoin the Union—by 1 January 1863, or their slaves 'would be declared thenceforward and forever free'[32]. On 1 January 1863 Lincoln sent a stern warning to the Confederates by signing the order and forced secessionist leaders of Confederate states to fall in line while not budging on the issue of ending slavery.

Deen Dayal invoked the concept of cultural nation to defend his argument and decry Nehru's position. 'Apart from temperamental weaknesses and hesitancy, there is a fundamental error in the thinking of the Prime Minister. He thinks within the frame-work of the Government of India Act of 1935 or the India Independence Act of 1946. The sovereignty of India accordingly is limited to the territories handed over to her by the Britisher and/or to States that join the dominion. In all other cases, the people of different areas are to be the architects of their fate and their future. If they desire to be independent, they must struggle. The status that they would enjoy is also to be determined by them. This line of thinking ignores the basic fact of India being one. It does not recognise the existence of an Indian nation, which by historical accident came under the dominion of a number of Western powers. If the tiny territory of Goa was, and is, ruled by Portugal while the rest of the country was under the British rule and now independent, it did not and does not in any way create a separate Goanese people. The people of Goa are a part and parcel of the *Bharatiya* Nation. The struggle for the liberation of these territories is therefore an integral part of our freedom struggle. Those who say that the people of Goa themselves should fight for their independence are propounding a theory which is dangerous and unnational,' he emphasised.[33]

TOWARDS A COMPREHENSIVE NEW VISION

By the early 1960s, Deen Dayal started articulating a new vision and philosophy for Jana Sangh. He would consistently use words like *Bharatiya* and *Dharma* in place of India, thus underscoring the fact that his party was based on ideals different from Western ones. In an article that he authored in the early 1960s, Deen Dayal had deliberated at length upon the rationale for the creation of the Bharatiya Jana Sangh and proposed that it was not just another opposition political party but an alternative socio-political philosophy.

'Bharatiya Jana Sangh was born out of this realisation that the party in power, or even others in the opposition, had completely neglected this fundamental basis of Bharat's life and culture. In their attempt to modernise the country, they were trying to devitalise it by changing its age-old values. If they posed as reformers, they were only deluding the people, and themselves. Dayanand and Gandhiji were great reformers, they brooked no social evil, but they never decried Dharma or minimised its importance. On the contrary, they appealed in the name of Dharma, and they succeeded.'[34]

'To Jana Sangh, indivisibility of the country, oneness of its people, and unity of their culture, are fundamental concepts of our Rashtra Dharma. It was on this basis that the whole country fought the Britishers untidily. This unity permeates our whole history, life and literature in spite of outward diversities. It is because of this faith that Jana Sangh opposed the idea of plebiscite in Kashmir, or discrimination between the people there and in the rest of the country in their rights of franchise and justice. In keeping with our traditional outlook of tolerance and respect for all religions we stand for full freedom to every citizen in the matter of worship and faith, but we consider it unnational to differentiate in politics on the basis of anybody's religious persuasion. We do not recognise minorities based on religion, in the sphere of politics. We would like Christians and Muslims to give up their separatism and be integral parts of the nation. Their insistence on right of minorities in matters of services, language, ministerial appointments, elections, etc. are a negation of the one-nation theory. Congress, by trying to champion their misconceived cause, is only obstructing the process of national integration, to suit its party ends.'[35]

Coming to the economic ideas of Jana Sangh, he declared that, 'Socialism and Capitalism are both foreign concepts. Jana Sangh rejects both.'[36]

As the stranglehold of the Congress over the political firmament of India started to weaken by the early 1960s, the Jana Sangh, under the leadership of Deen Dayal Upadhyay, emerged as a philosophical alternative to the Nehruvian ideology, the dominant theme of the first two decades of independent India.

The stage was set for the rise of a new and quintessentially Indian political philosophy, which would alter the course of Indian politics in the decades to come.

∾

3

The Four Lectures

Having established the Bharatiya Jana Sangh as a mainstream political party with a distinct political outlook, Deen Dayal set out to develop a philosophical doctrine for it. As a curious student of contemporary world politics, he closely observed the various politico-philosophical currents influencing the world at that time. He noticed the reigning confusion in the European political arena. Fascism and communism had proved to be dangerous for mankind. On the other hand, liberal capitalist nationalism, too, had turned out to be grossly inadequate to address the concerns of the masses. While the communist world was living in self-deception—claiming that the price in terms of human freedom and rights that groups in communist countries were paying was an essential prerequisite for the establishment of a Proletarian raj—the capitalist world was busy tinkering with its own model, not willing to accept failure.

From the wreckage of the Great Depression and the Second World War emerged a new thinking that classical political liberalism and nationalism needed a dose of welfarism and an element of state control, in order to make the dysfunctional model function well. 'The post-War order represented something historically unusual; Capitalism remained, but it was Capitalism of a very different type from that which had existed before the war—one tempered and limited by the power of the democratic state and often made subservient to the goals of social stability and solidarity, rather than the other way around,' wrote eminent political scientist Sheri Berman[1]. Berman called the neo-hybrid entity as 'social democracy'. Jan-Werner Miller labelled it 'Christian democracy', while Karl Ruggie referred to it as 'embedded liberalism'. 'Democratic liberalism' was how Karl Bracher spoke of it. While it was 'end of history' for Fukuyama, it became 'end of ideology' for Daniel Bell and Seymore Martin Lipset.[2]

This reigning confusion in the Western liberal world at that time was well summed up by Daniel Bell in 1960 thus: 'Few serious minds believe any longer that one can set down "blueprints" and through "social engineering" bring about a new utopia of social harmony. At the same time, the older "counter-beliefs" have lost their intellectual force as well. [A] few "classic" liberals insist that the state should play no role in the economy, and few serious conservatives, at least in England and on the continent, believe that the welfare state is "the road to serfdom". In the Western world, therefore, there is today a rough consensus among intellectuals on political issues: the acceptance of a welfare state; the desirability of decentralised power; a system of mixed economy and of political pluralism.'[3]

By then, European powers had established vast empires across the globe. They carried with them ideas and values prevalent in Europe at that time. This process of imposing European values and culture on the many different and beautiful cultures, value systems and civilisations in Africa, Asia and America began some five centuries ago through superior military force and imposition of scientific and technological advancement. In the eyes of the European colonisers, they were nurturing a universal, secular and materialist culture with the aid of science and technology, which would lead to better living standards and a new value system. In order to overcome local resistance, the colonisers did not just need superior military technologies, but also newer political philosophies.

This process of universalisation of the value system along European lines had led to severe destruction of countless local cultures and civilisations and unmitigable pain and suffering to local communities and societies. 'The dominant Euro-centric concepts are not easily applied to two-thirds world,' wrote Elise Boulding.[4] In the name of modernisation, two-thirds of the world was subjected to great upheavals of Westernisation. The science and technology that the colonisers had brought in had no context, but held a sort of magical attraction for the large masses; traditional patterns of social relations, landholding, agri-production and distribution, and in many cases, the traditional, yet progressive social customs, including the autonomy of women, had all been destroyed. Village self-sufficiency was replaced by landless urban poverty. So many beautiful cultures had to pass through so much suffering in the five centuries of European political and ideological colonisation.

Finally, in 1972, the UNESCO Bellagio Conference report on 'Reconstructing the Human Community' had to admit the need for 'a transcending of "only a European point of view" in regard to the origins of science, democratic development, nationalism and the United Nations, as well as transcending of the psychology of dominance, especially in regard to the power of science and technology.'[5]

INTEGRAL HUMANISM OF JACQUES MARITAIN

Deen Dayal studied most of these developments. He wanted to develop a twentieth-century Indian alternative to this European destruction. He was not alone. Within Europe too, there were philosophical dissensions to the 'European way' thesis during the twentieth century. One of the prominent ones was the thesis of a French academic by the name of Jacques Maritain. Maritain's dissent of the dominant contemporary European political trends of totalitarianism and communism was older by nearly three decades to that of Deen Dayal.

Jacques Maritain was a French philosopher who had, in his lifetime, traversed through Protestantism and atheism before finally settling down with Catholicism. He is regarded as the philosophical father of the Christian Democratic movements in Europe. Although he authored dozens of books, two of which stand out: *Integral Humanism,* written in 1936, and *Man and State* written in 1951. *Integral Humanism* was an effort to build the intellectual basis for a personalist theory of democracy. Like Deen Dayal, Maritain too had developed his integral humanism theory in the historical context of the rise of totalitarian ideologies like fascism, Nazism and communism. Deen Dayal would add capitalism to this list of evil challenges, all of which had their origins in European civilisational ethos. Like Deen Dayal, Maritain too believed that these challenges were 'destructive of human rights and of the family, as well as of a democracy of freedom and responsibility towards common good.'[6]

Maritain's critics observe: 'When he published *Integral Humanism,* those ideologies were already at work politically, and about to unleash the Second World War with the fanaticism of a racial and nationalistic imperialism. The "integral humanism" proposed by Maritain in 1936 aspired to lead the human person towards a full development under the "primacy of the spiritual" that would eventually be fulfilled in Christ'.[7]

'For, a society of free men implies basic tenets which are at the core of its very existence. A genuine democracy implies a fundamental agreement between minds and wills on the bases of life in common; it is aware of itself and of its principles, and it must be capable of defending and promoting its own conception of social and political life; it must bear within itself a common human creed, the creed of freedom,' Maritain opined.[8]

Maritain's philosophy had acquired a prominent place in Catholic theology in the latter half of the twentieth century. In a speech at Rio de Janeiro on 1 July 1980, Pope John Paul II invoked Maritain's 'integral humanism' to explain that 'culture must cultivate man and each man along the extension of an integral and full-fledged humanism, through which the whole man and all men are promoted in the fullness of every human dimension. Freedom must be understood in a more substantive sense than mere freedom of choice. The freedom which Christian democracy seeks to promote above all is what St. Augustine called *libertas maior*, namely freedom in its full development, freedom in a morally adult state, capable of autonomous choices in regard to the temptations coming from every form of disorderly love of self. The integral culture includes the moral formation, the education in values of individual, social and religious life.'[9]

Maritain argued, 'Once the spiritual dimension of human nature is rejected, we no longer have an integral, but merely partial, humanism, one which rejects a fundamental aspect of the human person.'[10] Accordingly, in *Integral Humanism*, he explores the prospects of a new Christendom, rooted in his philosophical pluralism, in order to find ways Christianity could inform political discourse and policy in a pluralistic age.

Although Deen Dayal based his initials thoughts on the contemporary historical context like Maritain, he gradually widened his canvas to draw inspiration from the age-old civilisational richness of India. While Maritain's integral humanism revolved around man, Deen Dayal made man, society, nature and the divine as the axes of his thesis. In Maritain's view, democracy and Christ were the guarantee for man's progress, while Deen Dayal's integral humanism proposed that it is the all-encompassing idea of Dharma that should be the basis for universal good.

Deen Dayal heavily drew from the wisdom of ancient Indian scriptures and traditions, thus making his brand of integral humanism more a philosophical school of thought rather than any ideology.

THE INTEGRAL HUMANISM OF DEEN DAYAL

Integral Humanism as an organised thesis and philosophy was first presented by Deen Dayal in April 1965, through a series of four lectures to Jana Sangh cadres in Mumbai. A few months prior to that, in January 1965, the Jana Sangh had held a major conference at Vijayawada in Andhra Pradesh. It was here that the party had adopted its manifesto, and for the first time stated that integral humanism would be the guiding principle of the party's politics.

Since the four lectures form the core of Deen Dayal's thoughts on integral humanism, it is important to understand the summary of each.

LECTURE 1: CRITIQUE OF THE WEST[11]

In his first lecture, Deen Dayal focused on the confusion prevailing in the country and bemoaned the polity's lack of direction. He attributed it to the self-delusion in the country in the wake of the onslaught of Western ideas and ideologies.

'Having attained Independence, the question naturally ought to have occurred to us, "Now that we were independent, what shall be the direction of our progress?" But it is amazing that serious thought has not been given to this question and today, even after seventeen years of independence, we cannot say that a definite direction has been decided upon,' he lamented.[12]

He described the Congress as a magic box in which a cobra and a mongoose lived together. His allusion was to the lack of any philosophical vision or commitment by the political establishment to the country's future. There were big and hoary slogans coined by all political parties, but they actually meant nothing. All that was seen being played out was opportunistic politics with the singular objective of capturing power by hook or by crook.

Deen Dayal attributed the root cause of the problems being faced by the country to neglect of its national identity. 'It is essential that we think about our national identity. Without this identity, there is no meaning of independence, nor can independence become the instrument of progress and happiness,' he said.[13]

Deen Dayal highlighted the growing influence of Western ideals and ways of life on Indian society and decried the notion that Westernisation was modernisation. He made a fine distinction between Western science and Western lifestyle. 'We had taken pride in resisting things British while they ruled us, but strangely enough, now that the Britishers have left, Westernisation has become synonymous with progress. It is true that a narrow sense of nationalism should not be allowed to obstruct the progress of the nation. However, Western science and the Western way of life are two different things. Whereas Western science is universal and must be absorbed by us if we wish to go forward, the same is not true about the Western way of life and values. In fact, thoughtless imitation of the West must be scrupulously discarded,' he had warned.[14]

Deen Dayal then went on to discuss the basis of various economic and political doctrines of the West and concluded that they had not succeeded in achieving any good for Western nations. Although democracy was universally accepted by all in Europe, the individual was continuously exploited, he observed. Deen Dayal was a quintessential democrat. His criticism of democracy in Europe was limited to the fact that it had failed to secure the rights of individuals, leading to the rise of revolutionary worker movements based on communist/Marxist ideologies.

'In some countries of Europe, there was social revolution. Even where Socialism was not accepted, politicians had to accept the rights of workers. "Welfare State" was accepted as an ideal. Nationalism, democracy, Socialism or equality—these three doctrines have dominated European social political thinking. Every now and then, apart from these, ideals of world peace and world unity also cropped up. All these are good ideas. They reflect the higher aspirations of mankind. But by itself, each of these doctrines is incomplete. Not only that, each stands opposed to the rest in practice. Nationalism poses a threat to world peace. Democracy and Capitalism join hands to give a free reign to exploitation. Socialism replaced Capitalism and brought with it an opposition to democracy and individual freedom. Hence the West is presently faced with the task of reconciling these good ideals. They have not succeeded to this day, in this task,' he analysed in the first lecture.[15]

Deen Dayal concluded his first lecture on the premise that the West was itself facing a dilemma over ideologies and institutions and that India should think in terms of sharing its own wisdom with the world rather than ape the West.

'We may indeed seek some guidance from the Western world, but the fact is, it has no concrete suggestions to offer. It is itself at [a] crossroads, unable to decide what is good. Under such circumstances we cannot expect guidance from the West. On the contrary, we must consider whether in this present state of the world, we can contribute something to resolve its dilemma. Having taken note of the progress of the world, can we add to the common store of knowledge? As a member of the world community, we must discharge our responsibilities. If we possess something that may prove helpful to world progress, we should not hesitate in imparting it to the world,' he concluded.[16]

LECTURE 2: BODY, MIND, INTELLECT AND SOUL[17]

Having talked about the ideological confusion reigning in the West in the first lecture, Deen Dayal turned to Indian culture in the second. 'To them their culture; to us ours' was the principle he advocated in this lecture. He reminded his listeners that each ideology in the West had a local context and hence, to assume that they were universal ideologies and should be emulated blindly, would be a mistake. '...those who would like to make Western ideologies the basis of our progress forget that these ideologies have arisen in certain special situations and time. These are not necessarily universal. They cannot be free from the limitations of the particular people and their culture, which gave birth to these "isms". Besides, many of these ideas are already out of date. The principles of Marx have changed both with the changing times as well as with varying conditions to the extent that parrot-like repetition of Marxism for problems facing our country would amount to a reactionary attitude rather than a scientific and pragmatic one. It is indeed surprising that those who claim to reform society by removing dead traditions, themselves fall prey to some outdated foreign traditions,' he lamented.[18]

He then added, 'Every country has its own peculiar historical, social and economic situations and its leaders decide the remedies to the ills that beset the country from time to time, taking into consideration its background. It is illogical to believe that remedies which the leaders of one country decided to try for their problems are likely to be applicable as such to all other peoples.'[19]

Deen Dayal was not fanatically discarding those Western ideas in toto. Instead, he exhorted that there could be some ideas one could find useful for one's situation and there was no harm in accepting them; but the bad and useless ones had to be discarded. Similarly, all those indigenous ideas weren't all necessarily holy; one should be wise enough to separate the relevant from the irrelevant ones, he suggested.

He was essentially referring to the essence of India's ancient wisdom:

> 'Puraanamityeva na sadhu sarvam; nachaapi sarvam navamitya vadyam;
> santah parikshaanyatarat bhajante; moodhah parapratyayaneya buddhi'

Meaning: 'All that is ancient need not be sacred; similarly, not everything new is holy; wise men examine the efficacy before accepting; fools just imitate.'

Since Western ideas such as nationalism, democracy, socialism, equality, etc. had in practice proven to be 'incomplete and mutually opposing,' Deen Dayal asked if we could turn to Bharatiya culture for answers to the confused world.

'From the national stand point, we shall have to consider our culture because that is our very nature. Independence is intimately related to one's own culture. If culture does not form the basis of independence, then the political movement for independence would reduce simply to a scramble by selfish and power-seeking persons. Independence can be meaningful only if it becomes an instrument for the expression of our culture. Such expression will not only contribute to our progress, but the effort required will also give us the experience of joy. Therefore, both from the national as well as human standpoint, it has become essential that we think of the principles of the *Bharatiya* culture. If with its help, we can reconcile the various ideals of the Western political thought, then it will be an added advantage for us,' he had further elucidated.[20]

A detailed discourse on the fundamental characteristics of the Bharatiya culture followed. Deen Dayal projected Bharatiya view as integral; not compartmental.

'The first characteristic of *Bharatiya* culture is that it looks upon life as an integrated whole. It has an integral view point. To think of parts may be proper for a specialist, but it is not useful from the practical standpoint. The confusion in the West arises primarily from its tendency to think of life in fragments and then to attempt to put them together by patch work. We do admit that there is diversity and plurality in life, but we have always attempted to discover the unity behind them. This attempt is thoroughly scientific,' Deen Dayal argued.[21]

Referring to philosophers as scientists, Deen Dayal presented the *Bharatiya* thinking of fundamental unity as a scientific argument. 'The Western philosophers reached up to the principle of duality; Hegel put forward the principle of thesis, anti-thesis and synthesis;

Karl Marx used this principle as a basis and presented his analysis of history and economics. Darwin considered the principle of survival of the fittest as the sole basis of life. But we, in this country, saw the basic unity of all life. Even the dualists have believed nature and spirit to be complementary to each other than conflicting. The diversity in life is merely an expression of internal unity. There is complementarity underlying the diversity. The unit of seed finds expression in various forms—the roots, the trunk, the branches, the leaves, the flowers and the fruits of the tree. All these have different forms and colours and, even to some extent, different properties. Still, we recognise their relation of unity with each other through seed,' he explained.[22]

Is conflict the basis of human relations? Can cooperation become the basis instead of conflict? Deen Dayal decried the Western notion of the 'survival of the fittest', calling it the 'law of the jungle'. *Kaam* (desire), *krodh* (anger), *lobh* (greed), *moh* (possessiveness/ attraction), *mad* (arrogance), *matsarya* (jealousy)—these six qualities are considered lowly in Indian tradition. They are also considered as the root cause of conflict in society. 'It is essential to save ourselves and the society from these elements. We cannot consider them as our ideals or standards for human behaviour. Survival of the fittest is the law of the jungle,' he had explained.[23]

Deen Dayal then got into the narrative of Dharma. The English word 'religion' is not the correct word for 'Dharma', he insisted at the very outset. Defining the concept of happiness, he went on to analyse that mere physical happiness alone doesn't constitute happiness.

'We have thought of life as integrated, not only in the case of collective or social life, but also in the individual life. Normally, an individual is thought of in the physical bodily forms. Physical comfort and luxury are considered happiness. But we know that mental worry destroys bodily happiness. Everyone desires physical comfort. But if a person is imprisoned and there, he is given finest of food etc., will he be happy? A person does not experience joy on getting nice food if it is also accompanied by a few abuses,' he said explaining it through the story of Krishna and Vidura.

There is a well-known story in the Mahabharata. When Krishna went to Hastinapur as an emissary of the Pandavas, Duryodhan invited him to enjoy his hospitality. Krishna declined his invitation and went to Vidura's house instead. Vidura was an uncle to both the Pandavas and the Kauravas and the prime minister of the kingdom. Overjoyed and exuberant in her enthusiasm to serve this revered guest, Vidura's wife mistakenly served banana skins to Krishna instead of the pulp, which she had thrown away. Krishna quietly enjoyed the meal of banana skin. That is why it is said, 'Even a modest meal, served with dignity and affection, tastes better than the best delicacies served with disrespect.'

Going beyond physical and mental happiness, Deen Dayal talked about intellectual happiness. According to him, if the body and the mind are happy, yet there is intellectual confusion, then it would be equivalent to madness. 'If he is involved in some intellectual confusion, he is reduced to a state almost similar to madness. And what is madness itself? A lunatic may have all physical comforts, he may be perfectly healthy and properly cared for by his relatives; but he does not possess intellectual happiness. Intellectual peace is also essential and important. We will have to take all these things into consideration,' he said.

Then comes the fourth element—soul. An individual human being is made up of these four elements—body, mind, intellect and soul. They are integral, not separate. He took his discussion to various philosophies in Europe and America.

Thereon, Deen Dayal's material man versus integral man analysis began. In classical Indian thought, human existence is explained as four-fold—body, mind, intellect and soul. Deen Dayal considered Western thinking to be compartmentalised. 'The confusion that has arisen in the West is due to the fact that they have treated each of the above aspects of a human being separately and unrelated to the rest,' he explained.[24]

Some countries considered man as a 'political animal' and extended voting rights to him. However, they couldn't offer him food. Marxist societies offered food to man, but not voting rights. People revolted in both situations. Countries like the US offered both food and voting rights; yet people were not satisfied. The USA has the highest number of suicides, highest number of mental patients, and highest number of drug addicts. 'Result of the failure to not think of man as an integral being,' he concluded.[25]

There is a misconception that whereas the West has concerned itself only about the body, the Indian thought has gone to the other extreme and bothered only about the soul and *moksha*. Deen Dayal stated that this is a gross misconception.

'While we recognize the need to pay attention to the soul, we do not neglect the body. *Upanishads* declare in unambiguous words that a weakling cannot realize the self. The body is the primary instrument to discharge the responsibilities that Dharma enjoins. The fundamental difference between our position and that of the West is; whereas they have regarded body and satisfaction of its desires as the aim, we regard the body as an instrument for achieving our aims. We recognize the importance of the body only in this light. The satisfaction of our bodily needs is necessary, but we don't consider this to be the sole aim of all our efforts. Here in Bharat, we have placed before ourselves the ideal of the four-fold responsibilities, of catering for the needs of body, mind, intellect and soul with a view to achieving the integrated progress of man. Dharma, *Artha, Kama* and *Moksha* are the four kinds of human effort. *Purushartha* means efforts which befit a man. The longings for Dharma, *Artha, Kama* and *Moksha* are inborn in humans. Of these four efforts too, we have thought in an integrated way. Even though *Moksha* has been considered the highest of these *Purusharthas*, efforts for *Moksha* alone are not considered to give benefit to the soul. On the other hand, a person who engages in action, while remaining unattached to its fruits, is said to achieve *Moksha* inevitably and earlier,' he explained.[26]

The rest of this lecture focuses on the Purushartha discourse.

'We have thus considered the life of an individual in a thorough and integrated manner. We have set the aim of developing body, mind, intellect as well as soul in a balanced way. We have tried to satisfy the manifold aspirations of man, taking care that efforts to satisfy two different aspirations are not mutually conflicting. This is the integrated picture of all the four-fold aspirations of an individual. This concept of a complete human being—integrated individual—is both our goal as well as our path,' Deen Dayal said in conclusion of his second lecture.[27]

LECTURE 3: EVOLUTION OF THE INDIAN NATION AND STATE[28]

Deen Dayal began his third lecture by questioning the Social Contract Theory put forward by John Locke and Thomas Hobbes. According to him, the theory is based on the description of society as 'a group of individuals brought into being by the individuals through an agreement among themselves,'[29] and it gives greater importance to the individual. If at all there were any differences in the West about this view, they were limited to questions like: If the individual produced a society, then in whom are the residual powers vested—in the society or in the individual? Does the individual have the right to change the society? Can the society impose a variety of regulations on the individual and claim a right to the allegiance of the individual to itself? Or is the individual free with regard to these questions?[30]

Whereas the West was debating these questions, Deen Dayal claimed that, in reality, the very premise that society is a creation of individuals through a contract itself was incorrect. The mere coming together of a few individuals doesn't automatically form a society, he insisted.

The Indian view is that 'society is self-born. Like an individual, society comes into existence in an organic way. People do not produce society. It is not a sort of club, or some joint stock company, or a registered co-operative society. Society is an entity with its own "SELF", its own life; it is a sovereign being like an individual; it is an organic entity,' he emphasised, adding, 'We have not accepted the view that society is some arbitrary association. It has its own life. Society too has its body, mind, intellect and soul. Some Western psychologists are beginning to accept this truth. McDougall has produced a new branch of psychology called group mind. He has accepted that the group has its own mind, its own psychology, its own methods of thinking and action.'[31]

William McDougall, an early twentieth-century psychologist, postulated the theory of the 'group mind'. Group mind is not merely the collective mind of the members of the group. According to the theory, 'the individual in the crowd loses his individuality and becomes a part of the crowd which comes to develop its own crowd consciousness. The crowd consciousness supplants the individual consciousness of the individuals. The members of the crowd participate in the crowd consciousness and act according to the stimulus provided by the crowd.'[32]

Deen Dayal then went on to use the example of students as a way to buttress his argument that individuals and collectives have different thinking and mind. An individual student may be a disciplined one, but as a group, students could be different, because the group mind is what operates in a group, not the individual mind. Deen Dayal then made another profound statement that even the group mind doesn't conclusively establish a social or national identity. The group mind can be influenced by historical memories of cohabitation, yet mere cohabitation over a period of time doesn't make a group into a society or a nation. Thus, Deen Dayal raised the vital question of what a nation was all about.

Deen Dayal's comparison between Greek and Jewish societies

is interesting and thought-provoking. The Greeks have been living as a society for millennia. There has been no interruption as far as the heredity of Greeks is concerned; the father-son tradition has continued from ancient to modern Greece without any other nation taking over or obliterating them. Yet, the Greece that had produced Alexander and Herodotus, Ulysses and Aristotle, Socrates and Plato, and present-day Greece, have hardly any comparison. The ancient nation of the Greeks is no longer to be found; in its place arose a new nation, although it was called by the same name. All the while people of the same stock have been living there. But, in case of the Jews of Israel, they hardly lived together as a group; they were dispersed all over the world for close to two millennia. However, they didn't simply melt away in the societies that they had lived in for centuries. They remained a nation and finally reclaimed their land in 1948. 'It is clear therefore that the source of national feeling is not in staying on a particular piece of land, but is in something else,' exhorted Deen Dayal, before launching his nationhood argument.[33]

Like individuals, nations too have souls. It was Swami Vivekananda who had first emphasised on the national soul. 'Every nation has a destiny to fulfil, duty to perform and mission to accomplish,' he had said.[34] Deen Dayal took the concept forward by saying that it was that mission, together with a motherland, that constituted a nation. He stated that the mission, the core idea behind the formation of the nation, becomes its soul. Nations develop cultures, traditions and even a personality. But that is not the soul of the nation. They are all the outward manifestations of the core idea that guides the nation. Deen Dayal called that core idea of the nation as 'Chiti'.

Indian history is replete with stories like Ramayana and Mahabharata, which were essentially stories of kings, kingdoms and battles. Even though the Pandavas and the Kauravas had both fought in the war, the Pandavas were praised as rightful; Krishna had killed his uncle Kamsa, but that killing was upheld as just. Vibhishan switched sides and helped Ram against his own brother, Ravan, in Ramayana; yet, it was never considered treason. How could these be explained? Deen Dayal's answer was 'Chiti'.

'If there is any standard for determining the merits and demerits of a particular action, it is this *Chiti*; [w]hatever is against *Chiti* is discarded as perversion, undesirable, and should be avoided. *Chiti* is the touchstone on which each action, each attitude, is tested, and determined to be acceptable or otherwise. *Chiti* is the soul of the nation. On the strength of this *Chiti*, a nation arises, strong and virile,' Deen Dayal argued.[35]

According to Deen Dayal, just as the soul in a body constructed various limbs or organs using '*Prana*', the life force, the national soul, Chiti, too had built its own national institutions for sustenance and survival. Deen Dayal compared them to different departments in a factory. These institutions are intended to fulfil the needs and aspirations of the nation. Deen Dayal listed some of these institutions as: family, caste, guilds, property, marriage, *gurukul* and *rishikul*. The state too, was an institution on the same lines, Deen Dayal stated.[36] In the Mahabharata, it is said:

Na rajyam naiva rajaaseet, na dandyo na cha dandika
Dharmenaiva Prajah sarvey, Rakshantisma parasparam.

It means: 'In the *Krita* Yuga, there was no state nor a king; no guilty and no punisher; it was Dharma that guided people to protect each other.' Later on, the nation had created the state. The West confuses these two and thinks that nation and state are the same.

Describing the process, Deen Dayal said, 'Interruption and disorganization came into existence. Greed and anger dominated. Dharma was on the decline and the rule "might is right" prevailed. The *Rishis* were perturbed over the developments. They all went to Brahma to seek counsel, Brahma gave them a treatise on "Law and the Functions of the State", which he had himself written. At the same time, he asked Manu to become the first King. Manu declined saying that a king will have to punish other persons, put them in jail and so on; he was not prepared to commit all these sins. Thereupon, Brahma said, your actions in the capacity of king will not constitute a sin, as long as they are aimed at securing conditions under which the society can live peacefully and according to Dharma. This will be your duty, your Dharma. Not only that, but you will also have a share of the Karma of your subjects, whereby you will gain Dharma considerably if your subjects maintain conduct according to Dharma. Thus, state came into existence as a contract. This contract theory can be applied to the state but not to the nation. In the West, it was exactly opposite. Society as a nation, according to them was a contract, but the king claimed a divine right and proclaimed himself the sole representative of God. This is wrong. In our Country, the king may have been first recognized in antiquity but the society as a nation is considered self-born. State is only an institution.'[37]

Deen Dayal then turned his attention to the relationship between man, society and the state. He negated the Western understanding that conflict and struggle were inherent to human existence. The capitalist West had envisioned man in perpetual conflict with society, state and nature in order to grow. The communist state believed that society was made up of two groups—the haves and the have-nots—and there would be a perpetual conflict between the two. In Deen Dayal's view, conflict was only a result of decadence, not the natural order.[38]

He saw perfect harmony in man, society, state and nature. He emphasised that various social institutions like community, caste, panchayat, etc. were only a harmonious extension of man and that they would fall, if conflict arose. The state was also, similarly, a key institution, whose importance was never understated in India. Acharya Chanakya would assist Chandragupta in statecraft; Swami Samartha Ramadas motivated Shivaji to become a strong ruler;

Vidyaranya Swami awakened manly qualities in Harihara and Bukka so that they would return to the warrior clan and become kings. Ignoring and undermining the role of the state is perilous.

However, while acknowledging this aspect, Deen Dayal also emphasised that the state was never at the centre of Indian national life. The state was one of the institutions to run society, not the only institution, he stated.

'We had not considered the state to be the sole representative of the nation. Our national life continued uninterruptedly even after the state went in the hands of foreigners. The Persian nation came to an end with their loss of independence. In our country, there were foreign rules, now and then, in various parts of the country. The Pathans seized the throne of Delhi, and then the Turks; the Mughals and the British too established their rule. Despite all this, our national life went on, because the state was not its centre,' he explained.[39]

The natural question that arises from it then is that if none of the institutions were at the centre of national life, then what was at the core of India? Swami Vivekananda's 'national soul' or Deen Dayal's Chiti was. 'The state is brought into existence in order to protect the nation; generate and maintain conditions in which the national ideal can be translated into reality,' Deen Dayal said.[40]

He then embarked on discussing the concept of Dharma. Dharma, according to him, was the manifestation of the eternal laws that maintain the Chiti. 'It is Dharma that is supreme. Dharma is the repository of the nation's soul. If Dharma is destroyed, the nation perishes. Anyone who abandons Dharma betrays the nation,' Deen Dayal said.[41]

Using Dharma synonymously with religion is wrong. It is a much wider concept than religion, which is essentially a way of worship. Religions in the West have not had such a hoary history. They were responsible for wars, conflicts and societal strife. Equating them with Dharma would undermine the vastness and virtue of Dharma. By equating it with religion, one would tend to look for it in temples and other shrines. Just as textbooks are not knowledge, temples alone are not Dharma.

Deen Dayal referred to the British dictum that 'the British Parliament can do everything except making a woman into a man and vice versa' and light-heartedly commented that it could not legislate that every Englishman must walk on his head. Nobody, not even the kings or the Parliament, shall have absolute sovereignty, he opined. Dharma is supreme, and all institutions should subordinate themselves to Dharma, he argued.[42]

Deen Dayal then made a strong pitch for a unitary system of governance rather than federal system as envisaged by India's Constitution makers. He took exception to the very first Article of the Indian Constitution which described India. 'India, that is Bharat, will be a union of states,' it read. However, his unitary idea involved greater decentralisation of powers to the lowest unit.

'A unitary State does not mean a highly autocratic centre nor does it entail the elimination of provinces. The provinces will have various executive powers. Even the various entities below the provincial level, such as the *Janapadas*, will also have suitable powers. The Panchayats too should have powers. In this way, the decentralization of power will be accomplished. The authority will be distributed to the lowest level, and will be fully decentralized. At the same time, all these entities of power will be centred around the unitary State. This arrangement will embody Dharma,' he explained.[43]

Deen Dayal then discussed the concept of Dharma *Rajya*. Dharma Rajya is not a theocratic state. However, in Dharma Rajya, the rulers are enjoined to subject themselves to Dharma. In the older times, during the coronation ceremony, the king would declare: '*Adandosmi, Adandosmi*', meaning 'No one can punish me'. Then, the royal priest would raise his staff and gently hit the king on the back, saying, 'Dharma *Dandyosi*'—meaning 'Dharma, the rule of law, will punish you'. The king would run around the sacred fire and the priest would follow him with the staff. Thus, after completing three rounds, the ceremony would come to an end, wherein the king would be unambiguously told that not he, but Dharma would be the absolute sovereign.

'Dharma *Rajya* doesn't mean a theocratic state,' insisted Deen Dayal. He described Pakistan as the most recent theocratic state of the time, where all non-Muslims were treated as second-class citizens. 'In a theocratic state, one religion has all the rights and advantages, and there are direct or indirect restrictions on all other religions. Dharma *Rajya* accepts the importance of religion in the peace, happiness and progress of an individual. Therefore, the state has the responsibility to maintain an atmosphere in which every individual can follow the religion of his choice and live in peace. Dharma *Rajya* ensures religious freedom and is not a theocratic state,' he declared.[44]

The discussion then turned to secularism. Deen Dayal raised a fine point about secularism and the Hindi equivalent of the word— 'Dharma *Nirapeksh*'. According to him, the entire problem lay in trying to equate the Western idea of religion with a very Indian concept of Dharma. Secularism is supposed to be a condition where the state doesn't have any religion. In the Indian context, it was interpreted as Dharma *Nirapeksh*—meaning 'a state indifferent to Dharma'. 'It is fundamentally erroneous,' exhorted Deen Dayal.[45] Dharma, as a set of universal and eternal values, should guide every aspect of the life of a society including politics. Thus, Dharma Nirapeksh Rajya—indifference to Dharma by the state—is an oxymoron. State must be guided by Dharma only; it can't be indifferent to or against the Dharma.

In Dharma *Rajya*, nothing—the state, the legislature, the judiciary, the Constitution, even the people—is sovereign. It is only the Dharma which is all-powerful. Everything else must abide by Dharma. Deen Dayal insisted that even the democratic principle of majoritarianism too was not above Dharma. He cited the example of France during the Second World War, where De Gaulle escaped to London to defy the decision of the then French prime minister, Marshall Petain, to surrender to the Nazi forces and declared that France would be independent always. De Gaulle didn't have majority support when he made the declaration. Neither did Lokmanya Tilak when he declared that freedom was the birth right of Indians. 'Elections and majority can decide as to who will form the government. The truth cannot be decided by the majority,' stated Deen Dayal.[46]

He finally gave a new definition to democracy. '... in the definition of democracy, to say that it is a government of the people is not enough. It has to be for the good of the people. What constitutes the good of the people? Dharma alone can decide. Therefore, a democratic Government—"*Jana Rajya*" must also be rooted in Dharma, i.e., a "Dharma *Rajya*". In the definition of "Democracy", which is "government of the people, by the people and for the people", "of" stands for independence, "by" stands for democracy and "for" indicates Dharma. Therefore, the true democracy is only where there is freedom as well as Dharma,' Deen Dayal argued as his third lecture came to a close.[47]

LECTURE 4: CONTOURS OF *BHARATIYA* ECONOMY[48]

After his elaborate discussion on the nation, state, democracy and related concepts in the third lecture, Deen Dayal turned to economy in his last lecture. He emphasised the Indian dictum, '*Rajaa Kaalasya Kaaranam*'—the king is responsible for the times— to argue that it was the responsibility of the executive to ensure that Dharma was properly institutionalised. However, unlike in Europe, kings and rulers were never accorded the place of God in the Indian system. In fact, the institution of state was regarded as one of the institutions—but not the only one—to promote the Dharma way of living. Deen Dayal referred to panchayats and

Janapadas, in the functioning of which even the mightiest kings desisted from interfering. Then there were trade associations that were also autonomous. 'The state never interfered with the affairs of these different institutions and associations. The function of the state was to ensure that the rules of Dharma were observed by the men running these institutions,' Deen Dayal opined.[49]

'We must have an economic system that helps in the flowering of human qualities in man. It should enable man to attain higher levels of perfection. In our conception it was believed that man attains God-like perfection through gradual development. We should have such an economic system that facilitates that goal,' he declared.[50]

Deen Dayal decried the Western economic model that, according to him, was based on the objective of not just fulfilling the needs of the man, but creating more wants and increasing desires. People are induced through various means into consuming more and more so that economy was propelled and profits were increased. But it had its evil consequences. When people stop consuming, economic depression sets in. Referring to the Great Depression of the 1930s, Deen Dayal had said, '... consumption oriented economic structure is leading to destruction ... It is fast disturbing the equilibrium of nature. As a result, new products are manufactured on one hand to satisfy ever increasing desires of the mankind, new problems arise every day on the other hand, that threaten the very existence of the mankind and civilisation.'[51]

Deen Dayal then outlined his idea of the economic system. One should use up only that much from nature which nature can replicate. The objective of our economic system should be not extravagant use of natural resources, but a well-regulated one, he declared.[52] God has provided for all the physical needs to lead a purposeful and happy life. But it is against His wishes to engage in a rat race of consumption as though that is the only objective of mankind, he voiced his belief. 'Keeping in view the aim of human life, we must endeavour to see how with minimum consumption, man proceeds to his goal with maximum speed. Such a system alone can be called civilization. This system will not think of merely a single aspect of human life but of all its aspects including the ultimate aim. This system will not thrive on the exploitation of nature but will sustain and nourish it. Milking, rather than exploitation, of nature should be our aim,' Deen Dayal said.[53] Alluding to the dictum from the *Isavasya Upanishad*, '*Tena Tyaktena Bhunjeetaah*'—Let us accept whatever is left off by *Isvara*—Deen Dayal said that the economic system should be such that it uses the overflow from nature to sustain our lives.

Both capitalist and communist models emphasised on profits. Their differences were limited to who the rightful owners of profits were. Capitalism believed that those who invested—the factory owners—were the masters and profits should belong to them, while the communists insisted that profits must belong to the labour since they were the ones who were responsible for the production activity.

Deen Dayal found fault with both models. For him, the very idea of profits that gave rise to the notion that 'one has to earn to eat' was flawed. He proposed the idea that those who were born shall eat, and those who earn shall feed. 'The right to food is a birth right. The ability to earn is a result of education and training. In a society, even those who do not earn must have food. The children and the old, the diseased and the invalids, all must be earned for by the society,' he argued.[54]

In Deen Dayal's view, education and healthcare were to be made available to all people free of cost. An educated person was an asset to the society while the uneducated would remain brutes and no society will be safer with uneducated people around, he said. Deen Dayal cited the ancient *Gurukul* system wherein education was free and the pupils would get their daily food through *Bhiksha*—seeking alms—which no householder denied. He called it an investment by society in its future. Similarly, he insisted that everyone should have access to free healthcare. 'The society must guarantee, to all its members, minimum requirements for the sustenance and progress of each individual including education and healthcare,' he said.[55]

If everything has to be made available freely, where would resources come from? Deen Dayal addressed that question subsequently by insisting that the concept of work should be such that every able-bodied person would get a job. 'Guarantee of work to every able-bodied member of the society should be the aim of our economic system. Today, we witness a very strange situation. On the one hand, a ten-year-old child and seventy-year-old man are toiling and on the other hand, youth of twenty-five is driven to suicide for want of work. We shall have to remove this mismanagement,' he declared.[56]

This raised the question of capital. For every able-bodied person to get a job, there needed to be a massive job-creation activity and that called for massive infusion of capital. Deen Dayal argued that machines represented capital infusion these days and warned that it had to be done judiciously. Machines reduce the quantum of human labour and increase the productivity of the worker. Excess production, which Marx described as surplus value, was what would form capital. Deen Dayal cautioned that the machine had to be treated only as an assistant to the worker, not as a competitor. 'However, where the human labour came to be considered as a commodity to be purchased with money, the machine became the competitor of the human being. The principal drawback of the Capitalist view point is the fact that by making the machine a competitor of human labour and thereby displacing and subjecting human being to privations, the very purpose of creating the machine has been defied. Machine cannot be blamed for this. It is the fault of the economic and social system,' he stated.[57]

He was not against using machines. His argument was based on his theory that the primary objective of the economic model had to be job creation. 'Work for every hand and water for every land,' he had said elsewhere. While scientific knowledge is universal, its application should be subject to time and place. It should take into account the condition of each country and its requirements. Machines should be tailored to avoid any conflict with our socio-political and cultural objectives, if not support them, Deen Dayal insisted.

He referred to eminent engineer M. Visvesvaraya's 'seven Ms' in economic production activity: man, material, money, management, motive power, market and machine. According to him, machines should be designed taking into account all the other six factors. 'Instead, we find now-a-days that we install the machines first and try to coordinate all other factors afterwards. Other countries of the world did not progress in this fashion,' he rued, and he was all for developing a 'Bharatiya technology'.[58]

Deen Dayal then discussed the place of man in the economic systems of capitalism and socialism. 'The economic theories of the past few centuries and the structure of society based on these theories have resulted in a thorough devaluation of the human being. His personality is altogether irrelevant to the economic set up. Capitalist economy recognizes only an "economic man", whose decisions are all based entirely on calculations of gain and loss, in terms of material wealth. He works solely to gain more wealth. For him, just like other commodities, human labour is a commodity to be bought and sold in the market. This is free enterprise. In the race, no one is prepared to stop and give a helping hand to the weak who is left behind; elimination of the weak is considered just and natural. He is uneconomic, marginal unit, not fit to exist.'[59]

He further stated, 'Even as regards the consumer's needs, the capitalist is guided not by the necessities and desires of the consumer but by his purchasing power. The needs of the wealthy and the well-fed are attended to rather than those of the poor and the hungry. As a result, where countless varieties of goods are produced for the needs of the wealthy, even the basic necessities of life for the poor become scarce. The centralization and monopolization of production totally undermine the influence of the consumer. The markets are so organized that the consumer has to go by standard products. This standardization is on the increase at such a pace that individual preference of the consumer is ignored. Like the books in the library, even human beings are allotted numbers as consumers. The system which boasts of giving highest importance to the individual has ironically destroyed all individuality. Clearly, the capitalist system is incapable of helping the development of an integral human being.'[60]

Having highlighted the flaws of capitalist economic thinking, Deen Dayal then turned to socialism and suggested that it arose as a response to the ills of capitalism. But then, even socialism had failed to establish the primacy of the human being, he declared. All that socialism did was to transfer the capital from the hands of the capitalists to that of the state. 'The Capitalistic system thought merely of the economic man, but left him free in other fields where he could exercise his individuality. The Socialist system went much further thinking only of the abstract man. After that, there was no scope for the development of the individual personality based on diverse tastes and abilities. The needs and preferences of individuals have only that much importance in the Socialist system as in a prison manual. There is no such thing as individual freedom in the Socialist system,' Deen Dayal said.[61]

He further analysed the grave flaws in the communist ideology by raising serious questions about Marx's theory of proletarian dictatorship to wither away to create a stateless society. 'The dialectic materialism of Marx, too, operates only so long as state is not established as supreme after destroying the capitalists. Thereafter, the state puts a stop to the operation of the principle of Dialectic Materialism. In the name of crushing counter-revolutionaries, the state becomes more and more totalitarian. The day when the state is to wither away yielding place to a stateless society remains a mere dream. In fact, according to the Marxist view, to obstruct the process of these antitheses is itself reactionary. Marx is thus falsified by his own standards,' he observed.[62]

Having explained his differences with both the capitalist and the communist/socialist economic theories, Deen Dayal embarked on proposing his own ideas about the economic system needed for India. The objective of the Indian system should be to 'aim at the progress and happiness of man, the integral man.' He continued, 'Man, the highest creation of God, is losing his own identity. We must re-establish him in his rightful position, bring in him the realization of his greatness, reawaken his abilities and encourage him to exert for attaining divine heights of his latent personality.'[63]

Deen Dayal set out six general objectives for the economic system that he had in mind. He uses two words to summarise them—*Swadeshi* and decentralisation.

The six objectives included:[64]

- An assurance of minimum standard of living to every individual and preparedness for the defence of the nation.
- Further increase above this minimum standard of living whereby the individual and the nation acquire the means to contribute to world progress on the basis of its own Chiti.
- To provide meaningful employment to every able-bodied citizen by which the above two objectives can be realised and to avoid wastage and extravagance in utilising natural resources.
- To develop suitable machines for *Bharatiya* conditions (*Bharatiya* technology), taking note of the availability and nature of the various factors of production (Seven Ms).
- This system must help and not disregard the human being, the individual. It must protect cultural and other values of life.
- The ownership—state, private or any other form—of various industries must be decided on a pragmatic and practical basis.

While concluding his four-day lecture series, Deen Dayal suggested that ideas like nationalism, democracy, socialism and world peace should be reconciled with the traditional values of 'Bharatiya culture'. This is what he called 'integral humanism'.

Deen Dayal was categorical that he had provided only a philosophy. But Jana Sangh was not supposed to be a club of philosophers. And hence, he advised the cadres to strive to build institutions in the light of this ideal of integral humanism. 'We shall be required to produce such institutions as will kindle the spirit of action in us, which will replace the self-centredness and selfishness by a desire to serve the nation, which will produce not only sympathy towards our brethren, but a sense of affection and oneness with them. Such institutions can truly reflect our *Chiti*,' he envisioned.[65]

He then brought in the concept of *Virat*. While Chiti is the soul of the nation, Virat is its life energy, or Prana. Virat is the manifestation of the Chiti of the nation. 'The place of *Virat* in the life of a nation is similar to that of *Prana* in the body. Just as *Prana* infuses strength in various organs of the body, refreshes the intellect and keeps body and soul together; so also in a nation, with a strong *Virat* alone, can democracy succeed and the government be effective. Then the diversity of our nation does not prove an obstacle to our national unity,' he explained.[66]

His final words in this lecture series were also very important. While he advised his followers not to imitate 'Russia or America', he also exhorted them not to 'make this country a shadow of some distant past'.[67]

'We have to undertake the task of awakening our nation's *Virat*. Let us go forward in this task with a sense of pride for our heritage, with a realistic assessment of the present and a great ambition for the future,' he concluded.[68]

4

Nationalism, Communism and Fascism in Twentieth-century Europe

At a time when many in India were viewing the West with awestruck eyes as the beacon of progressive ideas, Deen Dayal was suggesting that the West itself was in a dilemma and could hardly offer anything substantial to mankind, much less to India. Deen Dayal saw serious contradictions in the Western ideological movements of the time. He was of the opinion that the civilisational experience of the West was not enough for it to come up with any universally beneficial idea or model. Apart from a brief historical experience with nation-states, the West had not had any long tradition of nations and nationhood. The ideologies that had become dominant in the nineteenth and twentieth centuries, like liberalism, capitalism, fascism and communism, were all untested and mutually contradictory. That was what prompted Deen Dayal to state that, with a rich civilisational experience of living as a nation, India did not need to turn to the West for ideas on nationhood, unless it could find proven ones there.

What was the situation in the West at that time over questions of national identity and nation-states? Had the nearly two centuries old nation-states of the West been firming up their identity in Europe and elsewhere? Had the ideologies of capitalism and communism been helpful in achieving that objective? Deen Dayal's conclusions were negative. He was not impressed by Western political and ideological developments of his time. He was clear that India would do better by not imitating Western ideas as they did not fit Indian reality and genius. In his opinion, Western political thought, be it capitalism or communism, was essentially based on centralisation of power, while the Indian genius had all along been for decentralisation.

'The centralisation of political, economic and social powers in one individual or institution is a hindrance in the way of democracy. Generally, when power in a certain field gets concentrated in one individual, that individual tries, directly or indirectly, to concentrate in his hands power in other fields also. It is thus that the dictatorial governments of the Communists and the Khilafat were set up. Normally speaking, the various units of administration should concern themselves with administration and should not enter the field of economics. A Capitalist economy first acquires power in the economic field and then enters the political field, while Socialism concentrates power over all means of production in the hands of the state. Both these systems are against the democratic rights of the individual and their proper development,' he opined.[1]

NATION-STATES IN THE WEST

The emergence of nation-states in Europe and their expansion into other parts of the world dates back to just two centuries. It had nevertheless triggered an important discourse in the West over the concept of nation and nationhood. This discourse is still ongoing, with multiple definitions and interpretations, each changing with every new historical development. No single definition or explanation seems to be capable of fully and comprehensively defining the idea of nationhood in the West. In the late nineteenth and early twentieth century, nationalism was the flavour of the season and nation-states were seen as a panacea to the evil monarchies and empires. Then came the fascist dictators with ultra-nationalist ideologies in the early twentieth century and suddenly, nationalism became a sinister idea. Wise men of the world at that time had concluded that the era of nation-states had come to an end and the world had gone global. But by the turn of the twenty-first century, nationalism was back with a vengeance, forcing the thinking world to revisit the idea with an open mind. 'When historians abandon the study of the nation, when scholars stop trying to write a common history for a people, nationalism doesn't die. Instead, [it] eats liberalism,' warned Harvard historian Jill Lepore.[2]

One of the main reasons for this confusion about nationalism and nation-states in the West was its relatively recent exposure to this concept. 'The concept of nation-states, i.e., that the aspirations of the people that constitute a nation are best served by a common political entity is considered a relatively recent idea in Europe from the 18th century. Nationalism led to the formation of nation-states and modern countries. This development was followed up with a gradual hardening of state boundaries with the passport and visa regime that followed it,' wrote author and publisher Sankrant Sanu, in an enlightening article, 'Why India Is a Nation'.

Many European nations that we see today didn't exist 200 or 300 years ago. We have heard of monarchs and royals, but nation-states came into being much later. Their boundaries too kept changing over the last couple of centuries. The two world wars brought about great changes in the geographies of many of these nation-states. Many of them have disputes related to their boundaries; and their very existence is contested by many groups within, to this day. Take the example of the Scots in the UK or the Flemish in Belgium or the Kurds in Turkey. All of them challenge the nation-state they live in and insist that they belong to a different nation.

The history of the UK in the last 200 years is a glaring example of this nation-state dilemma. England, Scotland and Wales got together in 1702 to form what was called Great Britain. Even after coming together, they had retained different laws and held on to separate national churches. Scotland had an old Presbyterian Church order and many Scots continue to follow it. It is in a way the national church of Scotland and is known as Kirk in that country. It is essentially a Protestant Church. The British continue to have Anglican Christianity as their state religion. Although an Anglican Church, the Church of Wales has its own Archbishop, who is independent of the Anglican establishment of England.

Using political, military and religious power, Great Britain had abolished the Irish Parliament and annexed Ireland in 1801. Thus emerged the collective of nations that was called the United Kingdom of Great Britain and Ireland. However, the Catholic majority in Ireland had not accepted this arrangement and after a long, often bloody, struggle, the arrangement fell through. Areas of Southern Ireland with a Catholic majority had seceded from the UK following the Anglo-Irish Treaty in 1921 to re-emerge as the Republic of Ireland. By that time, the Anglican Church had ensured that its followers had become a dominant group in Northern Ireland and continued to show their allegiance to the UK. Northern Ireland, therefore, remained a part of the UK. Thus, the nation-state of UK that we see today can boast of not more than a century's history.

Moreover, its woes are far from over yet. It is still struggling with the question of Scotland's independence. The kingdoms of England and Scotland were united politically in 1707.[3] Campaigns for self-rule began in Scotland in the nineteenth century itself. Finally, the Government of the UK was forced to conduct two referendums in 1979 and 1997 respectively and a separate Scottish Parliament was established by the Scotland Act of 1998 as a result.[4] The Scottish National Party continued to remain the dominant party in Scottish Parliament and under pressure from it, a referendum was conducted once again in 2014. Over 44 per cent Scots supported independence while 55 per cent voted against it.[5] The issue was settled in favour of a unified UK. But the demand for another referendum has picked up momentum after the UK government decided to quit the European Union in 2016 through a Brexit vote. The nationalism question hangs by a delicate thread in the country today.

American history has a similar story. Anglo-Saxon voyagers, who had sailed to the shores of the east coast of America and anchored near Boston in the eighteenth century, were in control of less than 10 per cent of the geographical entity that is today called the USA. At the time of the great American Revolution in 1776, when the 13 British colonies had decided to come together under the leadership of Thomas Jefferson and declare independence from the British Parliament, their geographical area was limited to the states that line the east coast of the USA today. Texas and California joined the union in 1845 after the Mexican War, and Hawaii became a state in 1900. Seen from this historical background, the USA as a nation-state is not more than two centuries old.

It is also important to note here that there is an ongoing discourse about whether or not the nation-state called the USA had emerged as a nation yet. Thirteen British colonies in America had come together from 1774 to 1789 at the Continental Congress in Philadelphia. The First Continental Congress met in 1774 to oppose the Coercive Acts, a series of measures imposed by the British Government on these colonies in response to their resistance to new taxes. The Second Continental Congress was convened the following year. In 1776, it took the momentous step of declaring independence from Britain. The Congress had acted as the government until a new Constitution was promulgated for the united entity of the 13 colonies in 1789. It described the new country as the USA. The present American Constitution came into effect on 4 March 1789. Liberal ideas of individualism, freedom, equality and human rights became the founding ideas of the American Constitution, a product of 'The Federalist Papers' of James Madison, Alexander Hamilton and the lesser-known

John Jay. During the course of its Constitution-making process, America had undergone a revolution from 1776 to 1783. The American Revolution was the result of a series of social, political and intellectual transformations in American society, government and ways of thinking. The Americans had rejected the aristocracies that dominated Europe at the time, championing instead the development of Republicanism based on the understanding of liberalism from the Enlightenment era. After the adoption of the new Constitution in 1789, the First Amendment, ten articles constituting the Bill of Rights, was adopted in 1791. The most important part of the US Constitution, the Bill of Rights keeps the diverse American people together. For the Americans, the essence of their liberal dogma lies in the First Amendment. It epitomises the freedoms that Americans enjoy today—freedom of religion, speech, media, assembly and freedom to petition.

However, sceptics like Samuel Huntington had raised serious questions over this feeble foundation of the American nation. In his important work, *Who Are We*, Huntington raised the crucial question as to whether the USA had really emerged as one nation. 'Globalisation, multiculturalism, cosmopolitanism, immigration, sub-nationalism, and anti-nationalism had battered American consciousness. Ethnic, gender and racial identities came to the fore. In contrast to their predecessors, many immigrants were ampersands, maintaining dual loyalties, and dual citizenships. A massive Hispanic influx raised questions concerning America's linguistic and cultural unity. Corporate executives, professionals and Information Age technocrats espoused cosmopolitanism over national identities. The teaching of national history gave way to the teaching of ethnic and racial histories. The celebration of diversity replaced emphasis on what Americans had in common. The national unity and the sense of national identity created by work and war in the eighteenth and nineteenth centuries and consolidated in the world wars of the twentieth century seemed to be eroding. By 2000, America was, in many respects, less a nation than it had been for a century. The Stars and Stripes were at half-mast and other flags flew higher on the flagpole of American identities,' Huntington bemoaned.[6]

One may or may not agree with his remedy that the core American identity for nearly 200 years has been the 'Protestant ethic minus organised church', but Huntington's thesis underscores the simmering disquiet in the American academic world over the fundamental question of the core national identity of America.

The nation-states in Africa were a creation of the Colonists. During 1884–85, European colonisers had held a meeting called the Berlin West Africa Conference to discuss the partitioning of Africa. It was agreed that European claims to parts of Africa would only be recognised if Europeans provided effective occupation. In a series of treaties in 1890–91, colonial boundaries were completely redrawn. All of sub-Saharan Africa was claimed by European powers, except for Ethiopia (Abyssinia) and Liberia. Germans too were major players in this game at that time. But what is most noteworthy is that not a single representative of the African people was involved when the colonial masters were redrawing boundaries and creating the nation-states of Africa.

There are a few countries in the world that can claim to have a much longer history. For example, countries in South America like Mexico and countries in Eurasia like Egypt and Turkey, to name a few. But here again, the nation-states of all these countries are of very recent origin and had nothing to do with their ancient civilisational past. The ancient Mayan culture that was predominant in Mexico since the eight century BCE or the Aztec culture of the medieval period have largely remained as museum artefacts and a symbol of pride while present-day Mexican society has become Hispanic in language, religion and culture. Same is the case with countries like Egypt and Turkey. The ancient kingdoms of Mesopotamia, Egypt, etc. have lost all traces of their origins to the modern nation-states of Egypt, Italy and Turkey.

All this points to the fact that global understanding of the concept of nation and nationhood is based on models that are short-lived and shifting bases constantly. Yet, based on the experience of the last two centuries, various scholars have tried to develop theories for nation and nationalism. Ethnicity, language, kinship, culture, territory and several other factors have been enumerated as the basis for nationalism. However, there is hardly any unanimity among political scientists and scholars over its definition. In the West, all this has ended in definitional confusion with regard to nation and nationality.

BIRTH OF NATION-STATES IN EUROPE

Until the advent of a full-blown democratic polity in the latter half of the twentieth century, the nationalism discourse in the West was largely controlled, especially in the eighteenth and nineteenth centuries, by intellectual, political and financial elites. Broadly speaking, the European concept of nationalism was based, in the initial phases, on religious identities. Later on, in the eighteenth and nineteenth centuries, the Germans, French and the British started defining their identities in terms of language, ancestry and culture, rather than religion. The European nationalism discourse acquired secularist credentials gradually, and only in the last two centuries. A popular revolution broke out on the streets of Paris on 5 May 1789, leading to the deposition of the centuries-old Ancien Régime led by King Louis XVI. Famously known as the French Revolution, this historic event established a Constitutional government in France and laid strong foundations for a liberal democratic order based on the famous principles of liberty, equality and fraternity. It is another matter that it survived only for a decade.

In the medieval period, the influence of the Catholic Church started waning in Western Europe. The church's and Rome's political dominance was being challenged by movements for reformation and renaissance. The Reformists had vehemently argued that there was no need for the church to reach heaven and thus, the road to wisdom and heaven need not pass through Rome. That was the time when the Catholic priests were selling certificates of lineage to Adam and granting remission of temporal punishment for sins committed by the high and mighty for a price. Salvation was up for sale and the riches thus collected were being used by the Catholic establishment to build lavish institutions across Europe. Martin Luther King, Sr was one of the first to raise his voice against this outrage. 'Why does the Pope, whose wealth today is greater than the wealth of the richest Crassus, build the basilica of St. Peter with the money of poor believers rather than with his own money?' he questioned the Bishop, Albert of Mainz. Enclosed with that letter was a document that came to be known as 'The Ninety-Five Theses'. In his revolt against the Catholic Church, Luther had set in motion the movement of Reformation, which became the progenitor of Protestantism in Europe and laid the ground for the formation of secular nation-states.

In his illuminating article 'The Rise of the Nation-State', Bowen quoted Lynn Buzzard to state that '… the Protestant Reformation helped shatter the religious unity of Europe, and it was linked with the emergence of nation-states with their own boundaries, legislatures, jurisdiction, and therefore, laws. It was a time of growing national consciousness. In place of the authority of Rome or the Papacy or some universal principle, the source of the law's authority now became the state.'[7]

Many Western scholars consider the Treaty of Westphalia of 1648, that brought the Thirty-Year War to an end, as the birth date of the nation-states in Europe. Europe was largely under the symbolic control of Roman emperors until the Treaty in the mid-seventeenth century. One of the first actions of the Roman Emperor, Ferdinand II, after his ascension to power in 1619, was to force citizens to adhere to Roman Catholicism. Tensions were already simmering between the Catholic and the Protestant sects of

Calvinism and Lutheranism. Ferdinand's action led to an open war between the two religious sects. Kings and royals who were adherents of those faiths engaged in brutal wars in several places. The Treaty of Westphalia ended that bloody Thirty-Year War between the Protestants and Catholics, fixed boundaries of territories and made the kings and rulers the sovereign authority over their respective territories, replacing the authority of the Catholic Church. Thus began the journey of the European nation-state and nationalism.

In fact, European nationalism was a product of wars and conflicts. They needed the 'other' to define and fortify their national identities. Wars with France had brought the English, the Welsh and the Scots together to form a 'Protestant nation' called Great Britain against 'Catholic' aggressions. In his work, 'War and the Nation-State', historian Michael Howard argued that 'No nation, in the true sense of the word, could be born without war ... no self-conscious community could establish itself as a new and independent actor on the world scene without an armed conflict or the threat of one.'[8]

In present times, the nationalism discourse in Europe has entered a new phase with the formation of the European Union (EU) through the coming together of 27 different European nations. The formation of the EU had led to an extraordinary amount of economic integration among member countries in the region. Fifteen of them have turned to a single currency, Euro. However, efforts to transform the alliance into a political one had been met with stiff resistance from member-countries.

'European leaders have made significant efforts in recent years to boost the political infrastructure of the European Union, but it has been a bumpy and arduous road,' wrote Dani Rodrik in *The Globalisation Paradox*. 'An ambitious effort to ratify a European Constitution failed after voters in France and the Netherlands rejected it in 2005. In the wake of this failure came the Lisbon Treaty, which entered into force in December 2009, but only after the United Kingdom, Poland, Ireland and the Czech Republic secured exclusions from some of the requirements of the treaty,' he explained further. The treaty was intended to reform the voting rules in the Council of Ministers, give more powers to the European Parliament, render the EU's Human Rights Charter legally binding, and create a new executive position of the President of the European Council. Dani observed that there are 'significant' differences among member states on the 'desirability of turning Europe into a true political federation.'[9]

WESTERN ACADEMICS ON NATIONALISM

Despite definitional and institutional worries, there was some amount of agreement among modern Western scholars about what is historically the most typical, paradigmatic form of nationalism. It is one that features the supremacy of the nation's claims over other claims to individual allegiance, and which features full sovereignty as the persistent aim of its political programme. Territorial sovereignty has traditionally been seen as a defining element of state power, and essential for nationhood. It was extolled in classical modern works of Hobbes, Locke and Rousseau. Nationalism as a politico-territorial concept, however, didn't stand the test of time. Under this definition, a nation was seen as a political contract among individuals sharing a common territory. This was the Enlightenment period version of the definition of nationalism. In fact, Rousseau raised a pertinent question contradicting this argument. 'If Sparta and Rome perished, what state can hope to endure forever?' he asked.[10]

The territorial state as a political unit is seen by nationalists as centrally 'belonging' to one ethno-cultural group, and actively charged with protecting and promulgating its traditions. This form is exemplified by revivalist nationalism, that was most prominent in the nineteenth century in Europe and Latin America. In other words, a nation is any group of people aspiring to a common political state-like organisation.

Some scholars have added a cultural dimension to the definition. Michel Seymour, in his proposal for a 'socio-cultural definition', stated that a nation is a cultural group, possibly but not necessarily united by a common descent, endowed with civic ties.[11] By this definition, nation became a somewhat mixed category, both ethno-cultural and civic, but still closer to purely ethno-cultural than to the purely civic extreme.

Definitional variations abound. Early German elaborations talked about 'the spirit of a people', while somewhat later ones, mainly of French origin, talked about 'collective mentality'. Renowned British political scientist and philosopher Isaiah Berlin, writing as late as in the early 1970s, stated that his definition of nationalism consists of the conviction that people belong to a particular human group, and that '... the characters of the individuals who compose the group are shaped by, and cannot be understood apart from, those of the group....'[12]

There are some scholars who believed that the concept of nation itself is artificial and imagined. British anthropologist and philosopher Ernst Gellner observed that nationalism was an invention or fabrication. 'Nationalism is not the awakening of nations to self-consciousness; it invents nations where they do not exist,' he dismissively stated.[13] Anglo-Irish political scientist and historian Benedict Anderson authored a book claiming that nations were 'imagined communities'.[14]

Some modern-day critics like Prof. S.N. Balagangadhara of Ghent University in Belgium have argued that the European concept of nation-state has its origins in Christianity. They cite the story from Genesis of the Old Testament. In Genesis 11:1–9, there is a narrative of the City of Babel: 'Everyone on earth spoke the same language. As people migrated from the East, they settled in the land of Shinar. People there sought to make bricks and build a city and a tower with its top in the sky reaching Heaven, to make a name for themselves, so that they were not to be scattered over the world. God came down to look at the city and tower, and remarked that as one people with one language, nothing that they sought would be out of their reach. God went down and confounded their speech, so that they could not understand each other, and scattered them over the face of the earth, and they stopped building the city'. Thus, the city was called Babel. Land and language had thus been prescribed as the basis for 'one people' by the Bible.

Ethno-political or ethno-cultural form of nationalism has led to the creation of a large number of nation-states in the eighteenth and nineteenth centuries. It was also central to many-a-conflict in the world in the last century. It might have benefitted some, like the Israelis and Belgians, and continues to be seen as beneficial by groups like the Scots in the UK, the Flemish in Belgium, the Kurds in Turkey and Iran, and the Tamils in Sri Lanka.

The nationalism question became the pivot of twentieth-century politics. Empires and kingdoms started giving way to emerging nation-states and democracies. In just a century's time, the number of democracies in the world rose from around a dozen to more than a hundred. However, the political journey of mankind in the last century has been anything but smooth. Although starting as a fad, nation-states soon degenerated into zones of conflict. As economics became the driving force for people and governments alike, economic upheavals started taking their toll on political systems. Newer ideologies and political models started emerging in different countries, each claiming to address the misery and sufferings of their subjects and promising them welfare at an individual level and peace at the community level.

Nation-states, when they appeared on the global stage in the late nineteenth century, were essentially seen as a beneficial arrangement by the elites of those respective countries for their economic security and prosperity. In fact, there was a tacit understanding between the rulers and the elites over the governance arrangement. But then, as economic disparities grew, a new version of populist politics reared its head. The era of mass politics had begun. Democracies in nation-states that were hitherto controlled by the elite of those countries, started witnessing the rise of demagogues and populist politics. That led to the emergence of a new era of political theories and concepts based on mass politics and welfarism in the early decades of the twentieth century. This new form of politics was not at all peaceful. Elitist politics based on profiteering and economic prosperity had led to competition between nation-states. Nationalist expansionism had led to conflicts and wars. Two world wars in succession had had a devastating effect on world polity. Amidst all of this, chauvinist leaders with clumsy ideas rose to power. Fascism, Nazism and communism held sway over large swathes of territories and populations. Liberal democracies were struggling with the onslaught of such totalitarian ideologies and also with economic depression and its aftereffects. The Great Depression of the 1930s had taken a great toll on the liberalist ideology and politics. The world was at a crossroads. It was around this time that Deen Dayal Upadhyay set out to articulate his integral humanist thought as a quintessential Indian response to this global confusion and lack of direction.

LIBERAL CAPITALIST POLITICAL ORDER

Deen Dayal spoke at length about the failures of existing political theories and models like communism and capitalism in serving the purpose of mankind. He then embarked onto the task of defining an Indian alternative to them. Not just he, but many Western scholars too were engaged in serious scrutiny of these models in their respective countries, pondering over the inadequacies and incompetencies in them.

Deen Dayal was categorical that while there was nothing wrong in understanding Western models, they shouldn't be allowed to overwhelm the Indian thought process. 'Today, the democracy and the Socialism that we had been trying for, are basically resting on a Western foundation and are therefore incomplete. These two thoughts express different aspects of life and the truths related to them. Their synthesis is possible, but only when our point of view is synthesising. It would not be proper to press our entire life into the institutions and traditions of democracy as developed in the West, or into the ready-made moulds of Socialism pronounced by Marx and practised by Lenin, Stalin, etc. The life of this country is higher than both these ideas. Instead of foisting Western politics on India, we will have to develop our own political philosophy. While doing this, we can benefit from the thinking done in the West. But we must neither be overwhelmed by it nor must we consider it the eternal truth,' he said.[15]

Before the advent of the capitalist ideal in the eighteenth and nineteenth centuries, the world was largely divided into traditional communities guided by communal institutions that were influenced by religion in most cases. Hierarchies of clans, communities, religions and kingdoms had been tightly controlling people and imposing a form of discipline that hardly left any scope for individual freedom and material prosperity. A dense web of relationships, 'inherited from the past and sanctioned by the religion', as Gideon Rose, the editor of *Foreign Affairs* put it, were the governing forces behind the entire socio-political life of communities. Then came capitalism and it started eroding hierarchies and communal solidarity. Markets and profits became the defining feature of human relations. In the process, traditional community institutions were broken down and new concepts like freedom, profit, material welfare, etc. took their place. Classical liberalism, the mother of liberal democracies, was the product of this capitalist ideology.

Renowned economic historian Karl Polanyi described it as 'the great transformation'. This transformation had, no doubt, brought new benefits to mankind. It allowed for man's innate urge for freedom and progress to flourish. It opened up new avenues for economic prosperity and material development. It minimised the role of the government and allowed for flowering of individual enterprise based on the rule of law instead of the whims of kings or hierarchical elders. But soon enough, the world realised that the liberal capitalist order had its costs too. People were robbed of their stability as well as social and psychological security since supporting traditional institutions like family, clan, caste, etc. had been weakened. Market-controlled life and profit-centric economic activity had unleashed the beast of selfishness and materialism in man, leading to social and economic inequalities, exploitation and self-centred activities. Traditional family and community values got systematically undermined, which led to severe friction between tradition and modernity, resulting in acute social unrest. By the turn of the twentieth century, the market forces of liberalism had unleashed their own enemies in the form of demagogues preaching mass politics in the name of either communism or narrow nationalism. Karl Marx's warning that the '... bourgeoisie would produce its own gravediggers' came true by the end of the first quarter of the twentieth century.[16]

Capitalism's woes didn't end there. By the late 1920s came the economic nightmare called the Great Depression. It had caused massive economic mayhem in the West, which was a result of unregulated liberal capitalist policies pursued by the newly prosperous nation-states of Europe and America. The Great Depression, which lasted for about a decade until the Second World War propelled the war economy, had an impact not only on the economic prospects of nation-states, but on their democratic polity too. Demagogues from both sides—fascists and communists—had harangued against liberal virtues and successfully provoked sentiments against them among the masses in different countries. Where liberalism failed, communism or fascism would deliver, they promised. Sections of European populations started looking at these ideologies as viable alternative social, political and economic models. But what they got in these two ideologies was, to quote Gideon Rose again, an 'organised barbarism'.

When the Great Depression struck, capitalism was in its heydays. Capitalist countries were in a thrall. President Hoover of America had even declared pompously in 1928 that America had solved the problem of poverty for good. But in just a few years' time, everything turned upside down. America, together with several other capitalist countries, had been caught in the intense whirlpool of economic depression, leading to millions of job losses. Pessimism was so pervasive that men started talking about the collapse of civilisation itself. It was the time of some of the great scientific inventions and innovations that should have promoted more production and propelled the economy. But the opposite happened. Unbridled capitalism had led to unregulated markets and uneven distribution mechanisms. It had resulted in greater inequalities; merriment to some and misery to countless more. The world was in for serious economic and political insecurity, unseen until then.

Interestingly enough, the catalyst for all the twentieth-century ideologies in Europe was the two-centuries-old ideal of liberalism. It was the forerunner of capitalism in its emphasis upon limited government and free market economics. Liberalism is a deceptive word. It was first used in the early nineteenth century in Europe. It was essentially a movement led by the noblemen and rich citizens against state and church control. Liberalism was projected as though it cared for the ordinary people whereas what it really cared for, at least in the last two centuries, was high birth, gentlemanliness and munificence. An English language dictionary of 1768 had described the word Liberal as: '1. Not mean, not low in birth; 2. Becoming a gentleman; 3. Munificent, generous, bountiful'. Liberals were supposed to be the gentlemen class of society, who needed full freedom to prosper through free trade practices and were not to be controlled by any political or religious authority. The first champions of liberalism were the aristocrats of Europe.

The mass politics of the twentieth century had decimated

aristocratic liberal classes. Before the advent of mass politics, the French experiment with liberalism had led to the rise of Napoleon Bonaparte. The French Revolution of 1789 was a clumsy affair. In an effort to unshackle from the clutches of the monarchy on one side and the Catholic religious orthodoxy on the other, French deputies had revolted and thrown out King Louis XVI, who was eventually executed in 1793, attracting massive protests from all over the world. The liberal French Revolution in the first decade was to be a massively violent and unstable affair that would culminate in the rise of Napoleon Bonaparte towards the end of the eighteenth century. The liberals of his time had hoped that Napoleon would be the new messiah of liberalism. But soon, he turned France into a war machine and towards the end of his rule, around 1815, he actually returned to the old conservative politics of the monarchy by befriending the Catholic Church again.

Early liberalism had done no good to Europe or to mankind. The French Revolution had witnessed massive violence, executions and killings. Anarchy ruled the roost until Napoleon took over. Edmond Burke, godfather of European conservatism, was the first to harshly criticise the French Revolution. He refused to call the French revolutionaries as liberals, branding them 'illiberal' instead. In his pamphlet on 'Reflections on the Revolution in France', Burke used harsh language for the leaders of the revolution—the French deputies—for their 'presumptuous ignorance' and 'savage manner'. He bemoaned that the destiny of France had fallen in the hands of a 'swinish multitude'. Whether it was proper for Burke to use such uncivil language was a hot debate in his time. Many scholars had condemned Burke for his choice of words. But the fact remains that liberalism as a political idea had not had a hoary entry on the world stage in Europe.

Capitalism was the by-product of liberalism. Freedom from, and rejection of, the state and religious control became the hallmarks of early capitalist order. It had resulted in a situation which English philosopher Thomas Hobbes had described at least a hundred years ago as a 'war of every man against every man'. Some capitalist thinkers had argued for a laissez-faire economic system, with no interference of the government in matters of the economy in any form. Laissez-faire and free trade intellectuals were vehemently against the socialistic ideas of workers' interests, among other things. They were capitalists of the highest order. According to them, the sufferings of the working class were their own providence. Any idea of state intervention to protect the interests of the working class was absurd. Giving in to workers' demands wouldn't be charity, but plunder, these intellectuals argued. They suggested that the government's role should be limited to providing physical protection and justice, while the rest should be left to God.

One of the foremost laissez-faire intellectuals was a French political economist called Frédéric Bastiat. For Bastiat, the poverty and sufferings of the working class were their own doing because they were 'lazy, irresponsible, and prone to prodigality'. In fact, for him, they were a part of 'the providential plan'. 'Government had nothing to do with their hardship. Nature assigned each person to his position in society, and the only way to better one's condition was by improving one's own character,' Bastiat argued.[17]

The liberals entered the twentieth century with such quixotic ideas bordering on absurdity. They were opposed to universal adult suffrage because they didn't agree with the maxim that men and women were born equal. American liberals were even opposed to Abraham Lincoln on the grounds that Lincoln had used emergency measures such as arrests of suspected traitors, suspension of habeas corpus writs, overlooking several constitutional provisions, etc. The liberal campaign gradually acquired arrogance and superiority complex. They even defended colonialism in the name of 'civilising the world'. By the time of the Second World War, liberals were convinced about their greater global mission. American magazine moghul Henry Luce had declared in 1941 in an editorial in *Life* magazine, 'We (American liberals) are the inheritors of all the great principles of Western civilisation. It now becomes our time to be the powerhouse.'[18]

Europe had responded to this liberal capitalist project in the early twentieth century through a twin response. Mass politics of two kinds had erupted—the fascism and Nazism of the radical nationalist kind and communism of the Marx-Engels kind. Fascists had adopted national socialism while it was international socialism for the communists. Fascism had never been articulated in any coherent manner whereas communism was a well-articulated response to the liberal capitalist order. These responses were more short-lived than imagined by their preceptors. But they had nonetheless catalysed a major ideological churning in the twentieth century. The world was divided into two camps—one led by Western liberals and the other by fascists and communists in Europe.

COMMUNISM AS THE ANTIDOTE

Communism made a grand entry into Europe with the opening statement of the Communist Manifesto of Marx and Engels proclaiming, 'A spectre is haunting Europe—the spectre of Communism. All the powers of old Europe have entered into a holy alliance to exorcise this spectre.' As an ideology, communism had envisaged a world split vertically into two—the haves and the have-nots. It was a response to the liberal capitalist dogma of free market and less governance. Communism had proposed that there would be perpetual conflict between the haves and the have-nots and this conflict would end in the establishment of a 'proletarian dictatorship'. Coined by a socialist revolutionary and a military officer in Prussia, Joseph Weydemeyer, this phrase was adopted by Karl Marx to indicate the intermediate stage between capitalist control and the communist ideal of the 'withering away of the state'. Marx used the word 'proletariat' to denote the working class who had nothing but their two hands to live. While the liberals wanted the working class to accept their plight as fate, Marx insisted that the working class should rise up in revolt against the liberal capitalist order in order to overthrow exploitative regimes and establish the rule of the collective working class.

Marx's ideology achieved temporary success in 1871 when Paris was captured by the socialists and was converted into a commune. The commune that controlled Paris from 18 March to 28 May 1871 was a revolutionary socialist government. During their two months of governance, the communards[19] implemented policies of social democracy. Feminist, socialist and anarchist currents played important roles in the commune. It was eventually suppressed by the national French Army during *La semaine sanglante* (The Bloody Week) beginning on 21 May 1871. Around 20,000 communards were killed in battle. In Engels's judgment, the Paris Commune was history's first example of the 'Dictatorship of the Proletariat'.

Marx had predicted that the proletarian revolution would occur in industrialised countries like Britain and Germany where working class populations were present in large numbers. But his predictions didn't prove to be right. While the labour in the industrialised West did get organised into a political force, democracies continued to flourish in the industrialised world. However, predominantly agrarian economies like Russia and China fell to communism in the twentieth century. It was Vladimir Ilych Ulyanov, popularly known as Lenin, who had succeeded in establishing a communist government in Russia in 1917 through the famous October Revolution. Interestingly, Lenin was not a proletariat. He was born into a middle-class, well-to-do family and studied law. Influenced by the Marxist ideology, he moved to Europe and became the theoretician for revolutionaries in Russia. The Tsar regime in Russia was overthrown by revolutionary forces in February 1917 and a provisional government was established. Soviet history described it as the Bourgeois Revolution. It was followed by another revolution in October in the same year, which is called the Great October

Socialist Revolution. It was this second revolution that had the imprints of Lenin. Lenin was not physically present when the revolution took place and only returned after the capture of power by the Bolsheviks was complete. The regime, put in power by Lenin after the October Revolution in Russia, was the first communist regime of the world.

The Leninist Communism project, which ostensibly came as a response to the bourgeoise exploitation of the capitalist regime of Tsar rulers like Nicholas II, turned out to be the bloodiest regime in the twentieth century; bloodier than its ideological cousins like the Nazis in Germany. As soon as he captured power, Lenin began a violent purging of 'class enemies'. It began with the brutal execution of the entire family of Tsar rulers including Nicholas II at Yekaterinburg in July 1918 through shooting and bayoneting. In the ensuing seven years, until the death of Lenin in 1924, thousands perished in brutal executions. Stalin, who took over the communist regime of Russia in 1924, took this brutality to newer heights. American historian Timothy Snyder gathered modern data from the Soviet archives that became available after the collapse of the Soviet regime in the 1990s and concluded that the number of victims of the brutal Soviet communist regimes exceeded nine million. More than six million had been targeted by the regime under various pretexts while another three million perished due to man-made famines, harsh imprisonments at Gulags, etc. It became so brutal that historians started parodying the dictum 'war is a continuation of politics' by stating that in Communist Russia, 'it is politics which is the continuation of the war by other means'.

Soviet communism was not just a government; it was an experiment in human organisation. The focus of the communist experiment in Russia was the man. The individual man was sought to be replaced by a collective man. The whole attempt was to suppress every aspect of individuality of man and mould him into an economic and political communal being. This required a massive machinery for the regimentation of man. Lenin, and the leaders after him, had used centralised control of all aspects of the Soviet life—political, economic, social and media. Lenin described media freedom as a bourgeois hoax. Through a state-controlled media, Soviet citizens were repeatedly told that the world outside was in total anarchy and that the future of mankind lay in turning to communism. Those who disagreed were dealt with in a manner of utmost brutality. Hundreds of Gulags—forced labour camps—were established across the Soviet Union and indiscriminate and selective deportations to them became the order of the day. Gulags were death traps. Millions perished there due to harsh conditions, rough weather and famines. Those who were forced into Gulags included many intellectuals and rich people who were projected as class enemies of the proletariat.

Lenin had his own justification for the brutality of the communist regime. Democracy, for Lenin, was a bourgeois institution, only for the exploitation of the working class. Similarly, freedom, equality, etc. were also seen as myths perpetuated by the bourgeois class. He believed that none of these should have any place in the communist revolutionary scheme of things. Lenin contended that iron dictatorship of the proletariat was essential for the revolution to succeed. Revolution would provoke counter-revolution, and those counter-revolutionaries had to be dealt with in a ruthless manner through execution, imprisonment, Gulags and gagging of press freedom. Revolution was war and war is founded upon terror, he declared. He argued that since communism was the obvious choice for mankind and it was more than mere rejection of the Western civilisation, all means for achieving it were valid and all costs involved, including human costs, were inevitable. That was how Lenin and subsequent communist leaders defended their autocratic and cruel regimes.

Lenin believed that the revolution shouldn't have any boundaries. 'To struggle by all available means, including armed forces, for the overthrow of the international bourgeoisie and the creation of an International Soviet Republic as a transition stage to the complete abolition of the state' was declared as the global mission of communism by the Second Congress. When the Comintern was established as an organisation in 1919 at Moscow, over 35 countries that lent their support were represented at the conclave. By the time of the eruption of the Second World War, a good number of countries had already turned communist or were well on the path to communism. At its peak, communism had over 40 countries under its spell. Russia had annexed some neighbouring territories to create the USSR in 1922 and used the Comintern to spread communism in Eastern Europe before the Second World War. Comintern was disbanded in 1943 and the Labour parties in different countries were freed from Soviet stranglehold. But that didn't end the spread of communism. Instead, the communist ideology started expanding into East Asia. China, Vietnam, Cambodia, Lao and North Korea became communist in subsequent decades.

The ideology of communism based on hatred and violence, with a weird theory of class struggle, didn't last long. Unlike liberal capitalism which had the elasticity to reinvent itself from time to time, the rigid dictatorial nature of communism was not able to hold on for long. By the late 1980s, communist states started collapsing one after the other. The major collapse happened when the USSR had disintegrated in the early 1990s. Today, only a handful of countries including China, Vietnam, Cuba, Cambodia and Lao follow the communist form of one-party rule. The radical anti-state, anti-democracy ideology of communism had spawned a number of guerrilla movements leading to anarchy and violence in many parts of the world. Some of them still survive in countries like India and some Southeast Asian countries in the name of Maoism.

RISE OF FASCISM

Around the time that communism was spreading its tentacles in Eastern Europe, countries like Germany and Italy in Western

Europe came under another kind of anti-liberal worldview in the form of fascism. Where Marxism-Leninism was a dictatorship of the party, fascism was the dictatorship of an individual. Fascist regimes in Italy and Germany that sprung up after the First World War had one thing in common—the unrest generated by the Treaty of Versailles that was signed to end the war. Interestingly, the two countries had fought in opposite camps during the war.

The Treaty of Versailles was seen as a let down by Italian nationalists because the territories that they had been promised by Britain before the war were denied under the treaty. War had led to economic strife, unemployment and civic unrest, which was exploited by Mussolini to establish the first Fascist government in Italy through the establishment of the National Fascist Party in 1921 and the capture of power in 1922. Originally a member of the Socialist Party of Italy and a soldier during the war, Mussolini had organised his own army after the war from among the soldiers and also the youth of Italy who were restless about the happenings in the country under the nationalist leadership. Mussolini's supporters wore military uniform and displayed discipline and absolute loyalty to their leader. By the time he established his National Fascist Party, Mussolini had already mobilised a cadre of over half a million soldiers. With this military force, he marched towards Rome and captured power by forcing the cabinet to resign and leaving no option for the king. Thus, Mussolini became the Prime Minister of Italy without ever having majority in parliament.

Fascism had never pretended to have any ideology of its own, nor had it any pretensions about democracy or rule of law. Brute power of the uniformed cadre and demagogy of the unchallenged leader were the only strengths of Fascist regimes. 'He had openly thrown overboard all the pretence of majority rule. He will obtain power not because the mass of the electorate supports his views, but because his followers will not allow opposition to make itself heard. Government, for him, exists to fulfil needs, not to give effect to wills; and its first requirement is an overwhelming strength incompatible with liberty. For liberty indeed, Mussolini professes no affection. He has called it a nineteenth century concept which has exhausted its utility. Liberty, for him, is the parent of anarchy if it implies hostility from opponents, and the proof of disloyalty, involving expulsion from his party, if it comes from his declared supporters,' wrote Harold Laski, an eminent political scientist of those times, in 1923.[20]

Like Lenin, Mussolini too believed in ruthless power. He emphasised patriotism, rejected communism and guarded his country against falling prey to Comintern Bolshevism. He believed in law that suited his rule, not the rule of law. Like Lenin, he too argued that all methods, including violence, were justified in achieving the objective, in this case, 'national reconstruction'. Fascists were not coherent in their thoughts and ideas. Nevertheless, they were articulate, pretending to be visionaries. They coined new phrases that seldom had any real meaning. Mussolini had coined the slogan, 'A new heaven and a new earth', whatever that might have meant. He insisted that whoever was opposed to his ideas was a traitor. He believed that the entire wisdom of Italy since ages was consummated in his party and in the movement he led.

In his famous article on Lenin and Mussolini that appeared in *Foreign Affairs* in 1923, Laski compared the two: 'Lenin and Mussolini have established a government not of laws but of men. They have degraded public morality by refusing to admit the terms upon which civilised intercourse alone becomes possible. By treating their opponents as criminals, they have made thought itself a disastrous adventure; and that at a time when what is needed, above all, is inventiveness in social affairs. They have penalised sincerity in politics. They have given rein to passions which are incompatible with the security of life. They have insisted on the indispensability of themselves and their dogmas even though we cannot afford to pay the price incurred in the enforcement of that notion.'[21]

Harold Laski was witness to history as it unfolded in later decades. By the early 1930s, Germany had seen the rise of another fascist regime under Adolf Hitler. Like Mussolini, Hitler too fought the First World War as a soldier of Weimar Germany. He joined political activity after the war and was imprisoned for his anti-government activities. After his release in 1924, Hitler started his Nazi party. In the 1932 elections to the German Parliament, when no party could secure majority, the conservatives encouraged Hitler to run the country with their support. Thus began the more than a decade-long disastrous rule of Hitler in 1933. As soon as he became the Chancellor of Germany, Hitler unleashed his Nazi ideology on friends and foes alike. Political parties were abolished and a one-party rule with the slogan of national socialism became the creed of the country. Hitler was opposed to both capitalism and communism and believed that both were the conspiracy of Jews and Zionists. Like Mussolini, Hitler too believed in his indispensability and the spiritual superiority of the German nation. Like all Fascists, he too was a demagogue and used his oratory skills to mobilise the German nation in support of his philosophy of German racial superiority. He too had undertaken massive purges of opponents.

Hitler had utter disregard for institutions. One by one, all democratic institutions were disbanded. He equally disregarded history, culture, art and theatre. Everything was bent to suit the Nazi ideology. Media was completely taken over and filled with news of the revolution, statements by Hitler and other leaders and accounts of Nazi celebrations. Nazis had discarded a large part of German history. For them, history began with Nazism in 1919. Kaiser to Marx were non-entities in the new history of Nazi Germany. Hitler wanted Germany to be big. *Lebensraum*—'living space'—became his slogan. He began purging Germany of Jews— Jewish accounts claim the elimination of over six million Jews in what is known as the Holocaust. Then, Hitler turned his attention to the neighbourhood. His invasion of Poland on 1 September

1939 in the name of *Lebensraum* had led to the commencement of the Second World War, which lasted for six years and culminated in unheard of miseries.

Deen Dayal had closely watched these developments in the world. The end of the Second World War had seen the collapse of fascist regimes in Germany and Italy. However, the world was regrouped into American and Soviet camps, and the era of the Cold War followed. Western capitalism and Soviet communism had started competing with each other for dominance over as large a territory of the world as possible. No single country could escape the impact of this ideological Cold War. India was no exception. The political jargon in India too was hovering around the two ideological opposites. Institutions, political as well as social, were coming under the strain of these competing ideologies.

Having studied the history of twentieth-century ideologies, Deen Dayal came to the conclusion that if India were to progress, it ought to find a third path, a path of its own, based on its own wisdom and genius derived from the experience of the millennia of its civilisational history.

৵

5

Rashtram: The Indian Concept of Nationhood

After Independence, when the leaders of India set out to make a constitution for the country, a couple of things weighed heavily on their minds. The world was just out of the horrors of a war forced on mankind by ultra-nationalist dictators and that had made nationalism a retrograde idea. Within India, the country was divided on the nationality question, with the majority of Muslims opting out of India's civilisational nationhood idea. In addition to these two mental preoccupations was the immediate challenge at hand in the form of the integration of over 560 princely states with either the dominion of India or Pakistan. Given the circumstances, leaders including Jawaharlal Nehru and Babasaheb Ambedkar preferred making a secular nation-state out of the newly independent and partitioned India. They were reluctant to revisit the Gandhian idea of India as a cultural nation. Although Jawaharlal Nehru, in his famous 'Tryst with Destiny' address on the midnight of 14–15 August 1947, talked about 'the soul of a nation, long suppressed, finds utterance …,' he too was not sure as to what that national soul was. Decades of the British propaganda that India was not a nation had had enough impact on the minds of the leaders who were embarking on building the architecture for the future of the country.

The British, who had ruled over India for more than two centuries, were at the forefront in arguing that India was never a nation in the European sense of the term. Sir John Strachey, a member of the Council of the Secretary of State of the British Government, wrote in 1888: 'This is the first and the most essential thing to learn about India that there is not and never was an India or even any country of India possessing, according to European ideas, any sort of unity, physical, political, social or religious. No Indian nation, no people of India of which we hear so much.'[1] The seven-member Indian Statutory Commission, popularly known as the Simon Commission after its chairman Sir John Simon, which came to India in 1928 to study the possibility of constitutional reforms in the country, had referred to India as a 'conglomeration of races and religions'.[2]

It was not just the British who took forward this European discourse on India's nationhood, but some eminent Indian leaders too were of a similar opinion. Surendranath Banerjee, a senior leader of the Indian National Congress, was prominent among them. Banerjee had authored a book titled *A Nation in the Making*, in which he observed that India was being made into a nation largely due to British efforts. Surendranath Banerjee had started his career as a British civil servant, but later on became a freedom fighter. He was one of the founders of the Indian National Congress in 1885–86 and served as its president for a couple of terms. Banerjee was more of an apologist for the British and never in sync with the mainstream Congress movement of the twentieth century. He was knighted by the British for his services.

These ideas were echoed in the Constituent Assembly of India. It is instructive to revisit the debates from the Constituent Assembly over several of these issues. The creation of a Constituent Assembly for India was the result of the Cabinet Mission Plan of 1946. Accordingly, an elected Assembly was formed by August 1946. It had 208 members from the Congress and 71 from the Muslim

League. But by then, talks about India's partition had gained momentum and the Muslim League had decided not to join the Assembly which was dominated by the Congress. After Partition and Independence, the first formal meeting of the Assembly for drafting the constitution of independent India took place on 31 December 1947. The 299-member body had held sittings on 114 days spread over close to three years. While the Assembly was chaired by senior Congress leader Dr Rajendra Prasad, the drafting committee of the constitution was chaired by Dr Ambedkar.

The Indian Constitution does not call India a nation. It uses the word 'Union' in its place. The Preamble of the Constitution starts with the statement, 'We, the people of India....' Article 1 of the Constitution describes India, 'that is Bharat', as a union of states. Both these expressions—people and union—were borrowed from the constitution of America. The preamble of the American Constitution begins with the statement, 'We, the people of the United States...' The American Constitution was an improvement on the Articles of Confederation that existed earlier. The effort was to build a 'more perfect union' than the one that existed among the Confederate states. The makers of the Indian Constitution depended heavily on those concepts, even though the Indian situation warranted a different approach. There were prolonged deliberations in the Constituent Assembly over these core concepts with some members insisting on taking a quintessentially Indian approach while some others favouring concepts borrowed from outside. When Dr Ambedkar presented his first draft of the Constitution to the Assembly in the latter half of 1948, heated debates ensued over some of the core concepts. The total and unambiguous departure from Gandhian and Congress principles like united and strong nationhood, village empowerment, etc. did not go down well with several members who attacked Ambedkar. There were several others who believed that Ambedkar should have been more liberal in allowing a much looser federation than the one he had proposed.

Maulana Hasrat Mohani, a member of the Communist Party, vehemently argued that the Indian states should have autonomy like the American provinces and India should become a 'Federation' of 'independent states' as in America.[3] There were many opposed to the idea of autonomous states. As a compromise, along with the word 'nation', the word 'federal' was also avoided in the Constitution. Mahboob Ali Baig Sahib Bahadur, a member from the then Madras Presidency, rued that provinces had been reduced to 'glorified District Boards'.

'People seem to think that the Centre must be strong, and that unless the Centre is very strong the provinces will always be an impediment in the way of the Centre becoming strong. That is a wrong view. If provinces are made autonomous, that does not necessarily mean that the Centre will be rendered weak. What do we find here? My view is that the provinces will be nothing but glorified District Boards. All these clearly show that in the hands of a Central Government which wants to override and convert this federal system into a unitary system, it can be easily done. Now there is a danger of this sort of Government becoming totalitarian,' he argued.[4]

On the other side were many who were unhappy that the traditional Indian system was completely ignored by Ambedkar. 'I must confess, I am very disappointed. I see nothing Gandhian in this Constitution,' complained Mahavir Tyagi.[5]

'We have forgotten whom we repeatedly call the Father of the Nation,' stated K. Hanumantaiah.[6] 'Sir, to the utter disappointment of myself and some of us who think with me, this Draft Constitution has drifted from point to point until, at last, it has become very difficult for us to understand where we are, where the country is, where the people are, what is it that they are going to derive out of this Constitution when it is put on the statute book,' T. Prakasam bitterly argued.[7]

Dr Ambedkar chose to use his concluding address to the

Constituent Assembly on 25 November 1949 to dwell at length over these issues. He bemoaned that India was found wanting in its recognition of the principle of fraternity. 'Fraternity means a sense of common brotherhood of all Indians—of Indians being one people. It is the principle which gives unity and solidarity to social life,' he said. He then referred to a story narrated by James Bryce in his volume on the American Commonwealth about the United States of America to buttress his point about how difficult it was to achieve fraternity.[8]

'The story is—I propose to recount it in the words of Bryce himself—that—"Some years ago, the American Protestant Episcopal Church was occupied at its Triennial Convention in revising its liturgy. It was thought desirable to introduce, among the short sentence prayers, a prayer for the whole people, and an eminent New England divine proposed the words, 'O Lord, bless our nation'. Accepted one afternoon, on the spur of the moment, the sentence was brought up next day for reconsideration, when so many objections were raised by the laity to the word nation as importing too definite a recognition of national unity, that it was dropped, and instead there were adopted the words 'O Lord, bless these United States'."'[9]

Ambedkar relates this story to the Indian situation. 'There was so little solidarity in the U.S.A. at the time when this incident occurred that the people of America did not think that they were a nation. If the people of the United States could not feel that they were a nation, how difficult is it for Indians to think that they are a nation. I remember the days when politically-minded Indians, resented the expression "the people of India". They preferred the expression "the Indian nation." I am of opinion that in believing that we are a nation, we are cherishing a great delusion. How can people divided into several thousands of castes be a nation? The sooner we realize that we are not as yet a nation in the social and psychological sense of the world, the better for us. For then only we shall realize the necessity of becoming a nation and seriously think of ways and means of realizing the goal. The realization of this goal is going to be very difficult, far more difficult than it has been in the United States. The United States has no caste problem. In India, there are castes. The castes are anti-national in the first place because they bring about separation in social life. They are anti-national also because they generate jealousy and antipathy between caste and caste. But we must overcome all these difficulties if we wish to become a nation in reality. For, fraternity can be a fact only when there is a nation. Without fraternity, equality and liberty will be no deeper than coats of paint,' Ambedkar explained.[10] On a different occasion, Ambedkar insisted that nationalism was a 'spiritual' idea.

The idea of a 'nation in the making' thus secured constitutional accord in India. The discussion in the Constituent Assembly was dominated by references to the making of the American nationhood or even the Irish nationhood. Many talked about the Australian and Canadian constitutions as reference points. Those modern nation-states were sought to be examples for India in its nation-making endeavour.

However, the European concepts of nation and nation-state are alien to the Indian reality. 'The concept of nation itself is, in fact, alien to the Hindu temperament and genius. It is essentially Semitic in character, even if it arose in Western Europe in the eighteenth century when it had successfully shaken off the Church's stranglehold. For, like Christianity and Islam, it too emphasizes the exclusion of those who do not belong to the charmed circle (territorial, or linguistic, or ethnic) as much as it emphasizes the inclusion of those who fall within the circle. Indeed, the former, like the heretics and pagans in Christianity and Islam, are cast into outer darkness,' wrote Girilal Jain, eminent Indian author and renowned editor of prestigious publications.[11]

Rabindranath Tagore too was critical of the Western thought. 'The civilisation of Ancient Greece was nurtured in the city walls.

In fact, all the modern civilisations have their cradles of brick and mortar. The walls leave their mark deep in the minds of men. Thus, in India, it was in the forests that our civilisation had its birth, and it took a distinct character from this origin and environment. It was surrounded by the vast life of nature and had the closest and most constant intercourse with her varying aspects. Her aim was not to acquire but to realise, to enlarge her consciousness by growing into her surroundings. The West seems to take pride in thinking that it is subduing nature as if we are living in a hostile world where we have to wrest everything we want from an unwilling and alien arrangement of things. This sentiment is the product of the city wall habit and training of mind. But in India the point of view was different; it included the world with the man as one great truth. India put all her emphasis on the harmony that exists between the individual and the universal. The fundamental unity of creation was not simply a philosophical speculation for India; it was her life object to realise this great harmony in feeling and action.'[12]

In fact, a land of such extreme diversity in language, religions, rituals and customs is a nightmare for any scholar to explain in terms of the modern nation-state concept. That leads us to the question of what is India all about, if not a nation in the European sense?

INDIAN APPROACH TO NATIONHOOD

Sri Aurobindo, one of the greatest philosopher-saints of the twentieth century, described the Indian approach to nationalism in the following words: 'In Positivism, Europe has attempted to arrive at a higher synthesis, the synthesis of humanity; and Socialism and philosophical Anarchism, the Anarchism of Tolstoy and Spencer, have even envisaged the application of the higher intellectual synthesis to life. In India, we do not recognise the nation as the highest synthesis to which we can rise. There is a higher synthesis, humanity; beyond that there is a still higher synthesis, this living, suffering, aspiring world of creatures, the synthesis of Buddhism; there is a highest of all, the synthesis of God, and that is the Hindu synthesis, the synthesis of Vedanta. With us today, nationalism is our immediate practical faith and gospel not because it is the highest possible synthesis, but because it must be realised in life if we are to have the chance of realising the others. We must live as a nation before we can live in humanity.'[13]

Sri Aurobindo rejected the theory that the essential conditions of nationality were unity of language, unity of religion and life, and unity of race. He pointed out that the English nation itself was built out of various races; that Switzerland had distinct racial strains speaking three different languages and professing different religions; that in America the candidates for the White House had addressed the nation in fourteen languages at that time, that Austria was a congeries of races and languages and that the divisions in Russia were hardly less acute. He argued that the idea that unity in race, religion or language was essential to nationality was an idea that would not bear examination. He referred to the example of the Roman Empire, which had created a common language, a common religion and way of life, and tried its best to crush out racial diversities under the weight of its uniform system. But it had failed to make one great nation. In an illuminating passage, Sri Aurobindo defined the essential elements of nationality. He wrote: 'We answer that there are certain essential conditions—geographical unity, a common past, a powerful common interest impelling towards unity and certain favourable political conditions which enable the impulse to realize itself in an organized government expressing the nationality and perpetuating its single and united existence. This may be provided by a part of the nation, a race or community, uniting the others under its leadership or domination, or by a united resistance to a common pressure from outside or within. A common enthusiasm coalescing with a common interest is the most powerful fosterer of nationality.'[14]

Deen Dayal had discussed this subject in detail in his lectures and writings. He identified four elements that constitute a nation—one, land and people, which we could call as the country; two, common aspirations and collective will; three, a well-organised system of dos and don'ts, rules that guide the actions of the collective, which can be described as Dharma; and four, certain ideals of life that are common to all those people. All four were required to make a nation, according to him. Mere land and people don't constitute a nation automatically. There are many territories in the world where people live, but they don't automatically become nations. The North and South Poles can't be called nations by transporting people there, Deen Dayal used to quip. There needs to be a sentiment that binds those people together for centuries. There should be shared feelings, shared sense of history and shared vision for the common future of people to emerge as a nation. It takes centuries and calls for relentless and selfless efforts by countless great saints, scholars and social reformers to nurture that sentiment, he stated.

Deen Dayal's ideas on nation and nationhood were different from the Western understanding of these concepts. According to him, '...when a group of people lives with a goal, an ideal, a mission and looks upon a particular land as motherland, the group constitutes a nation. If either of the two—an ideal and a motherland—is not there, then there is no nation.'[15] Deen Dayal called nation a 'living organism' that evolves over millennia through historical and civilisational experiences. 'When a human community living in a certain tract of land for centuries starts experiencing a certain identity with it; customises the special qualities of its life; develops a common set of traditions; a common life mission; common feelings of happiness and sorrow; common experience of friends and foes; a common history through which its great saints and sages nurture that great civilisation through their penance and sacrifice—it is then that a nation with distinct cultural life is born,' he explained.

According to his concept, nation is a spirit, a feeling and an emotion. It is not just about the land, not even about the people. A land and a people together constitute a country. In the West, besides these two prerequisites, a common racial or historical identity was described as the basis for nationhood. But Deen Dayal differentiated between a country, which is a product of land and people coming together through a legal document like a constitution and a government, etc., and a nation, which is all of these put together but much more. He used to cite the example of Israel to emphasise that for centuries, even when they didn't have the land and a united people, much less a government of their own, did the Jewish nation not exist?

The Jews were living on the lands of Palestine, but they were never satisfied. They were dispersed all over the world in first century CE; they suffered great ignominy in many countries except perhaps in India, and generations had passed without them being able to return to their motherland. Yet, successive generations of Jewish leadership had kept the fire of freedom alive in the hearts of millions of Jews across the globe. Every year, the Jews would meet at one place in the respective countries they were living in, remember their history, triumphs and travails, and while departing, would say to each other : 'Next year in Jerusalem.'[16] For generations, year after year, the Jews had prayed for their return, and never gave up. And finally, when that moment came, towards the end of the Second World War, millions of Jews started pouring into Palestine. They had no knowledge of the Hebrew language; nor did they have any knowledge of Jewish customs and traditions; yet, they left everything behind in the countries that they were living in and returned to the 'Promised Land', almost empty-handed. What was that sentiment that had lived on for centuries even when there was no country and no government that they could call their own? What was that sentiment that had motivated them to return to their fatherland, leaving behind their hard-earned wealth and prosperity?

That was the sentiment of nationhood, and Deen Dayal called it an 'eternal reality'.

RASHTRAM: THE ENLIGHTENED PATH

The Indian word for denoting this eternal emotional and spiritual idea of nationhood, as distinct from the European racial, political and geographical idea of the nation, is '*Rashtram*'. Rashtram is the Indian concept of nationhood. It is a very ancient idea of nationhood, developed by Hindu seers and sages through persistent experimentation and analyses of social life. It all happened long before European political scholars and practitioners had started pondering over ideas like nation and nationalism. 'Common enthusiasm coalescing with a common interest' as the basis of nationhood has been realised in India several millennia ago.

To differentiate between the European and Indian understanding of the nation, one can refer to a profound observation made by the eminent Indian author and novelist, K. Raja Rao. 'It is not the Indian who makes India, but India makes the Indian,' he had cryptically observed once.[17] The Europeans had developed the idea of a nation with man at the centre, whereas the Indian idea of Rashtram is just the opposite.

Rashtram is etymologically explained as a firm, enlightened path for the welfare of a community. The word is derived as a combination of two roots: *rasmi*—'the sun' and *sTha*—'firm, placed in'. This led to an extraordinary evocation in the Vedas: *rashtram me datta* (Give me that lighted path).

In India, the concept of nation existed in the form of a pan-Indian, spiritual-emotional identity since millennia. References to Rashtram can be found in many places in ancient Indian literature. In the *Rig Veda*, the most ancient work of Hindu seers, the word 'Rashtram' was used to describe the national identity of the people of the land called Bharatavarsha. Rashtram as an idea is a unifying and development-oriented (*Abhyudayam*) concept as against today's conception of a nation, in which the basic urge to live together in harmony is not developed, and which has been a major source of political conflict and violence throughout the history of the last several centuries.

RASHTRAM: THE DIVINE MOTHER

Rashtram has been invested with divinity and motherhood in the Vedas. Sage Vak, one of the many women composers of hymns in the Vedas, said in the Pratham Mandala of the *Rig Veda*:

> *Aham Rashtri Sangamani Vasunam Chikitushi Prathama*
> *Yagyiyanam*
> 'I am the beholder of this *Rashtra*; benefactor of the gods; and
> first among the worshipped.'

Thus, an effort was made to infuse a sense of divinity, sacredness and motherhood in Rashtram from the times of the *Rig Veda*. Nation is a feminine entity in India in contrast to the common Western masculine understanding of the country as fatherland. This Vedic hymn is, in a sense, the origin of the concept of *Bharat Mata*—the motherland. Sri Aurobindo described her as *Jagajjanani*—the mother of all mothers—the Universal Mother.

In the foreword to R.K. Mookerjee's *The Fundamental Unity of India*, late Sir J. Ramsay MacDonald, the former prime minister of Britain, wrote: 'The Hindu regards India not only as a political unit naturally the subject of one sovereignty—whoever holds that sovereignty, whether British, Mohammedan, or Hindu—but as the outward embodiment, as the temple—nay, even as the goddess mother—of his spiritual culture.... He made India the symbol of his culture; he filled it with this soul. In his consciousness, it was his greater self.'[18]

EVOLUTION OF RASHTRAM

This distinct idea of nation as Rashtram was not a product of any theory; nor was it an overnight phenomenon. It evolved in

India through the efforts of countless saints, sages and wise men. Max Weber, eminent German philosopher and sociologist of the twentieth century, had said in his *The Protestant Ethic and the Spirit of Capitalism* that the mission of the states is the 'preoccupation not so much with the well-being of people in the future as with the "quality" of future people's character.' In other words, the so-called 'fatherland', according to Weber, was not exactly the land of the fathers, but of the future generations. Many millennia before Weber, ancient Hindu sages had also deliberated upon this mission of the nation and had come up with the concept of *bhadra iccha* (benign wish). There is a beautiful shloka in the *Atharva Veda* which states that the Rashtram, or the national identity of the people of India, was the product of that bhadra iccha of those sages.

Bhadram icchhantah rishiyah
swar vidayah, tapo dikshaamupanshed agre.
tato raashtram, bala, ojasya jaatam
tadasmai devaupasannmantu

It means that a benign wish had originated in the minds of ancient seers during the course of their penance. This benign wish was for Abhyudayam, the welfare and glory of all. This is not divisive and not guided by any selfish desire for personal pleasures. These *rishis* (sages) were supremely learned, and it was their benevolent wish for mankind. Abhyudayam is the material and spiritual well-being of mankind. The sages concluded that even gods bowed before such a consciousness. The sages had seen themselves as harbingers of this consciousness. *Vayam Rashtre Jagruyama Purohitah*—'We are the priests of enlightenment of the nation,' they declared. Now what is Rashtram here? This is not a political idea, but it is spiritual. Welfare of all is its motto.

BHADRA ICCHHA: BENIGN WISH

But the most important question that arises is how can bhadra icchha be explained? A doctrine of Dharma was developed on the basis of this bhadra icchha.

Sage Kaṇāda in *Vaiśeṣika Sūtra* notes a definition of Dharma by its beneficial impact, focusing on the discharge of one's responsibility:

Yatobhyudaya nisreyasa siddhihi ca dharmah

'That which leads to the attainment of *Abhyudaya* (material prosperity in this world) and *Nihśreyasa* (total cessation of pain and attainment of eternal bliss hereafter) is Dharma.' The bhadra icchha of the sages was to secure this two-fold objective.

Dharma, the set of eternal principles and values, is essentially meant to protect and uphold the nation and its people. In fact, everything in the social life of an individual has been linked to the well-being of the Rashtram through Dharma. For example, when a marriage is solemnised, the mantras used are:

dhruvam te raja varuno dhruvam devo bruhaspatih |
dhruvam ta indrashchagnishcha rashtram dharayatam dhruvam

Oh king! May Varuna give stability;

May the divine Bruhaspati give stability;

May Indra and Agni give stability;

May the entire nation be held in stability!

It is this Dharma which is the soul of the Rashtram. Swami Vivekananda described India as '*Dharma Praana Bhaarata*', meaning Dharma is the soul of Bharat. This concept of national soul, which Deen Dayal described as Chiti, is unique to India and that soul manifests in Rashtram—the quintessential national identity. Jawaharlal Nehru, the first prime minister of India, despite his Western upbringing and socialist convictions, had to appeal to this concept of the national soul in his famous 'Tryst with Destiny' address. He had said:

'Long years ago, we made a tryst with destiny, and now the time comes when we shall redeem our pledge, not wholly or in full measure, but very substantially. At the stroke of the midnight hour, when the world sleeps, India will awake to life and freedom. A moment comes, which comes but rarely in history, when we step out from the old to the new, when an age ends, and when the soul of a nation, long suppressed, finds utterance.

'It is fitting that at this solemn moment we take the pledge of dedication to the service of India and her people and to the still larger cause of humanity.

'At the dawn of history, India started on her unending quest, and trackless centuries are filled with her striving and the grandeur of her success and her failures. Through good and ill fortune alike, she has never lost sight of that quest or forgotten the ideals which gave her strength. We end today a period of ill fortune and India discovers herself again.'

The ideals that Nehru referred to as those that had given India strength were the ideals of Dharma. Dharma can be understood as a set of values that define the ethical and spiritual life of India as a Rashtram. They include its outlook to life, creation, universe, god, state, wealth and everything else. It is these ideals on which the Indian nationhood—*Rashtriyata*—was founded and thrived. It is these ideals that India has 'never lost sight of' in her long journey through victories and vicissitudes.

THE ENTIRE WORLD IS ONE RASHTRAM

However, one important dimension needs to be understood here. Rashtram is not a political concept in the sense that it doesn't define any geographical boundaries. It is more an ethical, spiritual concept—a view and way of life. The sages of India had concluded that the whole of earth, surrounded by oceans, is one Rashtram.

   prithivyah samudra parayantaayah eak raat iti

Therefore, the idea and concept of Rashtram is a philosophy here. It delineates the principles of life that define man's relationship with the entire universe and creation. This expansive understanding of the concept of Rashtram had led to notions like '*Krinvanto Viswamaryam*', or Let us Ennoble the World, and '*Vishwa Kutumb*', meaning World as One Family. It is not about expansionism or colonialism. It is about spreading the noble message of this Rashtram to all corners of the world.

STATE UNDER RASHTRAM

What is state under Rashtram? Deen Dayal makes a clear distinction between the two. Unfortunately, in present-day political discourse, state and nation are used identically and interchangeably, as though they are synonyms. Where Rashtram, the Indian nationhood, is a spiritual-emotional concept, state is a political entity. Highlighting this distinction, Deen Dayal used to say that even the name United Nations Organisation was an anomaly as it was, in reality, just the United Organisation of the States. This crucial distinction needs to be understood carefully in order to grasp the concept of Rashtram fully. In the West, nation-states constituted the identity of the people. State—the political leadership—provided required combustion for the people to survive as a nation. In European political thought, state absolutism still holds sway. The state claims divine omnipotence there and draws its authority from the writings of Aristotle and other ancient European political philosophers. Aristotle had proclaimed that the state was a natural entity and that man had found his fulfilment in and through the state. The theory of state absolutism, wherein it is conceived that the state is the repository of all powers and is entitled to undivided obedience of its subjects, had its roots in the political theories of Hegel and Rousseau and John Austin's legalism.

With the collapse and decimation of political sovereignty, many nation-states ceased to exist. It had happened in the long history of the world, compelling the famous twentieth-century Urdu poet and politician of India and Pakistan, Mohammad Iqbal, to ask:

Yunan mishra roma, sab mit gaye jahan pe—kuch baat hai ki
   hasti mitati nahi hamari

Nations like Egypt, Iran and Rome have vanished with the collapse of the sovereign political powers of the day; whereas, how come the nation (in India) doesn't show any signs of decay! Similar is the history of twentieth-century nation-states like Yugoslavia and the USSR. Once the binding political power collapsed, the nation-states collapsed like a pack of cards. The lifeline of these nation-states was in their political power, whereas the lifeline of the Rashtram is outside of it. The Rashtram views the state as one of the many institutions that help society pursue the path of Dharma. State, described as *Rajya*, is thus not synonymous with Rashtram.

Elaborating on this difference, Deen Dayal had said, 'The nation is a self-governed entity. It appears on its own and establishes various institutions to fulfil its needs in social, economic and political spheres. State is one such institution.'[19] The state is thus one of the representative institutions of the nation. It is not the nation by itself. Even if it ceases to exist, the nation shall still remain. Vibrant nations survive and prosper outside the government and state than under them. Bill Clinton, as the President of the United States of America, had once made an interesting distinction between the government and nation. 'We have moved past the sterile debate of those who say that the government is the enemy and those who say that the government is the answer. My fellow Americans, we have found a third way. We have the smallest government in 35 years, but the most progressive one. We have a smaller government, but a stronger nation.'[20]

In its long history, India was very rarely ruled by one sovereign ruler. No single ruler had ever held complete sovereignty over the entire Indian nation. Events like *Rajasuya* would occasionally give rise to emperors with suzerainty over their subjects, but never a single state. Multiple kingdoms had existed here. They too were not uniform in structure or nature. The *Aitereya Brahmana*, one of the ancient texts of India, describes ten kinds of Rajyas under one Rashtra:

> samrajyam. bhaujyam. svarajyam. vairajyam.
> parameshthyam. rajyam. Maharajyam Adhipatyamayam.
> samantaparyayi syat. sarvabhauma sarvayusha antadaparardhat.
> prithivai

There were autocratic monarchs, hereditary kings and democratic republics living side-by-side. There were instances when foreign aggressors had occupied some of these states and established kingdoms. Greek conquerors like Alexander, Seleucus, Huns, Shakas and Kushans came here. They established their kingdoms for some time over parts of the territory of this country. Then came the Islamic hordes. Muhammad bin Qasim was the first Islamic invader to occupy the Sindh province in today's Pakistan in the early eighth century CE. From then to the eighteenth century, many parts of the Indian nation were under Muslim rule. After that came the British, who continued to rule over almost the entire Indian territory for over two centuries. During all these times, state was under alien control. Yet, the nation didn't cease to exist. The soul of this nation existed elsewhere, in its religions, culture, pilgrimages, social institutions and many other entities.

In fact, the state as a political institution was even seen as dispensable. In the Mahabharata, there comes a narrative about the first epoch of the Hindu almanac—the *Krita Yuga*.

The relevant verse reads:

Na Rajyam Naiva Rajasit Na Dando na ca Dandikaha
Dharmenaiva Praja Sarvaha Rakshantisma Parasparam

There was no state; no king. There was none to be punished and none to punish. People have protected each other through the eternal principles of *Dharma*.

Thus, aeons before Marx envisaged 'withering away of the state', the Indian nation had experienced such a state of statelessness. Yet, national life had continued.

Chanakya, the great Indian political philosopher, stated that the king was a servant of Dharma. Unlike in nation-states, the Rajah enjoys no special privileges whatsoever. He is mandated to live like a commoner. The happiness of the Rajah lies in the happiness of his subjects. Even his powers as a ruler are subject to the scrutiny of Dharma.

MILLENIA-OLD EXPERIENCE OF INDIA AS RASHTRAM

In India, this kind of Rashtram existed for several millennia as an ethical and spiritual idea pervading the entire national life of Hindus. Innumerable political units had existed in the form of kings, vassals, principalities, self-governed republics and, occasionally, monarchs. But they never interfered in the national life of the people. Their duties were limited to safety, order and development. In fact, while kings were waging wars, society had carried on with its daily chores, unhindered.

As a Rashtram, it had the enormous catholicity to welcome and absorb any number of outside elements, whether they came as aggressors like the Hunas, Kushans, Greeks and other kings, or as refugees like the Zoroastrians and Jews. When its boundaries were threatened, the kings of the Rashtram rose against the enemy. In fact, the kings were mandated to secure the borders, not only of their kingdoms, but also of the Rashtram. A state is only as safe as its borders, Chanakya had cautioned Chandragupta Maurya.

To put it succinctly, the nation doesn't exist for the state; the state exists for the nation. The state, like all other institutions, should be such that it nourishes the nation. An alien-controlled state, however welfare-centric it may be, can't be considered as nurturing the nation. That is the reason why alien rule was opposed through various means by the natives of this country. There is more to a nation than just material well-being. Deen Dayal highlighted this aspect by differentiating between *Swa-rajya* and *Su-rajya*. Swa-rajya is self-rule. Su-rajya is good governance. 'A Swarajya—self-rule with difficulties is still more appropriate than a Su-rajya—good rule which is foreign,'[21] he had said. According to Deen Dayal, a Swa-rajya should perform three obligations towards the nation. The first is that it should be governed by people belonging to the nation. Second, all policies that the state makes should benefit the entire nation. Third, the state shouldn't be influenced by alien thinking or rulers. It should have the ability to chart its own course, uninfluenced by external factors. If a state comes under foreign influence or pressure, it will cause harm to the fabric of the nation, although it might appear to be delivering material benefits to the people.

Talking about the relationship between the nation and the state, Deen Dayal had said, 'Self-rule is only useful and effective until the point that it fulfils the requirements of the motherland. This can only happen when national society progresses from the worship of the state to the worship of the nation. True capability lies not in the state, but in the nation. That is why those who love the nation, worship national values over politics. The nation is the sole truth. Devotion to this truth has been described as a cultural duty. Political duties can only be successful when these intensive national values are bolstered by the strength of cultural duties that accompany them.'

In order to sustain this spirit of ethical and spiritual ideals, various institutions were devised in India. Innumerable sacred places were developed across the length and breadth of the country. Pilgrimages, festivals, etc. became important institutions in the life of the Rashtram, instead of politics and statecraft. A unique band of renounced individuals became the vanguard carrying this ethical, spiritual ideal across the country from place to place, time to time and generation to generation. They authored a number of *Dharma Shastras* to guide the society in upholding the spirit of Rashtram in the contemporary age. Great epics like Ramayana and Mahabharata along with their innumerable forms in later ages became powerful instruments of carrying the message of the Rashtram through generations.

Through the spirit of the Rashtram, the ethical spiritual nationhood, an evolved national life has developed in India. The uniqueness of this Rashtram has been captured by many-a- scholars and travellers in the past. No one could have encapsulated it better in prose than Max Müller, the renowned German Orientalist of the nineteenth century. Max Müller never visited India during his lifetime, but his knowledge about the country and its civilisational history was unparalleled. In his famous essay on India, he wrote: 'If I were asked under what sky the human mind has most fully developed some of its choicest gifts, has most deeply pondered on the greatest problems of life and has found solutions to some of them, I should point to India. And if I were to ask myself from what literature we, in Europe, may draw the corrective which is most wanted in order to make our life more perfect, more comprehensive, more universal, in fact more truly human, a life not for this life only, but a transfigured and eternal life—again I should point to India.'[22]

6

Chiti, the National Soul, and *Virat*, the National Life-Force

Renowned English writer and philosopher, famously known as the 'Prince of Paradox', G.K. Chesterton had once described America as a 'nation with the soul of a church'.[1] The immediate provocation for Chesterton's observation were the questions that he had been asked for his entry into America. When he went to the American consulate to secure papers for travelling to America, the application form contained questions like: Are you an anarchist? Are you a polygamist? Irked and amused by these questions, Chesterton started pondering over the traits of Americans, and the result was an autobiographical essay titled 'What is America'. 'America is the only nation in the world that is founded on a creed,' he concluded.[2]

DO NATIONS HAVE SOULS?

Chesterton's observations sparked a major debate in the world. Do nations, like individuals, have souls? Not just political scientists, but even psychologists had jumped into the fray. Chesterton had based his analysis of America on the document of the Declaration of Independence and opined that 'it enunciates that all men are equal in their claim to justice, and that governments exist to give them that justice, and that their authority is for that reason just. It certainly does condemn anarchism, and it does also by inference condemn atheism, since it clearly names the Creator as the ultimate authority from whom these equal rights are derived.'[3] More than a century-and-a-half after Chesterton, it was the Harvard professor and author Samuel Huntington who had returned to the topic by proclaiming that the soul of America lay in the 'protestant ethic' minus the church.[4]

Decades before Chesterton was to call America's soul as the church, another great Englishman from Chesterton's country, Benjamin Disraeli, a conservative strongman and two-time prime minister of Britain, had championed the idea of a national character. Disraeli was the only Jew to have risen to become the prime minister of Britain. He had built strong foundations for Conservatism in British politics. 'Nations have characters,' Disraeli insisted, adding '… and the national character is precisely the quality which the new sect of statesmen in their schemes and speculations either deny or overlook.'[5]

Some psychologists had disagreements over the efforts to find a common characteristic of nations. The so-called national character, to them, appeared an over-generalisation leading to stereotyping of nations. Their criticism of the national character argument has been focused on the trivialisation of the external character of the peoples of various nations. There is an element of truth in their criticism. National character was made into an aspect of fun and ridicule by resorting to stereotyping of nations based on human behaviour.

'Germans don't laugh', one stereotype goes, because they are 'sticklers for order to the point of absurdity'. The French are 'typical playboys' always 'thinking of wine and women'. The Americans are fond of expensive cars. The Russians are uncouth, pugnacious and reckless, fond of vodka and street brawls. The Hindus are lazy; hence, their slow economic growth was 'Hindu rate of growth'.

There exist several jokes built around such stereotyping. One such joke in Russia goes something like this: What will people of different nationalities do when they see a fly in their glass of beer? The German, being a practical guy, will remove the fly and drink the beer. The Frenchman, being an idealist, will fish out the fly, wipe it, allow it to fly away and discard the beer. The Russian will drink the beer along with the fly, while the American, a guy conscious about his rights, will summon the waiter, scold him to his heart's content and demand another glass of beer.

West European stereotypes are well illustrated in the following joke: Paradise is where the cooks are French, mechanics—German, policemen—British, lovers—Italian and it is all organised by the Swiss. Hell is where the cooks are British, policemen—German, lovers—the Swiss, mechanics—French and it is all organised by Italians.

Such stereotyping of the national character is no doubt incorrect. However, while deriving national character based on external individual behavioural traits may look absurd and out of place, to deny that nations have their own character like individuals, and it is reflected in their social mores, customs and traditions will be taking the argument to the other extreme. Historical experiences mould the character of nations and when nations fail to produce wise men to guide them through those experiences to a higher national purpose, those experiences may have a negative impact on the country's character. Anton Chekhov, renowned Russian writer, quipped that the deep-seated flaw in the Russian personality was 'the slave that lives within every Russian soul'—the psychology of a victim. He believed that centuries of the oppressive Tartar yoke and the subsequent Soviet command system under which Russians had lived for so long left a deep imprint on the country's social and political psyche and is hard to erase.

Two great philosophers of the world, Sri Aurobindo from India and Georg Hegel from Germany, had alluded to the concept of national soul in their writings. 'The nation or society, like the individual, has a body, an organic life, a moral and aesthetic temperament, a developing mind and a soul.... [I]t is a group soul that, once having attained a separate distinctness, must then become more and more self-conscious...,' wrote Sri Aurobindo.[6] Hegel saw 'pure Spirit incarnating into the world, not just as one great beam of light, but as refracted light of many different rays.' He described these rays as incarnating into particular geographical regions that have an ecological integrity or clear boundaries. 'The local ecology—fauna, flora, and humanity—interacts with the incoming ray of Spirit, and the result of that interaction eventually becomes a nation. Thus, each geographical community has its own ray of Spirit, which, as it incarnates, creates the emergence of the *volkgeist*, or folk soul. The national folk soul, which has also been described as an overlighting angel, carries the unique energy of its people and can be seen manifesting in the culture, songs, and myths of its people. This loose-knit grouping of peoples eventually unifies as the Spirit of the nascent nation incarnates more fully. Eventually the soul of the nation begins to express through the sophisticated form of the state, with all its social forms and complex laws which embody the ever-growing collective learning of its people.'[7] To put it simply, Hegel believed that nation was nothing but a spirit, a folk soul, which manifested through the culture, myths and at a sophisticated level, even in the form of the state.

Deen Dayal used the word Chiti for describing the national soul. It is one of the foundational concepts of Deen Dayal's integral humanist thought. Every nation and every culture has its own Chiti, which is like the soul of an individual, he said. 'Chiti is fundamental and is central to the nation from its very beginning. *Chiti* determines the direction in which the nation is to advance culturally. Whatever is in accordance with *Chiti* is included in culture. *Chiti* is the touch-stone on which each action, each attitude is tested, and determined to be acceptable or otherwise. *Chiti* is the soul of the nation. It is on the foundation of this *Chiti* that a nation arises and becomes strong and virile ....,' he wrote.[8]

POLITICS AND CULTURE IN THE MAKING OF A NATION

The history of the world, if analysed correctly, will convey the same message—that nations respond in different ways to similar questions, based on their cultural and civilisational experiences. Conservatives, world over, have agreed to the proposition that national cultures play an important role in shaping the destiny of nations. Alexis de Tocqueville, the nineteenth-century French diplomat and author of *Democracy in America*, had concluded that Americans were culturally democratic because of the religious morals they imbibed in churches. 'I sought for the greatness and genius of America in her commodious harbours and her ample rivers—and it was not there ... in her fertile fields and boundless forests and it was not there ... in her rich mines and her vast world commerce—and it was not there ... in her democratic Congress and her matchless Constitution—and it was not there. Not until I went into the churches of America and heard her pulpits aflame with righteousness did I understand the secret of her genius and power. America is great because she is good, and if America ever ceases to be good, she will cease to be great,' he wrote.[9] 'Americans are so enamoured of equality, that they would rather live in slavery with equality than in freedom with inequality,' he added.

One of the outstanding works in this century on the question of culture's role in nation-making was produced by two Harvard professors. In their thought-provoking symposium on the role of culture in shaping human progress, Lawrence E. Harrison and Samuel P. Huntington discussed this question at length. The symposium papers were compiled into a publication titled *Culture Matters: How Values Shape Human Progress*. Harrison and Huntington had studied how much cultural factors influence the economic and political development of different nations.

This Conservative idea was, of course, contested by the Liberals. They believed that it was politics that defined the destiny of nations, not culture. Daniel Patrick Moynihan, renowned American politician and diplomat, famous for his 1965 report on black poverty in the US, commonly known as the Moynihan Report, had once wryly quipped, 'The central Conservative truth is that it is culture, not politics, that determines the success of a society. The central Liberal truth is that politics can change a culture and save it from itself.'[10]

In the last one century, many efforts have been made to build a world order based on democracy, development and human rights. Theodore Roosevelt, the President of America during the first decade of the twentieth century, had talked about building an 'international political order'. Woodrow Wilson, who succeeded him, had delivered a significant speech to the joint meeting of the US Congress on 8 January 1918. The First World War was coming to an end and Wilson outlined his vision for long-lasting global peace. The speech became famous as the 'Fourteen Points Speech'.[11] Although all his points were not accepted by American allies, his initiative had led to the creation of the first ever international governing body for nations by the name of League of Nations.

Wilson's successor in later years, Franklin D. Roosevelt, who was the President of America during the Second World War, had made 'democratisation' of the world his mission. 'Democracy alone, of all forms of government, enlists the full force of men's enlightened will,' he declared.[12] His successors, right up to George Bush, Jr had invested heavily in this mission of carrying democracy to every country in the world. Successors of Roosevelt and of Marx and Lenin, through Marshall Plan or Five Year Plans, tried to take development and scientific and technological progress to every nook and corner of the world. The politics of Cold War was as much about human development and progress as about a fight between capitalist and communist world orders.

But to the dismay of all, after more than half a century of concerted post-War efforts for human progress and development, when the twenty-first century dawned, global reality seemed something totally different. With honourable exceptions like Hong Kong, Singapore and Taiwan, a vast majority of countries in the Third World continued to be backward, struggling with large populations and poverty. Of the over six billion people living on this planet, only a sixth live in the developed world.[13] Two-thirds lived in countries that the World Bank categorises as low- or middle-income countries. The campaign for democracy, launched by America immediately after the Second World War, too didn't seem to succeed much. Although dozens of countries have come out of the yoke of colonialism and dictatorship in the second half of the last century, largely through the Gandhian way of non-violence, democratic institutions haven't been able to gain a strong foothold in many of them. In the Islamic Middle East, democracy is abhorred. In Africa it is either weak or non-existent. In Latin America, it swings between a cruel dictatorship and a failed democratic leadership. The story of many Asian countries too is not very encouraging. As Fareed Zakaria pointed out in his book, *The Future of Freedom: Illiberal Democracy at Home and Abroad*, democracies in many countries, led by strongmen, have become a major challenge for human freedom and liberty. 'In sum, the world at the end of the twentieth century is far poorer, far more unjust, and far more authoritarian than most people at mid-century expected it would be,' wrote Lawrence Harrison in his foreword to the book, *Culture Matters*.[14]

To strengthen his point that it was ultimately the culture of a nation that determined its progress, Huntington compared two countries, Ghana in Africa and South Korea in Asia, that had almost identical economies in the 1950s. Economies of both these countries had almost identical per capita GDP, and were receiving almost the same amount of external aid in the 1950s. Half a century later, South Korea had emerged as one of the top fifteen economies in the world with a per capita equalling that of several developed countries in Europe. Moreover, in spite of serious provocations in the neighbourhood, South Korea remained strongly wedded to democratic institutions of governance. But Ghana remained where it was, with a per capita gross national income almost six times lower than that of South Korea. On the question of democratic institutions too, its credentials are questionable. 'How could this extraordinary difference in development be explained?' Huntington questioned, adding, 'Undoubtedly, many factors played a role, but it seemed to me that culture had to be a large part of the explanation. South Koreans valued thrift, investment, hard work, education, organization and discipline. Ghanaians had different values. In short, cultures count.'[15]

CULTURAL NATIONALISM IN INDIA

India offers a classic example of a unique culture that has contributed to shaping its national life. Its view of everything—people, morals, social order, environment—is distinctly different from that of the rest of the nations in the world. Even in being different, it has its uniqueness which was aptly described by Swami Vivekananda while addressing the World Parliament of Religions in 1893. 'I am proud to belong to a religion which has taught the world both tolerance and universal acceptance. We believe not only in universal toleration, but we accept all religions as true,' he exhorted.[16] At a time when the world was discussing the virtues of tolerance, Swami Vivekananda stood up to tell the world that India, in its thinking, didn't stop at tolerance alone. Tolerance has an element of arrogance in it. 'I am superior, yet I tolerate your inferior being', was how the Semitic religions had presented the concept of tolerance at that time. But Indian cultural experience has been not only about tolerance, but acceptance and validation of all the different religions and thought processes as true; and to further celebrate this diversity.

Many Western scholars too have acknowledged and appreciated this uniqueness in Indian culture. Michael Wood, a famous British historian, had said, 'India was one of the earliest of the great civilizations and it defined the goals of civilized life very differently from the West. The West raised individualism, materialism, rationality, [and] masculinity as it ideals. India's great tradition insisted on non-violence, renunciation, the inner life, [and] the female as pillars of civilization. And through all the triumphs and disasters of her history she hung on to that ideal, an eternal quest to identify humanity with the whole of creation, a unity in diversity … History is full of empires of the sword but India alone created an empire of the spirit.'[17]

Margaret Elizabeth Noble was an Irish woman who met Swami Vivekananda in 1895 at London and became his disciple. She later arrived in India in 1898 and became a monk. Swami Vivekananda gave her a spiritual name as Bhagini (Sister) Nivedita. Her scholarship and depth of understanding about India and Hinduism was in no way inferior to that of her guru. In one of her speeches, she had raised an interesting question to highlight the cultural uniqueness of India. 'Had Niagara been situated on the Ganges, it is odd to think how different would have been its valuation by humanity,' she stated, and went on to say, 'Instead of fashionable picnics and railway pleasure trips, the yearly or monthly incursion of worshipping crowds. Instead of hotels, temples. Instead of ostentatious excess, austerity. Instead of the desire to harness its mighty forces to the chariot of human utility, the unrestrainable longing to throw away the body, and realise at once the ecstatic madness of Supreme Union. Could contrast be greater?'[18]

'The life of spirit' that Nivedita talked about was what Deen Dayal described as the Chiti, inner soul, of India. Events in India's past reflect the manifestation of this inner soul. The Chinese had built the Great Wall over a period starting from seventh century BCE. Chinese history claims that it took 1,600 years and hundreds of emperors to build this wall and its supposed length varies from 8,000 km to 21,000 km. The ostensible reason given for building such a mammoth wall was to protect Chinese empires from the aggressions of nomads from the north. If we look at Indian history, all major invasions into India happened through one major mountain pass called the Khyber Pass. Why did it not occur to any Indian king to close the pass by building a wall across it? The ethos of India, its belief in the dictum *Vasudhaiva Kutumbakam*—the entire world is but one family—doesn't allow the idea of shutting off from the rest of the world. Not until recently did India consider sealing its borders on some fronts.

'All warfare is based on deception,' declared ancient Chinese general and strategist Sun Tzu in his acclaimed treatise, *The Art of War*.[19] Deception and cunning were integral to warfare, according to him. On the other hand, in India, the epic Bhagavad Gita that discusses the philosophy of war through the Mahabharata, begins with a verse *'Dharma Kshetre Kuru Kshetre'*. It describes the battlefield of Kuru as 'Dharma *Kshetra*', meaning 'a field of righteousness'.[20]

The decision of the Indian leadership to pass on the membership of the UN Security Council to China despite it being offered to India; or its refusal to take over the Gwadar port from Oman when the Emir wanted to sell it to India—while these actions attracted genuine criticism, they also demonstrated the specific cultural trait of the country. Even in day-to-day life, even in the remotest of villages and the poorest of families, the day will most likely start with prayer to rivers and nature and end with *'Lok Kalyan ho'*—Let there be glory to mankind. Not about self, nor family, nor caste, nor country, but the well-being of all of humanity. This is the manifestation of Chiti in the daily life of an average Indian.

CHITI AND VIRAT, SOUL AND LIFE FORCE OF A NATION

'The shape of a nation is determined by the collective fundamental nature of the "one people". No matter what changes occur in the outer structures according to the times and situations, the fundamental characteristics of the nation do not change. As long as the principles, for the vindication of which the nation took birth, are followed, the *Chiti* will remain alive and conscious. It will be ready to face daunting challenges and move on. It will be prepared to make greatest sacrifices for the global good,' wrote Deen Dayal.[21]

Can Chiti then be equated with patriotism? Yes and no. Chiti is sublime and invisible. It is an emotion and spirit. It manifests through the actions of people. Patriotism is one such action. Chiti is concerned with the happiness of the individual soul. Famous Greek philosopher Aristotle had said, 'Man is by nature a social animal; an individual who is unsocial naturally and not accidentally is either beneath our notice or more than human. Society is something that precedes the individual.'[22] Individuals can't survive in a vacuum. They are dependent on relationships for survival. It can be contested as to whether an organised society had been a reality from the beginning. But it is indisputable that societies and nations have evolved over time, demonstrating varied qualities and characteristics. These qualities and characteristics that make a nation are the Chiti of that nation.

The Chiti has the potential to awaken the organised spirit of the nation. People of a nation can't be motivated by principles that are alien to their inner soul. But the Chiti can motivate them to make supreme sacrifices in achieving the lofty goals of its national mission. This kind of awakening of the inner Purushartha, life-force of a nation, on the basis of its Chiti was described by Deen Dayal as the Virat—the superior being. The Virat—the consolidated mega power of a nation stirred up by the Chiti—manifests only after a mammoth effort. It calls for the creation of 'one people' out of the multitude of masses on the basis of the national inner soul— the Chiti. Mahatma Gandhi's efforts at using cultural symbolism to mobilise national power during the freedom struggle was an example of that. Speaking in the Constituent Assembly of India, T. Prakasam, a member of the Madras Presidency, highlighted Gandhi's contribution to the freedom movement by calling him

a 'seer'. 'I had a talk with the great Lala Lajpat Rai more than
forty-five years ago in England. He was the earliest of the sufferers
for freedom and he said: "Look at the organization and discipline
and the way in which people here conduct themselves. Can we
ever hope to send away these British people from our country and
establish freedom?" That was my feeling when I touched that shore.
Under those circumstances it was, that this man, Gandhiji came as
a Seer and lifted us up.'[23]

Once the Virat of a nation wakes up, its success can't be stalled.
Waking up of the Virat of this nation, inspired by its Chiti, has been
witnessed on several occasions after independence too—during the
wars against the neighbours and campaigns like Swachch Bharat
(Clean India).

Waking up of the Virat—consummate inner power of the life-
force of a nation—is not an easy task. Deen Dayal's prescription
was that it was only the Chiti—the enlightened national soul—
that could achieve this awakening. There are occasions when the
very survival of nations is challenged. Nations that rise up to the
challenge on the basis of their inner soul will succeed in warding
off these threats. Nations that fail to do so or resort to dependence
on alien powers and philosophies will eventually perish. Failure
to realise the national soul, Chiti, and the subsequent failure to
awaken the inner power, Virat, on the strength of that Chiti is the
reason why nations perish.

Prime Minister Lal Bahadur Shastri's call of *Jai Jawan—Jai
Kisan* likely found greater resonance with the people of India than
the many speeches laced with modern scientific terminology made
by his predecessor Jawaharlal Nehru. This was so because Shastri's
appeals were not just about material wealth but also about the
wealth of character and national unity. 'We can win respect in the
world only if we are strong internally and can banish poverty and
unemployment from our country. Above all, we need national
unity. Communal, provincial and linguistic conflicts weaken the

country. Therefore, we have to forge national unity. I appeal to all to work for national unity and usher in a social revolution to make our country strong. In the ultimate analysis, the strength of the country does not lie in its material wealth alone. It requires people like Mahatma Gandhi, Jawaharlal Nehru and Rabindranath Tagore. It requires the force of character and moral strength. I appeal to our young men to inculcate discipline in themselves and work for the unity and advancement of the nation,' he had said in his first Independence Day speech in 1964 that had stirred the conscience of the entire nation.[24]

Another significant effort at awakening national power through the appeal to the emotions of the national soul could be found in the famous address of Prime Minister Winston Churchill to the British Parliament on 4 June 1940. The Second World War was at its peak. European powers in the British neighbourhood, like France and Belgium, had fallen to the *Wehrmacht*—the German war machine. Next in line was the British island. Churchill was elected as the prime minister that year when the country was faced with the worst challenge in the war. The self-esteem and confidence of the British government was at its all-time low. The leadership was preparing for the eventuality of a German victory. The cabinet was in a state of disillusionment. That was when Churchill decided to use his oratory skill to rekindle the national spirit. His famous speech, which left several parliamentarians shedding tears of emotion and joy, remains one of the greatest speeches in world history even to this day.

'Even though large tracts of Europe and many old and famous States have fallen or may fall into the grip of the Gestapo and all the odious apparatus of Nazi rule, we shall not flag or fail. We shall go on to the end. We shall fight in France, we shall fight on the seas and oceans, we shall fight with growing confidence and growing strength in the air, we shall defend our island, whatever the cost may be. We shall fight on the beaches, we shall fight on the landing grounds, we shall fight in the fields and in the streets, we shall fight in the hills; we shall never surrender, and if, which I do not for a moment believe, this island or a large part of it were subjugated and starving, then our Empire beyond the seas, armed and guarded by the British Fleet, would carry on the struggle, until, in God's good time, the New World, with all its power and might, steps forth to the rescue and the liberation of the old,' thundered Churchill.[25] History was witness to how a rejuvenated Britain finally emerged victorious in the war.

Chiti and Virat are thus unique concepts that Deen Dayal had introduced in the national discourse in the last century.

7

Dharmic vs Semitic:
Worldviews at Variance

What are the characteristics of Chiti and how does it manifest and preserve itself? Deen Dayal's answer was 'through Dharma'. 'The laws that help manifest and maintain Chiti of a nation are termed Dharma of that nation. Hence, it is this Dharma that is supreme. Dharma is the repository of the nation's soul. If Dharma is destroyed, the nation perishes. Anyone who abandons Dharma, betrays the nation,' he had said.[1] In other words, according to Deen Dayal, Dharma was the legal and constitutional framework around which the Chiti of the nation would manifest, and by which it would be protected.

DHARMA: THE DEFINITIONAL CHALLENGE

Before understanding what Dharma is all about and how, in Deen Dayal's opinion, it formed the basis for India's national identity, it is important to distance it from the English word 'religion'. This easy but inaccurate translation of the quintessential Indian word— Dharma—into a commonly used English word—religion—has led to serious doctrinal confusion in India and around the world too. Authors like Rajiv Malhotra have argued that Indian scholars should be wary of the 'digestion' of their language in the name of global culture. 'The distinctiveness of the cultural and spiritual matrix of dharma civilizations is under siege from something insidious: the widespread dismantling, rearrangement, and digestion of dharmic culture into Western frameworks, by disingenuously characterizing the latter as "universal",' Rajiv Malhotra argued in his book *Sanskrit Non-Translatables*.[2]

Deen Dayal too warned about the dangers of wrong interpretations arising out of internalisation into a Western language system. 'Religion means a creed or a sect. It doesn't mean Dharma. Dharma is a very broad concept. It is concerned with all aspects of life. It sustains society. It sustains the whole world. That which sustains is Dharma,' he said.[3] Deen Dayal attributed the confusion around the concept of Dharma to foreign education. 'The distortions of Dharma that we nowadays see all around are largely the result of foreign education. The English word "religion" has substantially contributed in distorting the pure meaning of Dharma. The British first heard this word when they came to India. They had no word of an equally comprehensive meaning. So, they translated it as religion. Such translations have distorted the meaning of Indian words,' he insisted.[4]

For want of a better word, even Gandhi was compelled to use the word 'religion' to denote Dharma. But he would make it a point to differentiate his concept of religion from how it was commonly understood. 'Religion must pervade every one of our actions. Here religion doesn't mean sectarianism. It means a belief in ordered moral government of the universe. It is not less real because it is not seen. This religion transcends Hinduism, Islam, Christianity etc. It doesn't supersede them. It harmonises them and gives them reality,' Gandhi wrote.[5] And in Sri Aurobindo's words, 'Hinduism gave itself no name, because it set itself no sectarian limits; it claimed no universal adhesion; asserted no sole infallible dogma; set up no single narrow path or gate of salvation; it was less a creed or cult than a continuously enlarging tradition of the god-ward endeavour of the human spirit. An immense, many-sided and many-staged provision for a spiritual self-building and self-finding, it had some right to speak of itself by the only name it knew, the eternal religion, Sanatana Dharma.'[6]

However, definitional problems continue to abound. Essentially, concepts that have originated in classical Indian thought like Rashtram and Dharma continue to elude Westerners and English-influenced Indians alike. The Collins dictionary describes religion as 'belief in a god or gods and the activities that are connected with this belief, such as praying or worshipping in a building such as a church or temple'.[7] The Oxford dictionary defines religion as the 'belief in and worship of a superhuman controlling power, especially a personal God or gods'.[8] The encyclopaedic meaning of religion is 'a way of worship'. It denotes man's relationship with the almighty God through a particular way of belief and worship.

Dharma doesn't prescribe any one particular way of worship, nor does it prescribe any one single God. Like the word religion, the word 'God' too is understood differently in the West and in India. Seeing a huge pantheon of god-heads in Indian civilisation, the Semitic religions have attempted to describe the Indian religion as 'polytheistic'. It was for them a contradiction between 'one God and many gods'. Dharma is neither monotheistic nor polytheistic; it is omni-theistic, meaning, it sees divinity all over and everywhere. It is not about 'one God versus many gods'; it is about 'One God versus only God'. 'Sarvam Khalvidam Brahma', meaning 'Whatever is there is Brahman—the divine', is the core message of Dharma[9] (Chandogya Upanishad).

The Supreme Court of India was faced with a significant question relating to the definition of religion in a peculiar election-related petition. The election of the leader of a regional party in Maharashtra called Shiv Sena was challenged on the grounds that the candidate, Manohar Joshi, had invoked Hindutva in his election campaign, which was tantamount to invoking religion.[10] Indian electoral laws prohibit the use of religion in election campaigns. The Supreme Court was saddled with the question of the difference between the Western concept of religion and the Indian concept of Dharma. The word Hindu is always appended with the word Dharma and called Hindu Dharma. It is understood and misinterpreted as Hindu religion.

In a landmark judgement, describing Dharma as a consortium of values, the apex court had held that the word Hindutva cannot be automatically understood to be denoting any religion; instead, it is to be understood as a 'way of life', and not as a 'way of worship'. In the judgment delivered on 11 December 1995, setting aside the earlier decision of the Bombay High Court to that petition, the five-judge Constitution Bench of the Supreme Court headed by Justice J.S. Verma had observed: 'These Constitution Bench decisions, after a detailed discussion, indicate that no precise meaning ascribed to the terms "Hindu", "Hindutva", and "Hinduism"; and no meaning in the abstract can confine it to the narrow limits of religion alone, excluding the context of Indian culture and heritage. It is difficult to appreciate how in the face of these decisions, the term "Hindutva" or "Hinduism" per se, in the abstract, can be assumed to mean and be equated with narrow fundamentalist Hindu religious bigotry....'[11] The learned judges had added that: 'It is a fallacy and an error of law to proceed on the assumption that any reference to Hindutva or Hinduism in a speech makes it automatically a speech based on Hindu religion as opposed to other religions or that the use of the word Hindutva or Hinduism per se depicts an attitude hostile to all persons practising any religion other than Hindu religion ... and it may well be that these words are used in a speech to emphasise the way of life of the Indian people and the Indian cultural ethos.'[12]

However, even this definition—of Hinduism being a way of life and not just worship—doesn't fully address all concerns. Which religion is not also a 'way of life'? Semitic religions command every aspect of the believer's life, and so do many Indic religions like Buddhism, Jainism, Sikhism and Vedic Hinduism. In that sense, they too are qualified to be not just 'ways of worship' but 'ways of life' too.

The closest English equivalent for Dharma, thus, cannot be 'way of life' as against 'way of worship'. Dharma can be uniquely understood as a 'view of life'; a worldview that is eminently different from religious and theological concepts that emanated from the Semitic region or materialist European concepts like capitalism and communism. It probably talked about the very same things that the other religious and material philosophies have been talking about in all these millennia. But it has a different take on each and every one of those, a different vision and conception, that is based on a value system which is a product of the age-old wisdom of national life in India.

UNDERSTANDING DHARMA

Religions in the West have focused on morals and dos and don'ts for mankind. 'Monotheism transformed the vision of human nature and the character of moral thinking. All three monotheistic faiths developed during times of great social dislocation, each fashioned in such circumstances a distinct kind of moral anchor. There was a new reason to be moral: because God, all-seeing, all-knowing, loving yet wrathful, requires it of you. Monotheism made humans both greater and lesser than they had been before. They had been created by God in His image. Yet they were now seen as weak, corrupt, flawed and broken; reason had become subservient to faith,' wrote Kenan Malik.[13] If you forgot god, your moralism was dead, the monotheists insisted.

Dharma, on the other hand, is not about mere dos and don'ts. It is not about morals, but about values. Dharma propounds a value system that binds society together, and gives it a direction and a life mission.

Shimon Peres, the legendary leader of Israel and its former prime minister, in his latest book, *No Room for Small Dreams*, made an interesting observation about the Jewish nation. 'The Jewish people have lived by the guiding principle of *tikkum olam*, the ambition to improve the whole world, not just ourselves. We lived in exile for two thousand years, without land, without independence, held together not by borders, but by this simple set of values that have echoed through history—in Hebrew, in Yiddish, in Ladino—in every language of every country into which the Jewish people dispersed. It is the basis of our identity. And it is from this moral code that we knew, fundamentally, that Israel was not born to rule over other people, that to do so is in profound opposition to our heritage.'[14] The choice of words shouldn't be missed—'set of values', 'identity', 'moral code', 'heritage'. It is those words that constitute a distinct worldview, on the lines similar to Dharma.

Does that mean religion has nothing to do with Dharma? Are they two altogether different entities and concepts? Janaki Abhisheki beautifully answered this question in her book, *Religion as Knowledge*.[15] Components of religion also form part of Dharma, but it is not limited to or by them. It goes beyond holy scriptures and their teachings and injunctions. It is about practise and penance. It is a journey inwards as much as it is outwards.

'How was man to understand Dharma?' asked Abhisheki, and explained: 'Four sources are given by the composers of the *Dharmashastras*—the sacred texts, viz., the *Vedas*, *Smritis* (authorities in regard to rule of law and behaviour), *Sadaachaara*—the good examples set by the good, and fourthly, doing that which is "good for the soul".'[16] Thus, according to her, Dharma is as much about scriptural wisdom as it is about one's actions guided by the soul.

Talking of one's actions being in line with Dharma, Deen Dayal exhorted that even the gods couldn't go against it. 'God cannot act contrary to Dharma. If he does, he is not omnipotent. Strength lies not in unrestrained behaviour, but in well-regulated action.

Therefore, the god, who is omnipotent is also self-regulated, and consequently, fully in tune with Dharma. God descends in the human body to destroy *Adharma* (against Dharma) and re-establish Dharma, not to act on his own whims and fancies. Even at the risk of being misunderstood, one can say that Dharma is superior to god. The universe is sustainable only if the god acts according to Dharma,' he emphasised.[17]

Dharma as a value system includes actions, not only of humans but even gods. Does that mean rigidity? Does that mean controlling the 'way of life'? If so, then what is the difference between Dharma and the Semitic religions that control each and every individual action as part of their religious worldview? It is important to understand this distinction.

Dharma as a value system is not static; it is not stuck in some historic past. It doesn't insist upon a 'certain type of behaviour'. It is flexible. 'The Vedic religion has always undergone transformation. It is dynamic and living. It is not like a stagnant pool,' Deen Dayal had said, adding 'The fundamentals of Dharma are eternal and universal; however, their manifestation can vary based on time, place and situations.'[18] The Dharmic worldview believes in an ever-changing social order based on unchanging eternal values.

Since it is 'ever-changing', there needs to be an authority to create synthesis between the 'ever-changing' and the 'unchanging'. That authority in Dharma traditions is vested in the institution of Gurus. The institution of the Guru is unique to Indic religious traditions only. Others have teachers, but the Indic people have masters. A master does not teach; they show the way. A teacher or a preacher teaches the past; a master or a Guru envisions the future. A teacher narrates; a Guru lives. Gurus in the Dharma traditions are endowed with Dharmic knowledge on one hand and the authority to interpret it to changing times on the other. No other religion in the world has this unique institution.

The value system that is described as Dharma is a product of the

Indian genius that evolved over centuries of penance and dialogue. Yet, it is universal. In fact, Hindus call it Sanatana Dharma, meaning an eternal value system, universal in time and space. In the course of a long history, the sages and saints of India have defined and interpreted the concept of Dharma in multiple ways.

In the *Shanti Parva* of the Mahabharata, it was stated:

Yah syatprabhavasamyuktah sa dharma iti nischayah—That which is able to bring about evolution is called Dharma.[19]

Adi Shankara described Dharma as:

Jagatah Sthitikaranam Praninam Sakshat Abhyudaya Nishreyasa Heturyah sa Dharmah—Dharma is that which accomplishes exceptional administration of the entire world, brings about worldly progress of every living being and causes progress in the spiritual realm as well.[20]

Sage Valmiki proclaimed in the *Aranya Kand* of the Ramayana: *Dharmasaram Idam Jagat*—This entire universe is the essence of Dharma.[21]

THE DHARMIC WORLDVIEW

In his famous poem 'The Ballad of East and West', Rudyard Kipling, a British journalist of the last century who was born in India, had quipped, 'East is East, and West is West, and never the twain shall meet.' Dharma as a view of life goes about enumerating a set of moral and ethical values for mankind. It is these values that distinguish the Dharma worldview from the Western worldview.

1. On the question of creation, the Dharma worldview believes: *Sarvam Khalvidam Brahma* (*Chandogya Upanishad*).

The entire universe, animate and inanimate alike, is pervaded by the *Brahman*—the divine consciousness.

The Semitic or Western worldview attributes divinity only to the Trinity—God, His son and the Holy Ghost, whereas the Dharmic worldview sees divinity everywhere.

2. On the question of ethnic, racial, linguistic and other differences in the world, Dharma proposes:

Vasudhaiva Kutumbakam

The entire world is one family. The West has, so far, only reached the idea of 'global markets', whereas the Dharmic worldview proposes the concept of a 'global family'.

3. On the economic question, Dharma talks about 'sustained consumption':

tena tyaktena bhunjitah (*Isavasya Upanishad*, Ch. 4)

One should acquire only as much as was left to them by *Isvara*.[22]

There has been a lot of discussion around 'sustainable development' in the world in recent times. 'Sustainable consumption' as a means for sustainable development is a new idea that mankind is embracing now, whereas Dharma had talked about it ages ago.

4. On the welfare question, it states:

sarve bhavantu sukinah—sarve santu niramayah

Let all be happy and free from diseases.

As against the Western idea of 'maximum benefit to maximum number', the Dharma view insists on the principle of 'happiness for all'.

5. On environment related questions, its proposition is:

Mata bhumi putro'ham prithvyah (*Atharva Veda* 12|1|12)

This earth is my mother, and I am her son.

Where the Western philosophies propagated the idea of 'subduing of nature' (Genesis 1:28), the Dharmic worldview proposed the idea of 'milking nature' just as a child draws milk from their mother.

6. On the question of religious diversity in the world, it explains:

Ekam Sadvipraa bahudhaa Vadanti maatarisvaanamaahuh—(Rig Veda)

Truth is one; wise men interpret it in different ways.[23]

The greatest idea of the Dharma school is the universal acceptance of religious diversity as against the condescension and intolerance of Semitic philosophies.

Dharma worldview also insists:

nana vibrati bahudha vivacasam
nana dharmanam prithivi yathaukasam
sahasra dhara dravitasya ye duham
dhruvena dhamurenk pasphuranti

'The earth is full of variety; it contains people speaking different dialects and speech, of diverse religious customs, each living according to what they think is right. The earth contains innumerable valuable things. It bears trees and plants of great diversity. We should pay homage to that Earth.'[24]

SEEKERS VS BELIEVERS

It is interesting to note that on most fundamental concepts, the Semitic and Western worldview is philosophically contrarian to that of the Dharma worldview. In fact, the differences are so deep and profound that the oft-repeated cliché 'All religions are equal' sounds very hollow. The Dharma worldview and the Semitic worldview differ from and disagree with each other on almost all aspects right from creation to salvation. It is a simple matter that two things, whose beginnings and ends are not the same, can't be 'equal'. Nevertheless, both deserve 'equal respect'.

Omnipresence of God is a unique fundamental of Dharma traditions. A very interesting anecdote about this concept comes up in the life of renowned Hindu saint Namdev. The anecdote goes thus: One day, Namdev returned to his temple at noon, only to find his Guru sleeping in the sanctum sanctorum, resting his legs on the Shiva linga. Rattled, Namdev wished his Guru to respond on why he had performed such a blasphemous act. His Guru's simple answer in the form of a counter-question reveals the great universal vision of the Dharma tradition. 'I agree that I had rested my feet on the sacred linga. But can you please show me a place that is not sacred, so that I can rest my legs there?' The Dharmic traditions not only see divinity all around, but also encourage humankind to seek union with that divine through rational human thinking.

The Dharmic worldview does not agree with the Semitic proposition that the final word has already been spoken by God. While viewing all of creation as leela (divine play), Hinduism also insisted upon a scientific and rational approach to life. Hence, seeking involves not just devotion but rational thinking too.

'Hindu thought has no mistrust of reason. There can be no final breach between the two powers of the human mind, reason and intuition. Beliefs that foster and promote the spiritual life of the soul must be in accordance with the nature and the laws of the world of reality with which it is their aim to bring us into harmony,' wrote Dr Sarvapalli Radhakrishnan in his famous book, *The Hindu View of Life*.[25] He went on to add: 'Precious as are the echoes of God's voice in the souls of men of long ago, our regard for them must be tempered by the recognition of the truth that God has never finished the revelation of His wisdom and love. Besides, our interpretation of religious experience must be in conformity with the findings of science. As knowledge grows, our theology develops. Only those parts of the tradition which are logically coherent are to be accepted as superior to the evidence of the senses and not the whole tradition.'[26]

Radhakrishnan emphasised that 'Hinduism is a movement, not a position; a process, not a result; a growing tradition, not a fixed revelation.'[27]

Semitic theology, on the other hand, encourages people to become 'Believers'. Reason should be subordinated to devotion. Both the Bible and the Quran were not creations of the messengers— Jesus and Mohammed—but their followers. Neither Jesus nor Mohammed wrote anything. Many of their contemporaries were illiterate too. Whatever is known about Jesus comes from the gospels of Matthew, Luke, Mark and John. How much of the gospels and the letters of St. Paul, the other source of Jesus's story, are true has been a matter of debate to this day. Similarly, the Holy Quran was created at least a decade after Mohammed's death. Caliph Uthman, who was a companion of Mohammed, commissioned a clerk in his kingdom to collect and collate various Suras and thus emerged the holy scripture.[28] These Semitic texts have been accorded the status of divine injunctions, which cannot be amended. Followers were asked to have unquestioning belief in them as the pristine word of God.

Semitic traditions are predominantly monotheistic. The case of the Dharmic traditions is very complex and Hinduism is the fountainhead of Dharmic traditions.

'In Hinduism, anthropomorphism (nature worship), polytheism, monotheism, monism and even atheism exist side by side. Hinduism is not a monotheistic religion. Buddhism and Jainism are religions without the concept of God as their central theme. Confucianism and Taoism in China, again are not religions in the Western understanding of the word. The idea of being "religious" is ultimately a Western idea. In the Hindu tradition, there were atheistic and materialistic schools of thought, like Charvaka, all of which get lumped under "Hinduism". Obviously, if we take the Abrahamic idea of religion, atheistic religion is absurd—you can't really be a "Christian atheist" or a "Muslim atheist"—not so long ago you would be hung for heresy,' an article in the online magazine *Veda* stated.[29]

FOUR-FOLD WESTERN BELIEF SYSTEM

Twentieth-century Western thought is a product of certain doctrinal fundamentals. These fundamentals are the outcome of the religious and philosophical thinking of the West from the last few centuries. Unlike Eastern civilisations, the experience of the West has been limited to a few centuries. From that limited experience came certain fundamental convictions like:

1. Struggle for existence
2. Survival of the fittest
3. Exploitation of nature
4. Individual rights

Struggle for existence

Right from the ancient Greek philosophers like Heraclitus of Ephesus, who wrote of struggle being the father of everything, to Aristotle, who saw struggle as a permanent feature for sustenance in the animal kingdom, and Thomas Hobbes' vivid description of 'a war of every man against every man', to Darwin's famous chapter of the same name in the book *On the Origin of Species*, Western thinkers have religiously believed in the idea that struggle and conflict are inevitable to human existence.

Darwin explained his beliefs on this question thus: 'A struggle for existence inevitably follows from the high rate at which all organic beings tend to increase [so that] on the principle of geometrical increase, its numbers would quickly become so inordinately great that no country could support the product. Hence, as more individuals are produced than can possibly survive, there must, in every case, be a struggle for existence, either one individual with another of the same species, or with the individuals of distinct species, or with the physical conditions of life. It is the doctrine of Malthus applied with manifold force to the whole animal and vegetable kingdoms.'[30]

Karl Marx too believed that conflict was inherent in human progress. In fact, he theorised it by claiming that human race progresses only through conflict. His theory of dialectic materialism proposed that the engine of progress is conflict. It is through conflict that societies change and progress. The more the conflict, the better the evolution of society, he had said. Dialectical conflict is the engine of social change, Marx concluded.

'Hegel put forward the principles of thesis, anti-thesis and synthesis; Karl Marx used this principle as a basis and presented his analysis of history and economics; Darwin considered the principle of survival of the fittest as the sole basis of life; but we, in this country saw the basic unity of all life,' said Deen Dayal.[31]

Dharma traditions believe that there is fundamental harmony
and order in creation. Conflict exists, but only as a result of
ignorance, not as a fundamental truth. Conflict represents the
degradation and downfall of a society, not its progress. It occurs
when societies ignore the fundamental oneness of creation and the
universe. The Vedantic concept of *Maya*—illusion—explains the
reasons for conflict in creation.

Survival of the fittest

The second concept of the 'survival of the fittest' was first coined by
renowned English philosopher of the nineteenth century, Herbert
Spencer. He deduced this idea from Darwin's concept of 'natural
selection' and applied it to the socio-economic sphere. 'This survival
of the fittest, which I have here sought to express in mechanical
terms, is that which Mr. Darwin has called "natural selection", or
the preservation of favoured races in the struggle for life,' wrote
Spencer.[32]

Again, Dharmic traditions have never accepted the theory of
'preservation of the favoured races in the struggle for life'. This
one concept, derived from the Darwinian theory of the struggle
for existence, has become the cause of countless wars, conflicts and
socio-political upheavals in human history. Deen Dayal used to
famously argue that the Western capitalist dictum—'whoever earns
will eat'—a product of Darwin and Spencer's ideas, should not be
accepted as valid. As per Dharmic traditions, 'those who are born
will eat; and those earn will feed'. It is not just the fittest who shall
survive; everyone who is born shall have a right to survive.

Exploitation of nature

'Exploitation of nature' has been the bane of mankind. In a way,
it has its origins in Semitic theories of creation itself. The story of
Adam and Eve eventually leads to the conclusion that nature is
created for human happiness and enjoyment.

In the Genesis 1:26-28, God instructs humanity to manage creation in particular ways. 'And God blessed them, and God said unto them, Be fruitful, and multiply, and replenish the earth, and subdue it: and have dominion over the fish of the sea, and over the fowl of the air, and over every living thing that moveth upon the earth.'

The idea of 'subduing' the earth and 'dominion' over everything that moves upon the earth is anathematic to Dharmic traditions that call the earth 'the mother'. Domination and exploitation are alien to Dharmic traditions. 'Nature has enough for everybody's need; not for everybody's greed', Mahatma Gandhi had famously admonished once.

Reverence for nature is integral to Dharmic traditions. In fact, Dharmic traditions are worship-centric traditions. Everything, animate and inanimate, is sacred for the people of these traditions. That is why, in Hinduism, there are as many temples for animal godheads as human gods. God in Hinduism is described in ten different manifestations, half of them being animal forms. Nature worship is integral to Dharmic traditions.

A recent Indian example of conflict between the Western concept of development through exploitation of nature and the Dharmic concept of reverence for nature was the Chipko movement of 1970. This movement, led by a Gandhian, Sundarlal Bahuguna, became a global inspiration for people fighting to protect forests and the environment. It all started when contracts were issued by the government for cutting trees in the forests of the present day Uttarakhand state at the foothills of the Himalayas. Aware that dangers like floods, landslides and reduction in rainfall were largely being caused due to indiscriminate cutting down of forest cover, residents of a village called Reni had decided to prevent the execution of this government order. Women were at the forefront of these unique protests. These women hugged the trees for days on end, preventing loggers from cutting them. *Chipko* in Hindi means 'to cling on'. Because the women clung to the trees and did not give up, the contractors were finally forced to abandon logging and the government too had to relent.

Individual rights

On the question of individual human rights, it will be very instructive to turn to an exchange of correspondence between Mahatma Gandhi and Dr Julian Huxley in mid-1947. 'I learnt from my illiterate but wise mother that all rights to be deserved and preserved came from duty well done,' wrote Gandhi.[33]

The rights discourse is very prominent in the West. In Dharmic traditions, this discourse always comes together with duties.

In fact, Western societies have faced some moral dilemmas for many centuries. What is important? Good of the man or good of the community? What motivates man? His selfish interest or subsuming it in the larger interest of the community? Just as the Dharmic traditions pondered over these questions and built a value system for universal welfare and well-being, ancient Western philosophers like Socrates too looked into these questions and concluded that 'men of reason' should rule the world.

Plato's eminent thesis, 'The Republic' chronicles Socrates' discourse with Plato's brother Glaucon. Glaucon challenged Socrates to prove that a just man with a bad reputation was happier than an unjust man widely perceived as good. Socrates approached this challenge with an analogy: Justice in a man is like justice in a city, he proposed. A just city is where there is harmony, cooperation and peace. An unjust city is where there is friction, exploitation and chaos. In order for a city to be happy, it must be ruled by philosophers who knew what is good for all, as against what is good for some. Philosopher kings are needed, he proposed. He then addressed the question of the individual on the same lines. Just as philosophers must rule a happy city, reason must rule a happy man.

If reason rules, then man understands what is truly good, not just what appears to be good.

Reason, morality and values are the extraordinary human capabilities that have made civilisations possible. The Dharmic order has been built on these capabilities over millennia and flowered into a unique view and way of life in India.

8

Institutions to Sustain Dharmic Social Order

INSTITUTION-BUILDING IN THE WEST

In Europe, man is seen as a self-centred and dollar-hunting animal. In his magnum opus *Politics*, Aristotle vividly discusses this nature of self-interest in man. 'Again, how immeasurably greater is the pleasure, when a man feels a thing to be his own; for surely the love of self is a feeling implanted by nature and not given in vain, although selfishness is rightly censured; this, however, is not the mere love of self, but the love of self in excess, like the miser's love of money; for all, or almost all, men love money and other such objects in a measure,' he argued. Both Plato and Aristotle believed that the good of the individual should be subordinate to the good of the collective. 'No citizen should think that he belongs just to himself. He must regard all citizens as belonging to the state, for each is a part of the state; and the responsibility for each part naturally has regard to the responsibility for the whole,' Aristotle had stated.[1]

John Stuart Mill was the first leading Western economist to conclude that man was essentially an economic being. This nineteenth-century British philosopher had proposed an arbitrary definition of man as 'a being who inevitably does that by which he may obtain the greatest amount of necessaries, conveniences, and luxuries, with the smallest quantity of labour and physical self-denial with which they can be obtained.'[2] That is how the idea of the 'economic man' was born.

Mill's money-hunting, selfish man became a 'symbol-using animal' in Edmund Burke's theories. He had said that man uses his intelligence to 'become better than what he presently is.' Sigmund Freud reduced man to a bundle of desires. The Austrian psychoanalyst, with limited case studies of his own self and of a few of his patients, theorised that humans were made up of desires and that even children desired 'objects'. It is the ego and desire that drive humans, and their repression or suppression in the name of social norms or culture would only lead to irrational behaviour, according to Freud.

Western socio-economic institutions were a product of this individual-centric discourse. Karl Marx was against this individual-centric social order, and 'maximum benefit to maximum people' became his maxim. He saw the existing society as an exploitative and hierarchical order where men with privileges would rule over men who were lesser privileged. A class struggle was inevitable, and violence was inherent in this kind of a bourgeois society, he believed. An ideal scientific socialist society was one in which every individual had equal stakes and where the society lorded over an individual, not any other person. 'The main condition for the liberation of the individual is the abolition of exploitation of one individual by another, of hunger and poverty, and the reassertion of man's sense of dignity. This was the kind of society of which the utopian socialists and the founders of Scientific Socialism dreamed. In contrast to bourgeois individualism, socialist collectivism starts off from the interests of the individual—not just the chosen few but all genuine working people,' he explained.[3] The first-ever experimentation with the Marxist idea of creating a collective man as against the individual man had happened in the Soviet Union under Lenin and Stalin, and it had turned out to be one of the greatest disasters in the history of mankind.

An individual's submission to a larger social good is envisaged in Eastern societies too. But it was always taught as a virtue and people were encouraged to strive for the welfare of others. However, the collective man in the Soviet Communist model was a creation of the state. Nations are shaped by a variety of institutions like family, clan, caste, school, religion, public institutions and the media. In the Soviet Union, the state had taken control of all those institutions. Families were not allowed to be formed because a family with relationships was seen as the source of individualism and selfishness. Instead, communes were created. Children born in communes were to be the property of the state, not the parents. Collective farms were created. All economic activity was taken over by the state. Factories, businesses and commercial activities like transport were all state controlled. Propaganda institutions like radio and newspapers too were in the hands of the government. Religion was banished and churches were destroyed. Young pioneers, sometimes as young as 10-year-olds, were recruited by brainwashing children and youth, in order to implement the policies of the collective. They would walk into any home, search for stocked-up grains and punish the householder if they found any. They would walk into any office and denounce an official who may have been as much as three times their age as a revisionist. This was followed by punishment. The concept and existence of individual man was completely abolished and, in his place emerged a collective man, who thought, acted and behaved as the state dictated. He was like a cog in the wheel of a huge machine called the Soviet state.

The West had created a man exactly opposite to this Marxist version of the collective man. If the Marxist man represented a collective, this man was on the other end of the spectrum— completely self-centred and individualistic. Immanuel Kant, the

German philosopher of the eighteenth-century Enlightenment Era, was, in a way, the father of the individualist doctrine, that had dominated the West in the last two centuries. Man must always be understood as a human individual, he insisted, and further qualified that by saying that man was an end in himself, not a means for any higher achievement. Western individualism is centred on ideas like self-wealth, self-reliance and self-esteem. In all these, self is of primacy. Individual is supreme. Western liberalism is based on these individualistic ideas. Man is at the centre of everything, yet he is disconnected from all other entities like society and universe. The state and other institutions exist to protect the individualistic rights of man. Religion that doesn't subscribe to individualism and emphasises on collective morality has no place, according to this school of thought.

As against the West's individual man and communism's collective man, the Eastern worldview has introduced the concept of the integral man. Not just Dharmic traditions, even Chinese traditions like Taoism have emphasised the virtues of integral life.

THE INTEGRAL MAN IN DHARMIC WORLDVIEW

The Dharmic social order stands on four pillars. At the physical level, they are: *Sharir*—body, *Mana*—mind, *Buddhi*—intellect and *Atman*—soul. At the professional level, they are the four *Ashramas*: *Brahmacharya*—Acquiring knowledge through celibacy and dedication to a Guru; *Grihasta*—Family life as a householder; *Vanaprastha*—Retirement from professional bonds and dedicating oneself to serving society; and *Sanyasa*—Total renunciation and Godward movement. At the societal level, they are the four Varnas (in the distorted form of castes today): Brahmana—devoted to seeking and disseminating knowledge; Kshatriya—devoted to activities related to valour; Vaishya—dedicated to trade and commerce; and Shudra—dedicated to physical labour and artisanship. At the spiritual level, they are four Purusharthas: Dharma—righteous behaviour; *Artha*—economics; *Kaama*—wants and desires; and Moksha—a state that breaks the cycle of birth and death. Dharmic traditions propose a fundamental unity at the individual level and a synthesis at the spiritual level. Talking about these pillars of Dharmic unity, Deen Dayal had said, 'Here in Bharat, we have placed before ourselves the ideal of the four-fold responsibilities of catering to the body, mind, intellectual [sic] and soul with a view to achieve the integrated progress of man. The longings for Dharma, Artha, Kaama and Moksha are in-born in man and satisfaction of these in an integrated way is the essence of Bharatiya culture.'[4] Deen Dayal's integral humanism is about the synthesis of the four-fold order that was envisaged by ancient sages in India.

While freedom, independence and self-interest formed the core of Western philosophies, unity and integralism were the focus of Eastern thinking. Confucius insisted that, 'The five relationships were emperor and subject, parent and child, husband and wife, older brother and younger brother, and between friend and friend.'[5] In other words, the Eastern philosophies saw the world as an interconnected whole.

The Dharmic social order looks at man as an integral being of the society and the universe. While Semitic traditions describe the fundamental state of all humans as 'sinners', Dharmic traditions believe that humans are 'born divine'. '*Amritsya Putrah Vayam*'—We are all begotten of the immortal[6]—is how the Vedas describe human existence. Both Deen Dayal and Gandhi envisaged man to be at the centre of their thinking. But unlike the Western individualist idea of man at the centre of several concentric circles, the inner-most being society and the outermost the universe, Deen Dayal's view was that man was at the epicentre of a spiralling evolution that ultimately leads to the cosmos and divinity. Between man and his ultimate goal of achieving eternal happiness or moksha, there is no straight line. He has to pass through society, humanity and the universe before finally realising the divine.

Many contemporary scholars have explained it as concentric circles versus spiral circles. In the concentric circle theory, although man is at the centre of the activity, he is independent and unconnected with the outer circles like society, humanity and the universe. In his famous work *Elements of Ethics*, second-century Stoic philosopher Hierocles talks about every individual standing at the centre of a series of concentric circles. The individual forms the first circle, while the immediate family, extended family, the local community, the country, and finally, the entire human race, form consecutive outer circles. Hierocles also suggested that in a virtuous society these circles should come together and constantly move people from the outer to the inner. The Stoic word for this process of drawing the circles closer was *oikeiosis*. Kenan Malik interpreted this untranslatable word as something similar to the process by which everything is made into your home.[7] However, the spiral theory that some scholars propounded to explain Deen Dayal's thinking, project man's evolution in a spiral manner from his individual self gradually moving into circles of society, religion, humanity and the universe with the ultimate aim of subliming into the infinite.

Western man is a material man. Deen Dayal's integral man is a synthesis of body, mind, intellect and soul. His ultimate happiness lies not in satisfying just either of the components, like bodily happiness or happiness of the mind. The ultimate and eternal happiness of man lies in the happiness of the soul. Jiddu Krishna Murthy, an eminent philosopher of the last century, used to say, 'It is in giving, not in taking, the eternal bliss is there.' Thus, in India, the social order was developed in such a way that man evolves not through acquisition but sacrifice.

One of the verses that Deen Dayal used to fondly refer to was:

Tyajedekam Kulasyarthe Gramasyarthe Kulam Tyajet
Gramam Janapadarthe Atmarthe Prithivim Tyajet

It means, for the sake of the welfare of the clan, one has to readily give up his individuality; a clan should be ready to give itself up in the interest of a community. In the same way, in order to attain ultimate happiness of the soul, one should be prepared to discard the entire material world.

The institutions that were built in India aimed at providing a social order that was focused on the welfare and well-being of each and every component of creation and not 'maximum benefit to maximum people'. They didn't minimise or discard the importance of man. But they saw his evolution and glory not in his individual self but in his larger integration with society and beyond.

Deen Dayal discussed this dimension at length in various speeches.

'The happiness of an individual is linked with the society; they are not distinct from each other. An individual is a part of the society and no discussion on society is possible without discussing about the people who constitute it. If a society is dynamic, it is because of the individuals in it. The vicissitudes of a society are manifest through its individuals and it is the society that inspires each individual to undertake the work for the society,' Deen Dayal explained, elaborating the relationship between the individual and society.[8] Insisting that it would be erroneous to separate the individual from society, Deen Dayal argued that man acquired language, values, education and behavioural aspects from society. 'It is necessary to examine concepts of happiness, success and welfare from the point of view of both the individual and the society. This is the holistic philosophy. I am body, mind, intellect and soul. We and I are the same. I am a Hindu; I am an Indian and I am a man. This is the crux of India's vision,' he elaborated.[9]

The conflict between the Western and Communist ideas of man and society was about who or which is important—individual or the society. But both agree on one premise that there exists a conflict between the individual and the society. The West has favoured individual over society's interests while the communists have advocated for collective interests as against the individual. This idea of conflict became the basis of development of the entire life system of the West. Even the nations became the products of conflict. The Darwinian evolutionary dogma that the fittest race or nation or individual alone will survive, guided the Western life leading to conflict and war.

INSTITUTIONS FOR INTEGRAL SOCIAL ORDER

The Dharmic view has been that the individual and society have an organic and living relationship. They are not two independent and exclusive entities. Instead, they are complementary. In order to achieve this complementarity, an institutional framework is needed. Over millennia, a conscious and thoughtful effort was made in India to develop institutions that would promote the idea of integralism.

Social organisation in India began with the building of the institution of family. Not the individual, but the family was seen as the basic unit of society. Marriage was made a sacred obligation, not a contract. In the West, marriage was seen as a contractual bond between two individuals, terminable at any time. Under the individualistic and liberal outlook, each partner enjoyed their rights and break up of families was seen as a result of the assertion of the individual's rights. The family system suffered greatly in the West as a consequence of this individual-centric thinking. Divorces became the order of the day and led to serious societal problems like violence and social unrest. Children became the worst victims of this unstable institution. The situation compelled the UN to step in and declare the year 1994 as the International Year of the Family. Noticing the collapse of the institution of the family and the consequent social problems engulfing the largely Christian Western world, Pope John Paul II too hosted a World Meeting of Families at Rome in the same year. The Catholic Church continues to host such celebrations once every three years. The objective behind this renewed emphasis on family in the West was to encourage individualistic men and women to realise the importance of family. Data suggests that younger American men and women are opting to stay out of marriage longer, while the rate of divorce too is on the rise.[10]

TEMPLES FOR EDUCATION AND SOCIAL COHESION

Besides the institution of family, religious institutions like temples, *maths* and pilgrimages were promoted in India as a means of developing social bonding and integral outlook. Hindu temples were not places of worship alone. They were the nuclei of social, economic and cultural life of a community. It was the temple that had bridged the gap between man and man, community and community, village and village and even ruler and ruler. They were major centres of social cohesion and unity. Temples were centres of cultural extravaganza and artistic exuberance, thus providing patronage and promoting the cultural and artistic life of a community.

Temples played an important role in promoting moral and ethical values in society through activities of literacy and education. They had teachers spreading knowledge from the Vedas, Shastras—scientific knowledge, *Agamas*—archaeology and architecture, Puranas and *Itihasas*—history, *Kavyas*—literary works and philosophy. They provided employment to many teachers. Education of the students included lodging and boarding. The Gurukul system where a student lived with the teacher for the period of his learning was a unique model developed in India. In his important work on the education system in ancient and medieval India, *Beautiful Tree*, eminent Gandhian Dharam Pal highlighted the fact that universal education had been the motto of the Gurukul system. Contrary to the propaganda that education was denied to certain castes and classes of society, Dharam Pal insisted that it was available to all sections of society, including women.

A British officer, William Adam, had undertaken an extensive survey of the indigenous education system in India in the nineteenth century before the British system took over and undermined it. Adam's reports were edited and published by Joseph Dibona under the title 'One Teacher—One School'. Talking of the report, Dibona wrote, 'The thousands of schools he saw and carefully reported, had in common the fact that they reflected the diverse cultures of the people. These institutions were entirely supported by local resources, unaided by the government in any way. Nor were they strictly communal but instead provided some mobility for disadvantaged castes and revealed an underlying harmony in which the major religious groups—Hindus and Muslims—studied with and [were] taught by teachers of different backgrounds. The vast system of indigenous schools was soon to wither before the power of the new English curriculum.'[11] Almost every village had a school, and majority of the students and teachers belonged to non-Brahminical castes, he observed.

Temples had also sustained the art and craft of India and were major centres of recreation. Artists, craftsmen and practitioners of various cultural forms were hosted and supported by temples. Through a variety of cultural activities, temples used to impart moral and ethical teachings to the community.

The temple was a place of free food too. *Prasada*, the sacred offering to the deity, was an integral part of the temple culture in India. After being offered to the deity, the prasada would be distributed among the devotees. *Annam Bahukurvita*—Abundance of food—was considered a sacred duty of the kings and the rich. Temples were the places that would ensure that nobody went hungry. They ensured that there could be economic disparities in the society, but not a single person, irrespective of caste or creed, would be denied food. Building temples and supporting the activities of the temples was considered a sacred obligation, especially for kings and the rich. They would provide big endowments in the form of agricultural lands and valuables like gold ornaments to temples, which, in turn, would shoulder the responsibility of providing sustenance for mind and body through spiritual education and food nourishment.

Today, the temple as an institution has diminished in importance. After Independence, Hindu temples in India have been placed under governmental control by various state governments. This practice of taking over Hindu temples and their properties and placing them under government control began during the British period. The first such attempt was made through the Madras Regulation VII in 1817. However, the East India Company had, in 1840, directed that the temples be returned to the trustees as the Christian missionaries had objected to them being managed by Christians on theological grounds. But the supervisory role was retained by the Company through the Board of Revenue. After the 1857 uprising and when the colonial power changed hands from the Company to the British Queen, a new act—The Religious Endowments Act, 1863—was promulgated. This Act had allowed the temples to be managed by their trustees, but the control over them was with the Queen's government.

Until the early twentieth century, the Queen's government had little time or interest in interfering in the affairs of temples. But in 1923 came the precursor to what became the prototype for state governments in independent India—The Madras Religious and Charitable Endowments Act, 1923. The original objective of the British government was to take control of all institutions of all religions. But after stiff resistance from Muslim and Christian leaders, the government was forced to exclude them from the Act's purview. It was restricted to Hindus alone and was renamed as The Madras Hindu Religious and Endowments Act, 1927. Thus began the discriminatory stranglehold of the government over Hindu temples and other religious institutions. Sweeping powers were acquired by the government in 1935 by way of Act XII through which it could take over any temple at any time.

This continued after Independence with a number of state governments setting up endowment departments to take over and control temples and their assets. This practice continues to this day. The logic applied was that Hindu temples should be deemed as public institutions, thus paving the way for their governmentalisation. The same didn't apply to other religions. Around the same time when the British had enacted The Madras Hindu Religious and Charitable Endowments Act, 1927 came another British law called the Gurudwara Act, 1925, under which the management of all Sikh shrines was handed over to an elected community body called the Shiromani Gurudwara Prabandhak Committee (SGPC). Gurudwaras and other Sikh institutions continue to be under the control of the SGPC to this day. Similarly, Christians and Muslims have their own bodies to manage their respective religious institutions.

The primary reason for governments trying to take over Hindu temples or not willing to give up control over them has been the size of properties they own and the revenues they earn. On 6 January 2013, the Supreme Court of India had delivered a landmark judgment setting aside a Tamil Nadu state government order of taking over a famous and ancient Nataraja temple in a town called Chidambaram. The Supreme Court had said that the government did not have the authority to arbitrarily take over temples and religious institutions. In an important article discussing the verdict, eminent politician and thinker Dr Subramanian Swamy indicated that corruption and diversion of funds of temples for non-religious purposes were the real motivations behind temple control.

He wrote: 'Tamil Nadu Hindu Religious & Charitable Endowments Department has control over more than 4.7 lakh acres of agricultural land, 2.6 crore square feet of buildings and 29 crore square feet of urban sites of temples. By any reasonable measure, the income from these properties should be in thousands of crores of rupees. The government, however, collects a mere Rs 36 crores in rent against a "demand" of mere Rs 304 crores—around 12 per cent realisation. How much is under the table only a court-monitored inquiry can reveal. In any corporate or well-managed organisation with accountability, those responsible would have been sacked. Yet, we have people rooting for "government administration".'[12]

'The Srirangam Ranganathar Temple paid the government a (yearly) fee of Rs 18.56 crores (2010-11) for "administering the temple"; for employees rendering religious services, like reciting Vedas, Pasurams during the deity procession, no salary is paid. There are 36 priests in Srirangam who perform the daily poojas—they are not paid a monthly fixed salary. They are entitled to offerings made by devotees and a share in the sale of *archana* tickets. Yet the temple pays a monthly salary ranging from Rs 8,000 to Rs 20,000 for the temple's government-appointed employees, like watchman, car drivers, etc. who perform no religious duties.'[13]

'Many large temples maintain a fleet of luxury vehicles, typically the "fully loaded Toyota Innova", for the use of VIPs! And for the use of assorted Joint and Additional Commissioners and, of course, the Commissioner himself. It is very difficult to understand the religious purpose such extravagance serves or even a "secular" purpose!'[14]

It is hence natural for the Hindu community to demand freeing up of Hindu religious institutions from government control. Those temples and maths that have remained outside government control have been doing yeomen service to society by way of promoting education, healthcare and other social services. Institutions run by temples and maths like Dharmasthala, Ramakrishna Mission, and Kanchi math have contributed enormously to the spread of Dharmic moral and ethical values besides rendering social service.

VARNASHRAMA

Social organisation on Varnashrama basis was another institution that had evolved in India with the objective of promoting an organised social order. Varna was the social order and Ashrama was the individual order. The early scriptural references to both these orders were essentially about a structured life and were never rigid. The four Ashramas recommended were: Brahmacharya—learning about Brahman, the divine reality as a student; Grihasta—householder; Vanaprastha—retirement into social service; and Sanyasa—renunciation. Later, scriptures made these four Ashramas into stages of life, but there always existed the flexibility to bypass one or more of them.

The ancient Varna order was partly linked to the Ashrama order. Like Ashramas, Varnas were also categorised into four, based essentially on vocation. Class-based organisation of societies was not exclusive to India in ancient and medieval times. It occurred in almost all parts of the world. Medieval Europe had its rigid classes like royals, clergymen, nobles, burghers and serfs. Serfdom was the lowest rung into which the peasants were pushed without any rights or privileges. The burghers had certain privileges, while all the powers were vested with the clergy and royals. Ancient Iran's society was divided into four: *Atharva*—priest, *Rathestha*—warrior, *Vastrya Fsuvant*—head of the family and *Huiti*—manual worker.

The origins and efficacy of the Varna system have been discussed elsewhere. This is one institution which has come under tremendous amount of scrutiny and criticism in the last several centuries. Even within the Hindu school of thought, there existed divergent opinions about the contemporary relevance of the Varna system. Although the differences were nuanced, it is clear that each had approached the question from a different perspective. Gandhi, Golwalkar and Deen Dayal were broadly sympathetic to, if not outright supportive of, the Varna system. They believed that, although afflicted with certain evils, the system per se was good for social organisation. On the other side of the spectrum were leaders like Savarkar, Ambedkar and Balasaheb Deoras, the third chief of the RSS, who had more or less endorsed the view that the system has no contemporary relevance.

Discussing the role of Varna in organising society on Dharmic lines, Deen Dayal had said, 'The *Varna* system was established with the view that every individual could give assistance to fulfil the needs of the society according to his qualifications, while simultaneously developing himself to build capacity to serve. In India, the system that has been in existence since ancient times for the development of the individual and for the fulfilment of his social needs is *Varna* system. This system was created on the premise that people could serve society according to their Guna Karma—division of work according to their talent and nature.'[15] Both Deen Dayal and Golwalkar were of the view that the Varna system was helpful in maintaining harmony in society. They viewed the description in *Manusmriti* of the *Virat Purusha*—the celestial being as having Brahmins as the head, Kshatriyas as the arms, Vaishyas as the abdomen and Shudras as the legs—from the point of harmonious social order. Harmony among the various limbs of the body would make a healthy man; similarly, different units of a society should have a harmonious co-existence. Just as various limbs of the body complement each other, so should all men.

Gandhi too viewed the Varna system with utmost respect. In his view, the Varna system was 'the law of life universally governing the human family'. '*Varna* is not a thing that is superimposed on Hindus, but men who were trustees for their welfare discovered the law for them. It is not a human invention, but an immutable law of nature—the statement of tendency that is ever present and at work like Newton's Law of Gravitation. Just as the Law of Gravitation existed even before it was discovered[,] so did the law of *Varna*. It was given to the Hindus to discover that law. By their discovery and application of certain laws of nature, the people of the West have easily increased their material possessions. Similarly, Hindus by their discovery of this irresistible social tendency, have been able to achieve in the spiritual field what no other nation in the world has achieved,' he wrote.[16]

CRITIQUE OF VARNA SYSTEM

Both Gandhi and Deen Dayal were aware of the degeneration of the Varna system into a rigid hereditary and hierarchical caste system. Deen Dayal's criticism of the caste system was a bit muted, though he did warn that any inequality in society was unacceptable and should be removed. He blamed slavery and blind imitation of foreigners as reasons for the decay in the Varna system. 'Undoubtedly this system has weakened due to constant blows that it has suffered through the rise and decline of the society over long periods spanning centuries. Due to external aggressions as well as centuries of slavery, the society has been thrown into disarray. Due to blind imitation of the foreigners, several incompatible and laughable things have crept into our society,' he had said.[17]

But Deen Dayal was not willing to outright reject the Varna system. He tried to differentiate between the distorted vision of society and the system itself and appeared to suggest that if the vision was corrected, the system could still work. 'It is said that if class discrimination has to be abolished, this system will have to be destroyed. This is an issue worth pondering over; will differences be erased by eliminating the system? After eliminating these differences, won't some social organisation be necessary again? A system is only manufactured. Differences are promoted because of the wrong way we perceive a system. If there is a problem in the vision, then a best system may also breed differences. If the problem in the vision is removed, then the differences get erased. But destroying an entire system just to remove its distortions—what kind of a wisdom that will be? If a doctor talks about killing a sick person to remove the ailment, can that be called wisdom?' Deen Dayal had argued.[18]

'The Varna system was created for the comprehensive progress of the individual and society and for the attainment of the temporal and other-worldly happiness. This is the greatest of all creations. Removing the distortions that have crept into it and bringing it back to its actual shape is expedient and preferable,' he concluded.[19]

Incidentally, Gandhi was more forthright. He decried the degeneration of the Varna into the caste system and used strong words to critique it. 'Varna has nothing to do with caste. Down with the monster of caste that masquerades in the guise of Varna. It is this travesty of Varna that has degraded Hinduism and India,' he bemoaned.[20]

Savarkar was a staunch proponent of a casteless Hindu society. He believed that the caste system was the greatest curse on the ideal of Hindu unity. 'Just as I felt I should rebel against the foreign rule over Hindustan, I also felt that I should rebel against the caste system and untouchability in Hindustan,' he wrote from Andaman jail in 1920.[21] He had campaigned actively among the depressed classes to reject the superiority of certain castes, arranged Yagyopaveet (cross-thread usually worn by Brahmins and some other castes) ceremonies and led temple entry movements for those classes.

Ambedkar, obviously, was the most important figure in India's battles against social stratifications and discrimination. Dhananjay Keer, who has authored one of the most comprehensive and authentic biographies of Ambedkar, calls him a 'social revolutionary'. 'A reformer rebuilds what is already present, while a revolutionary demolishes the old and rebuilds from scratch,' wrote Keer.[22] Ambedkar wanted the caste system to go lock, stock and barrel. He blamed Hinduism for providing ideological and theological justification to the caste system. He saw caste as a hugely debilitating institution for society and wanted nothing less than its complete annihilation. 'You cannot build anything on the foundations of caste. You cannot build up a nation. You cannot build up a morality,' he exhorted.[23] He didn't see it as merely an institution to be pulled down. He called it a state of mind, that needed to be purged.

The harshest critics of the caste system, like Savarkar and Ambedkar, find a place of utmost respect and reverence in the RSS and allied institutions. Madhukar Dattatraya Deoras, also known as Balasaheb Deoras, the third chief of the RSS and the most influential one, had opined that 'What exists now is not (Varna) Vyavastha but only Avyavastha! Hence we should all put our heads together and think out how to guide it—a system which has to die and is already dying a natural death—along the correct path to its termination.'[24]

Although some nuanced differences do exist among nationalist leaders and thinkers over the relevance of the Varna and caste systems, there is total unanimity over the rejection of hierarchisation of castes and social evils like untouchability. Savarkar and Deoras were at the forefront in rejecting it ideologically.

Gandhi was like a one-man army crusader against the evil of untouchability. 'I am a touchable by birth but an untouchable by choice … I have endeavoured to qualify myself to represent not the upper ten even among the untouchables … but my ambition is to represent and identify myself with as far as possible, the lowest strata of untouchables, namely, the "invisibles" and "unapproachables", whom I have always before my mind's eye wherever I go,' he stated in a public declaration once.[25] In his thought-provoking book *The Indian Conservative*, entrepreneur-turned-author Jaitirtha Rao makes an interesting observation about Gandhi. 'Gandhi … while paying lip service to the so-called *Varnashrama* doctrine, which presumably sanctioned rigid heritable caste differences, did everything possible to sabotage caste and debilitate fatally its most extreme feature—untouchability,' he wrote.[26]

The institutions that form the core of the Dharmic social order in India needed constant revision and upgradation. Even the sages had warned that '*Puraanamityeva na sadhu sarvam*'—Not everything ancient is noble. '*Taatasya Kupoyamiti bruvaanam*'—Only a biased fool drinks even very salty hard water from a well just because it was dug up by his forefathers, they ridiculed.

∾

9

Integral Economic Vision and Programme

Do Indian right-wing thinkers have an economic policy? Is Deen Dayal's Integral Humanism a mere critique of Western economic models of capitalism and communism, or does it have something better to offer as an alternative economic philosophy? These questions have perplexed not just critics but even supporters of the Indian Right. 'For the Indian Right, economics has always been an incidental extra,' wrote Swapan Dasgupta, eminent columnist and parliamentarian, himself a member of the same group.[1] Dasgupta opined that 'Since the 1970s, the Bharatiya Jana Sangh and the Bharatiya Janata Party (BJP) had favoured an approach that can loosely be described as national capitalism. This was personified by its adherence to swadeshi, an approach that had its origins in the freedom movement. The Rashtriya Swayamsevak Sangh (RSS), on its part, combined its disavowal of consumerism with a fascination for technology, welfarism, and a strong state. There were, in short, just too many contradictory strands in the thinking on economic policy in the Hindu nationalist camp.'[2]

Another Indian Right thinker Hindol Sengupta voiced similar opinions. 'Throughout its four-decade-long history, India's ruling Bharatiya Janata Party (BJP) has always been divided between two viewpoints on economics,' he opined.[3] Sengupta quoted Krzysztof

Iwanek of Hankuk University, Seoul who, in his book *The Political Economy of Hindu Nationalism: From V.D. Savarkar to Narendra Modi*, highlighted some early contradictions in the economic thinking of the RSS and argued that 'Golwalkar (the second chief of the RSS) probably really favoured capitalism, but he chose to hide it under the garb of some old Indian tradition of political economy which was somehow more ethical than modern Capitalism.'

SOCIALISM TO SWADESHI: BJP'S ECONOMIC EXPEDITION

There is room for this confusion. The founder of Bharatiya Jana Sangh, Dr Syama Prasad Mukherjee was considered an open market protagonist. He was the Industries Minister in Jawaharlal Nehru's interim government until 1950. Among other differences between them, he opposed the socialist economic model being championed by Nehru. Jana Sangh, at least in the initial years, was seen as a supporter of the open market system. It consistently raised hackles against Nehru's socialist policies and what used to be described as the 'licence-permit-quota raj'. In the process, it had even acquired the sobriquet of a 'Brahman and Bania' party. After a few years came Deen Dayal Upadhyay's Integral Humanist philosophy as an Indian alternative to both capitalism and communism.

When Bharatiya Jana Sangh became Bharatiya Janata Party in 1980, 'Gandhian Socialism' was declared as its ideological philosophy. For the first time, the very word 'socialism' had found a place of approval in the Right lexicon. Despite strong opposition from senior party leaders from the Jana Sangh era, like Rajmata Vijaya Raje Scindia, Atal Bihari Vajpayee, who led the Jana Sangh group's walk out from the Janata Party in 1980 and the subsequent formation of the BJP, went ahead and inserted the phrase in the new Party's Constitution. Article IV of the party's Constitution until a few years ago, used to read: 'The Party shall be committed to "Gandhian Socialism."It has now been replaced with Gandhian approach to socio-economic issues leading to the establishment of an egalitarian society free from exploitation.'[4] Vajpayee continued to reiterate his commitment to Gandhian Socialism even after he demitted office as Prime Minister in early 2004.

At the launch of former Prime Minister Chandra Shekhar's book, *The Quest, the Hurdles: A Socialist Testament*, in September 2004, Vajpayee asked why the nation had stopped talking about socialism. 'It is in the preamble of our Constitution and is a guiding goal for all parties. For the BJP, Gandhian Socialism is what we want to achieve and make society free of exploitation and full of opportunities. So, we need to start this debate again,' he insisted.[5]

When the Congress government, led by P.V. Narasimha Rao, introduced a programme of macroeconomic stabilisation through structural reforms in 1991 and clearly tilted towards economic liberalisation and globalisation, the BJP and the larger Sangh Parivar took up cudgels against it. A new outfit called the Swadeshi Jagaran Manch was created under the leadership of eminent trade union leader and senior RSS functionary, Dattopant Thengdi.

Interestingly, however, when the first opportunity for ruling the country came into the hands of the BJP in 1998, Atal Bihari Vajpayee as the Prime Minister of a 23-party coalition had actively pursued liberal economic policies. He faced a barrage of criticism from within his party and the Sangh Parivar for supporting and taking forward the globalisation policies of the Narasimha Rao government. Prime Minister Narendra Modi, as the Chief Minister of Gujarat, was also an ardent supporter of global trade and liberal and market-friendly economic policies for which he too had to endure criticism from within.

In fact, Modi's rise to become the Prime Minister of India has partly to do with his image as a leader with liberal economic credentials. Hence, there was all-round expectation, especially among the conservative circles, that Modi would unleash a slew of liberal economic reforms, including land and taxation reforms. When that didn't happen in an outright manner and Modi started treading cautiously on the country's economic path, the conservatives were annoyed and some of them turned into his bitter critics.

The reason for this confusion is over the assumption that economic policy has only two sides—you either are a free-market globaliser or a populist economic nationalist. But the BJP and the wider RSS Parivar belonged to what the Swadeshi ideologue Dattopant Thengdi described as the 'third way'. This third way, neither capitalist nor communist, usually denoted by the word Swadeshi, is broadly the guiding principle of the BJP's economic policies.

MAKING OF THE GLOBAL ECONOMIC ORDER

Global domination became the obsession of both capitalist and communist powers after the Second World War. While Stalin wanted a 'Communist International' or 'Comintern', Roosevelt wanted a capitalist equivalent of it. Stalin pursued a politico-economic agenda to spread communism globally. But Roosevelt, with the support of the newly victorious Western European powers, wanted to use the route of economics to create a global system of interdependence. In fact, in his address at the inauguration of the Bretton Woods institutions in July 1944, Roosevelt made it abundantly clear. 'The economic health of every country is a proper matter of concern to all its neighbours, near and far.'[6] The mandate for globalisation was thus set, in the form of the World Trade Organization (WTO) and the International Monetary Fund (IMF). While at Bretton Woods, foundations of the Western economic world order were being laid down, a post-war Western political order was taking shape at Dumbarton Oaks leading to the creation of the UN and its affiliates.

Interestingly, the American and Western European leadership had seen these institutional developments as their answer to what they called the 'Soviet Communism's quest for world domination'. President Truman of America was categorical. In a famous address on 12 March 1947, which later became popular as the 'Truman Doctrine', he declared America's intent of supporting 'the cause of freedom worldwide'. 'A fateful hour had struck,' declared Truman, '... and the people of the world must choose between the two alternate ways of life'. Leadership of the United States is inevitable, he said, warning that failing which 'we may endanger the peace of the world'.[7]

Post-war economic order was basically a competing one between the Soviet communists and free market capitalists led by America. Both had claimed to give the world a new economic order. But by the 1970s, it became clear that neither was going to benefit humanity in the long run. Communism got stagnated by the early 1980s with nothing new to offer to the world. The communist powers solely relied upon their military power to perpetuate political control. In fact, it is not an exaggeration to say that no new and original idea has come from communist intellectuals in the last few decades. Their new fads are theories like environmentalism, multiculturalism, feminism, critical theory, post-modernism and post-truth. 'The biggest problem with the Leftist agenda is a lack of credibility,' said eminent political scientist Francis Fukuyama. He further added, 'Over the past two generations, the mainstream Left has followed a social-democratic program that centers on the state provision of a variety of services, such as pensions, health care, and education. That model is now exhausted: welfare states have become big, bureaucratic, and inflexible; they are often captured by the very organisations that administer them, through public sector unions; and most important, they are fiscally unsustainable given the aging of populations virtually everywhere in the developed world. Thus, when existing social democratic parties come to power, they no longer aspire to be more than custodians of a welfare state that was created decades ago; none has a new, exciting agenda around which to rally the masses.'[8]

In the last few decades, the world's poor countries didn't

experience any economic development as promised by the Bretton Woods institutions. Those institutions became centres of greed. The only issues that interest the developed countries are investment and market freedom. Like the Marxist theory, the capitalist economic model too remained an utopia, forcing critics to declare the entire modernisation theory itself as dead. Globalised capitalism too has reached its tether. While countries in the world see the return of economic nationalism as the answer to this situation in the twenty-first century, Fukuyama called for a serious intellectual debate. 'Serious intellectual debate is urgently needed, since the current form of globalised Capitalism is eroding the middle-class social base on which liberal democracy rests,' he argued in an article in the *Foreign Affairs* magazine.[9]

THE SWADESHI MOVEMENT IN COLONIAL INDIA

Much before Stalin's campaign for a global communist order, and much before the birth of Bretton Woods institutions, a debate had begun in India in the early years of the twentieth century. It was centred on the concept of Swadeshi and targeted primarily at ending the exploitation of native resources by British colonisers. However, the debate was not just confined to opposing exploitation and injustice by the British alone. It was extended beyond economics, to political, social, cultural and religious spheres too.

Swadeshi as an economic idea was initially propagated by Congress leaders like Dadabhai Naoroji at the beginning of the twentieth century. Naoroji's book *Poverty and the Un-British Rule of India* was the first-ever open challenge to the exploitative economic policies of the British and their impact on India. It generated intense discussion in the country and finally laid the ground for the Swadeshi movement against the British in 1906. Speaking at the Calcutta session of the Congress in 1906, Aurobindo Ghosh, eminent freedom fighter, paid eloquent tributes to Naoroji for highlighting 'the terrible poverty in India and its rapid increase under the British rule'. 'It was necessary for the nation but to realise its increasing poverty under British rule. It was Mr. Naoroji who first forced the question of Indian poverty into prominence, and for this India owes him a debt of gratitude,' Sri Aurobindo had said.[10]

In 1904, revolutionary poet and author Sakharam Ganesh Deuskar had published a book in Bengali, titled *Desher Katha*. It vividly portrayed the exploitation meted out to the indigenous industry and trades under foreign rule. Like Naoroji's book, Deuskar's book too had immense impact in Bengal, especially among the youth, and became the harbinger for a future uprising among nationalists. By the time the British had decided to divide Bengal in 1905, there was already a massive resentment brewing among the masses against their exploitation.

It was in these circumstances that the All India Congress Committee had decided to host its annual session in 1906 at Calcutta. By then, Swadeshi had become an important buzz word in Indian political discourse. The Congress, at that juncture, was divided into two camps—the radicals led by Tilak, Aurobindo, Bipin Chandra Pal and others, and the moderates led by Gopal Krishna Gokhale, Rash Behari Ghosh, Dinshaw Wacha and others. The radicals had decided to use the 1906 session of the Congress to launch the Swadeshi movement against the British. The moderates, although not entirely against the economic idea of Swadeshi, were nevertheless dead against making it a political programme of the Congress. They even tried to enlist the support of Lord Minto, who was invited to inaugurate the annual Swadeshi exhibition. Minto started offering homilies to Congress leaders by saying that they should follow 'Honest Swadeshi', by which he meant that it shouldn't be politicised.

The radicals led by Tilak and Aurobindo were determined to make Swadeshi the political plank to oppose the partition of Bengal. A resolution was brought by them before the Calcutta Congress, which read: 'This Congress accords its most cordial support to the

Swadeshi movement and calls upon the people of the country to labour for its success by making earnest and sustained efforts to promote the growth of indigenous industries and to stimulate the production of indigenous articles by giving them preference over imported commodities at some sacrifice.'[11]

Although the body of the resolution was limited to economic exploitation under the British rule, nobody at the session had any doubt over its political message. It had gone way beyond the demand for annulment of the partition of Bengal and raised questions over British rule itself. Valentine Chirol, noted British journalist, observed: 'The question of partition itself receded into background, and the issue, until then successfully veiled and now openly raised, was not whether Bengal should be an unpartitioned province or two partitioned provinces under British rule, but whether the British rule itself was to endure in Bengal, for the matter of that, anywhere in India.'[12]

Bipin Chandra Pal categorically stated, 'A subject nation cannot have any free economic activity or what the economists call economic freedom. Every student of political economy knows that there can be no economics divorced from politics. Economics and politics are organically related to one another, and India cannot consider the two apart, separated from and unconnected with one another.'[13] He strongly opposed any foreign investment from Britain into India on the same grounds.

The Congress radicals of Bengal took the Swadeshi movement into the realm of culture and religion too. Leaders like Brahmabandhab Upadhyay, Aurobindo Ghosh and Bipin Chandra Pal launched a sustained campaign against what they called 'Western influence'. Upadhyay was at the forefront, writing extensively against the imposition of Western culture under the British rule. In *Sandhya*, an evening newspaper that he used to publish, Upadhyay wrote: 'With the spread of English rule and culture, India lost her own ideal of civilisation. Our educated classes think as they have been taught by *Firangi* masters. Our minds have been conquered, we have become slaves. The faith in our culture and love for things Indian are gone. India will attain *Swaraj* the day she will again have faith in herself. The whole mass of our people must now be made to appreciate things Indian and return to our ancient way. That is *Swadeshi* as opposed to *Videshi*.'[14]

He ridiculed the economic Swadeshi idea as 'salt and sugar *Swadeshi*' and derided it as 'something like cooking mutton curry by the Ganga water'. He demanded unalloyed Swadeshi, urging people to shake off foreign cultural influence totally. 'Noble India we want, Golden India, the India of Kapila and Gautama, Vasistha and Vyasa, Raghu and Dilipa, Rama and Yudhistira. And for the creation of such an India, freedom from slave mentality is necessary,' he exhorted.[15]

In Swadeshi, Aurobindo saw the rise of the East against the West. For him, it was an Asian renaissance with countries like Japan, China and the Muslim world against Western and imperialist powers. He linked the Swadeshi movement with India becoming a part of that Asian or Eastern glory. Years before the Congress formally launched the Swadeshi movement, Rabindranath Tagore, another Bengali doyen of India's freedom movement and a renowned literary figure, wrote about the concept of Swadeshi Samaj. The Swadeshi Samaj of Rabindranath had nothing to do with the Swadeshi political movement of 1906. It was a constructive programme for the upliftment of society, economy and culture of the villages along the lines of the traditional Hindu religion.

GANDHI'S ECONOMIC IDEAS

This initial push, for a more indigenous model of development, by Congress radicals at the beginning of the twentieth century found its greatest champion in Mohandas Karamchand Gandhi. Gandhi had been a steadfast advocate and champion of Swadeshi and indigenisation all through his life. Like the Bengal radicals, he too didn't limit his indigenisation ideas to economy alone, although he had articulated strong views regarding the economic model that independent India ought to adopt. His Swadeshi thought included moral and ethical dimensions besides economic and political ones.

'Can we evolve a new kind of economics?' Gandhi would repeatedly ask. Because for him, economics was not just about material prosperity; it was about 'manufacturing souls.'[16] 'I don't draw any distinction between economics and ethics. True economics should stand for social justice and moral values,' he used to insist.[17]

The first major articulation of Gandhi's economic vision can be found in his treatise, *Hind Swaraj*. Authored by Gandhi while on a ship journey from London to Durban in November 1909, *Hind Swaraj* was originally published in Gujarati. The Gujarati version was banned by the British for its so-called seditious potential. However, when the English version came out, the British realised that it wouldn't have much of an impact on the English-speaking population and hence decided against banning it. In this book, Gandhi discussed Swaraj, modernisation, village self-government, etc., in a conversational form.

Gandhi was an ardent advocate of village self-reliance. India lives in villages, he would insist, adding that the nation would die the day its villages became lifeless. *Gram Swaraj*—village self-rule—was an article of faith for him. It was not an obscurantist idea, nor retrograde as Nehru would later call it. Gandhi's village republics were well-developed and modern—he even talked about railways and telegraph services in villages; but they were not going to be the dens of Westernisation. He discussed his idea of Gram Swaraj in the 1909 treatise first but made a number of amendments subsequently.

'My idea of *Gram Swaraj* is that of a complete republic, independent of its neighbour for its own vital wants, and yet interdependent for many others in which dependence is a necessity. Thus every village's first concern will be to grow its own food crop and cotton for its cloth. It should have a reserve for its cattle, recreation and playground for adults and children. Then if there is more land available, it will grow useful money crops, but excluding tobacco, opium and the like. The village will maintain a village theatre, school and public hall. It will have its own waterworks ensuring clean water supply. This can be done through controlled wells or tanks. Education will be compulsory up to the final basic course. As far as possible every activity will be conducted on co-operative basis. There will be no castes such as we have today with their graded untouchability. Non-violence with its technique of *Satyagraha* and non-cooperation will be a compulsory service of the village community. There will be a compulsory service of the village guards who will be selected by rotation from the register maintained by the village. The government of the village will be conducted by the *Panchayat* of five persons annually elected by the adult villagers, male and female, possessing minimum prescribed qualification,' he wrote.[18]

Incidentally, it was a running theme with some Western developmental economists of that time too. Among them was the famed Swiss economist Friedrich Schumacher, whose book *Small Is Beautiful*, published in 1973, was considered an eye-opener for an entire generation. Schumacher also underscored the importance of 'sound villages' for the overall development of a nation. 'Yet it remains an unalterable truth that, just as a sound mind depends on a sound body, so the health of the cities depends on the health of the rural areas. The cities, with all their wealth, are merely secondary producers, while primary production, the precondition of all economic life, takes place in the countryside,' he had articulated.

'There is no answer to the evils of mass unemployment and mass migration into cities, unless the whole level of rural life can be raised, and this requires the development of an agro-industrial culture, so that each district, each community, can offer a colourful variety of occupations to its members,' Schumacher suggested.[19]

Gandhi suggested the same in a different conceptual framework.

He was an advocate of decentralisation. Many scholars, who studied India from the eighteenth century onward came to the conclusion that Indian villages represented the soul of India. 'The village communities are little republics having nearly everything that they want within themselves and almost independent of any foreign relations,' wrote Sir Charles Metcalfe, a British colonial administrator who served as the acting Governor General of India in the mid-nineteenth century.[20] Metcalfe spent considerable time in India and came to the conclusion that, 'Dynasty after dynasty tumbles down. Revolution succeeds to revolution. Hindoo, Pathan, Mogul, Maratha, Sikh, English are all masters in turn, but the village communities remain the same. In times of trouble, they arm and fortify themselves. A hostile army passes through the country. The village communities collect their little cattle within their walls and let the enemy pass unprovoked.'[21] But he also opined that village life was a static one.

Eminent Indian sociologist M.N. Srinivas observed that by studying a village, one could comprehend the 'social processes and problems to be found occurring in great parts of India'. Srinivas cited the 'Fifth Report from the Select Committee on the Affairs of the East India Company (1812)', in which the village was described as 'the most basic unit of social organisation in India, a sovereign whole, irrespective of the transfer of power from kingdoms to regimes at the national or regional level.'[22]

Gandhi believed that decentralised planning was critical to his rural reconstruction programmes. 'I must dissent from the view that the core of planning is centralization. Why should not decentralization lend itself to planning as centralization?' he argued.[23] India was to adopt Gandhi's rural empowerment programme much later, under the 73rd and 74th Amendment to the Constitution of India. This amendment, popularly known as the Panchayat Raj Amendment, was promulgated in 1992 and came into effect from 1993, a full 46 years after independence. Through this amendment, a three-tier elected local government structure was created, at village, block and district levels. District planning boards were created and village elected bodies were given financial and planning powers. However, the Panchayat Raj system faces criticism that it only provided financial powers but failed to devolve real decision-making powers to the village elected bodies and, in that sense, lacked the vision of Gandhi's Gram Swaraj.

Gandhi had reservations over technology and machines too. Although his views were a bit rigid initially, he gradually moderated them. From an earlier position of calling machines 'a great sin', he moved to a moderate opposition of machines 'mastering us'. Yet, his general rejection of large-scale industrialisation continued till the end. As late as in September 1946, he wrote: 'I don't believe that industrialization is necessary in any case for any country. It is much less so for India. Indeed I believe that independent India can only discharge her duty towards the world by adopting a simple but ennobled life by developing her thousands of cottage industries and living at peace with the world. High thinking is inconsistent with complicated material life based on high speed imposed on us by mammon worship. All the graces of life are possible only when we learn the art of living nobly.'[24]

Gandhi also wrote extensively on Swadeshi. His Swadeshi as an economic idea was akin to Buddhist economic theories. 'From the point of view of Buddhist economics, therefore, production from local resources for local needs is the most rational way of economic life, while dependence on imports from afar and the consequent need to produce for export to unknown and distant peoples is highly uneconomic and justifiable only in exceptional cases and on a small scale,' said Schumacher of the Buddhist view point on economics.[25]

Gandhi's Swadeshi was more about strengthening village and small industries as well as upholding the traditional life of the country than against things foreign. 'Swadeshi is that spirit in us which restricts us to the use and service of our immediate surroundings to the exclusion of the more remote. Thus, as for religion, in order to satisfy the requirements of the definition, I must restrict myself to my ancestral religion. That is the use of my immediate religious surrounding. In the domain of politics, I should make use of the indigenous institutions and serve them by curing them of their proved defects. In that of economics, I should use only things that are produced by my immediate neighbours and serve those industries by making them efficient and complete where they might be found wanting,' Gandhi had elucidated.[26]

Responding to criticism that he was promoting narrow thinking, Gandhi wrote in 1926: 'I have never considered the exclusion of everything foreign under every conceivable circumstance as a part of *Swadeshi*. The broad definition of *Swadeshi* is the use of all home-made things to the exclusion of foreign things, in so far as such use is necessary for the protection of home-industry, more especially those industries without which India will become pauperized. In my opinion, therefore, *Swadeshi* which excludes the use of everything foreign, no matter how beneficent it may be, and irrespective of the fact that it impoverishes nobody, is a narrow interpretation of *Swadeshi*.'[27]

Gandhi's important contribution to economic thought was the concept of trusteeship. Again, the justification came from '*tena tyaktena bhuñjitha*' of *Isavasya Upanishad*. He wanted the owners of wealth to become its trustees. 'The rich man will be left in possession of his wealth, of which he will use what he reasonably requires for his personal need and will act as a trustee for the remainder to be used for the society,' he proposed.[28]

Much before Gandhi came up with the trusteeship concept, Swami Vivekananda had an encounter with John D. Rockefeller, the billionaire businessman in America. Emma Calve, a French opera singer, who was privy to the meeting, wrote that Vivekananda told Rockefeller that the money he had accumulated was not his.

He further added that Rockefeller was only a channel and his duty was to do good for the world. This wealth was given by God so that he might have an opportunity to do good for the people. According to Calve's narrative, Rockefeller was not immediately impressed by this suggestion. Annoyed and irritated, he went away, she stated. 'But about a week after, again without being announced, he (Rockefeller) entered Swamiji's study, and threw on his desk a paper which told of his plans to donate an enormous sum of money toward the financing of a public institution. This was Rockefeller's first large donation to the public welfare,' Calve wrote.[29] After a few years, the Rockefeller Foundation took birth in 1913 with massive endowments provided by the businessman. J.R.D. Tata too was a believer in this concept. 'What came from the people should go back to them,' he has often said.[30]

Sarvodaya, another socio-economic philosophy propounded by Gandhi, was based on British economist John Ruskin's essay converted into a book called *Unto This Last*. Gandhi received a copy of the book from his friend Henry Polak in 1904. He read it during a twenty-four-hour train ride to Durban and claimed that he was so greatly influenced by Ruskin's ideas that 'he could not sleep at all'. 'I determined to change my life in accordance with the ideals of the book,' Gandhi wrote.[31] He got the book translated into Gujarati and developed the concept of Sarvodaya. It was based on three principles

- That the good of the individual is contained in the good of all.
- That a lawyer's work has the same value as the barber's in as much as all have the same right of earning their livelihood from their work.
- That a life of labour, i.e., the life of the tiller of the soil and the handicraftsman is a life worth living.

'The first of these I knew. The second I had dimly realized. The third had never occurred to me. Unto This Last made it clear as daylight for me that the second and third were contained in the first. I arose with the dawn, ready to reduce these principal to practice,' Gandhi stated.[32]

BIRTH PANGS AND THE REJECTION OF GANDHISM

In the Constituent Assembly, a detailed discussion took place over the Gandhian view of decentralisation and devolving major powers to the village Panchayats. Many members insisted that a strong centre and an empowered village Panchayat system was the way forward for India. H.V. Kamath quoted from Aurobindo's *The Spirit and Form of Indian Polity*: 'At the height of its evolution and in the great days of Indian civilisation we find an admirable political system, efficient in the highest degree and very perfectly combining village and urban self-government with stability and order. The State carried on its work administrative, judicial, financial and protective—without destroying or encroaching on the rights and free activities of the people and its constituent bodies in the same department. The royal courts in capital and country were the supreme judicial authority coordinating the administration of justice throughout the kingdom.'[33]

R.K. Siddhwa, a member of the Parsi community, argued that '… local authorities are the pivots of the social and economic life of the country and if there is no place for local authorities in this Constitution, let me tell you that the Constitution is not worth considering.'[34]

Villagers should be given their due share in the governance of the country. If they are not given their due share, I submit that they are bound to react to this,' warned Mahaveer Tyagi.[35]

But Ambedkar, as the chairman of the drafting committee, took an uncharacteristically strident line. He ridiculed the arguments of the members for village government institutions saying, 'The love of the intellectual Indians for the village community is of course infinite if not pathetic.'[36] Although the village Panchayats had been long surviving political institutions in India, their contribution to the affairs and destiny of the country were minimal, he opined. Then came his harshest observation, which was strongly criticised. 'That they have survived through all vicissitudes may be a fact. But mere survival has no value. The question is on what plane they have survived. Surely on a low, on a selfish level. I hold that these village republics have been the ruination of India. I am therefore surprised that those who condemn Provincialism and communalism should come forward as champions of the village. What is the village but a sink of localism, a den of ignorance, narrow-mindedness and communalism? I am glad that the Draft Constitution has discarded the village.'[37]

Nehru too was not an admirer of village self-governance. Centralised planning was fashionable in those days. The government, under Nehru and his statistician friend Dr Prasanta Chandra Mahalanobis, had adopted the Soviet model of centralised Five Year Plans for India. Nehru was inspired by the ideas of British economist and Labour Party politician Harold Laski. Mahalanobis and he together launched India's centralised planning establishment from the second Five Year Plan. A decision to disband the Planning Commission, set up for this purpose, was taken by the Narendra Modi government in 2014. The Planning Commission has now been replaced with the NITI Aayog.

Gandhi's economic ideas did not have many takers. In fact, concepts like Ruskin's *Unto This Last* were highly criticised in contemporary Britain for their impractical ideas. Some of those outside the Congress like Vinoba Bhave continued to pursue them through campaigns like Bhoodan. Gandhians, as a group committed to the socio-economic ideas of Gandhi, progressively lost prominence in Indian polity. They were largely confined to some social service projects and centres.

After his rather acrimonious exchange of letters with his protégé Jawaharlal Nehru, towards the end of 1945, Gandhi had realised that there existed a fundamental gulf between him and other Congress leaders.

The correspondence between Gandhi and Nehru towards the end of 1945 is important because it became the defining dialogue between the stalwarts over the path to progress of free India. Independent India's destiny was to be sealed in these dialogues. Nehru's rashness to embrace modernity, without pausing and reflecting on the vision of an aging ideologue, had denied India an opportunity to develop its own model for the challenges that mankind was facing.

Gandhi was aware of Nehru's dislike for his ideas for village development put forth in *Hind Swaraj*. On 5 October 1945, he wrote a letter to Nehru. 'The first thing I want to write about is the difference in outlook between us. If the difference is fundamental, then I feel the public should also be made aware of it. It would be detrimental to our work for Swaraj to keep them in the dark,' he wrote at the very beginning and went on to defend *Hind Swaraj* and his vision for village-centric development. 'I am convinced that if India is to attain true freedom and through India the world also, then sooner or later, the fact must be recognized that people will have to live in villages, not in towns, in huts not in palaces. Crores of people will never be able to live at peace with one another in towns and palaces. They will then have no recourse but to resort to both violence and untruth. I hold that without truth and non-violence there can be nothing but destruction for humanity. We can realize truth and nonviolence only in the simplicity of village life and this simplicity can best be found in the *Charkha* [spinning wheel] and all that the *Charkha* connotes. I must not fear if the world today is going the wrong way. It may be that India too will go that way and like the proverbial moth burn itself eventually in the flame round which it dances more and more furiously. But it is my burden to protect India and through India the entire world from such a doom,' he penned.[38]

Lest Nehru misunderstood his insistence on villages, Gandhi clarified, 'My ideal village will contain intelligent human beings. They will not live in dirt and darkness as animals. Men and women will be free and able to hold their own against anyone in the world. There will be neither plague nor cholera nor smallpox; no one will be idle, no one will wallow in luxury. Everyone will have to contribute his quota of manual labour. I do not want to draw a large-scale picture in detail. It is possible to envisage railways, post and telegraph offices etc.'[39] Gandhi was clear that he was for well-developed modern villages.

Nehru replied on 9 October 1945. He was categorical and blunt. 'I do not understand why a village should necessarily embody truth and non-violence. A village normally speaking is backward intellectually and culturally and no progress can be made from a backward environment. Narrow-minded people are much more likely to be untruthful and violent,' he retorted. Nehru tried to distance not only himself but the entire Congress Party from Gandhi's idea of *Hind Swaraj*. 'It is many years ago since I read *Hind Swaraj* and I have only a vague picture in my mind. But even when I read it 20 or more years ago, it seemed to me completely unreal,' he told Gandhi, adding, 'As you know, the Congress has never considered that picture, much less adopted it.'[40]

Nehru rejected Gandhi's suggestion that the public be made aware of their differences, saying, 'I should imagine that a body like the Congress should not lose itself in arguments over such matters which can only produce great confusion in people's minds resulting in inability to act in the present. This may also result in creating barriers between the Congress and others in the country. Ultimately of course this and other questions will have to be decided by representatives of free India.'[41]

Seven decades after this exchange of letters, India, even today, struggles with its villages. 'Approximation of the culture of town' that Nehru envisaged has happened in a different sense.

Villages have become poor country cousins of towns in terms of consumption levels, whereas they remain backward in all other economic indicators. Hundreds of millions of Indians have been stuck in a life of low expectations and lower means. Those who left villages and moved to cities in search of a livelihood have ended up in the black holes of economic and social depravity.

DEEN DAYAL: THE CHAMPION OF GANDHIAN IDEAS

Some of the ideas that Gandhi championed were picked up in unexpected quarters. Deen Dayal Upadhyay had incorporated many of Gandhi's ideas in the Integral Humanist philosophy and developed them further. Like Gandhi, Deen Dayal also insisted upon Swadeshi and decentralisation as the panacea for the Indian economy.

The initial years of the Bharatiya Jana Sangh saw economic issues getting less importance because of many other pressing issues, like Kashmir, dominating the discourse. Jawaharlal Nehru was championing the cause of a 'socialist pattern of society'. At the All India Congress Committee session held at Avadi near Madras (present-day Chennai), a resolution was passed proclaiming the socialist pattern of society as the goal of the party. A decade of Nehruvian socialism had left India more impoverished and backward. Between 1955 and 1965, India's poverty rate grew from 52.66 per cent to 58.60 per cent.[42] In absolute numbers, it meant that the number of poor people in India grew from 198.7 million in 1955 to 301.7 million in 1965.

Naturally, the Jana Sangh had focused on rejecting the Nehruvian socialist model with all its might. However, that didn't automatically amount to the party coming up with any alternative. It took almost a decade, until Deen Dayal articulated his economic vision in the famous lecture series on Integral Humanism at Mumbai in 1965, for the party to finally come up with a coherent alternative economic vision. Facing criticism that the Jana Sangh did not have any economic philosophy, Deen Dayal initially insisted, 'The Bharatiya Jan[a] Sangh has got a clear economic program. But its place in the overall scheme of things in our party is only that much as that of economics in Indian culture. Western culture is materialist, and hence economy-centric. But we are a nation that is a blend of materialism and spiritualism. Hence it is clear that Jan[a] Sangh will always lag behind those economists and parties that consider all other life values unimportant before economy.'

The Jana Sangh was decidedly against Nehruvian Socialism. When it became politically imperative to adopt socialism at a later stage as BJP, Vajpayee preferred Gandhi and branded Nehruvian Socialism as statism and state socialism. The Jana Sangh leadership had rejected the other economic model prevalent in those days too, i.e., the capitalist model, describing it as an exploitative and individual-centric one. Deen Dayal considered socialism and capitalism as two sides of the same coin. In his opinion, both theories were not conducive for the integral development of man. While capitalism kept man at the centre of its philosophy, it could visualise only an economic man. On the other hand, the socialist and the communist models kept man subservient to the state and dismissed all other dimensions of human activity. Deen Dayal believed that both philosophies fundamentally devalued the human being thoroughly.

'The Capitalist system thought merely of the economic man, but left him free in other fields where he could exercise his individuality. The Socialist system went much further thinking only of the abstract man. After that there was no scope for the development of the individual personality based on diverse tastes and abilities. The needs and preferences of individuals have as much importance in socialism as in a prison manual. There is no such thing as individual freedom in the Socialist system,' he wrote.[43] In his view, both the systems had failed to envision 'integral man'. Deen Dayal concluded that neither capitalism nor socialism understood man, much less cared for him.

INTEGRAL HUMANIST ECONOMIC PHILOSOPHY

Through Integral Humanism, Deen Dayal articulated a coherent economic philosophy. His attempt was to evolve a synthesis between socialism and capitalism and suggest a wholesome third alternative. He rejected the capitalist concept of economic man, yet put man at the centre of his economic philosophy. Man as a slave of the state under the socialist philosophy too was not acceptable to him, because he saw the integral man as the master of his own self. 'The Indian system calls for a blend of the two. We are individualists and also stand for the societies. In accordance with Indian philosophy we look to the interest of society even while not ignoring the individual. Because we care for society we are 'socialist' in that sense, and because we do not ignore the individual, we are also individualists. Because we do not consider the individual to be supreme, it is said that we are not individualists. On the other hand, we also do not think that society should rob the individual of all his freedoms and peculiarities. We are against the individual being used as a part of a machine and in that sense we are not Socialists. It is our conviction that society cannot be thought of without the individual, nor can an individual have any value without society. Hence, we want a synthesis of the two,' he argued.[44]

In fact, Deen Dayal's integral humanist economic thought can be summarised in one word—*Antyodaya*. It literally meant the uplift of the last man. While Gandhi talked about Sarvodaya, Deen Dayal propagated a more practical idea of Antyodaya as the basis of his political and economic philosophy. The state should focus on ensuring that the fruits of growth and development reach the last person in the chain, he explained. 'The measurement of economic plans and economic growth cannot be done with those who have risen above on the economic ladder but of those who are at the bottom,' Deen Dayal wrote. He stressed on Antyodaya to rid the nation of poverty and ensure a minimum standard of living for all individuals.

Deen Dayal was an ardent advocate of Swadeshi and self-reliance. He was also with Gandhi on the question of urbanisation. Deen Dayal believed that India should focus on its villages and reject urbanisation. Although Deen Dayal linked his Swadeshi and self-reliance to rejection of heavy industry and urbanisation, it called for a restatement in the changed socio-economic milieu in India and the world.

Deen Dayal categorised industry under two heads: small-scale and large-scale, and further classified them into four categories:

- Small-scale industries with less training: cloths, shoes, rubber, glass, etc.
- Small-scale industries with more training: engineering goods, etc.
- Large-scale industries with less training: cement and fertilisers, etc.
- Large-scale industries with more training: mineral oil, iron, etc.

'Instead of giving priority to large-scale industries, we must give priority to small size enterprises,' he advised.[45]

On the question of technology, Deen Dayal was closer to Gandhi, with the difference being that, unlike Gandhi, he wouldn't reject machines outright. He instead insisted on developing 'Bharatiya technology', a version of technology that is specific and suitable to India's conditions and needs. By Bharatiya technology, he meant technological incrementalism. He was against importing machines that replaced man. He agreed that spinning charkha manually would not be a permanent solution. But he also insisted that the spinning machine that completely replaced the hands of the weaver couldn't be the solution either. It is here that his idea of Bharatiya technology came into play—a technology that would enhance the productivity of weaving without replacing the weaver.

Deen Dayal was not a welfare statist like Jawaharlal Nehru. Yet, he insisted that the state should provide for minimum welfare of every citizen. Basic needs of people like food, shelter, clothing, healthcare and education should be taken care of by the economic system that the state devised, Deen Dayal opined. Also, just as the right to vote guided political democracy, the right to work should guide economic democracy, he would say. 'If a government provides these minimum requirements, then only it is a rule of Dharma. Otherwise, it is a rule of Adharma,' was how he articulated his view.[46]

Deen Dayal was averse to dependence on foreign capital. He was clear that dependencies on foreign import and foreign capital were detrimental for India. He averred that foreign investments would exploit domestic labour and also have the potential of influencing politics in the country. In his opinion, foreign capital would bring with it not just foreign money but also exploitative capitalist ideas. He feared that it would introduce all the evils of capitalism in society and play havoc with the social culture.

'Work to every hand and water to every land' was Deen Dayal's philosophy. By work, he didn't mean slavery. Work that gives happiness to the worker and allows him to nurture his skills and capability should be available to everyone, Deen Dayal emphatically stated. He would insist that the slogan of 'every worker must eat' should be replaced by 'everyone who eats must get work'. He further evolved this into a social philosophy by saying, 'Those who are born shall eat; and those who earn shall feed.'[47]

AGRICULTURE AND INDUSTRY

Deen Dayal placed a lot of emphasis on agriculture. He was an ardent advocate of family farms. He was not too keen a supporter of cooperative farming, a fad in those days under the socialist influence, which has made a comeback in a different form. 'In a cooperative, we are faced with the crucial problem of how to distribute the produce. When people with all sorts of lands and with no lands and those with varying rights in land are joined together, it is practically impossible to divide the produce equitably.' he would argue.[48]

Deen Dayal saw a relationship between agriculture and industry. His proposition was that unless agriculture became incentivised and profitable, industry couldn't survive.

Another area where Deen Dayal brought his spiritual and economic ideas together was with respect to consumption. Like Gandhi, he also advocated for restraint in consumption. He insisted that industrialisation had to be done in such a way that we cater to the needs of society but do not overproduce to induce demand. 'We are, on the one hand, exploring new means to satisfy ever-increasing desires, on the other hand, we are facing ever-increasing problems. This race is likely to destroy the human society in its humanness. It is therefore imperative to define the goal of economic system from the standpoint of consumption. This could be cognised at restraint in consumption,' he proposed.[49]

Deen Dayal had outlined several objectives for the economy:

- Minimum standard of living for every individual and preparedness for defence of the nation.
- Grow beyond the minimum standard of living so that nation acquires the means to contribute to world progress on the basis of its own 'chiti'.
- Provide meaningful employment to every citizen by which the above two objectives can be achieved.
- Natural resources should be used without wastage and extravagance.
- Develop Bharatiya technology keeping in mind availability and nature of various factors of production.
- Means of ownership—private or state or any other—should be decided on a pragmatic basis.

TOWARDS A SELF-RELIANT ECONOMY

It is important to examine how several of Deen Dayal's economic ideas can be interpreted and applied to the present economic reality. Although some of his ideas look outdated, his core concerns with respect to Swadeshi or self-reliance and decentralisation remain very much valid to this day. The concept of *Atma Nirbhar Bharat*—self-reliant India—that Prime Minister Narendra Modi propounded in May 2020 is an application of Deen Dayal's economic ideology for twenty-first century India.

Modi's Atma Nirbhar formula doesn't discard anything. It takes a rather macro view. Modi outlined five pillars of building a self-reliant India. They are: 'Economy with potential for quantum jump, infrastructure, technology-driven systems, demography and an intelligence-driven supply system.'[50]

Atma Nirbharta is the contemporary version of human-centric economic liberalism based on the integral humanist thought with self-reliance at its core. Modi first invoked the Atma Nirbhar concept in an address to the nation during the COVID-19 pandemic-related lockdown on 12 May 2020. In that speech, he talked of being 'Vocal for Local'. His emphasis was on promoting locally manufactured products. Later, during his Independence Day address in August of the same year, he spoke about 'Make for the World'. It was about brand-building and making India an important component of global supply chains. The Indian government has also consistently and aggressively pursued 'Make in India' programmes since 2014, encouraging more and more investors to look at the country as an investment destination. Modi's Atma Nirbhar concept revolves around these three important themes: 'Vocal for Local', 'Make in India' and 'Make for the World'.

Some insist that Atma Nirbhar is not a new concept. It is true that successive prime ministers from Jawaharlal Nehru to Indira Gandhi to P.V. Narasimha Rao had all spoken about it in the past. But each one of them had a different understanding and interpretation of it. Also, like Modi, they too were responding to specific economic situations of their times.

For Indira Gandhi, self-reliance remained a mere slogan. She went on a nationalisation spree initially, nationalising the banking system and abolishing privy purses of the erstwhile royals. Rajiv Gandhi did make some important moves in the direction of shedding the socialist past of his grandfather, but he lacked will power. By the time Chandra Shekhar became the Prime Minister, four decades of haphazard economic policies had caused so much damage that India had to mortgage its gold reserves to the Bank of England in 1991 to avoid the humiliation of becoming a debt servicing defaulter. When P.V. Narasimha Rao became the Prime Minister in 1991, he inherited an economy that was in tatters. For Rao's government, self-reliance thus meant the ability to service debts on schedule. In his famous address to the AICC in 1992, Rao summed up his vision for self-reliance as 'we should be indebted only to the extent we have capacity to repay.'[51] Rao couldn't fully unshackle the country from the Nehruvian mixed economy. Yet, with the support of his Finance Minister, Dr Manmohan Singh, he opened it up for global integration.

Prime Minister Vajpayee invoked the concept of *Atma Shakti*—unleashing inner potential—for achieving Atma Nirbharta. The Vajpayee era witnessed dismantling of the burdensome structures of the command economy through initiatives like disinvestment. In fact, the Vajpayee government was the first to make a determined push to shed the burden of public sector enterprises by creating a separate ministry for that purpose. Although short-lived, the disinvestment ministry during the Vajpayee regime, led by the tenacious minister Arun Shourie, became the cynosure of many eyes.

Deen Dayal had categorical views about the public sector in India. He saw them as the manifestation of the state's obsession with socialism. 'The state (in Socialist countries) comes forward to own all factors of production and the citizens, big and small, lose their identity. Following these traditional methods, the state in India is also extending its sphere of activity even beyond its capacity. It is on this basis that the public sector is accorded a preferential treatment and all others are relegated to a secondary and derogatory position,' he criticised.[52] He argued that the state should allow different authorities to contribute to the development of the nation. 'The history of the last decade shows that the private sector has shown greater virility and capacity to invest and produce. Why should its services be not utilized? If we can tolerate a Birla and a Tata, what is the harm if a few more spring up,' Deen Dayal pragmatically argued.[53] Disinvestment during the Vajpayee regime was an attempt at achieving the balance between public and private sectors.

Various controversies engulfed the disinvestment ministry and later governments converted it into a department in the finance ministry. But the process continued. While the Vajpayee government unburdened itself from running unnecessary businesses like hotels, it invested heavily in priority areas like infrastructure. Infrastructure projects like the Golden Quadrilateral and the Pradhan Mantri Gram Sadak Yojna (PMGSY)—the rural roads scheme—pushed demand up and accelerated the economy, which resulted in a solid GDP growth rate of 8.5 per cent by 2003–04.[54]

Modi envisioned a self-reliance model based on the new economic reality of the country and the world. He too believed in Vajpayee's vision of reducing government's public sector bulge. Addressing a group of over 300 businessmen in the US during his first visit as the Prime Minister in October 2014, he insisted that 'It is not the government's business to run a business'.[55] Explaining his idea of self-reliance, he stressed in his special address to the nation on 12 May 2020 that India 'does not advocate self-centric arrangements when it comes to self-reliance. India's self-reliance is ingrained in the happiness, cooperation and peace of the world.'[56]

SELF-RELIANCE: THE GLOBAL EXPERIENCE

Countries like Japan, China and Israel, which started their national reconstruction around the same time as that of independent India, have all adopted self-reliance as the foundation for their future growth. Japan came out of the devastation caused by the nuclear bombing of its industrial cities, Hiroshima and Nagasaki, at the end of the Second World War in 1945. It started rebuilding its economy in the 1950s. China was doing economically well under Chiang Kai-shek until a violent takeover by the Red Army led by Mao in 1949. The journey of Communist China began in right earnest. Israel too secured its independence from the British soon after India, in May 1948, and began a difficult journey of building a new nation of the Jews.

Each country had its own path to self-reliance. Sakuma Shōzan is considered the father of Japan's modernisation. His famous slogan in the nineteenth century, which Japan vigorously applied after 1950, was: 'Japanese morals and Western technology'. Towards self-reliance, Japan adopted a three-pronged approach in early 1950s and 1960s. It restricted the import of manufactured products; fostered domestic industries through protective measures; and promoted technology transfers from advanced countries. Japan depended heavily on Western technology in the initial decades without allowing Western culture to influence it. In a few decades, it became self-reliant in technology too.

The economic rise of China is seen by many as a miracle. It has many lessons for India because in the initial years, after independence, it was Mao's China besides the Soviet Union, which had inspired Nehru to pursue disastrous socialist economic policies. Interestingly, in the initial three decades under Mao Tse Tung, China too had immersed itself in suicidal socialist practices, leading to unmitigated economic disaster. Deng Xiaoping, who became the supreme leader in 1978, transformed the economy completely. 'Socialism with Chinese characteristic' became the euphemism for Deng's revolutionary opening up. China under him initiated economic revival in the early 1980s with single-minded focus on growth. A new concept of 'GDP-ism' was coined to suggest that the mission should be to toil for higher GDP growth. From the year 1982 onwards, for almost three decades, China maintained an annual GDP growth rate of above 8 per cent. GDP-ism became the mantra and an obsession for the government as well as the masses. Incidentally, China and India were at the same economic threshold in 1980, but in the following three decades, China surged ahead.

The start-up industry is a major player in the story of Israel's economic success. It is described as a 'Can-Do' nation. Israelis are never content with what they have; they always try to innovate and improve. In less than four decades, they transformed their tottering economy into one of the top twenty in the world. The Yom Kippur War of 1973—the three-week war in which the Israelis had fought against the combined forces of Egypt and Syria—had practically destroyed Israel's nascent economy. A severe stagflation plagued the country until the mid-1980s, when the Israelis finally decided to take on the economic challenge. Realising that a country of eight million cannot outdo bigger economies, the Israelis focused on niche areas and developed world-class start-ups in deep-tech areas like electronic surveillance. The determined push for economic revival was so intense that when Israel was invited to join the world's club of the opulent, the Organisation for Economic Co-operation and Development (OECD), in 2009, it had a GDP higher than that of the group's average.

These nations offer a fresh perspective. Many Indian leaders like Gandhi and Deen Dayal had their own vision of Atma Nirbharta. Atma Nirbhar is not a path, as many mistakenly assume it to be; it is an ambitious vision and goal. The path to that vision and goal should be pragmatic. If Deen Dayal's integral thought is applied to the current context, the Atma Nirbhar path should mean leaner government, ease of doing business, greater investments, massive employment generation and greater integration with the global economy, not just as a beneficiary, but as a contributor. India needs to focus on each one of these to achieve real Atma Nirbharta.

THE PRESENT CHALLENGE

India traditionally has been a people-centric nation. The state was one of the institutions guiding public life, not the sole one. The role of the government in the life of an average Indian had always remained minimal. For a large section of the population, the state was an alien institution. Various other institutions like caste groups, religious groups, village councils, temples, saints and savants played a more important role in attending to the life of an individual. The Westminster model that India adopted after independence changed all that. Suddenly, governments became omnipresent and omnipotent. The political leadership overrode all other institutional leadership. Citizens became prisoners in the hands of the capricious state.

This alien nature of an all-encompassing state needs to change. Prime Minister Modi took several policy decisions to reduce the undue interference of the government in the life of ordinary citizens. 'Minimum government—Maximum governance' is the motto of this government. Hundreds of obsolete laws have been done away with. Red tape and lethargy have been curtailed. Technology has been effectively used to reduce human interface in government's functioning, thus paving the way for reduced corruption and increased speed of governance delivery. India has climbed up on the 'Ease of Doing Business' index from the 133rd position to 63rd position in the first five years of the Modi government due to consistent efforts.

Investments are an important challenge for India's economic growth. Deen Dayal was not in favour of inviting foreign investments into key strategic sectors like defence, which he believed had to be fully in domestic hands. However, he was very much in support of technology transfers from outside. The inflow of foreign direct investment (FDI) into India has steadily increased and reached a substantial level today. However, most of it goes into the stock markets or towards acquiring stakes in existing companies. Alternatively, FDI inflow has been into real estate in India. In the final analysis, a significant section of FDI has been leading to acquisition of valuable assets in India by foreign investors. Instead of helping in creating assets, these investments are actually taking over assets in India.

Both Gandhi and Deen Dayal emphasised the need for meaningful employment for the masses in India. As a nation of young people, India's demand for jobs is massive. Around 20 million youth attain employable age (18 years) every year, while the job markets in India cannot cater to even one-fifth of the demand. India needs to target 150 million jobs in the next five years. Deen Dayal's emphasis was on village and small industries and agriculture. Traditionally, these two areas have provided maximum employment in India. Over 40 per cent of India's employment is agriculture based.[57] Of the remaining, over 70 per cent jobs are provided by micro, small and medium-sized enterprises (MSMEs). Encouraging investment flows into areas of employment generation is a critical priority today.

Gainful employment can be provided by infrastructure and manufacturing sectors. India has long neglected the manufacturing industry and remained content with its successes in the information technology (IT) and services industry. Growth of medium and heavy industries outside the government sector has been marginal. Countries like China, Vietnam and Bangladesh have built their economic fortunes on manufacturing and exports. Strengthening the agriculture sector on the one hand and, reducing overdependence on it on the other, should be the way forward to ensure 'work for every hand'.

Atma Nirbharta should be understood from that perspective.

It also should be understood that the economy should ride over the shoulders of the people, while government should be an able facilitator. Becoming Atma Nirbhar should not be a government programme. It is about people too. It follows in three stages—*Atma Gaurav*—self-dignity, *Atma Samriddhi*—self-sufficiency, and *Atma Vishwas*—self-confidence. 'Vocal for Local' is about self-dignity or Swadeshi. 'Make in India' is about self-sufficiency—building domestic capability for domestic needs. But the third theme of 'Make for the World' is also equally important. It is about India's self-confidence. From a raw material supplier, India's economy has to mature into a manufacturing hub and brand builder in the world. It has to become an important contributor to global supply chains.

In his fascinating book *Too Small to Fail*, R. James Breiding narrated how not just big economies like America and China, but even smaller ones like Finland, Singapore, Norway and Sweden have risen to play a significant role in the world economy through their global brands. India can learn many lessons from their experience.

Because India, as a big country, cannot aim at anything less.

10

Democracy, with Popular Moral Authority

Making a 'moral man' has been the quest of philosophers for centuries. Some believed that God and religion could achieve that; some believed in man's ability to reason. In the Old Testament book of Ecclesiastes, King Solomon found man's moral virtue to be just to 'fear God and keep his commandments'. But thinkers from the later Enlightenment era insisted on man's innate wisdom and power of understanding as the basis of his virtue.

DEMOCRACY AND THE QUEST FOR A MORAL MAN

The Greeks gave the world the roots of democracy. But early Greek philosophers too struggled with the question of individual morality and social happiness. In recorded history, the Greeks were the first to experiment with models of governance. Greek thinkers had delved deep into the questions of human identity, nature and dignity and sought to build institutions. The state as an institution was seen by ancient Greek philosophers as an instrument for the moral and personal development of man. The Greek tradition was intellectual. It put premium on reason, virtue and knowledge. The Greek city-states were not exactly run on the representative democratic model that we practice today in many countries. They followed the system of consultations, debates and discussions among the gentry. Citizen equality as a concept did not develop in ancient Greek political thought. Greek city-states were largely aristocracies, with enlightened and rich citizens partaking in the proceedings of statecraft. Many sections of the population, including the working classes, women and slaves were excluded from the affairs of the state as they were considered to have less free time and therefore with limited opportunities to think, which was given utmost prominence. Yet, the objective of the state was defined as human welfare including education, ethics and harmony.

There were monarchies, oligarchies and popular democracies among the Greek city-states in fifth century BCE. Aristotle, the ancient Greek philosopher, wrote that while monarchies were for the benefit of the monarchs and oligarchies for the benefit of men with means, democracies were for the benefit of men without means. Plato, Aristotle's guru, was not fully in agreement. The city state of Sparta was an oligarchy while Athens was a raw democracy. Spartans ruled over Athens for a few decades. When they left, the Athenians held a court to punish supporters of the Spartans. Twenty-one thousand Athenians, all men from privileged backgrounds, assembled in a stadium and democratically voted to declare the philosopher Socrates as a collaborator of the Spartans. He was given the option of suicide or death at the hands of the state. Socrates decided to take his own life, prompting his disciple Plato to dismiss Athenian democracy as a 'kleptocracy'—a state of unrestrained political corruption.

In the absence of men with morals, democracies could become a source of injustice was a dilemma that continued to bother statesmen as democratic institutions evolved over the centuries in the Western world. In the *Federalist Papers*, James Madison, one of the founding fathers of the American Constitution and the fourth President of the United States, highlighted this serious democratic dilemma. 'If men were angels, no government would be necessary. If angels were to govern men, neither external nor internal controls on government would be necessary. In framing a government which is to be administered by men over men, the greatest difficulty lies in this: you must first enable the government to control the governed; and in the next place oblige it to control itself.'[1]

Plato's answer to this dilemma was to have 'Philosopher-Kings'. Either the philosophers should become kings, or rulers should 'genuinely and adequately philosophize' for greater public happiness, Plato argued. Enlightenment thinkers like Immanuel Kant believed in the power of human understanding. '*Sapere aude*', the Latin phrase meaning 'dare to be wise', became the motto of Enlightenment thinking. Reason was the God for thinkers of the Enlightenment era.

This quest for the moral man—an enlightened and philosophically mature individual—had led to many experiments in the Western world. The philosopher-king idea, while allowing for some wise men to rule over their subjects judiciously in the name of God, also created dictators like Hitler and Mussolini. But when reason became God, the Bastille was invaded by French citizens in July 1789 to spark off the famous French Revolution. God was stripped of 'His Holiness' and reason occupied his place. 'One god only, *Le Peuple* (The People),' the French revolutionaries declared, paving the way for the subsequent rise of both the communist ideology and democratic institutions. Western civilisation finally settled for a religious-moral narrative, which Martin Luther King, Jr had beautifully summed up by saying, 'The arc of the moral universe is long, but it bends towards justice.'[2]

Deen Dayal's view was that Western democracy was a product of this historic progression in Europe. 'After nationalism, democracy is the second radical concept that had deeply affected European polity. In the beginning, nations were ruled by monarchs, but their tyranny led to an awakening among the people. In the wake of the Industrial Revolution and development of international commerce, the trading community became a demanding force. Naturally, the traders came into conflict with the nobility and monarchy. This conflict sowed the seeds of democracy,' he wrote.[3]

Churchill used to quip that democracy was the worst form of government 'except for all the others'. Nehru too held the same opinion. 'Democracy is good. I say this because other systems are worse. So we are forced to accept democracy. It has good points and also bad. But merely saying that democracy will solve all the problems is utterly wrong. Problems are solved by intelligence and hard work,' Nehru had opined.[4]

Deen Dayal was a quintessential democrat. Like his mentor, Guruji Golwalkar, Deen Dayal too was convinced that democracy was the least harmful and best available form of government as conceived by man. He too insisted that the best form of government needed to be invented yet and emphasised on developing an Indian model of democracy. Golwalkar's objection to the Western democratic model was that it was based too much on 'self-praise and vilification of others.'[5] Like Gandhi, he also argued that true democracy was one in which every voice was heard without outright rejection.

DHARMOCRACY OR DHARMA RAJYA

It is the quest for a moral man that had led Deen Dayal to his famous philosophy of Integral Humanism. Unlike Western philosophers, Deen Dayal did not find religion and reason to be opposite poles. His philosophy was about man's evolution through society and the universe towards the divine. Deen Dayal's integral man was a moral man, fully integrated with cosmic reality in a progressive realisation through nation and nature.

The West saw a complete separation of religion and state— 'Render unto Caesar the things that are Caesar's, and unto God, the things that are God's,' the Bible has said.[6] However, Deen Dayal viewed Dharma not as a religion but as the eternal law that should encompass everything including statecraft. He gave a new definition to democracy based on Dharma. 'Dharma is eternal. Therefore, in the definition of democracy, to say that it is a government of the people is not enough; it has to be for the good of the people. Dharma alone can decide. Therefore, a democratic government, "*Jana Rajya*", must also be rooted in Dharma, i.e., a "Dharma *Rajya*". In the definition of democracy—of the people, by the people and for the people—"of" stands for independence, "by" stands for democracy and "for" indicates Dharma. The true democracy is one where there is freedom as well as Dharma,' Deen Dayal argued.[7]

Ernst Barker and other Western scholars were not accurate in advancing the theory that the origins of political thought lay in Greek philosophy. Around the time that Greek city-states like Athens and Sparta were flourishing with significantly evolved political institutions, several thousand miles to the East existed the Hindu civilisation with its well-developed Dharmic socio-political ideas and institutions. The Dharma code was what distinguished the ancient Hindu nation from the Greeks. The Greeks had developed a sound body of laws and insisted that the state function be based strictly on those laws. Delivering justice to its subjects as per the laws became the *primus prioritus* of the Greek state institutions. The Dharma code of socio-political order was built on similar principles.

Renowned Indian economist and academic Prof. P.R. Brahmananda underscored ten principles of a Gandhian society. They are: 1. Swaraj—self-rule, which included Swadeshi—self-reliance; 2. Equal respect for all religions; 3. State should function on the basis of love, spontaneity and voluntarism, not on fear or force; 4. Openness to ideas and ideologies; 5. Non-violent humanism; 6. Autonomy of individuals and self-contained units; 7. Antyodaya—justice at the grassroots; 8. Trusteeship in wealth management; 9. *Sattvic* (sustainable) materialism; 10. Harmony with nature.[8] This is essentially all about the Dharma code of socio-political order.

Dharma, although a code, was not merely concerned with political justice. The conception of Dharma Rajya encompassed all the ten elements enumerated by Prof. Brahmananda. Dharma-based statecraft can thus be described as 'Dharmocracy'.

Articulating the distinction between democracy of Western origin and Dharma based on systems of India, Deen Dayal used to say that adult franchise and electoral processes alone do not constitute democracy. 'Democracy is not merely the rule of the majority. In a majoritarian government, there will at least be one segment of the public whose voice has been stifled even though it may be right. This form of democracy cannot work for everyone's welfare and good. Therefore, in any form of democracy in India, election, majority and minority … all must be combined and harmonized at one pace. Anyone, who has a different opinion from the majority, even if he is a single individual, his viewpoint must be respected and incorporated into the governance,' Deen Dayal said.[9] This is Dharmocracy or Ram Rajya.

Gandhi too expressed similar sentiments in his writings. 'The rule of majority has a narrow application, i.e., one should yield to the majority in matters of detail. But it is slavery to be amenable to the majority, no matter what its decisions are. … Democracy is not a state in which people act like sheep. Under democracy, individual liberty of opinion and action is jealously guarded. I, therefore, believe that the minority has a perfect right to act differently from the majority,' he wrote in *Young India*.[10] 'The rule of majority, when it becomes coercive, is as intolerable as that of a bureaucratic minority. We must patiently try to bring round the minority to our view by gentle persuasion and argument,' he averred.[11]

DEMOCRACY IN INDIA

After Independence, India opted for Western democratic institutions. There was scepticism in England over India's ability to govern itself. Winston Churchill was said to have made derogatory comments about India's ability to self-govern.[12] Clement Atlee, the then British Prime Minister, also expressed serious doubts over India's attempts to adopt a democratic constitution. 'The Asiatic republics are few and of recent establishment. Their record is not very encouraging. They tend to degenerate into dictatorships or oligarchies. They offer a prize for the ambitious authoritarian individual,' he warned Nehru in a letter.[13]

Yet, there was near unanimity in India over democracy as the way forward after independence. It was only the Communist Party of India (CPI), which was not so enthused by the prospect of India becoming a Westminster model democratic polity. As India was preparing for an independent polity, the CPI had, in what became popular as the Ranadive Line, denounced India's independence as fake. B. T. Ranadive, the Secretary of the CPI, had insisted, 'yeh azadi jhooti hai'—this independence is fake. He argued that India was ripe for an armed revolution. When the Red Army captured power in China, Indian communists were overjoyed by the prospect of it marching into India and 'liberating' them. Congratulatory messages poured into Peking, greeting Mao Tse-tung. Mao, in response to a message received from Ranadive, wrote, 'The Indian people is one of the great Asian peoples with a long history and a vast population. Her fate in the past and her path to the future are similar to those of China in many points.' He also suggested that the people of India should emulate people of China to 'end the imperialist reactionary era in the history of mankind.'[14]

The Indian leadership had made up its mind about democracy long before Independence. When the British Parliament passed the Government of India Act of 1935, extending limited franchise to only about one-fifth of the Indian population, Nehru grudgingly called it a 'slave constitution', and unequivocally declared that India was going to be a democratic nation. 'Obviously, we are aiming at democracy and nothing less than a democracy,' he stated firmly.[15]

In Nehru's view, democracy was the greatest gift from Europe.

But leaders like Ambedkar and Deen Dayal viewed democracy as a natural choice for India. Speaking at the Constituent Assembly on 25 November 1949, Ambedkar reminded members that democracies were not new to India. 'It is not that India did not know what is democracy. There was a time when India was studded with republics, and even where there were monarchies, they were either elected or limited. They were never absolute. It is not that India did not know Parliaments or Parliamentary Procedure. A study of the Buddhist *Bhikshu Sanghas* discloses that not only were there Parliaments— for, the *Sanghas* were nothing but Parliaments—but the *Sanghas* knew and observed all the rules of Parliamentary Procedure known to modern times. They had rules regarding seating arrangements, rules regarding Motions, Resolutions, Quorum, Whip, Counting of Votes, Voting by Ballot, Censure Motion, Regularization, *Res Judicata*, etc. Although these rules of Parliamentary Procedure were applied by the Buddha to the meetings of the *Sanghas*, he must have borrowed them from the rules of the Political Assemblies functioning in the country in his time,' he said.[16]

T. Prakasam, a member of the Constituent Assembly from the Madras Presidency, intervened to inform the House that even modern democratic practices were not completely unknown to India. 'The Honourable Mr. Madhava Rau said that the ballot box and ballot paper were not known to our ancestors. I would like to point out to him, Sir, that the ballot box and the ballot papers were described in an inscription on the walls of a temple in the villages of Uttaramerur, twenty miles from Conjeevaram. Every detail is given there. The ballot box was a pot with the mouth tied and placed on the ground with a hole made at the bottom and the ballot paper was the kadjan leaf and adult franchise was exercised. The election took place not only for that village but for the whole of India. This was just a thousand years ago. It is not known to my honourable Friend and that is why he made such a wrong statement—a grievously wrong statement and I want to correct it,' Prakasam said.[17]

Deen Dayal too would emphasise on the same point. 'Vedic *Sabhas* and *Samitis* were also organised on the basis of democracy, and many medieval states in India were completely democratic. We have confined the powers and privileges of kings and made them cater to the demands of the public,' he wrote.[18]

Deen Dayal viewed democracy as a potential tool for national unity. He believed in the power of democracy to reform and moderate hardcore secessionists and separatists. His pragmatism encouraged him to think that even social evils like casteism and regionalism could end if democracy was nurtured properly. He also believed that for a diverse country like India, only democracy could ensure unity of the nation. 'If democracy comes to an end here, it will spell the doom of national unity,' he averred, adding '... even secessionist and separatist forces will gradually move towards national unity in a democracy. Even when they win the elections on the basis of casteism and regionalism, they would realise that they cannot sit alone in the legislatures. Democracy is essential for national unity.'[19]

DEBATE OVER POPULAR WISDOM AND ADULT FRANCHISE

There was some debate and suspicion in the Constituent Assembly over the question of universal adult franchise as part of India's transition into democracy. There was some resistance to making the right to vote a fundamental right for all citizens. Dr Ambedkar was in its favour and vociferously argued that '... the main thing will be franchise. This is a fundamental right. Franchise is the principal thing of the Constitution.'[20] Ambedkar's efforts to bring universal adult franchise within the ambit of fundamental rights remained unsuccessful. Finally, it found place in Part XV on Elections in Article 326 of the Indian Constitution. Even that was not without opposition. Brajeshwar Prasad, a member from Bihar, argued that universal adult franchise was a '... violation of the tenets of democracy. Adult franchise presupposes that the electorate

is enlightened. Where the electorate is not enlightened, there
cannot be parliamentary democracy,' Prasad insisted.[21] K.T. Shah,
another member from Bombay (Mumbai), also felt that literacy
was the 'minimum requirement in democratic citizenship.'[22] The
Greeks had similar reasons for denying ordinary citizens the right
of participation in democratic institutions—that they were not
supposedly men of reason and knowledge. They thought that only
the wise and knowledgeable could participate in the affairs of the
city states.

But just like on the question of democracy, on this question
too, the Congress leadership had made up its mind long before
Independence. When the Simon Commission, which came to India
in 1928 to study the constitutional reforms needed for the country,
challenged the Congress leadership to prepare its own Constitution
for India, the leadership had accepted the dare and formed an All-
Parties Conference under the leadership of Motilal Nehru for the
very task. The draft of the constitution was soon ready, in which
it was categorically stated that—'...every person of either sex who
has attained the age of 21, and is not disqualified by law, shall be
entitled to vote.'[23]

Reassuring members who were sceptical about universal adult
franchise, Dr Rajendra Prasad, on 26 November 1949, in his final
address to the Constituent Assembly as its Chairman, stated that:
'Some people have doubted the wisdom of adult franchise. I am
a man of the village. I, therefore, know the village people who
will constitute the bulk of this vast electorate. In my opinion, our
people possess intelligence and common sense. They also have a
culture which the sophisticated people of today may not appreciate,
but which is solid. They are not literate and do not possess the
mechanical skill of reading and writing. But I have no doubt in my
mind that they are able to take measure of their own interest and
also of the interests of the country at large if things are explained
to them. I have, therefore, no misgivings about the future, on their

account.'[24] Seven decades of India's democratic experience bear
testimony to the political maturity of the Indian people.

WORDS OF CAUTION

However, senior leaders like Gandhi and Ambedkar had words of
caution for the constitution makers. Gandhi was not a big admirer
of the British parliamentary system. His view was that in the British
system, the parliament worked only for partisan interest, and not
for national interest. 'By political independence I do not mean an
imitation to the British House of Commons, or the Soviet rule of
Russia or the Fascist rule of Italy or the Nazi rule of Germany. They
have systems suited to their genius. We must have ours suited to
ours.... I have described it as *Ram Rajya*—sovereignty of the people
based on pure moral authority,' he wrote in *Harijan* in January
1937.[25]

Ambedkar too described democracy in India as 'only a top-
dressing' on an Indian soil 'which is essentially undemocratic.' His
insistence was that the people of the country needed to be trained
in imbibing democratic spirit. His 'Three Warnings', delivered to
the Constituent Assembly on 25 November 1949, were the most
remarkable upbraiding of the people of India. 'The first thing, in
my judgement, we must do is to hold fast to constitutional methods
of achieving our social and economic objectives. It means we must
abandon the bloody methods of revolution. It means that we
must abandon the method of civil disobedience, non-cooperation
and satyagraha. These methods are nothing but the Grammar of
Anarchy and the sooner they are abandoned, the better for us. The
second thing we must do is to observe the caution which John
Stuart Mill has given to all who are interested in the maintenance
of democracy, namely, not "to lay their liberties at the feet of even a
great man, or to trust him with power which enable him to subvert
their institutions". There is nothing wrong in being grateful to great
men who have rendered life-long services to the country. But there

are limits to gratefulness. As has been well said by Irish Patriot Daniel O'Connel, no man can be grateful at the cost of his honour, no woman can be grateful at the cost of her chastity and no nation can be grateful at the cost of its liberty. Bhakti in religion may be a road to the salvation of the soul. But in politics, Bhakti or hero-worship is a sure road to degradation and to eventual dictatorship. The third thing we must do is not to be content with mere political democracy. We must make our political democracy a social democracy as well. Political democracy cannot last unless there lies, at the base of it, social democracy,' Ambedkar had warned.[26]

Both Gandhi and Ambedkar were responding to the experiences of their times—Gandhi was referring to the tyranny of the British rule and Ambedkar was responding to the oppressive caste system. Neither was against democracy, but both were against the idea of 'majoritarian rule'. For Gandhi, democracy meant the weak getting the same chances as the strong. For Ambedkar, it was about giving a voice to the voiceless.

For democracies to succeed, both Gandhi and Ambedkar believed that parliamentary majorities need to be restrained through constitutional ethics and public morality. Constitutional ethics is about leaders respecting constitutional order, conventions and institutions. The Americans have a written constitution, the British do not. Yet, both developed healthy conventions that safeguard their democracies. There is a beautiful convention in America of the outgoing president leaving behind a handwritten letter for the incoming one, which the new incumbent of the White House would get to see on the first day in the Oval office. 'We are just temporary occupants of this office. That makes us guardians of those democratic institutions and traditions—like rule of law, separation of powers, equal protection and civil liberties.... Regardless of the push and pull of daily politics, it's up to us to leave those instruments of our democracy at least as strong as we found them,' Barack Obama wrote in his letter to Donald Trump in January 2017.[27]

Democracy has travelled a long way. In the course of the last couple of millennia, it witnessed the rise of cruel despots and dictators, and also many great democrats. Even today, Vladimir Putin in Russia and Joe Biden in America have got elected through democratic elections that are very different from one another. Democracy has finally evolved into a successful system by creating a fine balance between elected and non-elected institutions with enough safeguards for the voice of the non-elected sections— whether a majority or a minority.

Democracies developed checks and balances in the form of elected parliaments on one side and unelected institutions on the other. While elected bodies are meant to be the voice of the majority, non-elected bodies such as the judiciary, media and other public institutions are expected to be the refuge for non-majorities. Democratic ethics demand that the elected must protect all the unelected instruments of democracy. India's democracy, as envisaged by the makers of its Constitution, thrived essentially because of this respect for ethical constitutionalism and moral activism of grassroots activists. Neither should see the other as an enemy and try to bring them down.

The reform that democracies need today is two-fold. First, elected institutions need to become less majoritarian and more consensual. Second, non-elected institutions should not become the voices of the elected majority alone; there is a need to build a stronger non-elected institutional framework for greater balancing.

Joseph Story, a renowned American jurist, had warned about this long ago. '[The American] Constitution has been reared for immortality, if the work of man may justly aspire to such a title. It may, nevertheless, perish in an hour by the folly, or corruption, or negligence of its only keepers, the people.'[28]

PUBLIC EDUCATION FOR DEMOCRACY'S SUCCESS

Both Gandhi and Deen Dayal opined that the success of democracy lay in educating the masses and believed that failure to do so would lead to democracy degenerating into a mobocracy. Deen Dayal used to refer to Julius Caesar of Shakespeare to underscore the nature of unenlightened public opinion. When Brutus murdered Julius Caesar, the Roman public had celebrated it, but when Antony revealed Brutus' deception, they went after Brutus the next moment. 'It is difficult to keep democracy alive between the two forms of government—mobocracy and autocracy,' Deen Dayal emphasised.[29]

Plato too had entertained similar fears about democracy. Demagogues can indulge in 'false and braggart words' and turn democracies into staging points for tyranny, he feared.[30] That democracies could end up producing tyrants and authoritarian dictators was the experience of the world in the last few centuries. Alexander Hamilton, one of the founding fathers of the American Constitution, used to claim that the creation of the electoral college system in America in 1787 was meant to ensure that a man with 'talents for low intrigue, and the little arts of popularity' could never become president of the United States of America.[31] Thomas Jefferson, another founding father, claimed that they wanted to build democracy in America on the basis of 'rational debate, reason, and compromise.'[32] But the events in America in the last fifty years indicate that the contrary is also possible under the same democracy. Donald Trump represented the very negation of those three values.

Authoritarians abhor rational debate and reason. They revel in their own superciliousness and narcissism. Julius Caesar used to invite sculptors to prepare hundreds of his own sculptures. Whenever he came across a new name, Stalin's only question used to be as to whether that new individual was a 'genius'. If the answer was 'yes', that individual would disappear the next day. In her book, *Twilight of Democracy*, American author and journalist Anne Applebaum refers to Hannah Arendt as 'the original philosopher of totalitarianism,' who identified the authoritarian personality as a 'radically lonely individual who, without any social ties to family, friends, comrades or mere acquaintances, derives his sense of having a place in the world only from his belonging to a movement, his membership in the party.'[33]

That was why 'people should be trained as good citizens for democracies to succeed' has been an accepted proposition all over the world. The responsibility for that was put on the leadership—the philosopher kings. Ronald Reagan used to say that a good leader is one who makes his people do good things. 'The greatest leader is not necessarily the one who does the greatest things. He is the one who gets the people to do the greatest things,' he said.[34]

DEEN DAYAL FOR PUBLIC EDUCATION THROUGH OTHER MEANS

Deen Dayal viewed it from a different perspective. While acknowledging the need for creating 'popular moral authority', he would still argue that it could not be done by the rulers alone. Left to them, the rulers would like to brainwash the public into believing only in them. 'In India, the problem has been solved by taking away the right of building democracy from the government. Educating public opinion is the work of selfless ascetics. Ruling according to public opinion is the task of the government. The ascetics always have the upliftment of the public and their spiritual interests in mind, and, as such, they work according to these noble ideals,' Deen Dayal explained.[35] He called those noble ideals *Sanskaras*. People should be imbued with ideals like feeling for the nation, consciousness of their responsibility, and discipline, he said, warning that if these Sanskaras were absent in citizens, democracy would 'degenerate into an instrument of individual, class and party interest.'

Deen Dayal enumerated three basic Sanskaras for citizens in a democratic polity. They were: 1. Tolerance and discipline; 2. Selflessness; and 3. Respect for the law of the land. Describing tolerance as the basis of Indian culture, Deen Dayal called upon the people to respond in a disciplined manner to dissent. Discipline also involved standing up to tyranny and wrongdoings of the rulers, not meekly submitting to them. 'Indiscipline and irresponsibility go together. A democracy can be successful only when a citizen understands his responsibilities and discharges them to the best of his abilities. It is imperative that the people must be responsible and disciplined in order to make democracy a success,' he asserted.[36]

He gave five tips to citizens to keep in mind at the time of the elections: '1. Use your right of franchise not for the party, but for ideals; not for an individual, but the party; and not for money power, but for the individual; 2. Do not be misled by the hype associated with a candidate because he is certain to win. Whatever the outcome of the election, it will be your own defeat; 3. The right to vote is a test of your thinking and morality. Pay heed to this. Do not sell your right to vote; 4. The right to vote is symbolic of each citizen's freedom and you should exercise it not at the behest of someone but at your own discretion after judicious thinking; 5. People should keep this constantly in mind that they are the real builders of political parties.'[37]

Lure of power, in Deen Dayal's view, made leaders blind to popular will. He argued that leaders should be selfless. 'In a democracy, a high degree of selflessness is required in the government. Like *Bhagwan* Ram, the rulers must always be prepared to rule at people's behest and give it all up when required without any ill-feeling,' he emphasised.[38]

That is why Deen Dayal wanted political parties to set an example for ordinary citizens. Rule of law is a political mandate, but people should have respect for law. Disrespect for law will lead to anarchy and autocracy. 'In order to generate respect for the law in the public, it is necessary that the political parties should themselves set an example in this regard,' he said.[39] Deen Dayal noticed growing evils like money power and muscle power in Indian politics in the initial years of independence itself and cautioned that it would sound a death knell to democracy. He insisted that parties should put up candidates who were selfless and committed to public service. Deen Dayal bluntly stated that '... there is not a single political party in India that is worried about this. The only thing that matters to them is that their candidate must somehow win.... They only grant a ticket to the candidate who has the maximum chances of winning.'[40] He then turned his attention to the people and called upon them to remember that '... an ineligible candidate is not worthy of our vote even if he belongs to a good political party. It is possible that while granting the ticket to such a person, a political party may have been guided by immediate gains or it may even have made a grave mistake. It is, therefore, the duty of a responsible voter to rectify this mistake by his awareness.'[41]

Deen Dayal was aware of the critical role that political parties play in a democratic polity. He wanted political parties to develop distinct character, rather than becoming mere vote winning machines in their lust for political power. A good political party is one which is 'not a conglomerate of people lusting for power, but one which has its own distinct character apart from aspiring for political power. Such a party is dedicated to its own ideals and their implementation instead of merely contesting elections or coming to power,' he would say.[42] Deen Dayal decried the use of money, caste and community in elections. When he was himself forced to contest in an election, he expressly ordered his workers to not invoke his caste to garner votes. Ambedkar too insisted that keeping the country above the creed was the only way to guarantee the success of democracy. 'This much is certain that if the parties place creed above country, our independence will be put in jeopardy a second time and probably be lost for ever,' he warned.[43]

Like Ambedkar, Deen Dayal too feared that democracies, in the absence of such public awareness, could breed dictatorial tendencies in leaders. As a die-hard democrat, he insisted that power should not be concentrated in the hands of any single leader. He was a staunch votary of democratic decentralisation. 'The centralization of political, economic and social powers in one individual or institution is a hindrance in the way of democracy,' he believed.[44]

Deen Dayal's idealism is a tall order for present-day politics. But it is key to the survival of democracy. And, as Noam Chomsky pointed out, democracy is not merely an ideal to be valued, it is essential for our survival.

∾

11

Identity as Ideology

Dharmocracy gave a unique identity to the ancient nation of the Hindus. Deen Dayal insisted that this unique Dharmic national identity had to be preserved and promoted, without which there would be no real meaning of independence. 'The basic cause of the problems facing Bharat is the neglect of its "core national identity,"' he bemoaned.[1]

What is the name of that 'core' national identity? Interestingly, despite coming from the RSS school of thought, Deen Dayal had not used the word 'Hindu' to denote that core identity. Instead, he chose the word 'Bharat'. The word he frequently used was 'Bharatiya'. The three words—Hindu, Bharatiya and India—are used interchangeably and considered as synonyms in RSS parlance.

INDIANISATION TO CULTURAL NATIONALISM

The Jana Sangh started using 'Bharat' and 'Bharatiya' to denote Indian society in general. Critics saw the word 'Bharatiya' as an effort on the part of the Jana Sangh to promote Hindu politics. A massive, often acrimonious, debate ensued in the 1960s about the meaning of the words 'Bharatiya' and 'Bharatiyakaran', the latter denoting, in its nearest possible translation, Indianisation.

One of the strongest votaries of Indianisation was Prof. Balraj
Madhok, who became the president of the Bharatiya Jana Sangh
briefly in 1966–67 but parted ways later due to internal differences.
Madhok authored a book, *Indianisation*, in which he explained his
idea. 'Indianisation aims at making every citizen of India a better
Indian, a good patriot and a nationalist. Indianisation of Indians is
as much valid both literally and metaphorically as nationalisation
of industries and undertakings which are already national property.
That there are people in the country who want to weaken and disrupt
India and there are forces which are consciously or unconsciously
undermining the unity of the country is the greatest justification for
propagating the concept and program for Indianisation in India of
today,' he argued.[2]

Yet, political adversaries like the communists continued to
dub Jana Sangh's ideology as 'Hinduisation', linking it to the
views of RSS leaders on Hindu Rashtra. Golwalkar categorically
dispelled this propaganda in an interview with an Iranian scholar
Dr Saifuddin Jeelany in 1971. 'Indianisation was of course the
slogan given by Jana Sangh. Why should there be such confusion?
Indianisation does not mean converting all people to Hinduism.
Let us all realise that we are all the children of this soil and we must
have our allegiance to this land. We belong to the same society
and that our ancestors are common. That our aspirations are also
common. Understanding this is Indianisation in the real sense.
Indianisation does not mean that one should be asked to quit his
religious system. We neither said this, nor we are going to say so.
Rather we believe that a single religious system for the entire human
society is not suitable,' Golwalkar said. 'Follow your own religion.
The God of Islam, Christianity and Hinduism is the same and we
are all His devotees. Give people true knowledge of Islam. Give
people true knowledge of Hinduism. Educate them to know that all
religions teach men to be selfless, holy and pious. Indianisation does
not mean making all people Hindus,' he further explained.[3]

The Bharatiya Jana Sangh got dissolved into the Janata Party in 1977, when several political parties of different hues came together under one umbrella, guided by eminent freedom fighter Jaya Prakash Narayan, against the dictatorial rule of Prime Minister Indira Gandhi. Interestingly, in 1975, when Indian democracy faced one of its severest challenges, it was not just political parties that were at the forefront protecting the political ideals of India's constitution makers but citizens from all walks of life. Prime Minister Indira Gandhi had imposed an Emergency in June 1975 and curbed all fundamental freedoms and rights of citizens. This dark phase continued for a full 21 months until March 1977. During this period, thousands of political leaders were incarcerated using draconian laws, in the name of internal security and defence of India.

During those trying times, safeguarding and restoration of democracy fell on the shoulders of non-political institutions as the entire opposition political class was in jail. The campaign against the Emergency powers of Indira Gandhi and for the restoration of democracy was led by saints, scholars and socially conscious citizens of India, including the media. Organisations like the RSS were at the forefront, leading the charge against the dictatorship. Finally, when Indira Gandhi was defeated at the hustings and democracy was restored in India, those individuals and institutions simply withdrew from political activism. The saga of the fight against the tyrannical rule during the Emergency days of 1975–77 was a shining example of the *Dharmocratic* model as enunciated by Deen Dayal.

The merger of Jana Sangh in the Janata Party was a short-lived affair, as the ideological positions that the Jana Sangh leadership took did not go down well with the leaders of the other constituent parties in the new outfit. The Jana Sangh leadership was forced to quit the Janata Party. When that critical moment came in 1980, the Jana Sangh faction did not go back to the old Jana Sangh identity.

Instead, the leaders chose a new name—Bharatiya Janata Party—for the new entity.

With a new name came new parlance too. After a brief romance with the hazy ideology of Gandhian Socialism, the party leadership, under Lal Krishna Advani, turned to the term 'cultural nationalism' to describe the philosophy of Deen Dayal. Conceptually speaking, cultural nationalism was not a new idea, nor was it unique to the BJP in India. The idea that shared culture, rather than ethnicity, race and descent, would form the basis for nationalism was first discussed in nineteenth-century Europe. Cultural nationalism denoted 'the belief that each nation in Europe had from its earliest formation developed a culture of its own, with features as unique as its language, even though its language and culture might have near relatives over the frontier.'[4]

In the Indian context, Deen Dayal wrote, 'It is essential that we think about our national identity. Without this identity, there is no meaning of independence, nor can independence become the instrument of progress and happiness. As long as we are unaware of our national identity, we cannot recognize or develop all our potentialities. Under alien rule this identity is suppressed. That is why nations wish to remain independent so that they can progress according to their natural bent and experience happiness in their endeavor. Nature is powerful. Any attempt to go against the nature or to disregard it would lead to troubles. Natural instincts can't be disregarded, but it is possible to elevate this nature to the level of culture. Psychology tells us how by suppression of various natural instincts different mental disorders ensue. Such a person remains restless and dejected. His abilities slowly deteriorate, and he becomes perverted. The nation too, like the individual, falls a prey to numerous ills when its natural instincts are disregarded. The basic cause of the problems facing Bharat is the neglect of its national identity.'[5]

Cultural nationalism continues to be in vogue in the nationalist discourse in India even today. Whereas organisations like the RSS use 'Hindutva' or simply 'Hindu' to denote that core identity, the BJP and broader nationalist school use the phrase cultural nationalism.

NATIONAL IDENTITY IN NATION BUILDING: EXPERIENCE IN THE WEST

The concept of national identity has been a subject of serious debates and disagreements globally. The Left-Liberal discourse regards identity questions as dangerously divisive and parochial. Ethno or cultural nationalisms were on the rise in the early twentieth century when the First World War broke out. In fact, the unification of Germany, based on common language and culture, brought about in 1871 by uniting German-speaking city states around Prussia had given respect and honour to nations and nationalism in Europe and the West in the nineteenth century. This feat had made Otto van Bismarck the 'Iron Chancellor', who had brought about the union, a cult-like figure.

Almost a century before him came two other big experiments in nation-building—one in America and the other in France. The American constitution, promulgated on 22 June 1788, was the first major attempt at creating a unified American nation. Liberal ideas of individualism, freedom, equality and human rights became the founding ideas of the American constitution, a product of the Federalist Papers of James Madison, Alexander Hamilton and the lesser-known John Jay. It was not a perfect nation, with racial supremacy and exclusion built into its very constitutional structure. It took more than 150 years and countless struggles for the USA to build a much stronger American identity, one based on racial equality and justice. The problems, though, do not seem to be over yet.

The other major effort in nation-building took place in France around the same time. Some 6,000 km away from America, in feudal France, a popular revolution broke out on 5 May 1789 on the streets of Paris, leading to deposition of the centuries-old Ancien Régime led by King Louis XVI. Louis XVI was finally executed brutally, and a new French nation was born. Famously known as the French Revolution, this historic movement, although it survived only for a decade, established a constitutional government in France and laid a strong foundation for a liberal democratic order based on the famous principles of liberty, equality and fraternity. The constitutional experiment was not successful. In ten years, the first French Republic collapsed and a military general, Napoleon Bonaparte, rose to power in France by the end of the eighteenth century. Napoleon indulged in incessant wars to expand French territory and was eventually defeated by the alliance of the feudal kingdoms of Prussia, Austria and Russia at the Battle of Waterloo in 1815.

The nineteenth century remained a century of nations and nationalism. In fact, European countries were so smug and contented with their respective national governments that they didn't anticipate the breaking out of the First World War in the early twentieth century. It was the end of the First World War which paved the way for the birth of internationalism and multilateralism. The League of Nations was born in January 1920 at the Paris Peace Conference but lacked any real strength. Eventually, it failed to contain the rise of fascist nationalists like Hitler in Germany and Mussolini in Italy, who became responsible for the Second World War in 1939.

The two world wars have made ethno-nationalism a bad word in international politics. The League of Nations and its post-Second World War avatar, the UN, put more emphasis on institutions for global governance that would have the authority and powers to override nationalistic impulses which are seen as against basic human welfare and international peace.

Concepts like nationalism and national identity have been

demonised in Europe and the West by Enlightenment liberals. Ethnic and cultural notions of nationalism were branded as 'identity politics' by them. Any discourse on nation and national identity got immediately identified with the fascist politics of Hitler and Mussolini and dismissed. The entire nationalist discourse was forced on the defensive. Rise in international travel and large-scale immigration precipitated this upheaval over national identity.

MULTICULTURALISTS VS ASSIMILATIONISTS

The rise of economic prosperity of the USA and Western Europe and increase in modes of international travel in the last century led to large-scale migrations from the developing world to these countries. Immigrants brought new challenges of integration and assimilation. As the numbers of immigrants rose, debates over national identities made a comeback in the West. Fluctuating economic fortunes of several countries in the West have added fuel to the fire.

In Europe, identity debates are at a feverish pitch today, largely centred on immigrants. Europe is facing an unprecedented challenge of immigrants, mainly from the Arab world. This immigration is different from the previous ones, in the sense that it is massive in size and hence described by many as waves. Arab-speaking Muslims from several countries in the Middle East and North Africa today flee to relatively prosperous and definitely more peaceful countries in Western Europe.[6] A large number of them are illegal immigrants, sneaking into host countries through porous borders of land and sea or overstaying beyond visa periods. These migrations are caused by several reasons, including economic and socio-political ones, with the most prominent among them being oppression, terror and civil war in many countries. These immigrants are poor, mostly uneducated, represent an alien language and practice a religion that is looked at with suspicion, if not hatred, by the populations of the countries they migrate to.[7]

The resultant social and economic strife that immigrants cause to host societies is leading to the rise of stridently anti-immigrant ultra-conservative political movements in different countries in Europe. In Germany, it is Alternatives for Germany (AfG),[8] led by Alexander Gauland. In France, it is Jean-Marie Le Pen's National Front.[9] In Austria, it is Freedom Party of Austria,[10] led by Heinz-Christian Strache. In Netherlands, it is Geert Wilders' Party for Freedom.[11] It is Sweden Democrats,[12] led by Jimmie Akesson, in Sweden. It is Matteo Salvini of the League Party in Italy.[13] Several other European countries are also witnessing the revival of far-right parties and ideologies centred on the idea of a national identity based on ethnicity or race. These parties reject multiculturalism, unbridled immigration, racial and religious appeasement, and minority politics. They tend to overstate things and attract criticism for being xenophobic, racist, anti-Islamic and anti-immigrant. Their demands range from closing national borders for immigrants to closing down of Islamic schools in their respective countries.

The rise of these far-right parties in different countries together with the rise in violence, crime and terrorism indulged in largely by immigrants had led to countries waking up to the new challenge of national identity. The West's response has been two-fold. Multiculturalism, wherein the country's laws and political systems would tolerate and accommodate diverse cultures of immigrant populations, has been seen as the way forward by liberal intellectuals and the political class. Countries like the UK have gone to the extent of trying to provide prominent space for immigrants in their respective systems. At one point, some leaders of the Church of England too joined in the chorus in support of multiculturalism, calling for Sharia laws to be implemented in UK.[14] Decades of multiculturalist policies did provide political space for immigrants to rise, but they failed to address the core issue of integration of immigrants into mainstream national societies. If anything, multiculturalism has, rather than helping in greater integration, exacerbated racial and cultural differences, and further fortified diverse identities. Today, leader after leader in the West, from Angela Merkel in Germany[15] to Emmanuel Macron in France,[16] is declaring publicly that multiculturalism is a failure.

Multiculturalists and assimilationists, therefore, are at loggerheads. Where multiculturalists demand recognition and respect for diverse cultures of immigrants, assimilationists argue that immigrants must be made to assimilate with mainstream societies.

The West is struggling to find answers to this new challenge before it acquires more serious proportions and leads to civil wars. There could be some important lessons for the West to learn from the experience of the rest of the world in managing diversities without compromising with core unity.

Margaret Thatcher is believed to have hailed India as an example. Mikhail Gorbachev, the last President of the USSR, visited the UK and met Prime Minister Margaret Thatcher in 1984 and supposedly asked for suggestions. 'When the Soviet leader asked for some advice on how he could deal with a multi-national, multi-ethnic state, the British prime minister asked him to look no further than his Indian friends, who the Iron Lady believed were doing a very good job of managing diversity,' wrote Ajay Kamalakaran in *Russia Beyond*.[17]

Michael Aaron, former UK Ambassador to Sudan, in a thought-provoking article, 'Debating National Identity', summed it up beautifully: 'Some countries and governments consciously set out to create and foster a national identity—that is the purpose of the Pledge of Allegiance recited daily by many US school children. For others (the UK but also in the Gulf), a Royal Family is a major focus of national identity. In many cases, a historical event like a revolution or independence is an important element in developing a national identity. A national flag can also be a powerful emblem— consider New Zealand's intention to create a new flag to reflect their national identity and the success of Canada's Maple Leaf. But ultimately, a successful national identity depends on the citizens of the country concerned feeling pride in their country.' He also added a personal note to it, which eloquently explains the question of national identity. 'Personally, I am proud of being English (especially when it comes to football), British (at the Olympics) and European (and not just during the Ryder Cup golf competition).' What he intended to explain was that multiple sub-identities could happily co-exist within the ambit of a wider national identity.

CULTURAL IDENTITY AS NATIONAL IDENTITY

Deen Dayal and several thinkers of the nationalist school of thought in India have argued that national identity in India has to be based on cultural identity. This Indian value system has not indulged in a slugfest over glorifying diversity as multiculturalism on one hand and annihilating it in the name of assimilationism on the other. Instead, it has proposed the philosophy of 'unity in diversity'. The Bharatiya identity that Deen Dayal spoke about has celebrated diversity while nurturing united national life.

India's core identity doesn't lie in political ideologies and programmes. 'National union in India must be a gathering of its scattered spiritual forces, a union of those whose hearts beat to the same spiritual tune,' Swami Vivekananda had said.[18] Even Nehru had to admit it in one of his speeches. Dr Sampurnanand, eminent Congress leader from Uttar Pradesh and its chief minister from 1954 to 1960, had arranged a discussion with a number of eminent scholars in 1957 to discuss threadbare the question of India's future direction. Nehru had himself prepared a summary of the conclusions of that discussion session in which he said: 'In our craze for material development, we have completely neglected the spiritual aspect of our life. Human life has a purpose, an ultimate goal. We need to revive a philosophy of life with its spiritual base for which a man should be prepared to live and to lay down his life if necessary. We speak of a welfare state and advocate Socialism and democracy, yet we do not have a clear and unequivocal definition of either. Democracy and Socialism are merely the means, not the end. While thinking of our economic problems, the goal of life—as has been laid down in *Vedanta* on the foundation of which the entire creation rests—must be ever present before us.'[19]

This was Nehru, advocating for more than the political creeds of socialism and democracy, to meet the ends, and his conclusion was that Vedanta was the solution. Is that tantamount to mixing religion and politics? The secular argument goes for total and unequivocal separation of the two. However, cultural identities shouldn't be mistaken for religious beliefs. Alexis Tocqueville attributed the working of the American political system to the American culture, which is 'congenial to democracy'. Max Weber went one step further and declared that the rise of capitalism in the West was essentially a cultural phenomenon.[20]

Unlike the countries in the West, India did not face any big challenge of immigration in history. Invaders came in hordes, lured by the riches of the land, either to go back defeated or to get assimilated in the mainstream of this country. But India's brush with Semitic faiths exposed it, for the first time, to a conflicting narrative about its national identity. The questions that Western nations are facing today due to experiences with immigrants, were questions that India faced a long time ago. The Semitic religions of Islam and Christianity gained prominence in India through state power at different times in history. Christian clerics and Muslim traders came independent of state power and invading armies; yet, the spread of these Semitic faiths in India followed the state power that resulted in large-scale religious conversions of native people from their respective faiths to Semitic ones, many-a-times through allurement and coercion too.[21]

Does change of religion lead to change of national identity? In its long history, India had to find a categorical answer to this question once during the twentieth century. Until then, it was universally presumed that faith and religion did not impact national identity of the people. During the struggle against the British, there were many occasions when Hindus and Muslims would fight together. The biggest battle against the British that had ended the rule of the East India Company and brought the country directly under the British kingdom was fought in 1857. Famously called the First War of Independence, the 1857 revolt, primarily led by the soldiers of the British Indian Army and subsequently joined by several royals, saw Hindu and Muslim soldiers and royals fighting shoulder-to-shoulder against the British.[22] [23]

NEW CHALLENGE TO CULTURAL IDENTITY: THE TWO-NATION THEORY

The advent of the twentieth century saw the identity question acquiring new dimensions. Until then, the Semitic challenge to Indian national society was about iconoclasm and exclusive and supremacist dogmas. But a new political outfit, the Muslim League, came into existence in 1906 at Dhaka in present-day Bangladesh, which would change the entire discourse in the next four decades. The Muslim League had, for the first time, proposed that Hindus and Muslims were not just two religious societies but two distinct nationalities. It also insisted that the two could not live together under one roof as a united national society.

Mohammad Ali Jinnah and Mohammad Iqbal became the ideologues of what became famously known in later years as the two-nation theory. Iqbal, a renowned Urdu poet and philosopher, who became the President of the All India Muslim League in 1930, was the first to give the religious identity of Indian Muslims a politico-national colour. On 29 December 1930, while addressing the annual conference of the League, Iqbal had said: 'I would like to see Punjab, North-West Frontier Province [now Khyber Pakhtunkhwa], Sindh and Baluchistan amalgamated into a single state. Self-government within the British Empire or without the British Empire, the formation of a consolidated North-West Indian

Muslim state appears to me to be the final destiny of the Muslims, at least of North-West India.'[24] It was this idea of Mohammad Iqbal that became the basis for the creation of Pakistan, seventeen years later—a nation created purely on religious lines. However, the father of the 'Pakistan dream', Iqbal didn't live to see it come true. He passed away in 1938 after months of illness.

A decade later, Mohammad Ali Jinnah, who had by then become the supreme leader of the Muslim League and the 'sole spokesman' of Pakistan—to quote renowned Pakistani author Ayesha Jalal—had formalised the two-nation theory. 'Hindus and the Muslims belong to two different religions, philosophies, social customs and literature ... It is quite clear that Hindus and Muslims derive their inspiration from different sources of history. They have different epics, different heroes and different episodes.... To yoke together two such nations under a single state, one as a numerical minority and the other as a majority, must lead to growing discontent and final destruction of any fabric that may be so built up for the government of such a state,' he had stated at the League's convention in Lahore in 1940.[25]

Jinnah's argument was facetious. Going by the argument, Muslims could not co-exist with any other religious groups in any other country either. Jinnah's argument that Hindus and Muslims derived inspiration from 'different sources of history' and had 'different heroes' was erroneous and frivolous too. Muslims in India, with very few exceptions, were of Indian origin. What Jinnah's argument meant was that mere change of religion would change one's history, heroes and ancestors. It called into question fundamentalist Islam's tendency to reject all other national identities and promote the idea of Islamic *Ummah* (brotherhood).

Jinnah's two-nation theory did not stand the test of time. In just over two decades, Pakistan had again split up into two countries when the Bengali-speaking people of East Pakistan revolted against their Punjabi counterparts in the West and created an independent

Bangladesh in 1971. Today, the country is torn apart by the very same fundamentalist forces that play havoc with minority populations like Hindus, Sindhis, Baloch and Shias, besides oppressing women, liberals and free thinkers. The country is surviving because of the force of its army as there remains no other binding factor for it to survive as a nation.

The two-nation theory directly contradicted India's age-old nationhood concept of inclusive pluralism. Indian leaders had not accepted that proposition. During the making of the Constitution of India, there were some who argued in favour of a system of preferential treatment to Hindus since the country was divided on the basis of the two-nation theory. Participating in the debate on Article 5 of the draft constitution, regarding citizenship laws in India, P.S. Deshmukh argued, 'If the Muslims want an exclusive place for themselves called Pakistan, why should not Hindus and Sikhs have India as their home?'[26] However, the broader consensus was that independent India wouldn't give up its ancient identity of nationhood and fall into the trap of religious nationalist arguments.

Dr S. Radhakrishnan, who became the first Vice President of India, made a superb speech in the Constituent Assembly on 14 August 1947, in which he dwelt at length upon the question of India's ancient identity. 'The body politic may be divided but the body historic lives on. (Hear, hear.) Political divisions, physical partitions, are external but the psychological divisions are deeper. The cultural cleavages are the more dangerous. We should not allow them to grow. What we should do is to preserve those cultural ties, those spiritual bonds which knit our peoples together into one organic whole,' he exhorted.[27]

Dr Rajendra Prasad, the Chairman of the Constituent Assembly, who was to become the first President of independent India, also articulated similar sentiments in his address on 15 August 1947. 'It is undoubtedly a day of rejoicing. But there is only one thought which mars and detracts from the fullness of this happy event.

India, which was made by God and Nature to be one, which culture and tradition and history of millenniums have made one, is divided today and many there are on the other side of the boundary who would much rather be on this side. To them we send a word of cheer and assurance and ask them not to give way to panic or despair but to live with faith and courage in peace with their neighbours and fulfil the duties of loyal citizenship and thus win their rightful place. We send our greetings to the new Dominion which is being established today there and wish it the best luck in its great work of governing that region and making all its citizens happy and prosperous. We feel assured that they all will be treated fairly and justly without any distinction or discrimination. Let us hope and pray that the day will come when even those who have insisted upon and brought about this division will realise India's essential oneness and we shall be united once again. We must realise however that this can be brought about not by force but by large heartedness and co-operation and by so managing our affairs on this side as to attract those who have parted. It may appear to be a dream, but it is no more fantastic a dream than that of those who wanted a division and may well be realised even sooner than we dare hope for today,' he said.[28]

The very thought of Hindu-Muslim separation was agonising to Gandhi. It came as a blow to his life-long commitment to and conviction about Hindu–Muslim unity. He resisted it until the last moment, and in the end, laid down his life as a victim of its fallout. 'We must save our hearts from being sundered. Otherwise, Jinnah Saheb's claim that we are two nations will stand vindicated. I have never believed in it. When we are descended from the same ancestors, can our nationality change simply from changing our religion?' he questioned out of anguish.[29] He wrote in *Hind Swaraj*: 'Should we not remember that many Hindus and Mahomedans own the same ancestors and the same blood runs through their veins? Do people become enemies because they change their religion? Is the God of the Mahomedan different from the God of the Hindu? Religions are different roads converging to the same point. What does it matter that we take different roads so long as we reach the same goal? Wherein is the cause for quarrelling?'[30]

Nehru had once made a passionate speech to the students of Aligarh Muslim University (AMU) in 1948. 'I have said that I am proud of our inheritance and our ancestors who gave an intellectual and cultural pre-eminence to India. How do you feel about the past? Do you feel that you are also the sharers in it and inheritors of it, and therefore proud of something that belongs to you as much as to me? Or do you feel alien to it and pass it by without understanding it or feeling that strange thrill which comes from the realisation that we are the trustees and inheritors of this vast treasure? I ask you these questions because in recent years many forces have been at play diverting people's minds into wrong channels and trying to pervert the course of history. You are Muslim and I am a Hindu. We may adhere to different religious faiths or even none; but that does not take us away from that cultural inheritance that is yours as well as mine. The past holds us together; why should the present or the future divide us in spirit?'[31] Nehru exhorted the audience, invoking cultural oneness as the binding identity of the Indian nation.

From Gandhi to Nehru to Viceroy Wavell, every sensible leader opposed the two-nation argument and Jinnah's insistence on partitioning India along religious lines. 'Vivisect me before you vivisect India,' claimed Gandhi.[32] Sardar Patel went one step ahead further to declare: '*Talwar se talwar bhidegi*' (sword will clash with sword). He meant that India would fight till the end against partition.

Dr Rajendra Prasad, who was in jail during the Quit India Movement, went on to write a book, *India Divided*, in which he spoke about the ills of partition and how illogical the thought was. Even before the ink on that book could dry up, India was partitioned. Nehru, in his typical romantic style, proclaimed that the idea of partition was 'fantastic nonsense' and 'the idea of some mad people'. The irony was that it was the same Nehru who became a signatory to the partition agreement, called the June 3rd Plan. Sardar Patel remained a mute spectator.

Viceroy Wavell famously declared his opposition to the idea in 1944, stating that, 'India is a God-made triangle, you cannot divide it.' Even Clement Atlee's mandate as Britain's Prime Minister to Lord Mountbatten, the last Viceroy of India, was not to partition India. 'Keep it united if possible. Save a bit from the wreck. Bring the British out in any case'—these were Attlee's instructions to Mountbatten.[33]

POST-PARTITION DEBATE OVER NATIONAL IDENTITY

Partition had triggered a big debate in India over the issue of national identity. It dominated Jana Sangh's politics from the very beginning. 'One Country, One Nation, One Culture, Rule of Law'—these four principles were presented as fundamental to the Jana Sangh thought process by Dr Mukherjee in the very first meeting of the party.

While challenging the Nehruvian discourse of nationhood and national identity, the Jana Sangh stuck to its commitment of India's identity as an ancient nation of inclusive Bharatiya values. It opted for the word Bharat for India in its discourse and unequivocally declared that the doors of the party would be open to all citizens of India. 'We have thrown our party open to all citizens of India irrespective of caste, creed or community... People must be united by a bond of fellowship and understanding inspired by deep devotion to the spirit of common motherland. It is obvious for the vast majority of Bharat's population to assure all classes of people who are truly loyal to their motherland, that they will be entitled to full protection under the law and to complete equality of treatment in all matters social, economic and political. Our party gives assurance unreservedly,' Dr Mukherjee declared in his first address as head of the newly formed party in 1951.[34]

Eminent freedom fighter V.D. Savarkar, popularly known as Swatantra Veer Savarkar or simply Veer Savarkar, had a different take on the subject. Ambedkar quoted Savarkar as stating, 'The name "Hindustan" must continue to be the appellation of our country. Such other names as India, Hind, etc., being derived from the same original word Sindhu, may be used but only to signify the same sense—the land of the Hindus, a country which is the abode of the Hindu Nation. Aryavarta, Bharat-Bhumi and such other names are, of course, the ancient and the most cherished epithets of our Mother Land and will continue to appeal to the cultured elite. In this insistence that the Mother Land of the Hindus must be called but "Hindustan", no encroachment or humiliation is implied in connection with any of our non-Hindu countrymen.'[35]

In a sense the 'spiritual' that Ambedkar talked about was interpreted as Hindu by Savarkar. Historically, the people of India were recognised as Hindus in Western lands and also in China. The Persians were said to be the first people to use the word Hindu to denote people living on the other bank of river Sindhu or Indus. Thus, people of India came to be recognised as Hindus. Even the name India was derived from the word Indus, the Romanised version for the Greek word *Indos*. In any case, this word too was derived from the river Sindhu or Indus itself. Some nationalist thinkers argue that the origins of the word Hindu were not foreign, but very much indigenous.

'Iravatham Mahadevan, Indologist from Tamil Nadu, was the first one to point out the Vedic link while studying the Harappan unicorn and the cult object before it. Being a student of Sanskrit, he was familiar with the Vedic ceremony of the Soma filtering ritual. He says he was "reminded of the two most powerful images in the Soma chapter of the Rig Veda, Pavamana and Indu". Pavamana means the flowing Soma, and Indu, the Soma drops collected at the bottom of the filter. The word Indu, in the authoritative Monier-Williams Sanskrit dictionary, represents not only the Soma drop but also the Soma itself. In the Brahmanas, Indu is used for moon. In the famous river hymns of Rig Veda (Nadistuti Sukta नदिस्तुति सूक्त, X.75), the river Indus is named as "Good Soma" (Su-Soma). So, we have the droplets of Soma—Indu and the flowing Soma Sindhu. Both Indu and Sindhu refer to the central Vedic religious ritual—Soma,' argued Aravindan Neelakandan in an article in *Swarajya* magazine.[36]

He also referred to the work of seventh-century Chinese pilgrim Xuanzang or Hieun Tsang, who said that India was 'anciently called Shin-tu, also Hien-tau'. However, 'according to the right pronunciation, it is called In-tu'. He also pointed out that in Chinese the term also refers to the moon. This was appropriate, said the seventh-century pilgrim, because 'the bright connected light of holy men and sages, guiding the world as the shining of the moon, have made this country eminent, and so it is called In-tu.'[37]

HINDU-BHARAT-INDIA

This thread was picked up by Golwalkar and the RSS, in general, who argued that Hindu, Bharat and India were synonyms and could be used interchangeably. In modern India, that became a matter of contention, with many arguing that Hindu denoted only a religious system prevalent among a wider section of the people of India and hence could not be equated with its national identity. Hindu, Hindutva and Hindu Rashtra became points of heated debate largely due to misrepresentations by Marxist and Islamist intelligentsia. Over time, they succeeded in projecting Hindutva as a pejorative idea of anti-Islamist ideology.

In his 1923 work titled *Essentials of Hindutva,* Savarkar explicitly addressed the suspicion about the word being anti-Muslim. He called the suspicion that had 'crept into the minds of some of our well-meaning but hasty countrymen that the origin of the words Hindu and Hindusthan is to be traced to the malice of the Mohammedans' as 'singularly stupid'. 'Long before Mohmmad [sic] was born, nay, long before the Arabians were heard of as a people, this ancient nation was known to ourselves as well as to the foreign world by the proud epithet Sindhu or Hindu,' he wrote.

The RSS, on its part, held that Hindu and Hindutva were synonymous with India and Bharat. It insisted that the ancient cultural greatness that Nehru talked about in his famous book *The Discovery of India*, or the spiritual principle of the nation that Dr Ambedkar talked about, were the essence of all these different words. Mohan Bhagwat, the sixth Sarsanghachalak of the RSS, was more forthright on this issue.

Speaking at a three-day lecture series in Delhi in September 2018, Bhagwat elaborated on his thoughts about Hindu and Hindutva. 'The Indian philosophy is called Indic thoughts, and people belonging to this country are called *Bharatvasi*. These are all synonymous. They talk about same thing. This means Hindu,' the RSS chief said.[38] He emphatically stated that Hindutva was the only philosophy that was inclusive and respected diversity. '*Hindutva* is not only for Hindus, it is for the world and humanity, be it Sikh, Jains, Buddhists, who all were born here. We never saw state and nation as same. States can come and go, but nation, which is a cultural concept, stays. We believe in that,' Bhagwat stated.[39] While talking about a common ancestry and shared culture, Bhagwat even insisted that there was no Hindutva without Muslims. 'If we do not accept Muslims, it's not *Hindutva*. *Hindutva* is Indianness and inclusion,' he categorically emphasised.[40]

Speaking at the annual Foundation Day function of the RSS held on the Hindu festival of Vijaya Dashami in October 2020, Bhagwat once again dwelt at length on the pervasive confusion over the issue of Hindutva and the RSS. He rightly pointed out that confusion and misconceptions about the Sangh were largely due to lack of understanding of the Sangh's preference for a specific vocabulary and how it interpreted certain words.

Hindutva was one such word. It is generally understood as

a religious term. But the RSS uses Hindu and Hindutva in the classical cultural and civilisational sense, not in the conventional religious sense. 'To us, it is the word expressing our identity along with the continuity of its spirituality-based traditions and its entire wealth of value system in the land of Bharat,' Bhagwat explained.[41] Therefore, in the RSS's view, the word is applicable to all the 1.3 billion people of India. But Bhagwat added a couple of riders for 'being a Hindu'—'...those who call themselves the sons and daughters of *Bharatvarsh*, whose everyday life is striving towards an alignment with its moral and ethical code and who are proud of the heritage of their ancestors who successfully traversed the same spiritual landscape since time immemorial.'[42]

Dr Sarvapalli Radhakrishnan had also described Hinduism not as religion but as a 'commonwealth of religions'. 'Hinduism is not a definitive dogmatic creed, but a vast, complex, but subtly unified mass of spiritual thought and realization. Its tradition of the godward endeavour of the human spirit has been continuously enlarging through the ages,' he wrote.[43] Gandhi described Hinduism as the 'relentless pursuit after truth'. The Hindutva of the RSS too is akin to the description of these notable leaders.

The RSS does not view Hindu as any religion or sect or denomination. It is viewed as the psychological common denominator 'whose vast courtyard cradled human civilisation, and that which honours and encompasses innumerable distinct identities'.[44] Those who disagree with the insistence of the RSS that the Hindutva it propagates is the same as what the term Hindu stands for, try to make a distinction on the lines of what the West perceives as the difference between Islam and Islamism. While some of their arguments merit debate, their criticisms are largely hollow. The RSS has, over the decades, made efforts to address these criticisms and explain its position in more inclusive terms. In fact, it has assimilated the colloquial and global interpretations of the term Hindu into its own parlance. 'When Sangh says that

"Hindustan is Hindu *Rashtra*", it does not have any political or power-centred concept in its mind. *Hindutva* is the essence of this *Rashtra's* "*Swa*" (self-hood). We are plainly acknowledging the self-hood of the country as Hindu because all our socio-cultural practices are directed by its principles with their spirit percolating in the personal, familial, professional and social life of each one of us. Acceptance of this view of life does not require giving up one's faith, language, land or any other identity marker. It only mandates an abandonment of the quest for supremacy,' Bhagwat affirmed.[45]

Yet, confusion persisted over not just Hindutva, but even Hinduism. It continues to be viewed from an anti-minority prism. At the root of this confusion is a flawed discourse on secularism in India. When India became independent, Gandhi suggested that it become a 'Rama Rajya'. 'Friends have repeatedly challenged me to define independence. At the risk of repetition, I must say that independence of my dream means *Rama Rajya* i.e., the Kingdom of God on earth,' he wrote in *Harijan* in May 1946.[46] Although apologetic about equating it with Hinduism, Gandhi did insist that Rama Rajya was the essence of Hinduism. 'My Hinduism teaches me to respect all religions. In this lies the secret of *Rama Rajya*,' he wrote in October 1947 after India attained independence.[47]

SCARS OF PARTITION: A FLAWED SECULARISM DEBATE

However, the scars of partition were fresh in the minds of India's constitution makers. The Hindu-Muslim divide, successfully engineered, exploited and profited of by the Muslim League was to be defeated and buried. The priority was to end majority-minority divide and discourse. In a speech in the Constituent Assembly on 25 May 1949, Sardar Patel appealed 'to forget that there is anything like majority or minority in this country and that in India there is only one community.'[48]

The two-nation theory continued to haunt Indian policy-making. A new phrase '*Dharma Nirapekshta*' was inserted into the political lexicon, without too much thinking or understanding. It broadly meant keeping a distance from religion in public affairs. It was interpreted as the Indian equivalent of secularism. Some members of the Constituent Assembly like K.T. Shah, Lok Nath Mishra and Tazammul Hussain wanted secularism to be included in the Indian Constitution, although for different reasons. While Shah insisted that the state should have nothing to do with religion, Mishra argued that either the majority religion of the Hindus be accepted as the religion of the state or all religions be kept at a distance. There was unanimity in the Constituent Assembly over the Indian state remaining secular, but members had different views over its meaning. Was the secularism of the French version, where the state expressly rejects religion, to be accepted or the American model where the state accords equal freedom to all religions and presidents take oath in the name of religion with the Bible in their hands?

Everybody, including Nehru, agreed that while secularism as a principle had to be accepted, the insertion of the word into the Constitution could lead to confusion and difficulties for a deeply religious society like India later. Hence, the word did not find place in the Indian Constitution in the beginning. It was only in December 1976 that the words 'secular' and 'socialist' were inserted into the Constitution through the infamous 42nd Amendment, which was effected at a time when the entire Indian Opposition was in jail due to the Emergency. There was a consensus in the Constituent Assembly that in the Indian context, the secular state should not mean that the state would be against God or religion. K.M. Munshi, senior Congress leader from Gujarat, put it eloquently as, 'A secular state is not a godless state. It is not a state which is pledged to eradicate or ignore religion. It is not a state which refuses to take notice of religious belief in the country.'[49]

The dominant theme in the entire discourse though was about granting specific rights to minority religions. An explicitly secular state could not have done that by ignoring the majority religion. Despite Sardar Patel's exhortations about rejection of the minority-majority syndrome, the Indian Constitution ended up providing various educational and cultural rights to minority groups in the country. 'Freedom of Religion' became one of the fundamental rights of the people and that right included 'right to profess and practise' religion. Thus, in practise, Indian secularism acquired a fundamental flaw, of rejecting the practises of the majority religion while accommodating the same from minority religions.

Dharma Nirapekshta became a fad during the initial years of independence. After a long speech by a minister in the Parliament, Piloo Modi, a veteran Swatantra Party leader, was said to have pointed out the contradiction by drawing his attention to the Ashok Chakra—the national emblem of India—engraved on the wall behind the Speaker's podium. It contained the words '*Dharma Chakra Pravartanaya*', meaning let the wheels of Dharma continue to roll. This contradiction became the hallmark of Indian secularism for many decades to come.

Secularism was a European concept. British author George Holyoake used it for the first time in 1851. Holyoake was an agnostic. But he did not use the term in any exclusive sense. 'Secularism is not an argument against Christianity, it is one independent of it. It does not question the pretensions of Christianity; it advances others. Secularism does not say there is no light or guidance elsewhere but maintains that there is light and guidance in secular truth, whose conditions and sanctions exist independently, and act forever. Secular knowledge is manifestly that kind of knowledge, which is founded in this life, which relates to the conduct of this life, conduces to the welfare of this life, and is capable of being tested by the experience of this life,' he explained.[50]

Secularism became a movement in Europe mainly due to Enlightenment-era thinkers who wanted European society to be freed from religious orthodoxy. Semitic faiths, especially Catholic

Christianity, dominated all spheres of life in Europe in the medieval period, which led to revolts and the rise of national churches in many countries. A Protestant movement swept through European lands propagating that the road to heaven need not pass through Rome. Separation of religion and state became an important element of Enlightenment thinking. However, consensus over the definition of secularism and its application eluded the Europeans as well.

As a concept, secularism was not new to India. Its various definitions were widely discussed and interpreted here. Holyoke's definition of secularism as material and empirical knowledge was explored by the sage Charvaka at least three millennia ago. Secularism as separation of religion and state too was not new in India. In fact, the only king who pronounced a state religion was King Ashoka in the third century BCE. There was a dispute over whether he became a Buddhist through conversion after the infamous Kalinga War in 260 BCE or if he was a Buddhist when he waged the war. However, there is no dispute over the fact that Ashoka put to death thousands of non-Buddhists like Jains and others.[51]

Secularism in the West was a response to religious orthodoxy's domination in the affairs of the state. In India, there were no theocracies ever. A land of extreme religious diversity, India held all its religions in equal respect and granted individuals full freedom to pursue religious persuasions without fear. Two doctrines—'*Ekam Sat—Viprah Bahudha Vadanti*'—Truth is one; Wisemen interpret it differently; and '*Sarva Panth Samaadar*'—Equal respect to all religions—have been integral to Indian cultural life from time immemorial. They found expression in various articles of the Indian Constitution as well.

However, many argued that Articles 29 and 30 went against that spirit and created a divide between the majority and minorities on the question of fundamental religious rights. When Frank Anthony, a nominated member of the Indian Parliament from the Anglo-Indian community, demanded that English be included in the Eight

Schedule of the Constitution because it was the language of the 'Anglo-Indian minority', Deen Dayal contested it on the grounds that Indian society could not be divided into majority and minority. 'If Shri Anthony thinks as a national, he should cease to think in terms of minorities and majorities. After all, this dichotomy has a restricted purpose in parliamentary democracy. We cannot extend it to plague our entire national life,' Deen Dayal argued.[52]

In essence the RSS viewed secularism as equal respect for all and appeasement of none.

12

Symbols of Cultural Integration 1: The Ram Janm Bhumi

Cultural nationalists have traversed considerable distance in the decades after India's independence. Of the many milestones, two important ones need mention here. The first was the verdict of India's apex court, the Supreme Court of India, in the 1990s that Hinduism or Hindutva was not a religion but a way of life.[1] This judgment addressed the fundamental question about India's identity as a Hindu or Bharatiya nation. The second important milestone was the historic verdict of the Supreme Court in the Ram Janm Bhoomi–Babri Masjid case in 2019. It helped negate the decades-old two-nation theory of Jinnah by upholding the view that those who had invaded India could not be heroes of any community or individual.

MINORITY RIGHTS DEBATE IN CONSTITUENT ASSEMBLY

Sadly, pandering to minority sentiments came to mean secularism in India. It allowed for minority communalism to grow and created backlash from the majority community. 'Minority-ism' did to India what multiculturalism did to Europe. It bred opposite forces leaving mainstream society more fragmented and weakened. When the

Constituent Assembly debated the question of minority rights, what had bothered the members was how the majority-minority divide would ultimately be bridged.

Responding to criticism about minority rights, Ambedkar took the lead by explaining the rationale behind provisions in the draft constitution for minorities. He expressed hope that the provisions in the Constitution would lead to the ultimate merger of majority and minority into one national society. 'Speaking for myself, I have no doubt that the Constituent Assembly has done wisely in providing such safeguards for minorities as it has done. In this country, both the minorities and the majorities have followed a wrong path. It is wrong for the majority to deny the existence of minorities. It is equally wrong for the minorities to perpetuate themselves. A solution must be found which will serve a double purpose. It must recognize the existence of the minorities to start with. It must also be such that it will enable majorities and minorities to merge someday into one,' he said.[2]

The question of minorities and majority forging into one national society had generated heated debate in the Constituent Assembly. Ambedkar himself had caused quite a stir when he commented, 'To diehards who have developed a kind of fanaticism against minority protection I would like to say two things. One is that minorities are an explosive force, which, if it erupts, can blow up the whole fabric of the State. The history of Europe bears ample and appalling testimony to this fact. The other is that the minorities in India have agreed to place their existence in the hands of the majority. In the history of negotiations for preventing the partition of Ireland, Redmond said to Carson "ask for any safeguard you like for the Protestant minority but let us have a United Ireland". Carson's reply was: "Damn your safeguards, we don't want to be ruled by you." No minority in India has taken this stand. They have loyally accepted the rule of the majority which is basically a communal majority and not a political majority. It is for the majority to realize its duty not to discriminate against minorities. Whether the minorities will continue or will vanish must depend upon this habit of the majority. The moment the majority loses the habit of discriminating against the minority, the minorities can have no ground to exist. They will vanish.'[3]

Many members contested Ambedkar's observations. H.V. Kamat made a significant intervention by narrating his experience. 'In 1927, I, as a student, attended the Madras session of the Congress. Maulana Mahomed Ali and Pandit Malaviya were both present there. There was a question about safeguards and Pandit Malaviya made a moving speech that went straight to the heart. He said: "What safeguards did you ask from the Secretary of State for India or from the Government of India? We are here. What better safeguards you want?" After that speech, Maulana Mahomed Ali came to the rostrum, embraced Pandit Malaviya and said: "I do not want any safeguards. We want to live as Indians, as part of the Indian body-politic. We want no safeguards from the British Government. Pandit Malaviya is our best safeguard." If that spirit had continued to animate us, we would have remained as united India, a single country, a single State and a single nation,' he said.[4] Disagreeing with Ambedkar's statement that no minority in India has taken Carson's stand, Kamat argued: 'The majority has always been willing to grant them safeguards, adequate safeguards. But the minority would have nothing to do with it. The minority in India took the same stand as Carson took in Ireland. That is why, to the detriment of the Irish body-politic division was resorted to, as was done in India, resulting in disturbance of the peace and progress of the country.'[5]

Mahavir Tyagi, another senior member of the Assembly, also came down heavily on Ambedkar. 'I am sorry that Dr. Ambedkar made the statement that minorities are an explosive force which if it erupts can blow up the whole fabric of the State. I say that these minorities can do nothing of the sort. The reason is simple—they are not factual, they are a mere fiction having no existence. I throw them a challenge. They have no right to be separately represented here. Whom will they represent? The fiction of minorities was a British creation,' he argued vehemently.[6] Tyagi's contention was that those who described themselves as a minority had migrated to Pakistan, and those who believed in one nation remained in India. 'Therefore, Sir, there is no minority now and there should not be any provision for minority representation here, because this has proved ruinous to the so-called minorities themselves,' he averred.[7] He also refuted Ambedkar's observation that the majority in India was 'basically a communal majority' insisting that 'the majority party is Congress, which is purely political.'[8]

Members from the minority communities presented divergent views. Some like B. Pocker, Sahib Bahadur, demanded continuation of separate electorates as 'the proper remedy and the right method of giving protection to the minorities.'[9] Others like Kazi Syed Karimuddin rejected those proposals and insisted that the system of reserved seats for minorities had to go. R.K. Siddhwa, a Parsi member of the Assembly, said 'As far as our community is concerned, when the majority community offered the reservation of seats to the Parsi community, we said: "No thank you, we do not want". Similarly, all the groups, I expect, Sir, will refuse with thanks the offer of the majority.'[10]

Although Ambedkar believed that provisions for minorities in the Constitution would ultimately lead to 'merging into one' someday, post-Independence politics in India thrived on the division. Minorities came to be viewed as vote banks and a brazen version of appeasement politics came to be identified with nationalism and secularism.

An inglorious episode of minority appeasement was played out with the decision of the Rajiv Gandhi-led government in 1986 to amend the Indian Constitution to further fortify minority laws in the face of an adverse judgement from the Supreme Court of India.

Whereas the Supreme Court wanted to rescue Muslim women divorced through the Sharia law by insisting that the man pay alimony at par with the amounts received by women from other communities, the new amendment freed Muslim men from any such obligation.[11] A section of the orthodox Muslim community comprising of men, especially the clergy, hailed the government's decision. But it evoked serious resentment among the people of the country in general and Muslim women in particular.

Minority-ist religious orthodoxy and state patronage towards it was challenged by a rapidly growing popular movement for building a temple of Ram at his supposed birthplace in Ayodhya in Uttar Pradesh. A sixteenth-century mosque, built at Ayodhya by Mir Baqui, the commander of Mughal emperor Babur, known as the Babri Mosque, became the symbol of a spirited fight between minority communalists and cultural integrationists. The mosque was also known as Janmasthan Masjid because it supposedly stood on the very spot considered by Hindus as the sacred birthplace of Lord Ram. It is believed to have been built in 1526 BCE after demolishing a temple. Restoration of the temple became the symbol of rejection of Jinnah's two-nation theory and also of the flawed secularism of the Indian political establishment. Lal Krishna Advani, senior leader of the BJP, undertook a countrywide campaign in a car-chariot to challenge what he termed as the 'pseudo-secularism' of the ruling party. The surcharged resentment had culminated in the unfortunate demolition of the disputed Babri structure on 6 December 1992. However, the questions it had raised remained unanswered until recently.

THE RAM JANM BHUMI: REJECTION OF MINORITY-ISM

The dispute went from court to court for a full seven decades. The disputed Babri structure fell in between. Yet the case continued. It reached a conclusion when the Supreme Court of India ruled in favour of granting the disputed site for constructing a Ram temple in 2019. In a unanimous judgment in November 2019, the Supreme Court bench comprising of five judges—one of them a Muslim—concluded that while it (the Court) did not decide matters in such cases 'on the basis of faith or belief', but 'on the basis of evidence' alone, it had 'clear evidence to indicate that the worship by the Hindus in the outer courtyard continued unimpeded in spite of the setting up of a grill-brick wall in 1857. Their possession of the outer courtyard stands established together with the incidents attaching to their control over it,'[12] and as regards the inner courtyard, there is 'evidence on a preponderance of probabilities to establish worship by the Hindus prior to the annexation of Oudh by the British in 1857.'[13] On the basis of these evidences, the Court granted possession of the site to a public trust for constructing a temple.

One of the judges, whose name was withheld, deemed it necessary to give an addendum on the question of whether the disputed site could be adjudicated as the birthplace of Ram. In his 116-page addenda, he referred to the earlier mentioned judgement by Justice Gajendragadkar in 1966 in the case of Shastri Yagnapurushadji and others vs Muldas Bhudardas Vaishya and another, in which the following observation was made about the Hindu religion: 'When we think of the Hindu religion, we find it difficult, if not impossible, to define Hindu religion or even adequately describe it. Unlike other religions in the world, the Hindu religion does not claim any one prophet; it does not worship any one God; it does not subscribe to any one dogma; it does not believe in any one philosophic concept; it does not follow any one set of religious rites or performances; in fact, it does not appear to satisfy the narrow traditional features of any religion or creed. It may broadly be described as a way of life and nothing more.'[14]

The judgement was certainly a high point in the history of the nationalist movement. It was the culmination of a struggle of five centuries. Hindus had not accepted Babur's commander Mir Baqui's vandalism of the temple in 1526. As during the crusades in

Europe, the site kept changing from temple to mosque to temple. The last time it happened was in 1949, when idols of Ram durbar appeared under the domes of the dysfunctional mosque. Since then, it once again became a functioning temple. After seven decades, the final verdict came, handing the temple site back to the Hindus.

It was the reassertion not of any religion but a wounded civilisation. 'So, new people come up and they begin to look at their world and from being great acceptors, they have become questioners. And I think we should simply try to understand this passion. It is not an ignoble passion at all. It is men trying to understand themselves. Do not dismiss them. Treat them seriously,' warned Sir Vidia Naipaul, the Nobel laureate, talking about this reassertion.[15]

Renowned British historian Arnold Toynbee had taunted Hindus four decades before Naipaul commended them. 'Aurangzeb's purpose in building those three mosques (Ayodhya, Kashi and Mathura) was the same intentionally offensive political purpose that moved the Russians to build their Orthodox cathedral in the city centre at Warsaw. Those mosques were intended to signify that an Islamic government was reigning supreme, even over Hinduism's holiest of holy places. Perhaps the Poles were really kinder in destroying the Russians' self-discrediting monument in Warsaw than you have been in sparing Aurangzeb's mosques,' Toynbee said in a speech at Delhi.[16]

THE PRECEDENTS

The Russian Orthodox cathedral that Toynbee referred to was the Alexander Nevsky Cathedral built by the Russians in the Polish capital of Warsaw in 1912. Poland was not an independent nation at the time of the First World War. Parts of its territory were under the occupation of Germans, the Austro-Hungarians and Russians. When Poland unshackled itself from foreign yoke and emerged as an independent nation after the war, the Cathedral was demolished by the Polish authorities in the mid-1920s. It had taken the Russians 18 years to build the Cathedral, between 1894 and 1912, but it didn't survive even 15 years. Intense debate preceded the demolition. The Poles saw it not as a religious monument but as a symbol of Russian domination. As in the case of the Babri Masjid in India, there were a few voices opposing the demolition in Poland, mostly from the orthodox community. They were contemptuously dismissed as 'Cathedralists'. Not that the Poles were against Orthodox Christianity. There were several other Orthodox churches in Poland. A lot of remnants of the Alexander Nevsky Cathedral were later shifted to the Mary Magdalene Orthodox Cathedral in the Warsaw suburb.

The Poles took less than a decade after their freedom to demolish the Orthodox Cathedral. There was a precedent in India too. The Somnath temple in Gujarat, that was looted and destroyed by Mohammed Ghazni in 1024, had been restored in 1951 immediately after Independence. Its restoration had Gandhi's blessings and the initiative came from Sardar Patel and K.M. Munshi. Gandhi's only suggestion to Patel was that the reconstruction of the temple should happen with funds collected from people, not from the public exchequer. Incidentally, the new temple at Ayodhya too will be constructed with funds contributed by people.

Unfortunately, by the time the consecration of the Somnath temple happened, both Gandhi and Patel were no more. Prime Minister Nehru was opposed to the idea of the temple's reconstruction. He first tried to dissuade Munshi, but the latter did not pay heed. Nehru then tried to discourage President Rajendra Prasad from attending the consecration ceremony. 'I believe in my religion and cannot cut myself away from it,'[17] Rajendra Prasad told Nehru gently but firmly. Nehru then wrote to all chief ministers in the country stating that his government had nothing to do with the reconstruction and they too shouldn't have anything to do with it either.

The Somnath temple returned to its past glory on 11 May 1951, when it was inaugurated in a grand function. 'The Somnath temple signifies that the power of reconstruction is always greater than the power of destruction,' Dr Prasad said in his address, adding 'By rising from its ashes again, this temple of Somnath will proclaim to the world that no man and no power in the world can destroy that for which people have boundless faith and love in their hearts...'[18]

Seventy years after the resurrection of Somnath, the same spirit is bringing Ayodhya to life. The laying of the first brick for the temple at Ayodhya was a symbolic reiteration of what Dr Rajendra Prasad had said at Somnath. 'Today, our attempt is not to rectify history. Our only aim is to proclaim anew our attachment to the faith, convictions and to the values on which our religion has rested since immemorial ages.'[19]

Damnatio Memoriae is a Latin phrase which roughly translates to 'erasing bad memory'. Although the phrase came into vogue much later, the practice dates back to Greek and Roman periods in European history. Erecting statues, not of men of God or of wisdom but of those in power, was a practice during those times. At one point, historians have stated, there were over 3,000 statues of the emperors in Athens and Rhodes for a population of a few ten thousands. Then began the practice of Damnatio Memoriae with people demolishing the statues of evil emperors. The practice has returned to America and Europe again recently.

The Babri story is the Indian equivalent of Damnatio Memoriae. The structure, erected by demolishing a flourishing Ram temple at Ayodhya, was one such bad memory for many. Iconoclasm was a regular imperial practice during the medieval period for Semitic religions. The Crusades that the Christians and Muslims fought during the eleventh to fourteenth century witnessed large-scale destruction of sacred places of worship of both faiths. Thousands of such places still exist in Western European countries. Hagia Sophia, a cathedral of the Byzantine-era Constantinople (Istanbul), which was recently converted into a mosque by Erdogan's Turkey, is one such living example of iconoclastic history.

Babur and later Mughal emperors like Aurangzeb were fired by this imperialist iconoclastic zeal and destroyed many prominent Hindu shrines with an 'intentionally offensive political purpose', as Toynbee argued.

Ideally, a solution based on mutual agreement would have been the best solution to the issue. Efforts were made in that direction in the early 1990s during the regimes of prime ministers Chandra Shekhar and P.V. Narasimha Rao, but they did not yield any results. That larger consensus was seen after the Supreme Court judgement in November 2019. Ever since the judgment, both communities have displayed maturity and positivity. There has been no chest-thumping or triumphalism from Hindus, while there wasn't any unwholesome reaction from Muslims either.

Mohan Bhagwat had issued a statement on the day of the judgement calling upon people to 'forget all past controversies and work together to discharge our duty.' 'The verdict should not be viewed from a "victory or defeat" angle. The conclusion arrived through churning of truth and justice should be viewed and taken as a decision that will enhance the integrity and brotherhood of the entire Indian society. Forces which create discord among people and incite violence should not be patronised and kept away. One should express happiness with restraint, moderation and politeness, completely avoiding any provocative or instigating action or deed and staying within the limits of the Constitution and law,' Bhagwat exhorted.[20]

Dr Ram Manohar Lohia, the renowned socialist leader of the twentieth century, used to say that Ram, Krishna and Shiv signified India's civilisational identity. 'You just stand outside a temple in Rameswaram in the South or Badrinath in the North; you will find Hindustan there,' he would say. Ram is revered as *'Maryada Purushottam'*—Epitome of Virtue—for his supreme human qualities, by millions irrespective of religion. The only message emanating from Ayodhya is about that larger unity and goodwill among people.

'You will find Ram in different forms in different Ramayanas; but Ram is present everywhere; Ram is for all. That is why Ram is the connecting link in India's unity in diversity,' Prime Minister Modi had said at the Bhumi Puja for the temple at Ayodhya on 5 August 2020.[21]

Swamy Chinmayananda, founder of the Chinmaya Mission, once gave a unique definition to Ayodhya. He was one of the pillars of the Ram Janm Bhumi movement until his demise in 1993. 'Ayodhya—the word itself means—*Ayuddha*—that is, non-war or peace. It is for *Ayuddha* (no conflict) that we are fighting. Just as the World War was for peace, we are no doubt fighting, but only for establishing peace and progress in our country.'[22] The temple at Ayodhya should pave the way for Ayuddha—peace forever—among communities.

SACRED PLACES AND SPACES

Every nation has its sacred spaces and every religion, its sacred places. Cultures determine the sacredness of physical and metaphysical spaces. Cultures are the soul of nations. Nations create their sacred identities around cultural manifestations like language, history, religion and morals. During the years of the French Revolution, only half of its population spoke French and only 12 per cent spoke it 'correctly'. Renowned American historian Eugen Weber narrated how France toiled in the aftermath of the Revolution through a 'traumatic and lengthy process' for what he described as 'self-colonisation'. That effort had led to the creation of the modern French state and given birth to notions of 'French superiority over non-European cultures'.[23]

Theodor Herzl was the visionary founder of the Zionist movement in the early twentieth century that laid the foundation for the Jewish state of Israel. Herzl was non-religious. But he understood that Judaism was an inseparable aspect of the Jewish personal and public existence. The first Zionist Congress, held at Basel in France in 1903 under Herzl's leadership, had a special announcement on the invitation—'*Yesh Achsanya Kshera*'—which meant that 'there is a Kosher restaurant in Basel'. '*Sabbath* lives in the hearts of the people,' Herzl declared at the Congress and rejected the British offer for a Jewish homeland in Kenya, invoking a psalm from the *Jewish Book of Psalms*: 'If I forget thee, O Jerusalem! Let my right hand forget its cunning.'[24]

Mircae Eliade, the Romanian scholar of religion at the University of Chicago, had coined the term 'hierophany', meaning the sacredness attached to places brushed by God's presence. For the Jews, the Wailing Wall in Jerusalem, believed to belong to the temple built by Solomon in tenth century BCE, is sacred. Similarly, Jerusalem is sacred for the Christians because of its association with Jesus from childhood until after resurrection. For Muslims, Mecca is sacred as the birthplace of the Prophet. Even the Greeks still attach sacredness to classical sites like the shrine of Apollo at Delphi or the temple at Ephesus, the ancient Greek city, now in Turkey.

The history of Semitic religions has many instances of sacred places being defiled and restored. Whether it was during the early Babylonian conquests of Greek cities or Roman conquests of Jewish lands, or medieval religious wars between Christians and Muslims called the crusades, the sacred places had, all along, been a target of victors. As the fortunes of the crusading parties changed, so did the fortunes of those sites. Mosques became churches and cathedrals turned into mosques.

Non-Semitic lands like India too were subjected to invasions during medieval conquests. Countless temples were destroyed and converted. But hierophany in India is not about just the physical spaces associated with the divine persona—those are far too many— but about the values and morals they represent. Places like Ayodhya represent a universal sentiment of sacredness not merely because of their association with the Ramayana and Ram, but also because of a value system that it stands for.

The restoration of the temple at Ayodhya must be seen in the context of this sacredness of a value system that is at the core of this country. Ram and Ramayana are hugely popular across Asia. Robert Goldman, the Sanskrit professor from University of California, observed: 'Few works of literature produced in any place, at any time, have been as popular, influential, imitated and successful as the great and ancient Sanskrit epic poem, the Valmiki *Ramayana*.'[25]

RAM AND RAM RAJYA: THE MORAL SOVEREIGN

Ram is a God to many. But the sage Valmiki presented him both as an avatar of Vishnu as well as an ideal human being. 'Who is the most accomplished man on earth at the present time?' Valmiki is believed to have asked sage Narad, defining the word 'accomplished' as 'one who knows the secret of religion, one who knows gratitude, is truthful, one who is ready to sacrifice his self-interest even when in distress to fulfil a religious vow, virtuous in his conduct, eager to safeguard the interests of all, strong, pleasing in appearance with power of self-control, able to subdue anger, illustrious, with no jealousy for the prosperity of others, and in war, is able to strike terror in the hearts of Gods.' Narad's reply was, 'Ram, the son of Dashrath.'

Valmiki went on to describe Ram as '*Vigrahvaan Dharmah*' and '*Maryadaa Purushottam*'—epitome of Dharma and morals. For Gandhi, Ram was truthfulness. His Ram Rajya meant 'people first'. Ram became great not when he was ruling, but when he was struggling. Power, for him, was an object of worship. Two phrases that Valmiki used to describe Ram's rule were— '*Raamo Raajyamupaasitva*' (Ram worshipped his kingdom); and '*Aaraadhanaaya Lokasya*' (worship of the people). Ram represented the cultural ethos of India.

This culture is represented through India's language, literature, arts, music and traditions. Epic histories like Ramayana and Mahabharata are, besides being historic narratives, also representative of this hoary culture.

'There is scarcely a language in India into which the Ramayana has not been translated—or written with its own creative flavour. There is hardly a folk tradition, which does not immortalize the life and legend of Ram. There is no caste or region in India which does not have names with Ram in some form or the other. All the saintly personalities in Indian history—from Tulsidas to Surdas, from Kabir to Tukaram, and from Sankaradev in Assam to Kamba in Tamil Nadu—have sung the praise of Ram in their mission for social reform. Sikhs, Jains, Buddhists and Arya Samajists (who do not believe in idol worship) have their own version of Ram and the Ramayana. Guru Granth Sahib, the sacred scripture of the Sikhs, invokes the name of Ram about two thousand four hundred times. Many Indian Muslims, too, have seen in Ram an ideal ruler and an embodiment of great human qualities. Allama Iqbal, the renowned Urdu and Persian poet, described him as India's "Imam-e-Hind" in a famous eulogy,' wrote L.K. Advani.[26]

For Gandhi, devotion to Ram was a lifetime obsession. Advani added that Gandhi's lifelong devotion to Ram formed the spiritual soil in which the tree of his social and political mission received its nourishment. Reciting Ram's name, according to Gandhi, 'purifies while it cures, and, therefore, it elevates'. 'Gandhi did not look upon Ram purely as a Hindu deity, but rather as a divine force of universal brotherhood and, in the context of India, of national integration,' Advani added.[27]

Unlike Semitic religions, Hinduism is not a religion of 'believers'. 'Unless you believe, you will not understand,' St Augustine of Hippo exhorted early Christians of the Roman empire.[28] But Hinduism allowed inquiry and wanted men to be seekers, rather than mere believers. That was what Gandhi and Ambedkar did with Ramayana

and Ram Rajya. Both sought to explore it from their respective
moral perspectives. Both argued from a logical moral prism; not
from blind faith nor blind hatred. Gandhi called Ram his personal
deity. But Ambedkar did not so much agree with Ram on questions
of morality. He even challenged several aspects of the Ramayana,
going to the original of Valmiki, in his *Riddles in Hinduism*.

Whether Ram was a historical person or not did not bother
Gandhi much. What mattered to him was the concept of Ram
Rajya. In his view, Ram Rajya essentially meant equal rights to
'prince and pauper'. Even during his visits to Ayodhya, the abode
of his deity Ram, first in 1921 and then in 1929, Gandhi's rhetoric
was about standing up for the weak and meek. Addressing the
saints of Ayodhya on the banks of River Sarayu during his visit in
February 1921, he resorted to his favourite theme of Ram Rajya.
He chose cow protection as the point of reference. 'Praying to god
for our own protection is a sin as long as we do not protect the
weak.... We need to learn to love the way Rama loved Sita.'[29] 'There
is no way to achieve Ram *Rajya* or *Swaraj* without observing this
svadharma,' he told them.

Ambedkar's criticism of Ramayana was based on his perception
about certain events. He believed that Ram upheld the Varnashrama
system and killed a Dalit saint called Shambuka. 'Some people seem
to blame Rama because he ... without reason, killed Shambuka.
But to blame Rama for killing Shambuka is to misunderstand the
whole situation. Ram *Raj* was ... based on *Chaturvarnya*. As a
king, Rama was bound to maintain *Chaturvarnya*. It was his duty
therefore to kill Shambuka, the Shudra, who had transgressed his
class and wanted to be a Brahmin. This is the reason why Rama
killed Shambuka,' Ambedkar wrote.[30] Many scholars insist that the
story of Shambuka's killing was an interpolation. Ambedkar was
also critical, probably on more valid grounds, of Ram's treatment of
Sita. He saw Ram Rajya as unjust and patriarchal and commented
on Ram's dismissal of Sita to forests the second time as '...there are

not wanting Hindus who use this as ground to prove that Rama was a democratic king when others could equally well say that he was a weak and cowardly monarch.'[31]

Both Gandhi and Ambedkar were looking at the concept of Ram Rajya from their respective prisms—Gandhi from a more pragmatic prism and Ambedkar from a literal one. But both highlighted the fact that a just system should be one where the weak are protected and their voices heard. The search for such a just and equitable system where there is harmony between the ruler and the ruled has been the elusive effort of political pundits for millennia. Socrates was asked to consume poison for the 'crime' of supporting the oligarchy of the 30 ruling tyrants of Sparta, a neighbouring city state. Socrates believed that the rule by a select class of wise men, like the oligarchy in Sparta, was better than a democracy based on mass hysteria as that of Athens. Tyrants in the ancient Greek regime were those who usurped the role of the monarch, though not necessarily in the way we understand its meaning today. Plato and Aristotle detested both systems—the cruel authoritarianism of Sparta and the mobocracy of Athens.

Plato's panacea was 'philosopher kings'. As Bhishma tells Yudhistira in the *Shanti Parva* of Mahabharata, which was repeated by Chanakya in *Arth Shastra*:

Prajasukhe sukham ragyaha prajaanam tu hite hitam,
Naatmapriyyam hitam ragyaha prajaanam tu priyam hitam

'Happiness of the ruler lies in the happiness of his subjects. It is not what the ruler likes that matters, but only what people like.'

In the *Yudh Kand* of Ramayana, sage Valmiki narrated the characteristics of Ram Rajya—Ram's kingdom:

- While Ram ruled the kingdom, there were no widows to lament, neither was there any danger from wild animals, nor any fear of diseases. Every creature felt fulfilled.
- Everyone was intent on virtue. Turning their eyes towards Ram alone, creatures did not kill one another.

- While Ram was ruling the kingdom, people survived for thousands of years, with thousands of their progeny, all free of illness and grief.
- Trees there bore flowers and fruits regularly, without any damage by pests and insects. It rained on time and the wind was delightful to the touch.
- All people were endowed with excellent characteristics and were engaged in virtue.

Ram Rajya was that state of governance where the ruler was wise enough to place the good of the people above his own interests. But then, who is to determine what is good and bad? Nietzsche, the German philosopher, had interpreted 'good' as 'whatever augments the feeling of power, the will to power, power itself, in man.'[32] And inadvertently, he became the darling of Hitler and the Nazis. Plato's philosopher kings became authoritarians when the Romans invested divinity in them. Smugness and self-righteousness produced cruel authoritarians in history.

Ram presented a different ideal. He 'worshipped people' and 'worshipped kingdom'. He did not believe in his infallibility nor was he overpowered by any superiority complex. When mother Kausalya asked him after his return to Ayodhya as to whether he had killed Raavan, Ram's reply was: '*Mahagyani, Mahapratapi, Mahabalshali, Akhand Pandit, Mahan Shiv bhakt*, author of *Shiv Tandav Stotra*, mighty *Lankesh* was killed by his own ego.'

That is why Gandhi summed up Ram Rajya as 'the sovereignty of the people based on pure moral authority.'[33]

THE RAM JANM BHUMI MOVEMENT AND THE SANGH PARIVAR

Advani's connection to Ram was through his association with the Ram Janm Bhumi movement and the famous Rath Yatra (chariot procession) that he had undertaken in the 1990s. The Ram Janm Bhumi movement, a campaign launched by Hindu saints and social organisations in the 1980s, was aimed at building a massive structure at the birthplace of Ram at Ayodhya.

The controversy acquired national dimensions after organisations like the RSS and BJP had joined and supported it in the mid-1980s. While the RSS took the decision to plunge into the movement sometime in the mid-1980s, the BJP jumped into the fray after a resolution in 1989 at Palampur in the Himalayan state of Himachal Pradesh. At the party's national executive meeting, held on 9–11 June 1989, the BJP had endorsed the demand for handing over the Ram Janm Bhoomi to Hindus for the construction of a Ram temple there. The BJP had also stated in that resolution that the dispute at Ayodhya was to be resolved through mutual dialogue between the two communities or, if that was not possible, through an enabling legislation.

Deen Dayal was not alive at the time of this movement. However, the BJP chose to start Advani's nationwide Rath Yatra on Deen Dayal's birth anniversary, on 25 September 1989. Deen Dayal had all along been an advocate of 'cultural freedom' together with 'political freedom'. In a speech in 1949, he exhorted the virtues of culture and declared that without cultural freedom, freedom of India was meaningless. 'Every nation had its own individuality and some special feature for the development of which freedom was essential. We need economic, social, cultural, as well as spiritual freedom. Freedom must include self-realization, for, culture pervades every facet of our national life just as life pulsates while conquering the high peaks and deep pits of difficulties and hindrances coming in the way of life. Culture is not something static. It is always in motion just like the flow of a river. If we have acquired freedom, this stream of our culture transcends national boundaries and binds our nation with the rest of the humanity. Therefore, cultural freedom is most important. Without this, our freedom will be meaningless, and it will not last,' he said.[34]

Advani chose Somnath as the starting point of his yatra because the reconstruction of the shrine on the rubble of loot and plunder was the first chapter in independent India along the journey to 'preserve the old symbols of unity, communal amity and cultural oneness'. Years later, Advani would reminisce about the objective of the movement. 'Ram, therefore, is a unique symbol of India's national identity, unity and integration. He is one of the ideals for Indians' aspiration to live a life of higher values. The story of his life, the *Ramayana*, is both a source and a carrier of the continuity of India's cultural traditions. Is there any wonder, therefore, that the twin causes—reconstruction of the Ram Temple in Ayodhya and protection of the Ram *Sethu* in the south—are deeply cherished by crores of people in India?'[35]

DEBATE OVER SECULARISM AND CULTURAL IDENTITY

Although ostensibly linked to the construction of a temple at the Ram Janm Bhoomi, the aim of the yatra was to raise three fundamental questions that had all along lurked in the collective subconscious of the nation, but hadn't been asked, fearing retribution from the pseudo-liberal intelligentsia. These questions were:

- What is secularism? What is communalism?
- Can national integration be achieved by constantly pandering to minority communalism?
- Can the government not reject the cult of minority-ism?

One great service that the movement had rendered at that time was to generate an intense debate on the country's ethos: 'Cultural nationalism with true secular credentials based on equal respect and non-appeasement' versus 'minority appeasement as pseudo secularism'.

Eminent intellectuals like Nobel laureate V.S. Naipaul and Nirad C. Chaudhuri had lent their voice in support of the movement subsequently. In an interview to eminent Indian journalist Dileep Padgaonkar of the *Times of India*, Naipaul had said: 'The people who say that there was no temple there are missing the point. Babar, you must understand, had contempt for the country (that) he had conquered. And his building of that mosque was an act of contempt for the country. In Turkey, they turned the Church of Santa Sophia into a mosque. In Nicosia, churches were converted into mosques too. The Spaniards spent many centuries re-conquering their land from Muslim invaders. So, these things have happened before and elsewhere. In Ayodhya, the construction of a mosque on a spot regarded as sacred by the conquered population was meant as an insult. It was meant as an insult to an ancient idea, the idea of Rama, which was two or three thousand years old.'[36]

Highlighting the grassroots nature of the movement, Naipaul said: 'One needs to understand the passion that took them on top of the domes. The jeans and the tee shirts are superficial. The passion alone is real. You can't dismiss it. You have to try to harness it … What is happening now (Ayodhya movement) is different. The movement is now from below.'[37]

Nirad C. Chaudhuri, the celebrated author, had, in a separate interview to Padgaonkar, summed up the argument in favour of national self-respect. 'My point is that it is the very nature of things. That what happened in Ayodhya should not have happened is another matter. But I say that the Muslims do not have the slightest right to complain about the desecration of one mosque. From 1,000 A.D. every Hindu temple from Kathiawar to Bihar, from the Himalayas to the Vindhyas has been sacked and ruined. Not one temple was left standing all over northern India. Temples escaped destruction only where Muslim power did not gain access to them for reasons such as dense forests. Otherwise, it was a continuous spell of vandalism. No nation with any self-respect will forgive this. They took over our women. And they imposed the *Zazia*, the tax. Why should we forget and forgive all that? What happened in Ayodhya would not have happened had the Muslims acknowledged this historical argument even once.'[38]

Ayodhya is sacred not only for Hindus. At least five Jain *Tirthankars* came from Ayodhya. The city of Saket which finds mention in Buddhism is Ayodhya, where Buddha was believed to have lived for several years. Sikhism's connection with Ayodhya is much deeper. The Guru Granth Saheb, the sacred text of the Sikhs vividly describes Babur's invasions and iconoclasm. The tenth guru of the Sikhs, Guru Govind Singh, had sent his army to Ayodhya to support Baba Vaishnavdas, who was fighting to reclaim Ram Janm Bhumi from the Mughals. Sant Kabir, who did not believe in idol worship, declared *'Raam bina nahi dhaam'*—there is no place without Ram.

The foundation laid at Ayodhya on 5 August 2020 was for those great values, hidden in the fabulous tale of Ayodhya, that have over millennia been 'treasured as the common property of every Hindu—as well as that of many Muslims, Sikhs, Buddhists, Jains, and Christians,' to borrow the words of historian William Dalrymple.[39]

13

Symbols of Cultural Integration 2:
Akhand Bharat, Kashmir

In a judgement issued in 1984, in the Dr Pradeep Jain vs Union of India and Others case, Justice P.N. Bhagwati, the Chief Justice of India, wrote this: 'It is an interesting fact of history that India was formed into a nation neither on account of a common language nor on account of a single political regime over its territories; but on account of a common culture evolved over centuries. It is cultural unity—something more fundamental and enduring than any other bond which may unite the people of a country together—which has welded this country into a nation.'[1]

BHARAT MATA

This idea of cultural nationhood needed a land, society and an emotional bond that linked the two. That emotional bond in India's case was not through language or loyalty to a political regime, but through a culture whose footprints were all over the geography of the country. The culture manifested through a value system that defined both land and life as sacred. The country is seen not just as a piece of land but as a sacred mother. From there arose concepts like Bharat Mata, meaning Motherland Bharat, and Akhand Bharat, or integral India.

Deen Dayal used to regularly highlight these issues through his speeches and discourses. For example, the concept of Bharat Mata—India as the 'mother goddess'—is unique to the Jana Sangh politics. Jana Sangh had never seen the country as just a landmass or a political nation-state. Instead, reverence to the country as a divine femininity—the Motherland—became an article of faith. In fact, the daily newspaper started by Jana Sangh supporters in 1970 was called *The Motherland*.

'The basis of our nationalism is not simply Bharat, but "Bharat Mata,"' insisted Deen Dayal. 'Remove the word "*Mata*" (Mother) and Bharat would remain just a piece of land. The affinity between us and this land is established only with the relationship of the mother. No piece of land can be called a country so long as the relationship between it and the people living in it is not that of mother and son. This is patriotism,' he exhorted.[2]

In ancient Indian thought, the entire earth has been described as mother. This idea of attributing motherhood and thus, reverence to the earth and environment is one of the unique aspects of Indic thought. Over time, it was extended to the country as well. Swami Vivekananda, Sri Aurobindo and other saints used this symbolism to invigorate the masses in India. In fact, '*Bharat Mata ki Jai*'—Hail Mother India—became a powerful battlecry during the independence movement and even later.

The concept of motherland is not unique to India alone. Many societies in the world call their homeland as motherland. The concept of fatherland emanated largely from Germany. During the campaign for unification of Germany in the nineteenth century, the concept of *Vaterland*—meaning fatherland—was widely in use. A poem written by Ernst Moritz Ardnt in 1813 was titled '*Was ist des Deutschen Vaterland*' (What is German Fatherland?). This poem, and the idea of a fatherland, became the inspiration during the struggle for German unification. When Germany attacked Russia in the concluding years of the First World War in 1918, Lenin's decree to his people was 'Fatherland is in danger'. *Vaterland* became prominent during Hitler's regime in Nazi Germany. The Nazi propaganda machinery had used it to mobilise German people in support of Hitler's ultra-nationalist regime. The *Vaterland* was projected by the Nazis as something to be defended, protected, served, fought for and, if need be, to sacrifice one's life for.

Nazi usage of the concept of fatherland had the opposite impact on the rest of the world. The Russians too started using the concept of motherland in its place. During the Second World War, the famous recruitment posters in Russia carried the picture of a woman with a title '*Rodima*-mother calls', meaning 'homeland-mother calls'. Even the Germans shied away from the fatherland expression after the Second World War because of its association with Nazi Germany. In India, Savarkar was the only leader to have used the word fatherland to denote homeland.

Attributing motherhood to the nation goes back to the Vedic times in India. Through several millennia, its saints and sages, rulers and scholars, and poets and freedom fighters have used the term to inspire loyalty and reverence in the minds of millions of people. 'Sri Aurobindo always loved deeply his Motherland. He wished her to be great, noble, pure and worthy of her big mission in the world,' wrote the Mother at the Aurobindo Ashram.[3] 'Even if I have to face death a thousand times for the sake of my Motherland, I shall not be sorry,' declared revolutionary freedom fighter Ram Prasad Bismil.[4] 'I loved my Motherland dearly before I went to America and England. After my return, every particle of dust of this land seems sacred to me,' wrote Swami Vivekananda.[5] Bankim Chandra Chatterjee's *Vande Mataram* became the celestial song of patriotism towards the motherland for millions of Indians over more than a century.

Even foreigners who studied India closely realised the profundity of this concept of divine motherhood attributed to this country. 'India was the motherland of our race, and Sanskrit the mother of

Europe's languages; she was the mother of our philosophy; mother, through the Arabs, of much of our mathematics; mother, through the Buddha, of the ideals embodied in Christianity; mother, through the village community, of self-government and democracy. Mother India is in many ways the mother of us all,' wrote American historian Will Durant.[6]

AKHAND BHARAT

Countries deploy cultural and emotional arguments for national unity and integrity. Abraham Lincoln's inaugural address in 1861 was a testimony to the fact that for protecting the unity of the country, more than a mere geo-political appeal was required. In that address delivered on 4 March 1861, Lincoln had exhorted his countrymen: 'The mystic chords of memory, stretching from every battle-field, and patriot grave, to every living heart and hearth-stone, all over this broad land, will yet swell the chorus of the Union, when again touched, as surely they will be, by the better angels of our nature.'[7]

The matriarchal bond and sacredness nurtured by Indian culture between its people and the land had resulted in a strong commitment to its geographical unity and integrity. The concept of Akhand Bharat is a product of this unwavering commitment to the sacred geography. The partition of India in 1947 was sought to be explained away by some as sharing of property by siblings. Children divide property; but they don't partition their mother. For Deen Dayal, a partitioned India was unacceptable because, 'Akhand Bharat is the natural state of our nation. Divided India is unnatural. Today we deceive ourselves that we delight in this unnatural situation, but there is no joy for us.'[8]

But he would also insist that the unity or indivisibility— Akhandta—that he was talking about was the 'feeling' of fundamental unity of society here. 'The words "Akhand Bharat" include all those basic values of nationalism and an integral culture, that the Jan[a]

Sangh accepted. These words include the feeling that this entire land, from Attock to Cuttack, Kutch to Kamrup and Kashmir to Kanya Kumari, is not only sacred to us but also a part of us. The people who have been born in it since time immemorial and who still live in it may have all the differences superficially brought about by place and time, but the basic unity of their entire life can be seen in every devotee of *Akhand Bharat*,' Deen Dayal had written.[9]

Deen Dayal, like Gandhi, saw in Partition a defeat to the lifetime belief in one national society in India. Gandhi saw in it a setback to his cherished mission of Hindu–Muslim unity, whereas Deen Dayal saw a perpetuation of foreign rule and values. 'It would be wrong to consider Pakistan a separate independent state. It represents that attitude and tradition which wants to put an end to the national persona of India and establish foreign rule and foreign values. Hence Pakistan is a remnant of slavery in India,' Deen Dayal argued.[10] In his scheme of things, Akhand Bharat meant freeing people of Pakistan from that slavery. 'So long as we do not liberate our brethren there from the slavery, our political independence will remain incomplete.'[11]

Golwalkar, at a press conference in Delhi on 24 August 1949, termed Pakistan as an 'uncertain state' adding that '… If the partition is a settled fact, we are here to unsettle it. There is, in fact, no such thing as a "settled fact" in this world. Things get settled or unsettled solely by the will of man. And that will of man is steeled by a spirit of dedication to a cause, which he knows to be righteous and glorious.'[12]

VIETNAM AND GERMANY: UNDOING PARTITION

Golwalkar was right. Partition of countries by colonial masters was undone in several countries in the last century. Vietnam and Germany were two examples of how nations partitioned by imperial powers could reunite through the sheer willpower of people. Through that same willpower, the people of Vietnam were able to defeat a mighty war machine like America. Reunification of Germany too was a historic saga.

Immediately after the Second World War, the competition between the Soviets and the Americans for expanding their respective spheres of influence had led to partitioning of countries like Vietnam, Korea and Germany. Apart from that, the continental partition of spheres of influence in Europe into Soviet-controlled Eastern Europe and the NATO-led Western Europe too had taken shape. Americans and their Western allies were concerned about the spread of communism in different countries in Asia. On their part, both the Soviets under Stalin and China under Mao did everything possible to export the ideology of armed struggle to various countries in the Asian neighbourhood.

Germany was divided into East and West Germany immediately after the war. In Vietnam's case, the Geneva Agreement chaperoned by France was to conduct free and fair elections in communist-controlled North Vietnam and West-supported South Vietnam simultaneously in 1954 and facilitation of unity through an elected government. However, the Americans realised that an election meant victory for Ho Chi Minh-led North Vietnam forces which were wedded to socialism and hence thwarted efforts with the help of dictators in the South. The French withdrew from the scene in 1956, but the Americans sent their armies into the South to protect the government from occupation by the Northern forces. A prolonged war ensued for almost two decades and finally the people of the South too joined the North, forcing the Americans to leave Saigon in South Vietnam in April 1975. The two Vietnams were reunited by defeating Cold War geopolitics when Vietnam emerged as a reunited independent nation in 1976.

It will be interesting to look at the history of some European nations to understand the process of nations and their integration/disintegration here. Germany provides for an interesting case study. Political and administrative unification of all the German parts of the region into one nation-state happened on 18 January 1871 at Versailles in France where Wilheim I of Prussia was declared as the first emperor of unified Germany. Yet, as Germans discovered, grand speeches, flags, enthusiastic crowds, a constitution, a political reorganisation, and the provision of an imperial superstructure—all this still did not make a nation.

German efforts at nation-building began after administrative unification. In the name of *Kulturekampf*, the process of Germanisation began, which included coercive assimilation programmes of Jews and other non-German minorities, and rewriting of German history among other things. Nationalist historians like Friedrich Dahlmann (1785–1860), his conservative student Heinrich von Treitschke (1834–1896), and others less conservative individuals, such as Theodor Mommsen (1817–1903) and Heinrich von Sybel (1817–1895) are some relevant names to be mentioned in this context.

In about seven decades' time, Germany, yet again, faced the cruel reality of partition, this time on communist–capitalist lines. At the end of the Second World War, Germany fell into the hands of the four Allied powers, namely, the US, the UK, France and the Soviet Union. With Stalin refusing to join hands, the other three countries came together and decided to undertake reconstruction of Germany under the famous Marshall Plan. Thus, Germany was divided into East and West Germany, with the Soviet socialists tightening their grip over East Germany. In 1961, the socialist regime of East Germany decided to build a wall, later called the Berlin Wall, dividing Berlin—and so also the people of the country—into two inaccessible units.

However, the Wall built by Stalinists in the guise of 'fight against fascism', was pulled down by the people on both sides on the midnight of 2–3 October 1989. Finally, the two governments were also forced to join hands to end the tyranny of the artificial division in 1990.

Like in Vietnam's case, the big powers played intriguing roles till the end in the case of German unification too. Those opposed to the fall of the Berlin Wall and the reunification of Germany included the then prime minister of the UK, Margaret Thatcher, and the president of France, François Mitterand. On the other hand, the East Germans were surprised to see Mikhail Gorbachev, the Soviet president, strongly supportive of the idea of reunification. His foreign minister, Eduard Shevardnadze, had actually advised the East Germans to hurry up.

Margaret Thatcher was profoundly sceptical. In March 1990, she told the French ambassador to London that Kohl[13] 'sees himself as the master and is starting to act like it'.

The so-called '2+4' negotiations over German unification, that involved both Germanies together with the US, USSR, France and UK, saw French President Mitterrand trying to thwart reunification; both he and Thatcher were alarmed over the prospect of what a reunited Germany could do to Europe. Mitterrand reportedly warned Thatcher that a united Germany could cover more ground than Adolf Hitler did, and the consequences would have to be borne by all of Europe. In September 1989, Thatcher was said to have appealed to the president of the Soviet Union, Mikhail Gorbachev, that he shouldn't allow the Berlin Wall to fall. 'We do not want a united Germany. This would lead to a change to post-war borders, and we cannot allow that because such a development would undermine the stability of the whole international situation and could endanger our security,' Thatcher reportedly told Gorbachev.[14] The US president George H.W. Bush, however, vigorously supported the Germans' right to reunite. And in the end, Thatcher and Mitterrand had to give in not just to Bush but to the massive popular momentum for unification that was building up in East Germany.

PARTITION OF INDIA: POLITICAL VS SOCIAL DIVIDE

The partition of India in 1947 too was a result of a colonial conspiracy. As to who was responsible for it, is a subject of historical debate. In his book *Guilty Men of India's Partition*, eminent socialist thinker and leader, Dr Ram Manohar Lohia held three main players responsible for it: the British, the Congress and the Muslim League. Later, historians have argued about others too. India's partition was not a division of the people. It was more of a compromise of leaders representing different influential segments of the time.

Speaking about the acceptance of Partition by the Congress, Prime Minister Jawaharlal Nehru told Leonard Mosley in 1960: 'The truth is that we were tired men, and we were getting on in years too. Few of us could stand the prospect of going to prison again and if we had stood out for a united India as we wished it, prison obviously awaited us. We saw the fires burning in the Punjab and heard every day of the killings. The plan for Partition offered a way out and we took it.'[15]

However, was Partition also a division of the people? In the heat of it, probably a large number of people on both sides emotionally identified with the new political identities. Those political identities will continue to remain. But there is another broader identity—of a society that has lived on for millennia as one. Eminent historian Ayesha Jalal, in her book, *The Pity of Partition: Manto's Life, Times, and Work across the India-Pakistan Divide*, eloquently highlights this dilemma by invoking the idea of a 'cultural nation'. '... the extent to which the contours of the cultural nation, creatively and broadly construed, do not map neatly onto the limited boundaries of the political nation,' she has said of India and Pakistan.[16]

In fact, Saadat Hasan Manto, one of the best storytellers of the twentieth century, was among those on the Pakistan side who had never reconciled with the idea of the split. One of his Partition stories that Jalal refers to was 'Toba Tek Singh' in which non-Muslim patients of a mental asylum in Lahore agitatedly await relocation to India because of their religious affiliations. 'Portraying the inmates to be of sounder mind than those making the decisions for their removal, Manto deftly questioned the wisdom of Partition and the sheer madness it had let loose,' commented Jalal.[17]

That India's partition was 'fantastic nonsense', as dismissed by Nehru once, can be gauged from the extent of dissonance in the Pakistan body politic in the last seven decades. In just over two decades, the product of India's Partition got partitioned again to give birth to another nation, Bangladesh.

Over the decades, as national boundaries got fortified, the proponents of Akhand Bharat gave it a cultural interpretation. The Akhand Bharat discourse is based on solid cultural and people-centric foundations today. In the early 1960s, socialist and Jana Sangh leaders, Dr Ram Manohar Lohia and Deen Dayal Upadhyaya, interacted with each other on the subject. Dr Lohia told Deen Dayal that the Jana Sangh's and RSS's belief in the concept of Akhand Bharat caused uneasiness among Muslims in Pakistan and posed a hurdle in the progress of Indo-Pak relations. Lohia said: 'Many Pakistanis believe that if the Jana Sangh came to power in New Delhi, it would forcibly reunify Pakistan with India.' To which Deen Dayal's reply was: 'We have no such intentions. And we are willing to put to rest Pakistani people's concerns on this score.'[18] Out of those interactions between the two was born the idea of an India Pakistan Federation. The idea could not be taken forward due to the 1965 Indo-Pak war and the demise of Deen Dayal in 1968.

NATIONAL INTEGRITY: THE KASHMIR CHALLENGE

The partition of India on communal grounds opened up a Pandora's box in the country. Partition was effected in such a haphazard manner that it left several simmering flashpoints on both sides. For India, the biggest challenge came in the form of the integration of Jammu and Kashmir (J&K). Kashmir has been integral to India's cultural and spiritual life from time immemorial. It drew its name from the sage Kashyapa and an ancient reference of the land can be found in a prayer for Goddess Sharada. There existed a famous shrine for Goddess Sharada in Kashmir, which went to Pakistan after Partition. Kashmir had been a land of a distinct version of Shaivism until it came under the influence of Islam in the medieval period.[19] The Himalayas that form the northern-most boundary of Kashmir have traditionally been considered not just the abode of Hindu gods, but also the northern boundary of ancient India. Thus, the region has as much cultural significance to India as political.[20]

India's Partition entailed over 560 princely states being asked to opt to join one of the two dominions of India or Pakistan. All but three princes declared their choices by 15 July 1947. Besides Sardar Patel, who was handling the States Department at that time, Viceroy Lord Mountbatten also played a significant role in encouraging several recalcitrant princes to fall in line. Speaking about Mountbatten's contribution, Gopalaswami Ayyangar told the Constituent Assembly, 'I should say that the actual accession of practically the overwhelming bulk of Indian States, the credit for that should go to the statesmanship and the genius for what he himself has called open diplomacy with which Lord Mountbatten has roped them in. I say this advisedly, because I think that but for the energy and the consummate skill which he has employed in this matter, we might not have reached the result which we are so happy to see today.'[21]

Of the three remaining princely states, J&K was the first to accede to India on 26 October 1947. The Nawab of Junagadh, a princely state in Gujarat, Muhammad Mahabat Khanji III declared on 15 August 1947 that he would accede to Pakistan. Since the state was deep inside Indian territory with no geographical links to Pakistan and also since the majority population of the state was Hindu, a referendum was conducted in February 1948 and based on the result of popular will, the state was merged into the Indian dominion. In the case of Hyderabad, the intransigence of the

Nawab called for police action in September 1948, leading to the merger of that state with the Indian dominion. In the accession of both Junagadh and Hyderabad, Sardar Patel played a key role.

J&K fell into a different category. Here, the ruler, Maharaja Hari Singh was a Hindu Dogra while a majority of his subjects were Muslim. The Maharaja had entered into a Standstill Agreement with both the dominions of India and Pakistan. But Pakistan was suspicious of his intentions, and in a hasty move, sent in armed tribesmen and army irregulars to forcefully annexe the state. Pakistan's provocation led the Maharaja to move quickly and sign the accession papers to merge his princely state with India on 26 October 1947.[22] The Indian Army arrived in Srinagar immediately and launched a counter-offensive. By then, Pakistani aggressors had almost reached the outskirts of Srinagar city. The Indian Army continued its pushback of aggressors until the matter was referred to the UN Security Council by Nehru's government in January 1948.[23] A ceasefire followed, which resulted in the annexation of one-third of the territory of J&K by Pakistan. India refers to it as Pakistan-occupied Kashmir (PoK) while Pakistan describes it as Azad Kashmir (AK).

Meanwhile, Sheikh Abdullah, the popular leader of the Muslim majority of the princely state and the head of the National Conference (NC) party, entered into an agreement with Delhi and became the prime minister of J&K. He also managed to secure special constitutional protection for his state in the form of Article 370 of the Indian Constitution, through which he was able to have a separate constitution, a separate state flag and the designation of Prime Minister for J&K. This created a situation where one state had special powers that almost made it a country within the country. It started posing serious challenges to India's integrity and unity.

One of the first major questions of national integrity that the Jana Sangh had taken up was that of the status of J&K. It was opposed to Article 370 of the Indian Constitution on the grounds that it bred separatist sentiments in the population of the state, especially the Muslims of the Kashmir Valley. It saw Article 370 as a product of Nehru's politics of appeasement and held him responsible for the disorder in J&K.

Article 370 had a unique history. It became a part of the Indian Constitution in 1950 along with more than 390 other articles but did not allow those articles to be applied to the state of J&K. The Indian Constitution came into force on 26 January 1950. While it was fully applicable to the entire country, only two of its articles— Articles 1 and 370, were allowed to be extended to J&K. Through Part III of the Constitution of India, every Indian secured a set of Fundamental Rights. However, those rights were also denied to the people of J&K because of Article 370.

THE DELHI AGREEMENT

The Article created a major emotional wedge between the people of J&K and the rest of the country. Finally, after four years, a Presidential Order was promulgated in 1954, extending several parts of the Indian Constitution including Part III to J&K. The order, while extending the Union of India's laws to the state, also ceded a lot of space to the state administration. The roots of this order lie in an agreement reached between Nehru and Abdullah. Known as the Delhi Agreement, its terms were announced by Nehru in the Lok Sabha on 24 July 1952, and in the Rajya Sabha on 5 August 1952.

Under this agreement, the state was allowed to retain the nomenclature of Prime Minister, a separate flag and a separate constitution. Before their accession to the Indian Dominion in 1947, almost all the princely states of India had their own prime ministers and constitutions. But once they acceded to India, they voluntarily accepted the Indian Constitution in entirety. The legislatures of the princely states passed resolutions submitting

themselves to the Indian Constitution and abolishing their state
laws. J&K was an exception. Sheikh Abdullah got the state to elect
a new Constituent Assembly in 1951 and had it pass a resolution
stating explicitly that J&K would retain its constitution and separate
identity. Abdullah was explicit about the mandate in his address
to the state's Constituent Assembly on 5 November 1951. He
enlisted three alternatives for the state's future to be decided by the
Assembly: accession to India, accession to Pakistan and complete
independence. According to him, even after the Maharaja's signing
of accession papers in 1947—even after the state became a part of
the First Schedule of the Indian Constitution—the accession was
not final, and the J&K Constituent Assembly retained the power to
decide on the matter. It was Article 370 which gave him this power.

Nehru entered into the Delhi Agreement with Sheikh Abdullah
in 1952 under these circumstances. Abdullah was able to extract
maximum concessions from Nehru. Some of the clauses came to
mean the following: First, while all the other states would be ruled
as per the Indian Constitution, J&K would retain its constitution of
1939 and the state's newly formed Constituent Assembly would look
into making necessary amendments for it to become compatible
with the Indian Constitution. The power of legislation would be
with the state legislature only, not with the Union Parliament. Thus,
a separate constitution was allowed. Second, J&K would continue
to have its own citizens, called 'State Subjects', under a state law
that the Maharaja had promulgated in 1927. The state legislature
would have the power to make laws for conferring special rights and
privileges on the so-called State Subjects which was not available to
other Indian citizens living in the state. Thus, a separate citizenship
was allowed. Third, J&K would retain its state flag which would be
equal in status to the national tricolour. Thus, a separate flag was
accepted.

Interestingly, one of the first amendments made by the J&K
Constituent Assembly in 1952 was to abolish the monarchy. Thus

came to an end the famed Dogra dynasty of the state. The titles of Maharaja and Yuvaraj, being enjoyed by Hari Singh and Karan Singh respectively, were abolished. Karan Singh was the regent of the state. His position was renamed as Sadr-e-Riyasat, a post whose occupant would be elected by the state legislature and ratified by the President of India. This meant that there wasn't going to be a Governor for the state as the Union's representative. But then, Sheikh Abdullah did not want the nomenclature of his own position to be done away with. Hence, the Maharaja had gone but not his Prime Minister. Successive chief ministers of the state used to be called prime ministers until 1967.

Thus, the Delhi Agreement, which became the basis for the 1954 Presidential Order, had effectively facilitated a system of 'one country—two constitutions; one country—two flags; and one country—two prime ministers'. Once again, it was Article 370 which led to these anomalies. It provided judicial immunity to the J&K legislature for enacting laws for its State Subjects. It didn't allow the full application of the jurisdiction of many institutions, such as the Supreme Court, the Comptroller and Auditor General and even the Election Commission, for several years.

It was against these dangerous provisions that the leader of the Bharatiya Jana Sangh, Dr Mukherjee, had launched an agitation along with the Jammu Praja Parishad. 'Ek desh mein do vidhan; ek desh mein do pradhan; ek desh mein do nishan: Nahi chalenge' (Two constitutions, two prime ministers and two flags in one country are not acceptable) became the war cry of the agitation.

ARTICLE 370

Article 370 didn't allow Indian laws promulgated by its Parliament to be automatically extended to the state of J&K like the rest of the country. Every such Act passed by Parliament needed the consent of the J&K state legislature. In many cases, the state legislature would make its own amendments to a law before accepting it.

The amendments to the LGBT legislation, passed by the Indian Parliament in December 2018 and mandated by the Supreme Court, could not pass the scrutiny of the J&K legislature, subjecting the LGBT community to the same old harassment in the state.

The Article did not allow the creation of a Women's Commission or a Minority Commission in the state. In fact, Article 370 was inherently anti-women. For several decades, it didn't allow women freedom of choice in marriage. While men in J&K were allowed to marry any woman from anywhere—rest of India, or Pakistan, or Afghanistan, or even America—women in J&K were not allowed to marry outside the state. Even if a Kashmiri woman married a man from the same religion, if he were from outside J&K, she would stand to lose her status as State Subject or 'permanent resident'. After a lot of hassle, finally, the state had amended the law, allowing women to retain their permanent resident status even after marrying outside the state. But it came with a rider—children from such a marriage wouldn't be granted permanent resident status.

Article 370 was responsible for the denial of basic human rights to millions of people living in the state for decades. They included refugees who came from West Pakistan at the time of Partition and migrant workers like scavengers and other manual labourers who migrated to J&K from other parts of the country. Despite living in the state for several decades, they remained non-State Subjects, thus effectively being deprived of many privileges, such as government education, healthcare, employment, assets and land ownership. Important laws passed by the Union Government for the welfare of *safai karmacharis*—scavengers—didn't apply to the state. The Article had deprived these sections, largely from the Scheduled Castes (SCs), their basic human rights and human dignity.

Several other important laws that the Indian Parliament promulgated were not extended to J&K. The 42nd Amendment to the Indian Constitution in 1976 inserted the word 'secular' in the Preamble. The J&K legislature refused to incorporate this word in its constitution. J&K has had its own penal code called the Ranbir Penal Code. The Indian Penal Code was not applicable there. Laws like the Safai Karmachari Act, Right to Education Act, Prevention of Corruption Act, 1988, also have not had any jurisdiction in J&K.

Not just political rights, but even developmental rights of the people of J&K were seriously hampered as a result of Article 370. Since the Article has not allowed land to be owned by non-State Subjects, no major industry has gone there. The last major private industry to go to J&K was a cement factory in the 1950s. The public sector unit HMT went in the 1970s, but shut shop soon after. Only one company in J&K—that too a state-owned institution called the Jammu and Kashmir Bank—is listed on any stock exchange. There were no big private hospitals, nor big private educational institutions. Article 370 had denied ordinary Kashmiris the fruits of development that people of the rest of India enjoyed.

It was this discriminatory article—which denied development, political empowerment and dignity to the people of the state—that was done away with on 5 August 2019 when the government, led by Prime Minister Narendra Modi, brought amendments to the Constitution practically annulling the article.

ARTICLE 370: MANY NAYSAYERS

Article 370 was under a cloud right from the time it was promulgated. When the proposal for drafting a special article for J&K came up before the Constituent Assembly, almost everybody rejected it. When Sheikh Abdullah approached the architect of the Indian Constitution, Dr Ambedkar, with a request to draft the special law, he refused. 'Making limited application of laws made by Parliament for the state of Jammu and Kashmir would create lots of problems rather than solving,' he bluntly told Sheikh Abdullah. Nehru then entrusted that responsibility to his trusted colleague from the Madras province, and a former prime minister of Maharaja Hari Singh in Jammu, N. Gopalaswami Ayyangar.

Nehru's decision was strange. Sardar Patel was handling the
accession of over 535 princely states, including difficult ones
like Hyderabad and Junagadh. Nehru singled out Kashmir and
handed it over to Ayyangar. Patel was naturally miffed and raised
strong objections, stating that as the Union Home Minister he
should be allowed to handle Kashmir too. Nehru responded to
Patel's annoyance rather curtly: 'Gopalaswami Ayyangar has been
especially asked to help in Kashmir matters. Both for this reason
and because of his intimate knowledge and experience of Kashmir,
he had to be given full latitude. I really do not know where the
States Ministry [Patel's ministry] comes into the picture except that
it should be kept informed for the steps taken. All this was done
at my instance and I do not propose to abdicate my functions in
regard to matters for which I consider myself responsible. May I
say that the manner of approach to Gopalaswami was hardly in
keeping with the courtesy due to a colleague,' he wrote to Patel on
27 December 1947.[24]

Gopalaswami was a seasoned politician and an ardent
Congressman. But even he found it a challenge to deal with Sheikh
Abdullah. The draft article, originally called Article 306A, ran into
trouble with Sheikh Abdullah. Annoyed, Ayyangar threatened to
resign, saying, 'Our discussion this morning, as I indicated to you,
left me even more distressed than I have been since I received your
last letter from Srinagar.... I feel weighted with the responsibility
of finding a solution for the difficulties that, after Panditji left for
America and within the last few days, have been created, from my
point of view without adequate excuse.'[25]

Interestingly, when the draft Article 306A was placed before
the Congress Working Committee (CWC) in October 1949 for
its approval, the committee rejected it with near unanimity except
for two members—Ayyangar himself and Maulana Abul Kalam
Azad. The CWC's contention was that no such special provision
could be granted to any one princely state. Nehru was abroad. He

had to turn to Sardar Patel this time, seeking his intervention in convincing the CWC.

In politics, leaders sometimes follow the orders of their superiors irrespective of their personal views. Faced with the dilemma of championing a proposal that his heart was not into, or inviting criticism that he pursued policies against Prime Minister Nehru, Patel opted for the former.[26] He was not willing to allow any bitterness to creep in at the very dawn of independence among the top leaders of the government. He had the proposal brought back before the CWC. When members objected, Patel convinced them to honour it since it involved Prime Minister Nehru's personal prestige as he had already given his word to Sheikh Abdullah. When Nehru returned, Patel wrote to him: 'After a great deal of discussion, I could persuade the [Congress] party to accept.'[27]

Patel didn't live long enough to see the Article's ill-effects. But in his absence, Nehru distanced himself in Parliament in 1952 when he said: 'Sardar Patel was all the time dealing with these matters.' It surprised even Gopalaswami Ayyangar. V. Shankar, Sardar Patel's biographer, quoted Ayyangar as bemoaning, 'It is an ill-return to the Sardar for the magnanimity he had shown in accepting Panditji's point of view against his better judgment.'[28] Shankar also wrote that Patel was never in agreement with Nehru's approach and even commented: 'Jawaharlal *royega*' (Jawaharlal will repent).[29]

After the CWC, it was the Constituent Assembly's turn to oppose it. What happened in the Constituent Assembly with respect to the princely state of J&K, at the behest of Nehru, was considered by many as undemocratic. As per the agreement, the state was to get four seats in the Constituent Assembly: two members were to be nominated by the Maharaja and two would be from the state legislature called the Jammu Kashmir Praja Sabha. The Praja Sabha had held its elections in 1946. But Nehru refused to accept the nominations of either the Sabha or the Maharaja. His contention was that the Praja Sabha didn't represent the will of the people because the National Conference, led by Sheikh Abdullah, had boycotted it. It is true that the National Conference didn't participate in the 1946 election to the state legislature. At a time when the country was busy with the Quit India movement against the British, Sheikh Abdullah and his National Conference were busy spearheading the Quit Kashmir movement against the Maharaja. As part of the movement, the National Conference had boycotted the 1946 election and was unrepresented in the Praja Sabha of 1946.

Nehru insisted that the four seats in the Constituent Assembly be filled by Sheikh Abdullah's nominees. When members like K.T. Shah vehemently opposed this as undemocratic, Nehru rose to defend it as the 'correct' democratic practice: 'It amazed me to hear Prof. Shah propose that the so-called *Praja Sabha* of Kashmir should send representatives to this House…. [H]e should know that there is nothing more bogus than the *Praja Sabha*…. He ought to know that the whole circumstances under which the last elections were held [in 1946–47] were fantastic and farcical. He ought to know that it was boycotted by all decent people … and the type of people who got in [the *Praja Sabha*] was the type who had opposed the freedom movement throughout, who had done every injury possible to the idea of freedom of Kashmir till then…. I admit that it is not desirable for any members of this House to come by nomination or be selected by some narrow process… though the process suggested for Kashmir is not ideal, yet I do think that it is a process that has been adopted in regard to many States in India. It is a process where you get a popular government with the representative of the popular party at the head of it, recommending to the ruler that certain names should go. Even from the view of democracy, that is not an incorrect process,' Nehru argued.[30]

Seizing the opportunity, Sheikh Abdullah nominated himself as a member and included three of his party colleagues: Moti Ram Baigra, Mirza Mohammad Afzal Beg and Maulana Mohammad Sayeed Masoodi. All the other stakeholders in the state had been excluded and the National Conference's voice became the voice of J&K in the Constituent Assembly.

A discussion on Article 306A (which became Article 370 in the final draft) was brought before the Constituent Assembly in a hurried manner just a month before the final approval of the draft Constitution. When the discussion began, several members raised serious objections. The first to object was a member of the Communist Party from Lucknow and renowned Urdu poet, Hasrat Mohani. 'Why this discrimination, please?'[31] he asked Ayyangar, to which the latter's reply was: 'The discrimination is due to the special conditions of Kashmir.'[32]

'If you grant these concessions to the *Maharaja* of Kashmir, you should also withdraw your decision about the merger of Baroda into Bombay and allow all these concessions and many more concessions to the Baroda ruler also,' retorted Mohani.[33] Ayyangar went on to provide a long explanation for the special treatment accorded to J&K. Finally, the Article found a place in the Constitution under 'Temporary, Transitional and Special Provisions'.

It was to be a temporary provision. There were several occasions during Nehru's tenure when the demand for its repeal had arisen in Parliament. Even Bakshi Ghulam Mohammad, the prime minister of J&K, had once urged Nehru to repeal the Article. When a group of leaders from Kashmir called on Nehru and demanded that it be repealed, Nehru did concede that it was not serving any purpose. India's second spy chief, B.N. Mullik claimed that in a private conversation, Nehru made the extraordinary admission that he '...agreed with the Jana Sangh's views that Jammu and Kashmir should be fully integrated with India and was taking steps in that direction.'[34] In the Parliament, in an oral reply, he said that Article 370 had been 'eroded and Kashmir stands fully integrated.'[35]

Prakash Vir Shastri, a Member of Parliament from Bijnour in Uttar Pradesh, had moved a Private Member's Bill in Parliament in 1964 on Article 370. The bill received wide support from members cutting across party lines. Even Congress and National Conference members were seen supporting it. Of particular interest were speeches made by the associates of Sheikh Abdullah.

Abdul Ghani Goni from J&K, who had earlier been a staunch supporter of a separate Muslim identity for Kashmir, was surprisingly aggressive in demanding a repeal of the Article. 'The then Prime Minister of Jammu and Kashmir, Bakshi Ghulam Mohammad, had moved for abrogation of Article 370, but the Central Government was not agreeable to it at that time. I do not know whether the Central Government is under the influence of the West or wants appeasement policy towards Pakistan ... they want to please their neighbours at our cost. The Central Government, our Congress leaders, have not done justice to the people of Kashmir. The people of Kashmir had decided once and for all that Kashmir is an integral part of India, whether there is Article 370 or no Article 370. It is only a provisional provision and a temporary provision in the Constitution which can be removed at any time. But as far as the complete accession is concerned, that is final and nobody can challenge it,' he declared during the debate.[36]

Goni further added: 'So I dispassionately appeal to the members of this House and appeal not only to the Opposition Members but also to the Congress members to support this Bill and get it passed and have Article 370 abrogated from the Constitution of India, so that we may also be treated as equal citizens, as good citizens of India as any other citizen. Don't treat us as second-class citizens, and don't treat us as a colony of India. We are as much a part of India as other states.'[37]

Another member of Parliament from the state, Syed Nasir Husain Samnani, also rose to question the relevance of Article 370, saying, 'We, the people of Kashmir, never demanded that we should be treated differently. We do not want Article 370. I want to end this curse in my lifetime, for my safety, for my children's safety, for the safety of our future generations. We should have the same laws as Maharashtra, Madras, Kerala, Bengal. We did not believe in two-nation theory of Jinnah and hence we did not allow any branch of Muslim League to be formed in Jammu and Kashmir.'[38]

For Jana Sangh and Deen Dayal, the Kashmir issue was not just a political one. Many years later, writing in *Organiser* in 1960, Deen Dayal explained Jana Sangh's position on Kashmir. 'Sovereignty in Kashmir is supposed to reside in the people of Kashmir and the Government of the State. People are not allowed to deal with the Union in their individual right. They are represented in all matters connected with the Union by, and through, the Legislative Assembly and the Government of the State. The Union similarly cannot exercise any right in the state except with the concurrence of the State Government and State Legislature; so far as the Indian Constitution is concerned simply an order of the President under Art 270 is deemed sufficient to make all sorts of amendments in the provisions of the Constitution as applicable to Jammu and Kashmir State. The Parliament is not asked to pass or discuss it. But the President cannot make this order unless the State Legislature has already enacted in that behalf. The real power is not with the President, but with the State Government,' he wrote.[39]

Having discussed the problem, Deen Dayal highlighted the crux of the Jana Sangh argument. 'These anomalies indicate that the Constitution doesn't represent the national and emotional unity of the people of the State with the rest of India,' he insisted.[40]

He concluded his article by stating: 'The Bharatiya Jan[a] Sangh has therefore, at its Nagpur session, demanded that Article 370 of the Constitution, which was of temporary nature, should be repealed. So long as this Article continues, normalcy in Kashmir in the matters of constitutional arrangements vis-à-vis Bharat will not be restored. The so-called special position of the State only grants certain powers to the State Government, to the exclusion of the people. The discriminatory treatment is being exploited by anti-national elements to the detriment of India. We are losing both ways. It is therefore necessary that citizens of that State enjoy all those rights that we enjoy, and all discrimination is put an end to.'[41]

Deen Dayal and Jana Sangh's wish found fulfilment in 2019 when the Indian Parliament passed historic amendments, making Articles 370 and 35A redundant.

COW PROTECTION

The 1950s witnessed massive movements across the country for cow protection. Cow protection has always been a major emotive issue with the people of India. Cow is sacred to a majority of Indians across religions including Hindus, Jains, Sikhs and Buddhists. In an agrarian country like India, the cow occupied not only a place of reverence but also of economic importance.

One of the first to champion the cause of cow protection as a means of generating a sentiment of national unity and self-respect was Mahatma Gandhi. He used to freely deploy cultural symbols to motivate and mobilise the masses. This approach of his had led to the British and Muhammad Ali Jinnah accusing him of communalising or 'Hinduising' politics in India. But Gandhi knew that the soul of India was religious/spiritual. That's why he wouldn't hesitate to invoke symbols like Hari, Ram, *Gau Mata*, Satyagraha, *Upavaas*, Bhajan, and Kirtan during the freedom movement. In fact, it was Gandhi's popular politics, brimming with cultural symbolism, that had transformed the elitist, memorandum-pushing Congress movement into a grassroots mass movement for independence.

Cow protection was very dear to Gandhi. He saw it as the greatest civilisational gift that Hinduism had to offer to the world. 'Cow protection to me is one of the most wonderful phenomena in human evolution. It takes the human being beyond this species. The cow to me means the entire sub-human world. Man, through the cow, is enjoined to realize his identity with all that lives.... Cow protection is the gift of Hinduism to the world,' he wrote.[42]

But then he did not hesitate to make it an important agenda

of the freedom struggle either. 'I hold that the question of cow-slaughter is of great moment—in certain respects of even greater moment—than that of *Swaraj*. Cow-slaughter and manslaughter are, in my opinion, two sides of the same coin,' he declared once.[43]

Several members of the Constituent Assembly of India had argued for inclusion of complete cow protection as a Fundamental Right. However, due to resistance from some prominent sections and leaders of the political spectrum, allegedly including Nehru himself, it had to be included in the list of the Directive Principles of State Policy.

A big rally was organised in Delhi in 1958 by Gau Hatya Nirodh Samiti, an organisation consisting of the prominent saints of India of the time. The Samiti had launched a massive signature collection drive in the country in the mid-1950s seeking a complete ban on cow slaughter. Many social and spiritual organisations, including the RSS, had joined the campaign. In the end, more than 20 million signatures were collected and were brought in bullock carts to the Rashtrapati Bhavan—the presidential palace in Delhi. A delegation of saints had called on the president of India, Dr S. Radhakrishnan and submitted a memorandum. This popular uprising had had its effect within states as well. More than twenty states gradually come forward to introduce laws regulating cow slaughter.

Bharatiya Jana Sangh too had extended its support to the movement in the 1950s. Deen Dayal described the cow as the 'symbol of *Bharatiya* nationhood'. Swaraj—independence—without cow protection was futile for him. 'The concept of *Swaraj* presupposes the resuscitation of our values of life and points of honour. And the cow, by far, constitutes the centre of all our points of honour. The urge for our independence always flowed from our sentiment for cow protection,' he wrote, adding 'The slogan of cow-protection will not only help us realise the fulfilment of our long-cherished aspirations, but will send through the entire national life a new wave of self-consciousness.'[44]

From Gandhi to Deen Dayal, many eminent leaders had seen cow protection as having the potential to awaken and unite the people of the country. Eminent leader of the co-operative movement in India and co-founder of Amul in Gujarat, Dr Verghese Kurien narrated an incident in his autobiography, *I Too Had a Dream*.

'In 1967, as Chairman of NDDB (National Dairy Development Board), I was asked to be a member of a high-powered committee, set up by the Government of India, to look into cow protection. It was a collection of rather individualistic and interesting personages. Justice Sarkar, Chief Justice of the Supreme Court, was appointed its Chairman. Among the other members of this committee were Ashok Mitra, who was then Chairman of the Agricultural Prices Commission, the *Shankaracharya* of Puri, H.A.B. Parpia, Director of the Central Food Technological Research Institute in Mysore and M.S. Golwalkar 'Guruji', the head of the RSS, the organization which had launched the entire cow protection movement,' wrote Dr Kurien.

While Dr Kurien was against cow protection and in favour of slaughtering draught cows, he enquired from Golwalkar the reason for his support of the cow protection movement. Kurien narrated his reply verbatim:

'Then I saw that the cow has potential to unify the country—she symbolizes the culture of Bharat. So, I tell you what, Kurien, you agree with me to ban cow slaughter on this committee and I promise you, five years from that date, I will have united the country. What I'm trying to tell you is that I'm not a fool, I'm not a fanatic. I'm just cold-blooded about this. I want to use the cow to bring out our Indianness, so please cooperate with me on this.'

It is unfortunate that such a potential unifier of the society and a symbol of national reverence and self-respect has been seen as a conflict between Hindus and Muslims.

One of the rulers who had understood this aspect was the last Mughal ruler of India, Bahadur Shah Zafar. He realised that the issue of cow protection could be used as an effective instrument for cementing Hindu–Muslim concord. 'After accepting the leadership of the rebellious soldiers on 12th May 1857, he agreed to enforce a ban on cow slaughter. On 28th July, he confirmed it and announced that anyone slaughtering a cow would be shot dead. The announcement was repeated by the Mughal emperor on *Bakar-'id*,' wrote historian Mahdi Husain. Husain said that it enabled Bahadur Shah to 'maintain communal harmony in Delhi during the most crucial period of the war.'[45]

Why did identity issues that were discussed above become such an important part of the nationalist movement? Deen Dayal explained that the vitality and character of a nation depended on how strongly it was linked to its roots. 'Why is there no vitality in the country even after so many years of independence? Why have poverty, starvation, unemployment and a feeling of hopelessness increased? Why has national character degenerated? Why has there been a continuous fall in all fields—economic, political, social, literary—and why has the life of the nation begun to drift aimlessly?' Deen Dayal asked poignantly. His answer was that 'without doubt one reason is that we are not standing on our feet.'[46]

'Our entire national life has lost its roots. Without a pure feeling of nationalism, not only is national development impossible, but even our independence may be lost. We have fallen on these evil days because we have forgotten the awareness of nationalism that manifests itself in age-old history of our nation. To get out of this pit, we must clearly visualize the sentiment that is the basis of our nation. A strong force can be created if the roots of national ideals and aspirations are strengthened. The purpose of national life can be understood on a true realization of our nationhood. An absence of this true realization is the basic cause of our present fall as a nation,' Deen Dayal concluded.[47]

෴

14

Human Dignity and Human Rights

The Western man had to wage relentless battles to secure his dignity and rights. These struggles existed right from the ancient gods of the Greeks, to Semitic religions, and even to modern Enlightenment thinkers and post-Enlightenment ideologies like nationalism and communism. Not until the Universal Declaration of Human Rights (UDHR) in December 1948 did he finally secure his rights and dignity.

QUESTIONS OF HUMAN DIGNITY IN EUROPE: GOD OR MAN?

The ancient Greek gods were far too many. They were not too wise or judicious either. Unlike the later Semitic gods of Judaism, Christianity and Islam, the ancient Greek gods were '…capricious, vain, vicious and deceitful. But however savage and immoral the gods may be, they are also all-powerful,' wrote Kenan Malik in his book, *The Quest for a Moral Compass*.[1] The gods often forced humans to act against their wishes. Homer's epic poem *Iliad* was all about this poignant history of human suffering at the hands of ancient Greek gods.

Homer's poem was from eighth century BCE. But as the civilisation progressed, the Greeks started raising important questions about the relationship between gods and humans, religion and reason. Socrates, the founding father of the Western philosophy and 'its first martyr', was the first to raise fundamental questions about the relationship between man and God. Socrates did not write anything. But his disciple, another famous Greek philosopher, Plato, had chronicled Socrates' discourses in *Socratic Dialogues*. One such early dialogue was called 'Euthyphro'. It is a dialogue between Euthyphro of Prospalta, an ancient Athenian religious prophet and Socrates, on the question of 'what is pious?'

'What is dear to the gods is pious. What is not is impious,' Euthyphro proposed. Socrates first got Euthyphro to agree that '…the gods are in a state of discard' and then rejected his proposition by saying that some gods may see certain actions as pious, and others may not. Euthyphro then modified his definition, saying '… the pious is what all the gods love, and the opposite, what all the gods hate, is the impious'. Socrates continued the dialogue by putting the most important question before Euthyphro—'Is the pious being loved by the gods because it is pious, or is it pious because it is being loved by the gods?'[2] This is called the 'Euthyphro dilemma' in Western philosophy. Objectivity and rational thinking were thus made the cornerstone of Western philosophy by Socrates through the suggestion that goodness and morality of man should have 'an objective existence independent of either gods or humans.'[3]

Around the time when the Greeks were searching for reason and rationale to power human agency came the Semitic statement from Genesis 1:26: 'We are all made in God's image.'[4] God became central to human life in the Semitic world. Morals, virtues, duties and obligations of man became subjective to God. This Judeo-Christian understanding of creation had prompted an ardent atheist like Voltaire to quip, 'I want my lawyer, my tailor, my servants, even my wife to believe in God, because it means that I shall be cheated and robbed and cuckolded less often…. If God did not exist, it would be necessary to invent him.'[5]

The Judeo-Christian concept of God is different from the

ancient Greek gods not only in the insistence upon God-centrism, but also in the core belief in 'One God' as against the multiplicity of gods that allowed freedom of choice to man in Greek societies. It began with Judaism, which insisted that God was singular, and introduced intolerance towards polytheism. 'You shall have no other gods before me,' Judaism explicitly ordained in the Ten Commandments. Thus was born a jealous God, who denied not only the existence of plurality of faiths and gods but also insisted upon making Himself the centre of human life.

While the sacrifice of Socrates at the hands of overzealous Athenians had led to human capacity for rational thinking overcoming God-centric existence, another sacrifice, this time by Jesus Christ, at the hands of insecure Roman kings, brought man back into the vortex of God. The Romans, influenced initially by Greek notions of the power of humans for rational and objective thinking, could not stand up to the unleashing wave of Judeo-Christian faiths. Six centuries after Socrates, and by fourth century CE, religion returned to dominate reason. God and church came back to control human enterprise—temporal as well as spiritual. There were only a few thousand Christians in first century CE, but by the third century CE, their number grew to some six million. The Romans initially resisted and persecuted Christians, including Jesus Christ, by looking at them as offshoots of Judaism. Emperor Diocletian launched the most vicious persecution in 303 CE. But it was Emperor Constantine who elevated Christianity to the status of state religion by embracing it while on his deathbed, three decades later.

For the next millennium or so, Judeo-Christian God and his representatives in the Holy Tree dominated every aspect of human life in the West. Kings to commoners—everyone was at the mercy of the church, the sole representative of the singular God of Christianity. 'By the tenth century, the Church was the single largest landowner in Western Europe. Kings found their legitimacy through the conduit of the Church and battled with the Church to expand their own power; Holy Roman Emperor Henry IV walked barefoot in the snow to earn back the approval of Pope Gregory VII; Henry II of England had himself flogged in order to win back the approval of his Christian population after accidentally ordering the death of Archbishop Thomas Becket,' wrote Ben Shapiro in his book, *The Right Side of History*.[6]

Art and science, and every form of human creativity came under the onslaught of the God-centric religion of the church. All human activity that was not approved by the church came to be seen as heretical or dangerous to the domain of God. Galileo Galilei, the Italian philosopher, astronomer and mathematician, had to face the Roman Inquisition on the charge of heresy for advocating Copernican theory. Almost a century before Galileo, in 1543, Polish astronomer and mathematician Nicolaus Copernicus had published '*De revolutionibus*', in which he claimed that the universe was heliocentric with the sun at the centre and the earth rotating around it. The Church did not take his theory seriously until Galileo reiterated it a hundred years later. It did not, however, take his heretical theory lightly this time. Copernican theory was banned, and Galileo was imprisoned for not agreeing to recant. Put under house arrest indefinitely by Pope Urban VIII, Galileo spent the rest of his time at his villa in Arcetri, near Florence, until he died on 8 January 1642. Not just Galileo, but several others too had faced the Church's anger for articulating secular knowledge apart from Biblical narratives. Marsilius of Padua, another Italian scholar, became the target of Pope Clement VI for insisting on the sovereignty of citizens in place of that of the church. His teachings were banned by the Catholic Church, so was '*The Prince*', the famous treatise of Niccolò Machiavelli, renowned Italian Renaissance philosopher and diplomat.

Until then, the Christian worldview had allowed only 'natural rights' of humans like the right to live in accordance with God's creation. Secular knowledge, the product of man's creative mind, was not allowed freedom to flourish. Thinkers like Martin Luther and John Calvin attempted to challenge that worldview in the fifteenth century, but the church prevailed, eventually. It took another century for the Enlightenment-era thinkers to come forward to declare formal separation of the 'City of Man' and the 'City of God' and limiting the church's power to the latter.

Seventeenth-century Enlightenment thinkers like Thomas Hobbes and John Locke were the ones who finally freed man from the shackles of the church. While Hobbes raised fundamental questions about human rights beyond mere survival, Locke believed in the sovereignty of man. Locke insisted on 'life, liberty and property' as inalienable fundamental rights of man. These freedoms found their first expression in the creation of American constitutionalism and the Declaration of Independence in 1776. Thomas Jefferson, one of the founding fathers, declared that the unalienable rights endowed to man included '… life, liberty and pursuit of happiness'.[7]

POST-ENLIGHTENMENT DISCOURSE

The Enlightenment era that paved the way for establishing human freedom went to the other extreme of creating a God-free objective moralism. Courage to use one's own wisdom and knowledge were seen as the motto of the era. In the process, God was completely discarded and man became mere flesh and blood without any transcendent identity. Charles Darwin's treatise, *On the Origin of Species*, published in 1859, hit the final nail on the coffin of God-centrism by scientifically creating a notion of a 'world without God'. 'Darwinism was seen by the intelligentsia of the time as a final permission to break with the ways of the ancients. Finally, at long last, the superstitions of religion could be put aside; finally, at long last, the legacy of the ancient Greeks could be escaped. Mankind, in joining the animals, had finally liberated himself from the chains of the divine,' wrote Shapiro.[8]

Rights like life, liberty and happiness were to be obtained by men through an agency other than the church. That agency was the constitutional government formed through popular will. From Europe to America, post-Enlightenment decades witnessed the rise of various kinds of governing agencies, free from religious interventions and interpretations. Just four months after the newly created Senate of the USA first met, citizens of France stormed the Bastille, founding a Republic on the French Revolution ideals of 'Liberty, Equality and Fraternity'.

However, the experience of the next two centuries showed that various forms of government themselves were to become an impediment to man's quest for dignity and rights. As the experience suggests, the end of the kingdom of God did not automatically translate into human happiness. Collective human mind did not provide a path for human freedom as the Enlightenment thinkers had envisioned. Instead came jingoist nationalism of Hitler's kind, and collectivist communism of Lenin and Stalin. Bismarck had laid the foundations for romantic nationalism through his *Kulturekampf*—cultural struggle—for German solidarity. Even after the defeat in the First World War and collapse of the Weimar Republic, the romantic nationalism kindled by Bismarck did not dissipate. It found its manifestation in the Hitlerian creed of ultra-nationalism, fascism, anti-Semitism, and mystical notions of German race superiority.

George Orwell brilliantly summed up the insidious thinking of Hitler in an essay in 1940. 'Hitler, because in his own joyless mind he feels it with exceptional strength, knows that human beings don't only want comfort, safety, short working hours, hygiene, birth-control and, in general, common sense; they also, at least intermittently, want struggle and self-sacrifice, not to mention drums, flags and loyalty-parades,' he wrote.[9] Where the Semitic religion wanted men to live in accordance with God's will, 'Hitler-ism' wanted them to die in accordance with Hitler's whims.

While the West of Europe was experiencing the tumult of romantic nationalism, reaching its crescendo after the First World War, the East was experiencing another kind of tumult in the form of the collectivist dogma of communism. The fall of Tsarist Russia after the First World War paved way for the rise of communism under the leadership first of Lenin and then of Stalin. In country after country that it succeeded in spreading its tentacles to, communism replaced the individual man with the collective, and in the process, heaped unimaginable sufferings on mankind.

Communism loathed the very idea of human freedom. Marx had succeeded in giving the hopeless dogma the veneer of a path-breaking ideology. An interesting exchange occurred when the Russian Social Democratic Party held its annual meeting in 1903 at Brussels and London. Social Democrats were not allowed by the Tsar to operate on Russian soil. A delegate named Posadovsky inquired whether the emphasis of socialist hardliners like Lenin, for absolute authority of the revolutionary nucleus of the party, was not incompatible with those fundamental liberties that socialism was officially dedicated to? 'Can the sacrosanctity of the person be violated if the Party leaders so decided?' he asked. Georgi Plekhanov, one of the founders of the party in Russia and a highly venerated leader, answered the question saying—'*Salus revolutiae suprema lex*', meaning if the revolution so demands, everything, including democracy, liberty, individual rights must be sacrificed.[10]

Millions perished in the worst human rights disasters in recent history in communist states like Soviet Union and China. The cost of freedom under communism was tyranny. Lenin oversaw the execution of tens of thousands branded as oppressors, exploiters and capitalists. Stalin took this tyranny to a new level. Tens of millions perished under his rule. The agricultural collectivisation programme from 1931 to 1934 had caused the death of at least five million people out of starvation in Ukraine alone. In China, Chairman Mao dwarfed both Hitler, the nationalist, and Stalin, the communist, in mass murder. In one of the most ill-planned, and ill-fated programmes of collectivist modernisation called the Great Leap Forward, Mao had caused the death of millions of people in China between 1958 and 1962. Historian Frank Dikotter vividly described the events of the time in his book, *Mao's Great Famine*. Citing a dossier that the Communist Party of China had itself prepared during the famine, Dikotter wrote: 'What comes out of this massive and detailed dossier is a tale of horror in which Mao emerges as one of the greatest mass murderers in history, responsible for the deaths of at least 45 million people between 1958 and 1962. It is not merely the extent of the catastrophe that dwarfs earlier estimates, but also the manner in which many people died: between two and three million victims were tortured to death or summarily killed, often for the slightest infraction. When a boy stole a handful of grain in a Hunan village, local boss Xiong Dechang forced his father to bury him alive. The father died of grief a few days later. The case of Wang Ziyou was reported to the central leadership: one of his ears was chopped off, his legs were tied with iron wire, a ten-kilogram stone was dropped on his back and then he was branded with a sizzling tool—punishment for digging up a potato.'[11]

UNIVERSAL DECLARATION OF HUMAN RIGHTS

These were the circumstances under which the Western world turned its attention to securing basic human rights for citizens of all countries in the world, irrespective of the political or government systems they were living in. There was an urgency felt by not only the leaders of nations but also by civilian leaders, due to the excesses that the ordinary citizens were being subjected to because of the raging Second World War. President Franklin D. Roosevelt of America was the first to raise the issue in an effort to coax the American Congress into giving up its foreign policy of neutrality during the war and joining on the side of the Allied forces. Roosevelt watched with concern as the Allied powers struggled and failed to contain the progress of Hitler's Nazi forces. He realised that it was time America intervened to defeat fascist forces.

Roosevelt found his address to the 77th Congress, delivered on 6 January 1941, to be an opportunity for motivating Americans for a greater international role. His speech became famous as the 'Four Freedoms Speech',[12] because of his insistence that the people of all nations of the world shared Americans' entitlement to four freedoms: 1. Freedom of speech and expression; 2. Freedom to worship God in his own way; 3. Freedom from want; 4. Freedom from fear. After the demise of Roosevelt, his wife, Eleanor Roosevelt championed the cause of these freedoms and played an active role in the drafting of the Universal Declaration of Human Rights (UDHR) under the UNESCO charter.

As the Second World War was raging, another effort was made by English author and statesman H.G. Wells, to codify and secure the human rights of citizens of all countries. Among others, Wells also solicited the support of Mahatma Gandhi for his proposed Bill of Rights defining war aims. Wells should perhaps write a 'cosmopolitan charter of duties instead—a statement of what citizens of the world owe to each other', Gandhi opined in his reply.

'Received your cable. Have carefully read your five articles....' Gandhi wrote, and '... you will permit me to say you are on the wrong track. I feel sure that I can draw up a better charter of rights than you have drawn up. But what good will it be? Who will become its guardian? If you mean propaganda or popular education, you have begun at the wrong end. I suggest the right way.'[13]

'Begin with a charter of Duties of Man and I promise the rights will follow as spring follows winter. I write from experience. As a young man, I began life by seeking to assert my rights and I soon discovered I had none—not even over my wife. So, I began by discovering and performing my duty by my wife, my children, my friends, companions and society and I find today that I have greater rights perhaps than any living man I know. If this is too tall a claim, then I say I do not know anyone who possesses greater rights than I,' Gandhi argued.[14]

As the Second World War came to an end and more than fifty countries signed up to the United Nations in 1945, efforts had begun to draw up a Charter of Universal Human Rights. In May 1946, the United Nations Educational, Scientific and Cultural Organisation (UNESCO) constituted a Commission on Human Rights composed of members from 18 countries. India was a member of this first-ever Commission on Human Rights, which was charged with the task of drafting an 'international bill of rights'. The Universal Declaration of Human Rights (UDHR) was the result of those efforts, which stretched over a period of almost two years from January 1947; it was adopted by the UN General Assembly to 10 December 1948.

Dr Julian Huxley, the biologist-turned-internationalist who became the first Secretary General of the UNESCO, played an active role in the making of the Declaration. In the run up to the drafting of the Declaration, Dr Huxley reached out to 150 eminent thinkers across the world for their opinions on 'the utility of a universal instrument of human rights and whether different conceptions of human rights could be reconciled into a single universal document'.

One of the recipients of Huxley's letters was Jawaharlal Nehru. 'It is most important that we should obtain contributions from men like yourself, who have thought about these problems both theoretically and in relation to practical politics, and who are representative of another culture than that of Europe,' Huxley wrote. He also made a request: 'Might I also ask you very kindly to forward the enclosed letter to Mahatma Gandhi asking him for a contribution.' Nehru replied expressing regret that he could not contribute since, '...we have to face very difficult and intricate problems in India, and I have the misfortune to be tied up with these problems. I cannot find the time for any quiet consideration or writing'. However, he promised that he would forward Huxley's request to Mahatma Gandhi. 'Certainly, I shall urge him to write something, for his approach to these problems is always novel and interesting,' Nehru wrote.[15]

Gandhi too was busy. But he found time in a moving train on 25 May 1947. 'I learnt from my illiterate but wise mother that all rights to be deserved and preserved came from duty well done. Thus, the very right to live accrues to us only when we do the duty of citizenship of the world. From this one fundamental statement, perhaps it is easy enough to define the duties of man and woman and correlate every right to some corresponding duty to be first performed. Every other right can be shown to be a usurpation hardly worth fighting for,' Gandhi wrote back in a most revealing reply.[16] Gandhi always held duties above rights and believed that by fulfilling one's duties one could protect the rights of the other and there was no other way.

Upon Dr S. Radhakrishnan's advice, Huxley invited similar contributions from two other scholars in India—Prof. S.V. Puntambekar, a renowned political scientist from Benaras Hindu University, and Prof. Humayun Kabir, a poet and philosopher who was to become India's Education Minister after independence. Prof. Puntambekar sent a deeply philosophical response, articulating an essential Indian view of the issue.

'Human freedoms require, as counterparts, human virtues or controls. To think in terms of freedoms without corresponding virtues would lead to a lopsided view of life and a stagnation or even a deterioration of personality, and also to chaos and conflicts in society,' Puntambekar wrote. He underscored the early thinking of Hinduism and of Buddhism in his response: 'They have propounded a code, as it were, of ten essential human freedoms and controls or virtues necessary for good life. They are not only basic but more comprehensive in their scope than those mentioned by any other modern thinker. They emphasise five freedoms or social assurances

and five individual possessions or virtues. The five social freedoms
are (1) freedom from violence (*Ahimsa*), (2) freedom from want
(*Asteya*), (3) freedom from exploitation (*Aprigraha*), (4) freedom
from violation or dishonour (*Avyabhichara*) and (5) freedom from
early death and disease (*Armitatva* and *Aregya*). The five individual
possessions or virtues are (1) absence of intolerance (*Akrodha*),
(2) compassion or fellow feeling (*Bhutadaya, Adreha*) (3) knowledge
(*Jnana, Vidya*), (4) freedom of thought and conscience (*Satya,
Sunrta*) and (5) freedom from fear and frustration or despair
(*Pravrtti, Abhaya, Dhrti*).'[17]

In its more than a dozen sittings stretched over 30 months,
the Commission on Human Rights held detailed deliberations
on a number of draft recommendations submitted by eminencies
from different countries upon the request of Huxley. One of the
long-standing members from India in the Commission was Hansa
Mehta, a reformist and educator, who worked actively in the
Congress-led movement for independence. Minoo Masani[18] and
Lakshmi Menon[19] too participated in some discussions of various
sub-committees.

At the eighth meeting of the Commission, Mehta asked for
consideration of the draft resolution that had been submitted by
India. It contained the following human rights for incorporation
into the UDHR:

'(a) Every human being is entitled to the right of liberty,
including the right to personal freedom; freedom of worship;
freedom of opinion; freedom of assembly and association; and
the right to access to the United Nations, without risk of reprisal,
whenever there is an actual or threatened infringement of human
rights.

(b) Every human being has the right of equality, without
distinction of race, sex, language, religion, nationality or political
belief.

(c) Every human being has the right of security, including the right to work, the right to education, the right to health, the right to participate in government and the right to property, subject only to the over-riding consideration of public weal when the State or its appropriate organs acquire it after paying equitable compensation.'[20]

However, this process was not without debates. The major debate was over the question of inclusion or omission of reference to 'God' in the Declaration. Some of the representatives from Catholic nations like Brazil were insistent upon inserting the phrase 'created in the image and likeness of God'. The debate in the deliberations was, therefore, about how to resolve the 'bargain about God and Nature'.

This debate as to whether human rights were derived from God or should be seen as natural rights of human beings went on for many days. India's position, as articulated effectively by Lakshmi Menon, was that the Declaration was applicable to all the nations in the world and there were different conceptions of God and faith. There would be many who do not believe in God too. When the debate was taken up at the Third Committee on the amendments, Lakshmi Menon stated, 'Although different countries had different beliefs and political systems, they shared the same ideals of social justice and freedom. The purpose of the declaration was to set forth those ideals and to find a basis of agreement acceptable to all. As far as Article 1 was concerned, there was general agreement that all men should live together in freedom and brotherhood. In that connection, lessons could be learnt from the democracies of both the East and the West.' She also appealed to the Brazilian representative to withdraw his amendment for the sake of unanimity.[21]

The final text of Article 1 of the Declaration thus contained the following statement:

'All human beings are born free and equal in dignity and rights. They are endowed with reason and conscience and should act towards one another in a spirit of brotherhood.'

The Universal Declaration of Human Rights was finally signed and sealed in December 1948. It granted equal recognition to economic, social and cultural rights alongside civil and political rights. The Indian delegation insisted upon the 'universal' nature of human rights and did not allow any reference to political ideologies, faith references and social beliefs. 'It would have been illogical to insist on political convictions which could not be shared by all, while at the same time proclaiming religious tolerance. The right to hold different opinions was a sacred right and the prerogative of every truly democratic people. The Indian delegation had therefore upheld that right, though perfectly aware of the dangers inherent in it. India, like other countries, would never agree to restricting political rights in order to realize social aims, however noble those aims might be,' Lakshmi Menon said in the concluding deliberations of the Commission.[22]

HUMAN DIGNITY AND RIGHTS: THE INDIAN PERSPECTIVE

Having successfully contributed to the making of the Universal Declaration and becoming a signatory to it in 1948, India became duty bound to incorporate the same in its own constitution. The Constituent Assembly of India was also holding its sessions at that time. Naturally, the question of Fundamental Rights took precedence in Assembly deliberations. While Gandhi insisted upon duties, the Indian Constitution gave preference to rights. However, those rights were also to be understood as an effort to secure dignity and freedom for the citizens of the free country. Part III of the Indian Constitution enumerates the Fundamental Rights enjoyed by every citizen of the country. Commenting on this, former Chief Justice of India, Justice P. N. Bhagwati had said:

'These Fundamental Rights represent the basic values cherished by the people of this country since the *Vedic* times and they are calculated to protect the dignity of the individual and create conditions in which every human being can develop his personality to the fullest extent.'[23]

The Indian Constitution, as adopted in 1950, did not specify any fundamental duties for its citizens. It delineated certain Directive Principles of State Policy for governments to implement as their responsibility. Only in 1976 were Fundamental Duties incorporated into the Indian Constitution. Article 51A was inserted in the Constitution through the 42nd Amendment in August 1976, stipulating eleven fundamental duties of the citizens of India.

'Fundamental duties: It shall be the duty of every citizen of India,

(a) to abide by the Constitution and respect its ideals and institutions, the national Flag and the National Anthem;

(b) to cherish and follow the noble ideals which inspired our national struggle for freedom;

(c) to uphold and protect the sovereignty, unity and integrity of India;

(d) to defend the country and render national service when called upon to do so;

(e) to promote harmony and the spirit of common brotherhood amongst all the people of India transcending religious, linguistic and regional or sectional diversities; to renounce practices derogatory to the dignity of women;

(f) to value and preserve the rich heritage of our composite culture;

(g) to protect and improve the natural environment including forests, lakes, rivers and wild life, and to have compassion for living creatures;

(h) to develop the scientific temper, humanism and the spirit of inquiry and reform;

(i) to safeguard public property and to abjure violence;

(j) to strive towards excellence in all spheres of individual and collective activity so that the nation constantly rises to higher levels of endeavour and achievement.'

However, these duties remain legally unenforceable and voluntary in nature to this day.

ANCIENT INDIAN PERSPECTIVE OF HUMAN DIGNITY

This brings us to the central issue of what was India's original conception about human dignity and human rights. Whereas the Western conception of human beings stems from the Genesis statement in the Old Testament that humans were created in God's image, the classical Hindu perspective calls humans as the manifestations of the divine itself.

'*Amritasya Putrah Vayam*'—We are all begotten of the immortal—is how Hinduism introduces human beings.

'Every individual soul is potentially divine,' proclaimed Swami Vivekananda.[24] Thus, human beings are seen in Hinduism not as an image of the God, but as manifestations of divinity. Hence, they are divine and rational beings rolled into one.

It is necessary to delve into the fundamentals of Hinduism in order to comprehend its position on human dignity and human rights. The fundamentals of Hinduism are in those great dialogues that took place in the hills and forests several millennia ago, among the great saints and savants very much like the Socratic dialogues. They were not commandments; they were informed suggestions. Hinduism has the most liberal thoughts that the world has ever witnessed. One reason was that it evolved through the process of deliberations and democratic consensus. Ancient Indian rishis—great sages and saints—practiced deep solitary contemplation and penance and engaged in dialogues and discourses among themselves and came up with a worldview that was essentially Hindu, but also universal in nature.

These dialogues were not the kind that the French Enlightenment writer and philosopher Voltaire referred to, rather condescendingly, by saying: 'I disapprove of what you say but defend to the death your right to say it.'[25] Voltaire's statement is considered the essence of democracy. Deen Dayal differentiated it with the ancient dialogues that took place among the sages and saints. 'The tradition of debates is old in our country. But such a debate can be fruitful only when each party carefully listens to what the other had to say and has the desire to accept the truth in it. Else the debate is fruitless. When Voltaire said, "I don't agree with what you say, but I shall defend to death your right to say it", he was only accepting the futility of the debate. *Bharatiya* culture goes beyond this and looks at debate as a means of realizing the truth,' Deen Dayal had said.[26]

Indic thought is very profound, and yet very humble. It does not ordain any final word or demand that followers believe in it. Men in the Indic thought are not 'believers'; they are 'seekers'. Indic thought is man's pilgrimage, an unending exploration of the Absolute Reality.

Since men are seekers, they must always be open to new ideas. They should not assume that all the wisdom was available in a single book or a philosophy. Humility, the quality of accepting our inadequacy to realise the Ultimate Truth, and a constant yearning for the same, was best captured in the Indic concept of '*Neti Neti*'. In one of the most popular Upanishads called the *Brihadaranyaka Upanishad*, sage Yajnavalkya proposes this idea about the realisation of God in a conversation with his wife Maitreyi, who was also a scholar. In Hindu philosophy, God is truth. Yajnavalkya described that form of the 'supreme being' as 'truth of truth, the vital force of truth, and it is THE truth of that.' He explained that there was 'no other and more appropriate description....' than '...not this, not this' for Ultimate Reality.[27]

Scholars have interpreted it in many ways like 'Neither this nor that' etcetera. But Chaturvedi Badrinath's interpretation, 'Not just this alone', best captures Indic spirit. In seeking, the seeker must not forget that what was being explored was not the entire truth. One must respect the other; and continue to seek.

Chinese Zen Buddhism too proposes a similar idea about enlightenment. Zen masters insist that one should go beyond 'like' and 'dislike', 'for' and 'against' to gain wisdom. The eighth-century Zen master Sen-ts'an wrote:

'The Perfect Way is only difficult
For those who pick and choose;
Do not like, do not dislike;
All will then be clear.
Make a hairbreadth difference,
And Heaven and Earth are set apart;
If you want the truth to stand clear before you,
Never be for or against.
The struggle between 'for' and 'against'
Is the mind's worst disease.'[28]

KARMA: THE HIGHEST OBLIGATION

Another significant aspect of the Hindu view on human rights is its emphasis on duties. In fact, Hinduism does not support the idea of separation of rights and duties. Thus, in Hindu discourse, no right is absolute. All the rights bestowed upon a section enjoin upon another section of corresponding duties. For a Hindu, the highest obligation is Karma, or performance of duty.

Karma is misunderstood sometimes as fate. In ancient Western societies, fate played an important role in certain philosophical schools. For example, the Stoics believed that both good and bad were created by God and one should simply accept everything as divinely ordained fate. The bedbugs were there to 'awaken us out of our sleep'; the mice were there to 'encourage humans to be tidy', the Stoics argued. Chrysippus of Soli, a Greek Stoic philosopher, argued that it would have been impossible for good to exist without evil. Seneca, the Roman Stoic philosopher, presented the fate theory for human suffering by arguing, 'God has deemed us worthy instruments of his purpose to discover how much human nature can endure.'[29] The philosopher Zeno of Citium, from Hellenistic Greece, was considered the father of Stoicism. He was once flogging a slave who had stolen some goods. 'But I was fated to steal,' the slave protested. 'Yes, and to be beaten too,' Zeno responded.

Acceptance of pain and pleasure as one's fate was seen as the path to tranquillity by the Stoics.[30]

But for Hindus, Karma was not regarded as fate. They instead argued that proper performance of Karma was the basis for all basic rights of the citizens. For example, the right to happiness was prominently emphasised in the *Arthashastra* by Chanakya. But it also enjoined upon the king the obligation to ensure that those rights of all his subjects were protected.

In the Bhagavad Gita, Lord Krishna declared to Arjuna that all wants and desires, as long as they were not against Dharma, were all his manifestation: '*Dharmenaavirodheshu Kaamosmi Bharatarshabha*'—I am those desires that are not against the Dharma.

As an essential prerequisite for the right to happiness, and millennia before the UDHR proclaimed it, the *Rig Veda* unequivocally stated that all human beings were equal. The *Atharva Veda* went further and talked about various rights and obligations or duties.

Samani Prapaa Saha Vonnabhagah
Samane Yoktre Saha vo Yunajmi
Aaraah Nabhimivaabhitah[31]

'All have equal rights to articles of food and water. The yoke of the chariot of life is placed equally on the shoulders of all. All should live together in harmony supporting one another like the spokes of a wheel of the chariot connecting its rim and hub.'[32]

In an important article, 'Happiness for All to Secure Social Harmony', Justice Rama Jois wrote: 'The *Vedas* and *Upanishads* were the primordial source of Dharma, a compendious term for all human rights and duties, the observance of which was regarded as essential for securing peace and happiness to individuals and society. The *Smritis* and *Puranas* were collections of the rules of Dharma including civil rights and criminal liabilities (*Vyavahara Dharma*) as also *Raja Dharma* (Constitutional Law). There were also several other authoritative works on *Raja Dharma*, the most important of them being the *Kamandaka, Shukra Niti* and Kautilya's *Artha Shastra*. All of them unanimously declare that the objective of the State was to secure happiness of all.'[33]

ANANDA: THE ULTIMATE GOAL OF LIFE

Alexander bumped into Diogenes, a half-naked man lying on the banks of a river. He asked the man, 'Who are you?' The man said he was Diogenes and then asked Alexander who he was. A little surprised and a lot annoyed, Alexander replied, 'I am Alexander the Great.' On hearing his reply, Diogenes laughed out aloud. 'I am seeing a man for the first time who calls himself "the Great",' he taunted. They both then engaged in a discussion. At the end, impressed by Diogenes' philosophy, Alexander promised to become his disciple. 'Do it today, or it will be too late,' warned Diogenes. Alexander hesitated, 'I have a mission to conquer the world. I shall come back after that,' he promised. 'You can never,' Diogenes replied. 'Can I do something for you?' asked Alexander. 'Yes! I am enjoying my beautiful sun bath. You are coming in the way. Please get off,' shouted Diogenes.

Alexander was looking for happiness in wars, conquest and subjugation. Diogenes, a saintly man, found it in his freedom to lie down by the side of the river. Freedom, absolute and unmitigated, is the Indic way.

'God is dead; Man is free', exclaimed German philosopher Nietzsche. 'No. God is here, and hence man is free,' exhorted Indian philosophers. 'God is all around. He is in you; and he is in me. I *am* the God, the unbound. Hence I am free'. India is a society that cherishes freedom in omnipresent divinity.

While emphasising on the fundamental unity of the *Atman* (consciousness), Hinduism does recognise that there exists diversity in God's creation. This diversity is not seen by a Hindu as a misnomer. Neither do they set out to destroy this diversity in the quest for uniformity when they talk about innate oneness. Diversity in form and unity in spirit is what Hinduism stands for.

OMNITHEISM

For the Semitics, God has been an invisible phenomenon. In the exodus story of the Old Testament, Moses was tending his sheep on the slopes of Mount Horeb one day when he suddenly saw 'the angle of Lord' in a bush nearby. Moses wanted to go closer when the Lord ordered him, 'Draw not nigh hither—Do not come closer.' Moses 'hid his face, for he was afraid to look upon God'. Although that was supposed to be the key moment for man's realisation of God, the Semitic God remained an unreachable phenomenon, only available through his messenger. God is singular and alpha male for the Semites. 'The new God was a transcendental deity, inhabiting a realm distinct and distant from humanity. Ancient gods had always been immanent in nature, and companions in everyday life. Not so Yahweh, who was separate and other. "For my thoughts are not your thoughts," the Lord told the prophet Isaiah, "neither are your ways my ways",' wrote Kenan Malik.[34]

However, the ancient Greeks and Babylonians had gods as humans. The Greek gods were capricious, egoistic and violent. There were good gods and not-so-good ones. They would frequently engage with humans, but with superior power and authority. The Semitics called the Greeks and Babylonians as polytheists for having a multiplicity of gods.

Looking at the multiplicity of godheads among Hindus too, the West has wrongly portrayed Hinduism as a polytheistic religion. Some Hindus mistakenly described this multiplicity as pluralism. Pluralism means existence of parts that are not interconnected. However, the Hindu ideal of respect for and celebration of diversity in creation stems from its core belief that whatever exists in the universe is nothing but the manifestation of one Supreme Reality.

The *Chandogya Upanishad* describes it beautifully as: '*Sarvam Khalvidam Brahma*'—All that we see in this universe is Brahman (Supreme Consciousness) only. The *Mundaka Upanishad* says that this Atman—Consciousness-existence or Bliss-absolute—has interpenetrated everything in the universe.

Lord Krishna referred to the omnipresence of the divine in his discourse to Arjuna in the Bhagavad Gita: '*Mayi Sarvamidam Protam Sutre Manigana Iva*'—I have interpenetrated the universe like gems threaded together.

It is interesting to observe scientific developments in Quantum Physics that seem to proceed along the same lines. After successful experiment on Bell's Theorem, eminent physicist David Bohm wrote: 'The essential new quality implied by the quantum theory is non-locality, i.e., that a system cannot be analysed into parts whose basic properties do not depend upon the whole system. This leads to new notion of unbroken wholeness of the universe.'[35]

Swami Dayananda Saraswati of the Arsha Vidya Gurukulam used the term 'Omnitheism' to describe it. 'The purpose of life for a Hindu is to realize the presence of divinity all around, feel oneness with it, and through this feeling, liberate spiritually. Omnitheism guides the Hindu way of life. He sees the divine everywhere, in trees, in rivers, in serpents and even in the vacuum. For him, all creation—animate and inanimate—is sacred. He worships a river and calls it *Ganga Mata*—Mother Ganges. He worships a cow and calls it *Go Mata*—Mother Cow. Even if he were to cut a tree for laying up a road, he would do that only after offering his obeisance to that tree and seeking pardon from it. Hence every Hindu might have a personal deity like patron saints culled from historical figures enshrined in folk memory. This is not polytheism as these deities are as divine as any in the creation and merely parts of the Whole.

'We not only tolerate, but we Hindus accept every religion.... Knowing that all religions, from the lowest fetishism to the highest absolutism, mean so many attempts of the human soul to grasp and realize the infinite, each determined by the conditions of its birth and association, and each of them marking a stage of progress,' exhorted Swami Vivekananda at the World Parliament of Religions in Chicago in 1893.[36]

In fact, the *Narada Smriti*, one of the many constitutions Hindus have had in the course of their long history, enjoins upon the king to protect non-believers too.

Pashandanaigama sreni poogavraata ganadishu
Samrakshet samayam Raja Durge Janapade Tatha

'The king should accord protection to compacts of associations of believers of *Vedas* (*Naigamas*) as also the non-believers (*Pashandis*) and others.'[37]

In a nutshell, the Hindu perceives global diversity as the 'Divine Game' and sets out to preserve and enrich it rather than trying to establish a 'Global Standard Culture'.

ETHICAL-SPIRITUAL IDENTITY OF HUMAN BEINGS

Human dignity cannot be ensured merely through constitutional means. It must be embedded in the basic Sanskaras, the value system of the society. Deen Dayal warned that in the absence of Sanskaras, even democracy can degenerate into an instrument of self-interest. 'There is no conflict between the individual and the society; if it exists, it is only an aberration. It is not necessary to curb the freedom of the individual in the interest of the society. On the other hand, unbridled liberty does not lead to the development of the individual. It actually leads to his ruin. Complete identification of the individual with society is itself a state of complete development of the individual. Freedom of the individual and the interests of the society are not contradictory. Democracy is but an instrument for the fulfilment of the duty of the people. The effectiveness of the instrument depends upon the feeling for the nation in the life of the people, consciousness of responsibility, and discipline. If these *Sanskaras* are absent in the citizen, democracy degenerates into an instrument of individual, class and party interest,' he said.[38]

The ancient sages of Bharat have thus visualised the grand idea of the oneness of Atman and *Paramaatman*—and universal oneness of human beings based on *Chetna*, the collective consciousness.

That the same consciousness pervades all creation is the greatest contribution of the Hindu classical thought to the wisdom of the world.

After many experiments in physics and neurophysiology, the Nobel Prize winning Austrian Physicist Erwin Schrödinger concluded in his book, *My View of the World,* 'In all the world there is no kind of framework within which we find consciousness in the plural. This is something we construct because of the temporal plurality of the individuals. But it is a false construction…. The only solution to this conflict, in so far as any is available to us, lies in the ancient wisdom of the *Upanishads.*'[39]

Upanishads are the fountainhead of Hindu philosophy which the great German philosopher Arthur Schopenhauer described as 'the solace of my life.'[40] Vedic and Upanishadic literature abound in ideas that proclaim universal oneness and universal well-being. These ideas have shaped and guided the Hindu socio-religious life for centuries.

The Indic thought does not recognise human beings as mere material beings. Its understanding of human identity is more ethical-spiritual than material. That is why a sense of immortality and divinity is attributed to all human beings in Hindu classical thought.

'The fundamental difference between our position and that of the West is that whereas they have regarded body and satisfaction of its desires as the aim, we regarded body as an instrument for achieving our aims. Satisfaction of our bodily wants is necessary, but we do not consider this to be the sole aim of all our efforts. Here in Bharat, we have placed before ourselves the ideal of the four-fold responsibilities of catering to the needs of body, mind, intellect and soul, with a view to achieving the integrated progress of man. *Dharma, Artha, Kama* and *Moksha* are the four layers of human endeavour—the *Purusharthas,*' said Deen Dayal.[41]

'Consistent with the depth of Indian metaphysics, the human

personality was also given a metaphysical interpretation. This is not unknown to the modern occidental philosophy. The concept of human personality in Kant's philosophy of law is metaphysical entity but Kant was not able to reach the subtler unobserved element of personality, which was the basic theme of the concept of personality in Indian legal philosophy,' observed Prof. S.D. Sharma.[42]

An invisible Atman, dwelling in each body as the quintessential identity of all creatures, forms the basis for all discussions on the status of human beings in Indic classical thought, starting from the times of the Vedas, indisputably the ancient-most literature of the world. When Jefferson, father of the American constitution, talked about the happiness of human beings, he was limiting it to body and mind. But the Hindu concept included happiness of the soul as an important element of human dignity.

The individual soul—*Jeevatman*—is not unique; it is universal at the level of the material world, and integral with the Divine Whole—Paramaatman—at the spiritual level. It is on this principle of non-dualism and integralism of the soul that the Vedas unequivocally emphasise non-discrimination of human beings:

Ajyesthaaso Akanisthaasa Yete
Sam Bhraataro Vaavrudhuh Soubhagaya[43]

'No one is superior or inferior; all are brothers; all should strive for the interest of all and progress collectively.'[44]

The *Rig Veda* is the first of the four Vedas and is considered the essence of all knowledge—*Jnana*. In fact, the Vedas emphasise the quintessential oneness of all creation.

Samaani va Aakootihi Samaanaa Hridayaanivah
Samaanamastu vo Mano Yathaa Vah Susahaasati[45]

'Let there be oneness in your resolutions, hearts and minds; let the determination to live with mutual cooperation be firm in you all.'[46]

Three famous ideals that inspired the French Revolution—

'Liberty, Equality and Fraternity'—have subsequently found place in almost all democratic constitutions of the world, including India. Liberty and equality can be achieved through constitutional means; but not fraternity.

'What does Fraternity mean?' Ambedkar, the architect of India's Constitution asked, and went on to explain that 'Fraternity means a sense of common brotherhood of all Indians—of Indians being one people. It is this principle that gives unity and solidarity to social life.'[47]

VARNASHRAMA AND HUMAN DIGNITY

No discussion on human dignity and rights with respect to Hinduism can be complete without taking up the question of the caste system and the hierarchical arrangement therein.

The Hindus perfected social organisation. The Hindu Varnashrama, grouping people into four Varnas, was the most scientific principle of social organisation. The Varnashrama was not the same as the present-day caste system. Plato had divided humanity into three classes: labourers who produce material needs of society; soldiers who guard the state; and the rulers who rule.

In the *Purusha Sukta*, an important hymn in *Rig Veda*, *Purusha*, the Cosmic Being, is described as the progenitor of creation. One of the verses that some, including the renowned Indic scholar Max Müller, find controversial, described the four Varnas as the creation of the Cosmic Being—from his mouth, arms, thighs and feet. Interestingly, Plato too resorted to an identical description of a tripartite division of the soul into appetitive, spirited and rational parts. 'The appetitive part of the soul is linked to bodily desires, such as the yearning for food and pleasure. The spirited is concerned with honour, and with anger and indignation. The rational is driven by a desire for knowledge and truth,' wrote Kenan Malik on Plato's conception. 'The common people are driven by base desires, soldiers by a yearning for honour, while rulers look to reason. Upbringing may help an individual regulate his soul and thereby change the group to which he should belong. Mostly, though, it is a matter of birth—we are born to be blacksmiths or soldiers or philosopher kings,' he explained Plato's division logic.[48]

The present-day caste system in India is a rigid birth-centric arrangement in line with Plato's classes. However, the Varnas were not hereditary. Untouchability and birth-based discrimination were unknown to the ancients during the Varnashrama days. No one was high and no one low, to quote the *Rig Veda*.

Shankara Digvijaya by Madhavacharya proclaimed:
Janmanaa Jaayate Shudrah Sanskaraat Dwija Ucchate
Vedapaathi Bhavet Viprah Brahma janaati Brahmanah
'By birth all are Shudras. By actions men become Dwija—twice born. By reading the Vedas, one becomes Vipra and becomes Brahman by gaining the knowledge of God.' For Adi Shankara, not birth, but knowledge became the basis for social arrangement.

A passage in the *Van Parva* of the Mahabharata ran thus: 'He, in whom the qualities of truth, munificence, forgiveness, gentleness, abstinence from cruel deeds, contemplation, and benevolence are observed, is called a Brahmin in the *Smriti*. A man is not a *Sudra* (low Caste) by being born a *Sudra* nor a *Brahmin* by being born a *Brahmin*.'

The *Shanti Parva* in the Mahabharata categorically rejected the idea of some Varnas being superior to others.

Na Visheshosti Varnanaam Sarvam Braahmyamidam Jagat
Brahmanaa poorva Sristhim hi Karmabhih Varnataam Gatam
'There are no distinctions of *Varnas*. Divine consciousness is omnipresent in the world. It was *Brahmanic* entirely at first. The *Varnas* have emerged in consequence of men's actions.'

In his paper read before the International Congress of Orientalists at Berlin in 1881, renowned freedom fighter and scholar, Shyamji Krishna Verma said: 'We read in the *Aiteriya Brahmana* (ii.3.19), for example, that Kavasha Ailusha, who was a *Sudra* and son of a low woman, was greatly respected for his literary attainments, and admitted into the class of *Rishis*—the pre-eminent Hindu sages. Perhaps the most remarkable feature of his life is that he, *Sudra* as he was, distinguished himself as the *Rishi* of some of the hymns of Rig-*Veda* (*Rig.*, X. 30-40). It is distinctly stated in the *Chandogyopanishad* that Jabala, who is otherwise called Satya Kama, had no *gotra*, or family name whatever (*Chan. Upa.*, IV. 4). Though born of unknown parents, Jabala is said to have founded a School of the *Yajur Veda*. Even in the *Apasthambha Sutra* (II. 5-10) and *Manu Smriti* (x. 65) we find that a *Sudra* can become a *Brahman* and a *Brahman* can become a *Sudra*.'[49]

From Vyasa, Valmiki and Vishva Karma to present-day saints, one finds countless eminent rishis who were Shudras by Varna. Even Megasthenes, the great Greek historian, wrote that there were four castes among Hindus and a Hindu of any caste could become a Sophist (Brahmin). Transmigration was not an exception as in Plato's classes, but a definite possibility in Hindu Varna order.

Caste hierarchy and privileges based on caste had no sanction in Hinduism. They are the result of the distortions that crept into the Hindu body-politic during the medieval period. Hinduism has witnessed a continuous stream of social reformers who strove to uproot this malice like Narayana Guru, Swami Vivekananda, Jyotiba Phule, Mahatma Gandhi and B.R. Ambedkar.

'Wherever you go, there will be caste. But that does not mean that there should be these privileges. They should be knocked on the head. The duty of the *Advaita* is to destroy all privilege. The days of exclusive privileges and exclusive claims are gone, gone forever from the soil of Bharat,' exclaimed Swami Vivekananda.[50]

Interestingly, the caste system is no longer the exclusive appendage of Hinduism. Almost all religions in India have these castes today, and they are afflicted by the system of caste-based privileges leading to conflicts within. Dalit Christians is a word frequently used to refer to those who converted to Christianity from the so-called low-caste Hindus. These Dalit Christians complain that they suffer several disabilities and severe discrimination within the Christian church establishment in India. There were instances when it led even to violence and separation of parishes on caste lines as in the South Indian city of Pondicherry in March 2008.

Deen Dayal Upadhyay's views on Varnashrama sounded supportive of the concept. However, he did not agree that the anomalies and evils that have crept into the system had to be eradicated. 'Many anomalies could have crept into the *Varna Vyavastha* today. They all must be eradicated. However, as far as its core idea is concerned, it cannot be understood from a Western prism. The West has held unhealthy competition and conflict as the basis of the social structure. Hinduism does not see conflict, discrimination and competition among different organs of the society; instead, it sees complementarity. Those who find discrimination in *Varna Vyavastha* fail to see the truth. *Varna* is not a discriminatory institution, but an organised structure. It is a grave mistake to look for high and low or superior and inferior in it,' he had said.

The fact remains that the Varna Vyavastha of ancient times, in which transmigration among castes was also a possibility, no longer exists. Its place has been taken over by a system that is based on birth. *'Janmanaa Jaatihi'*—caste by birth—is the present order. In Bhagavad Gita, Krishna had said:

catur-varnyam maya srstam guna-karma-vibhagasah

'According to the three modes of material nature and the work ascribed to them, the four *Varnas* of human society were created by Me.'

But the present-day caste is based neither on Guna (material nature) nor on Karma (work). A so-called cobbler by caste can be a professor in a university today, and a so-called Brahmin could be running a shoe store. Yet, caste identity remains the same, as it is acquired by birth. The sad reality about present-day India is that the

Varnashrama system has ceased to exist, and the caste system has outlived its utility.

Any society that lives on for millennia will acquire certain malevolent characteristics. One such evil characteristic that has crept into the body politic of the Indic society is the sin of untouchability. Its origins are yet suspect. It does not have any kind of scriptural sanction. Countless social reformers have fought against this social evil. 'Who reduced the *Bhângis* and the *Pariahs* to their present degraded condition? Heartlessness in our behaviour and at the same time preaching wonderful *Advaitism*—is it not adding insult to injury?' thundered Swami Vivekananda angrily.[51] Ambedkar's fight for dignity of life for the so-called untouchables is well-known. Gandhi spent his whole life educating people against this evil practice. He not just preached but showed the way by living it.

A particularly important reform in this regard came about when prominent saints and sages of India joined together under the auspices of the Vishwa Hindu Parishad at Udipi in Karnataka in 1969 and unequivocally declared that no one was inferior or superior by virtue of his birth in a particular caste. It was a turning point in the history of contemporary Hinduism when a large number of prominent religious and spiritual leaders of India came together to decry untouchability and caste discrimination by declaring—'*Hindavah Sodarah sarve*', meaning all Hindus are siblings; and '*Na Hinduh Patito Bhavet*', that is, no Hindu shall be considered inferior'.

Balasaheb Deoras, the third Sarsanghachalak of the RSS, delivered a series of lectures called the Vasant Vyakhyan Mala at Pune in Maharashtra in 1973. In a significant statement about the caste system, he said: 'Whatever be the origin, all of us consider untouchability as a terrible folly. It must be thrown out lock, stock and barrel,' he insisted. His statement, 'If untouchability is not a crime, nothing in this world is a crime,' continues to inspire millions of social activists in India in their work for social harmony and cohesion.[52]

It also brings us to the bigger question of how to deal with the caste system. It has its protagonists who continue to argue that the caste system is a wholesome organisation of society. Swami Vivekananda had a pragmatic suggestion: 'The only way to bring about the levelling of castes is to appropriate the culture, the education which is the strength of the higher castes.'[53] But that was more than a century ago. Experience shows otherwise. In any case, as Deen Dayal himself argued, if it is a system, it should be liable to change. Popular British poet Lord Alfred Tennyson had said, 'The old order changeth yielding place to new, and God fulfils in many ways, lest one good custom should corrupt the world.'[54] Varnashrama might have been good in a particular period. But it has outlived its utility. And the caste system has today become the single-most lethal challenge to social harmony and cohesion.

There were efforts to break the caste system as late as in the twentieth century. Ambedkar wrote about annihilation of caste. Socialists have experimented with groups of caste-less citizens. They even started bodies like Jaati Paati Todak Mandal—Society of Breakers of Caste Barriers. But tragically, in a few years' time, the Jaati Paati Todak Mandal became a caste.

Caste is a system of social organisation. Society cannot live in a disorganised manner. There cannot be systemic vacuum either. Hence the need of the hour is to 'replace' the caste with something else, rather than trying to 'remove' it. Golwalkar had suggested that trade and professional 'guilds' could replace castes. In a way, that is happening in Indian society, slowly but gradually.

෴

15

Womanhood in Western and Indic Traditions

'There is no chance of welfare of the mankind unless the condition of our women is improved. It is not possible for a bird to fly on one wing,' said Swami Vivekananda.[1] This is applicable to all nations and cultures of the world. Women played a central role in the rise and fall of many civilisations. For Hindus, creator-gods like Brahma, Vishnu and Shiv are incomplete without their female counterparts—Saraswati, Lakshmi and Shakti. They are also described as Jaganmata or Jagajjanani—the progenitors of the universe. Western civilisations have their own female ancestors. It was Pandora for ancient Greeks and Eve for Judeo-Christians. If Helen's beauty was the cause of the Trojan War in ancient Greece, Hindus have their Sita and Draupadi at the root of the wars in Ramayana and Mahabharata. But are the conditions of women the same in the Orient as well as the Occident? Are they treated in the same way in different civilisations?

STRUGGLES OF WOMEN IN THE WEST

A long struggle ensued before mankind secured fundamental human rights in the West in 1948. The UDHR emphatically states that all rights should be equally enjoyable by both men and women.

In fact, the Declaration was to begin with the statement 'All men are born free and equal in dignity and rights. They are endowed by nature with reason and conscience, and should act towards one another like brothers.' However, Indian delegates like Hansa Mehta insisted on replacing the word 'men' with human beings, although Eleanor Roosevelt argued that 'men' included 'women' too. Finally, Article 1 was amended to begin with: 'All human beings are born free and equal in dignity and rights. They are endowed with reason and conscience and should act towards one another in a spirit of brotherhood.' India's insistence had also helped in introducing rights related to healthcare, motherhood, etc. in the Declaration.

In Western civilisations, women had to endure enormous indignity and ignominy over several millennia. However, the status that women in Oriental civilisations enjoyed was much superior to their Western counterparts. Herbert Spender, the British politician and a great apostle of individual freedom, insisted that the position of women supplied a good test of the civilisation of people.[2] In India, women have always occupied a position of high esteem. Prof. H.H. Wilson had said: 'It may be confidently asserted that in no nation of antiquity were women held in so much esteem as amongst Hindus.'[3] The same was the case with pre-Confucian China. In the Shang dynasty that ruled during 1700–1100 BCE, evidence in the form of oracle bone inscriptions suggests that women even enjoyed leadership positions. One such leader was Fu Hao, who was a military leader.[4] As Confucianism spread in the country, women lost their equal status and were deemed unworthy and incapable of education.[5] The Han empire of the second century BCE treated women as subservient to men.[6]

Ancient civilisations of the West were dismal in this matter. Societies were primarily male-driven and patriarchal throughout history. The Minoan Crete civilisation, which existed from 2000 BCE to 1400 BCE and is considered by historians as the oldest European civilisation, is probably the only exception. In the Minoan

Crete society, women were held in remarkably high respect. There were no restrictions on them and they were actively involved in all aspects of life. The Minoan religion was based on a Great Mother Goddess as the supreme deity; was highly matriarchal and controlled by priestesses.

That was not to be the case with other civilisations of ancient Europe. In ancient Mesopotamia (2000–1200 BCE), the Babylonians were a patriarchal society where women were under the control of their husbands. The ancient Babylonian hymn *Gula* (the goddess of healing) describes a woman's life as 'I am a daughter, I am a bride, I am a spouse, I am a housekeeper.'[7] Ancient Egypt (3100–1087 BCE) too was a male-dominated society. Women did not have the freedom to serve in the government. Description about the status of women in ancient Egypt can be found in *The Instruction of Ptahhotep*: 'If you are prosperous, you should establish a household and love your wife as is fitting. Fill her belly and clothe her back. Oil is the tonic for her body. Make her heart glad as long as you live. She is a profitable field for her lord.'[8] Ancient Rome (800–500 BCE) and the Byzantine empire (400–1500 CE) were no exception.

Most influential and controversial myths about women were those from ancient Greeks and Judeo-Christians. The depiction of Pandora in ancient Greek mythology and Eve in the Judeo-Christian creation myth speak volumes about the way women were viewed and treated in those societies.

Pandora, like Eve or Havva in the Judeo-Christian tradition, was the first mortal female formed out of clay by the gods. The myth goes something like this: 'The Titan Prometheus was once assigned the task of creating the race of man. He afterwards grew displeased with the mean lot imposed on them by the gods and so stole fire from heaven. Zeus was angered and commanded Hephaistos (Hephaestus) and other gods to create the first woman, Pandora, endowing her with beauty and cunning. He then had her delivered to Prometheus' foolish younger brother Epimetheus as a bride. Zeus gave Pandora a storage jar (*pithos*) as a wedding gift which she opened, releasing the swarm of evil spirits trapped within. These would forever after plague the mankind.' This is also the mythical story about Pandora's box.[9]

This theme of a beautiful and cunning woman continues through the story of the Trojan Wars and the fall of Troy in Homer's epic poems *Iliad* and *Odyssey*. Supposedly written in eighth century BCE, these classical works of Homer set the tone for future historians like Herodotus and Sophocles and give us a peep into the glorious yet ghastly Greek history. *Iliad* was about a beautiful woman named Helen, queen of Sparta and wife of king Menelaus. She eloped with the Trojan prince Paris at the prodding of goddess Aphrodite. Some of the ancient Greek gods and goddesses were vicious. Aphrodite was one among them. She was grateful to Paris for recognising her as the most beautiful goddess. In return, she decided to fulfil Paris' evil desire of capturing Helen. She persuaded Helen to go to bed with Paris. Helen initially refused, allowing room for the possible interpretation that she was abducted by Paris. But Homer's poem indicated that Helen relented finally. Enraged, Menelaus sought the help of his brother Agamemnon to avenge the action of the Trojans and bring back Helen to him. Agamemnon set out with other Greek heroes like Achilles, Odysseus, Nestor and Ajax with a fleet of more than a thousand ships and lay siege to the Trojan city of Troy, demanding the Trojan king Priam for Helen's return. A 10-day war ensued, and Agamemnon succeeded in destroying Troy and killing Paris and Hector, the Trojan heroes. Helen was returned to Menelaus.

All through the Homerian narrative, Helen comes across as a hapless and weak woman. With the excavation of the archaeological remains of the city of Troy in western Turkey recently, Homer's epic poems acquired historical significance. When forced by Aphrodite into Paris' bed against her will, Helen retorted by sneering at her: 'Go sit by him yourself. Abandon the paths of the gods, never again turn your feet back to Olympus; no, stay with him, for ever whimpering around him and watching over him, until he makes you his wife—or else his slave.' She insisted that going to bed with Paris would bring shame on her and added, 'I have misery enough in my heart.' Yet, she knew she was powerless to resist the gods and conceded.[10]

Judeo-Christians, who were contemporaries of ancient Greeks, were equally appalling in their treatment of women. The story of Eve, the female companion of the first male, Adam, as described in the *Book of Genesis*, has had a profoundly negative impact on women in the West, throughout the history of the last two millennia. Eve was held up by several historians as well as Christian scholars as a quintessential evil who disobeyed Adam, and as the cause of human suffering. Eve's sin was that she disobeyed God's injunction and came under the evil spell of the serpent, encouraging Adam to eat the forbidden fruit in defiance. God punished them for their disloyalty and expelled them from the Garden of Eden. A greater punishment was reserved for Eve, since she was the one who came under Satan's influence. Adam was only misled by Eve. The original sin was that of Eve, the woman made by God out of the ribs of Adam, hence an inferior creature. God condemned Eve to a lifetime of painful childbirth and subservience to her husband: 'I will greatly increase your pangs in childbearing; in pain you shall bring forth children; yet your desire shall be for your husband; and he shall rule over you,' the Genesis book commanded.

This narrative had influenced the Judeo-Christian world for many centuries until recently. Women had to endure great discrimination and enormous suffering at the hands of the religious establishment as well as the believer world. Women were not allowed to open their mouths in any assembly, not empowered at the pulpit and generally treated as lesser humans. There were even debates until the middle of the last millennium about whether women should be treated as humans or animals as they were created out of the rib of the man and not a complete creation of God. Thousands of women were branded as witches and put to brutal death in medieval Europe.

As per the New Testament of the Bible, in his letter to Timothy, one of the apostles of Jesus, St Paul made a non-negotiable pronouncement that women could not teach at the pulpit because of their inherent sinfulness and moral corruption. They could not even communicate their faith or sense of self from a public platform. The saint declared: 'Let the woman learn in silence, with all subjection. But I suffer not a woman to teach, nor to use authority over the man: but to be in silence. For Adam was first formed; then Eve.'

In a moving article about the condition of women in Western religious societies that appeared in the *Washington Post*, Pamela Milne wrote in 1989: 'In the second century, Tertullian taught that all women share the ignominy of Eve. Like Eve, all women are "the devil's gateway ... the unsealer of that forbidden tree ... the first deserter of the divine law" who destroyed "God's image, man". Ambrose, a 4th-century bishop and one of the four great "doctors" of the Latin church, refers to Eve as a procreative "helper for the purpose of generating human nature" and concludes that "this then is the way in which a woman is a good helper of less importance."'[11] Thomas Aquinas significantly extended the argument in the thirteenth century, claiming that women were defective by nature. The consequence of such thinking can be seen in works like *Malleus Maleficarum* (Hammer Against Witches). This fifteenth-century document, which draws heavily on Genesis Three, provided the Inquisition its principal theological justification for persecuting women as witches. In the decades following its publication, thousands of women were executed. The themes of inferiority, evil and seductiveness continued to be emphasised in the writings of Luther, Calvin and Knox and remain disturbingly prominent in the twentieth century in places as diverse as papal encyclicals and TV fundamentalist preaching. The consequences for women of our day can be devastating. There are still men who refer to Genesis 2-3 to justify their right to physically 'discipline' a wife who is not properly subordinate. And there are some battered women who continue to accept such abuse because they think it is a husband's divinely sanctioned 'right and duty'.

No wonder then that the West needed a powerful movement for the liberation of women from this oppressive cycle. There was nobody to challenge the traditional interpretations of the Genesis, hence women themselves had to take up cudgels against it. That was how the Western feminist movement was born and it started challenging the misogynist and patriarchal interpretations of the Bible. Some early feminists believed that the portrayal of Eve is at the root of the problem and can be corrected through reinterpretation, although most believed that the religion itself was anti-woman. Elizabeth Cady Stanton (1815–1902) was one of the early feminists who published the *Woman's Bible* in 1885, attempting a reinterpretation of the story. 'It is amazing,' she wrote, 'that any set of men ever claimed that the dogma of the inferiority of woman is here set forth. The conduct of Eve from the beginning to the end is so superior to that of Adam.'[12] But such efforts did not really solve the problem for the women in the West, who had to continue their battles for long. In America, women secured voting rights only in 1919. The UDHR, which was released towards the end of 1948, sought to address the issue of women's rights comprehensively.

IMPOSITION OF VICTORIAN MORALS ON THE EAST

Incidentally, the regressive thinking of the West with respect to women reached the non-Western world too through colonists and missionaries. Traditional societies like India and other Southeast Asian nations have had a vibrant history of freedom and empowerment of women. But centuries of Semitic influence have left their imprints on societal mores and behaviours of those

societies also. Victorian morality, a highly discriminatory social
and moral code that prevailed in nineteenth and early twentieth
century Britain, had come to influence the thought and behavioural
patterns of traditional societies like India greatly.

What came to be known as 'Victorian morality' was an orthodox
and conservative social order that was strictly implemented in
England during the reign of Queen Victoria from 1837 to 1901.
It was a highly discriminatory social order based on status and sex.
Women were the worst victims while the social underclasses faced
tougher controls than the rich and privileged. While boys attended
the best schools and were groomed for various professions, girls were
not allowed public education. The entire learning process for girls
was restricted to homes and they were expected to learn managing
household chores like cooking and cleaning and some fine arts like
drawing, singing and playing the piano. Marriage, the supportive
role that women had to play for their husbands, and child-rearing
were deeply ingrained in the minds of girls. Victorian morality, in
that sense, was a highly discriminatory and inequal system loaded
heavily against women.

Victorian men were supposed to be strong, ambitious and
independent while women were weak, dependent and submissive.
Men had freedom to choose professions while women were
constrained to managing the home, rearing children and supporting
husbands. In line with the Judeo-Christian doctrine, women were
seen as the property of men. They could neither own property nor
have any political rights like voting. All this repressive and anti-
woman social order ironically flourished under a female ruler. Like
in America, women in England too waged a long struggle to secure
certain fundamental rights like the right to property and political
participation.

Certain aspects of this Victorian morality had come to influence
societies like India too, due to prolonged colonial subjugation.
Women were confined to homes and limited freedoms were

accorded to them. Freedom of women came to be identified with promiscuity. Birth of a girl became a stigma and burden and female foeticide became a regressive practice, especially among certain communities. Women were denied education, discouraged from intermingling with boys, married off at a tender age and confined largely to the limited role of managing home and family. Although these influences of Victorian morality were largely limited to certain sections of India, they called for a major reform, which was attempted by many in the last couple of centuries.

Gandhi was one among them. He wrote a letter to a fellow freedom fighter from Punjab, Raj Kumari Amrit Kaur, in October 1936 from his Wardha Ashram, in which he insisted that women themselves should resist from being 'slaves' of men. 'If you women only realize your dignity and privilege, and make full sense of it for mankind, you will make it much better than it is. But man has delighted in enslaving you and you have proved willing slaves till the slave and holders have become one in the crime [of] degrading humanity. My special function from childhood, you might say, has been to make women realize their dignity. I was once a slave holder myself but *Ba* (Kasturba Gandhi, his wife) proved an unwilling slave and thus opened my eyes to my mission,' he wrote in that letter.[13] He insisted that a daughter too should get an equal share as a son would in inherited property, a reform yet to be fully implemented in India. He upheld women's right to live separately from an unjust husband. 'I admit no distinction between men and women except such as has been made by nature and can be seen with human eyes,' Gandhi used to say.[14]

For his times, Gandhi's views on women were revolutionary. He had once said that for him true independence meant a day when a woman could go out on to the streets alone at midnight and roam about freely. Gandhi was not referring to security of women alone, but also to societal attitudes. Are women in any such conditions respected? Or suspected?

In 2008, Soumya Viswanath, a journalist, was waylaid and murdered in Delhi. The attack took place in the wee hours of the night, at 3 o'clock to be precise, when the journalist was returning home in her car. The then Chief Minister of Delhi, herself a woman, was reported to have commented that the girl was partly to blame because it was 'adventurous' on her part to be alone on the streets at three in the morning. 'All by herself till 3 AM in the city ... you should not be so adventurous,' the chief minister is quoted as commenting.[15] Gandhi had argued several decades ago that this attitude had to change.

There is no doubt that security of women is a major concern in India and other developing societies. At a time when atrocities against women are on the rise, it is important that there are stricter laws, stronger security measures and more stringent punishments. But mere laws or security measures cannot protect women.

Carry P. Meek, a Black Democratic Congresswoman from Florida, had once said it so poignantly: 'Let us stop pretending we can arrest our way to safety and security. Despite all the fine work that policemen and women do, we have got to find other solutions to deter crime.'[16]

SAFETY, HONOUR AND RESPECT

What is actually needed is a mindset change. Gender equality in actions and gender neutrality in perception is the need of the hour. 'Don't look at my lipstick; listen to what I am saying'; 'Don't teach us how to dress. Teach men how to see'—read the placards at a rally for women safety. Objectification of womanhood is a matter to be addressed seriously. Hillary Clinton had once jocularly commented, 'If I want to knock a story off the front page, I just change my hairstyle.'[17]

Another slogan that is common at women's rallies is very pertinent in this context: 'If you talk to your daughter about safety, talk to your son about consent.'

Safety of women lies not in restricting their lives, but in reforming the attitudes of men. Where there is a sense of dignity and respect for women, there her security is automatically ensured. Once Swami Vivekananda was asked about his views on protection of women. As soon as he heard the words 'protection of women', he laughed out loudly. 'Protection of women? You will protect her? She is Durga; she is Kali; *Mahishasura Mardini* and *Sakshat Jaganmata* herself. And you want to protect her?' Swami ridiculed and added, 'Respect her, so that her safety is automatically taken care of'.

Whatever new trends the new-age feminists may have picked up of late, the real battle of feminism has been for respect and safety. A renowned Australian feminist author, Dale Spender beautifully summed up the challenges that women, particularly in the developed Western societies face, and how feminism should be understood: 'Feminism has fought no wars. It has killed no opponents. It has set up no concentration camps, starved no enemies, practiced no cruelties. Its battles have been for education, for the vote, for better working conditions ... for safety on the streets ... for childcare, for social welfare ... for rape crisis centers, women's refuges, reforms in law. If someone says "I am not a feminist", I ask, "Why? What is your problem?"'[18]

If what Spender says is all about feminism, then probably India has more feminists than anywhere else. But neo-feminism has come to represent negation of social order, indiscipline, individualism to the detriment of the interests of others and rejection of family. Nobody's safety and honour can be ensured in a climate of disorder, indiscipline and collapse of institutions. Both should go together. No freedom is absolute. As the maxim goes, 'your freedom ends where my nose begins.'

Family is an important institution that mankind has invented and nurtured. It calls for continuous reform. But it cannot be rejected outright. In Indic thought, family has been made an important institution for pursuing Dharma. Like Yin and Yang, wife and husband together constitute the whole. In fact, the institution of family is the one that sustains creation through the continuum of generations.

Lebanese American writer and poet, Kahlil Gibran wrote in a poem that family was an institution created out of life's longing for itself. He said it beautifully:

'Your children are not your children
They are the sons and daughters of Life's longing for itself.'[19]

WOMEN THROUGH THE AGES IN INDIC TRADITIONS

The Semitic God is formless. Yet, descriptions about that formless God are always made as a 'He'—an alpha male. In Hinduism, God is *Ardha nareeswara*—half woman-half man—in form; and gender-free in formless. In Hinduism, man and woman are not seen as two different entities in creation, neither inferior nor superior. Ancient Hindu scriptures like *Sankhya Darshana* describe *Purusha* and *Prakriti*—man and woman—as eternal. They are complementary. No Hindu ritual is complete without the equal participation of man and wife.

Indian contemporaries of the ancient Greek and Judeo-Christian women were a much freer and cosmopolitan lot. Women of those times enjoyed equal respect, freedom and opportunities in India. They were highly educated, competed with men in Vedic knowledge and generally enjoyed dignity and respect at par with men of the times. They were active, not only in literary pursuits as authoring Vedic hymns, but also in politics. Their social life was in their own control. They even had the liberty to reject males during marriage ceremonies in a system called the *Swayamvara*—selection of the groom by the woman's choice. Swayamvara was one among the eight different types of marriages permitted in ancient Hindu system. Under this system, the woman would announce the date and place of her test and lay out the conditions that had to be fulfilled by a prospective candidate to be eligible to become the groom. Many men would turn up to face the test and the woman would choose the one who emerged victorious and garland him. Epic Indian women like Sita, Kunti and Draupadi had followed this system to choose their life partners. Vedic life celebrated the beauty and gaiety of women. There were festivals designed for young men and women to celebrate together, explore partnerships and marry after seeking the blessings of elders. Such practices are still prevalent among certain tribal communities in central India.

Despite several interpolations and definitional distortions, the *Manusmriti*, an ancient book of Hindu social law and codes, prescribed by sage Manu, unequivocally declares that women should be honoured and accorded dignity: '*Yatra Naryastu Pujyante Ramante Tatra Devatah*'—Where women are worshipped, that is where the angels tread. This great law-giver of Hinduism even granted rights of separation to women under specific conditions:

1. If a wife dies, her husband may marry another wife.[20] If a husband dies, a wife may marry another husband.[21]

2. If a wife becomes fallen by drunkenness or immorality; her husband may marry another.[22] If a husband becomes fallen, a wife may re-marry another husband.[23]

3. In particular circumstances, a wife may cease to cohabit with her husband.[24]

4. If a husband deserts his wife, she may marry another.[25]

Women of the Vedic age were epitomes of knowledge and wisdom. There were two types of women Vedic scholars—the *Brahmavadinis* were the ones who never married and dedicated their lives to Vedic learning; and the *Sadyodvahas* who were students of the Vedas till the time they got married. There were at least 30 women sages who were credited with authoring Vedic hymns. It is said that there were 27 women seers—Brahmavadinis and Sadyodvahas—who contributed to the *Rig Veda* itself. Some famous women authors like Gargi, Maitreyi and Lopamudra were known. But there were lesser-known ones too like Apala, Bindu, Dakshina,

Divya and many others. Women contributed significantly to other ancient literature as well, apart from the Vedas. Although Buddha did not talk much about women empowerment, Buddhism has had a living tradition of female monks spreading Buddhist knowledge. Emperor Ashoka, after turning to Buddhism in his later life, encouraged both his daughter Sanghamitra and his son Mahinda to dedicate themselves to spreading the religion far and wide. Sanghamitra was the one who took Buddhism to foreign lands like Sri Lanka.

Indic religions have provided leadership positions for women. At a time when Semitic religions were struggling with the question on whether to allow women to occupy pulpits, Indic religions saw great spiritual leaders among women. Women had risen in all walks of life in Indian society; they became judges, scientists, chief ministers, and even prime ministers and presidents.

Women played an active role in politics in ancient India too. In a well-researched paper on ancient Indian women, Prof. Naresh Raut writes: 'Women often enjoyed prominent roles in politics. Megasthenes mentioned the Pandya women running the administration. The Satavahana queen Nayanika ruled the kingdom on behalf of her minor son. So did Pravabati, daughter of Chandragupta II, on behalf of the minor Vakataka prince. A little after the Gupta period, queens used to rule in Kashmir, Odisha and Andhra. Princess Vijaybhattarika acted as the provincial ruler under the Chalukya King; Vikramaditya I. Women were provincial and village administrators in the Kannada region.'[26]

WOMEN IN RECENT HISTORY

Recent centuries of Indian history too have witnessed the rise of many prominent women in leadership roles. There was Ahilyabai Holkar (1725–1790), the ruler of Malwa for 30 years. She was intelligent, benevolent and valiant. She used to be called a 'philosopher queen'. She also had the credit of leading her armies from the front. A Scottish poet of the nineteenth century, Joanna Baillie, wrote a poem about Holkar:

> 'For thirty years her reign of peace, The land in blessing did increase;
>
> And she was blessed by every tongue, By stern and gentle, old and young.
>
> Yea, even the children at their mothers' feet, Are taught such homely rhyming to repeat
>
> In latter days from Brahma came, To rule our land, a noble Dame,
>
> Kind was her heart, and bright her fame, And Ahlya was her honoured name.'[27]

Another such powerful woman was the queen of Jhansi, Rani Lakshmi Bai. Historians compare her with Joan of Arc, who led the French army against the invading English in the famous Hundred Year War in 1429. Writing about the chivalry of Lakshmi Bai, General Hugh Rose, who defeated Rani's forces and captured Jhansi, wrote: 'The Ranee was remarkable for her bravery, cleverness and perseverance; her generosity to her Subordinates was unbounded. These qualities, combined with her rank, rendered her the most dangerous of the rebel leaders.'[28] Begum Hazarat Mahal (1820–1879), the ruler of Awadh, too was a part of the heroic battles of 1857 against the British along with Lakshmi Bai and others.

Indian history is replete with stories of many such heroic women. There were rulers like Rani Rudrama Devi of the Kakatiya dynasty in South India in the twelfth century or Begum Razia Sultana (1205–1240), queen of Delhi, who defended their kingdoms efficiently. Jijabai Bhosale (1598–1674) inspired her son Shivaji to establish *Hindu Pad Padshahi*—an independent Hindu nation. Tarabai (1675–1761), the widow of Rajaram Bhosale, Shivaji's son, took it upon herself to ward off continued Mughal efforts to take over the kingdom.

Tuluva queen Rani Abbakka Chowta (1525–1570) defended Ullal in Karnataka from Portuguese invaders for 40 years. Velu

Nachiar (1730–1796), queen of Sivaganga, fought and defeated the British. In fact, the British could not come back to take over Sivaganga as long as she was alive. Rani Chennamma (1778–1829) of Kittur fought the British until her death in 1824 to defend her freedom. Rani Durgavati (1524–1564), queen of Gondwana, fought against Mughal invaders for several years.

Not just in wars, but in all other areas of social life as well, women in India had full freedom. There was Anandi Gopal Joshi (1865–1887), the first female doctor with a medical degree from the US; Arati Saha (1940–1994), the first Asian woman to swim across the English Channel in 1959; Asima Chatterjee (1917–2006), the first female scientist with a PhD in Organic Chemistry; Capt. Prem Mathur (1910–1992), the first female pilot, who had to withstand several rejections because she was a woman until she finally secured a job in Deccan Aviation; and Justice Anna Chandy (1905–1996) who became the first woman judge in 1937 during British rule.

Despite these inspiring examples, the medieval period in India subjected women to different kinds of discrimination and handicaps including denial of education, child marriages, and general lack of freedom and respect at par with men. But the essential philosophy of India has always been of great freedom and dignity for women. Two great epics of India—the Ramayana and the Mahabharata—present the ideal characterisation of womanhood in ancient India. The two great battles in these epics revolve around the question of the dignity and honour of two women—Sita and Draupadi. The portrayal of these two women in those epics stand testimony to the fact that unlike Helen in the Trojan Wars, these women were never submissive or tolerant of oppression. Instead, they stood up and fought back for their dignity and respect, for which they were accorded a high place of honour.

DRAUPADI AND SITA: THE EPITOME OF INDIAN WOMANHOOD

Draupadi in Mahabharata is portrayed as a liberal, self-willed and courageous woman. She was married to five brothers, four of whom had other wives too. Throughout the epic, her projection has been that of a strong-willed woman. But for her insistence, the Mahabharata war would not have taken place. The Pandava brothers were offered five villages as compensation to settle the dispute. Being Dharmaraj, Yudhisthira would have gone for it. Aware of the fact, Krishna took the proposal to Draupadi. Draupadi reacted with righteous indignation. The brothers could accept the offer if they wanted to; but she was not going to settle for anything short of the blood of Dushasana, who humiliated her publicly in front of the entire assembly of noble men in the palace court by attempting to disrobe her. The proposal was thus rejected, and war ensued. Nobody called her an arrogant and obdurate woman. Instead, she was respected and called *Maha Sadhvi*—woman of epic virtue.

In the *Shanti Parva*, after the war was over, came an interesting incident. Bhishma, the grand old man, was lying on the bed of arrows, awaiting his death. Yudhisthira came to visit him. He had won the war and regained the kingdom from the Kaurava clan. He sought to learn *Raj Dharma*—wisdom of statecraft—from Bhishma. Draupadi was passing by and laughed out aloud on hearing Yudhisthira's request. Yudhisthira, considering Draupadi's laughter inappropriate, chided her. But Bhishma stated that Draupadi's laughter was justified. 'In the full royal court, when she was being disrobed, I too was present, but did nothing. Am I qualified to teach you *Raj Dharma*? That is the meaning of her laughter. It is justified,' Bhishma said to Yudhisthira.

In the Ramayana, one comes across an equally strong personality in Sita, the wife of Ram. The contemporary portrayal of Sita is of a woman who suffered indignities silently. Whereas all of India celebrates Ram, one region spread across India and Nepal, called Mithilanchal, prefers to celebrate Sita. Sita is the divine consort of Ram for the world, but for folk in Mithilanchal, she is their daughter, sister and simply, their girl. They call her *Kishori*—meaning a youthful girl. Mithila was the ancient kingdom of

King Janak, the adoptive father of Sita. He had found her in an agricultural farm near a place called Sitamarhi, in present-day north Bihar. The people of Mithila, the Maithils, are proud of their Kishori but also carry great pain in their hearts, for all the suffering that she had to endure. So much so that although Sita belonged to Mithilanchal, the people there hesitate to name their girls after her, out of sentimentality associated with Sita's lifetime

Unfortunately, it became the universal portrayal of not only Sita, but women in general in India. They are projected as '*abala*'— feeble and born to suffer. Sita epitomised those sufferings. This kind of portrayal of women as weak and destined for suffering and submission is of medieval origin. Several writings of the medieval period, including the sixteenth-century literary work of Tulsidas— the *Ramcharitamanas*—suffer from this anomalous portrayal of women as weak and needful of protection from men.

Medieval distortions apart, the Indian understanding of womanhood has been that of equality, divinity, self-respect and self-assertion. Sita epitomises not weakness or meekness, but these qualities. In fact, her very name Sita can be expanded to highlight her qualities—Strong, Intelligent, Transparent, Assertive.

To understand the personality of Sita, one must turn to the original Ramayana, authored by sage Valmiki. Sita's portrayal in Valmiki's Ramayana was that of a woman of courage, wisdom and knowledge, self-esteem and astuteness. She was discarded by her parents and found by king Janak in an agricultural farm. She was raised as a Kshatriya woman, and married into the noble Kshatriya family of Dasarath. She was kidnapped by Raavan, rescued by her husband Ram, only to be rejected again. She was sheltered and nursed by sage Valmiki in the forests and re-joined mother earth.

To understand this journey of Sita, the best source, other than the original Valmiki's Ramayan, is the series of lectures delivered by acclaimed scholar-politician Rt. Hon. V.S. Srinivasa Sastri. His *Lectures on the Ramayana* is a fascinating read; and among them, the three lectures on Sita are a treat.[29]

Sita comes out as a strong-willed woman in Srinivasa Sastri's narration. Sita was, in a way, singularly responsible for the war between Ram and Raavan. 'I had a dream,' she declared to Anasuya, that '...I would lead my life in forests'. When Ram tried to persuade her to stay back in the palace during his 12-year sojourn to forests—the *Vanvas*—Sita fiercely resisted the idea, castigating Ram for trying to get rid of her. 'I am a *Kshatriya* girl. I won't go under the control of other people, be it Kaikeyi or Bharat,' she declared firmly. Ram too admitted that Sita was a courageous woman. 'You wonder why I said "no" at first? I did not know what a courageous woman you really were. I thought you might be like ordinary women. Now I see who you are and what you are,' he said. Together they left for vanvas, along with Lakshman.

This courage Sita did not lose throughout her life. Even in the face of unbearable hardships in Raavan's court, Sita remained steadfast, not losing her courage and composure. Some narratives portray Sita as a disheartened and weeping woman in the Ashoka Van—the pine forest in which Raavan had imprisoned her. Ashoka Van was described by zealous writers as *Shoka* Van—garden of sorrow. But the original narrative goes differently. Sita did suffer, and may have even cried, but her courage did not diminish. She withstood all hardships. And when Raavan came to force her to accept his proposal for marriage, Sita refused to even look at him. Instead, she held up a blade of grass and addressed Raavan through that. 'I have so much power in me that if only I care to direct it against you, you would be a mass of ash. But I refrain from doing so because I want to preserve my *Tapas*—divine power. Besides, I have not received an order from Ram to defend myself. The burden rests upon him, and he himself should come and save me,' she confidently declared.

Here, Sita was reminding Ram of his Dharma as a Kshatriya and also as a husband. There were occasions when Sita would engage in a discourse on Dharma with Ram. She even taunted Ram for his eagerness to go to the rescue of the sages who were suffering at the hands of the Rakshasas. 'When a *Kshatriya*, trained to fight, finds his weapons ready, or when *Agni*—the fire finds fuel near, then there is danger. It provokes him to an exhibition of strength,' she warned. It could as well be a universal lesson for all countries. This demonstrated Sita's knowledge and wisdom. When Hanuman wanted to punish the women guards at Ashoka Van after Raavan's death, Sita prevented him by saying that they were not the cause of her misery as they were only obeying the orders of their master. Then came her jewels of wisdom on non-harming and non-retaliation. 'The righteous man ought not to be turned from the right by the sin of the sinner. The rule of honour is inviolable. Good men have only one jewel, their unblemished conduct, and they must guard it, come what may. Be they good men or bad, be they deserving of death, still must they be pardoned and treated with mercy by one claiming to be an Aryan. For, no one is above error,' she told Hanuman.

Sita's courage, coupled with her wisdom, manifested in her self-respect and self-confidence. In fact, the portrayal of Sita and Draupadi in the Indian epics indicates the respect and honour that the Indian society had accorded to women's self-esteem. Sita was submissive only to the extent that her self-honour was not violated, whether the violator was Raavan or Ram. Ram raised questions over her fidelity not once, but twice. The first occasion was after the defeat and death of Raavan. Sita was aghast. 'You are not a lowly man, nor am I a lowly woman,' she chided him. Her hurt self-respect came out in her words. 'You have let your ill-temper run away with your judgement, and like a low-bred man, esteemed me lightly as though I was no better than the ordinary type of woman,' she accused him. 'Only in name am I of Janaka's family. I came out of the pure ploughed earth,' she thundered. Agni, the Fire God stood testimony to Sita's purity by refusing to touch her. Thus, she came out of Ram's first fidelity test, but not without warning him about his lack of wisdom.

This courageous self-assertion of Sita can be seen time and again in Ramayana. The second time when Ram wanted her to leave was immediately after his return to the throne in Ayodhya. This time the excuse was that the citizens had suspicions about her. Sita was pregnant at that time. Ram could not muster the courage to ask her to leave. It fell upon Lakshman, who took her in a chariot to the banks of the river Ganges and conveyed the decision of the king. Lakshman was heart-broken, but Sita was stunned, yet composed. She asked Lakshman to convey to Ram that she would live until she gave birth to the children and proved her chastity.

Sita was given shelter and protection by sage Valmiki in his Ashram in the forests. Sita gave birth to twins, Luv and Kush. She raised them as warriors, taught them archery and other war skills. She would personally guide and supervise their military training as there was no one else to do that. During the Aswamedha Yagna that Ram had conducted, the ritual horse entered the forest and Sita's twins withheld it. War ensued and Ram's army was defeated by Luv and Kush. Surprised by the stories of the valour of the children, Ram himself came to the hermitage and realised that the children were his own. He then wanted Sita back. Here again, Sita came out as a woman of high self-esteem. She categorically refused Ram's invitation. 'This earth is not for me,' she told Ram, and clearly adding, '… nor this husband, nor the subjects whom no proof can ever convince.' She seeks for mother earth to open up and rejoins her.

This was quintessential Sita, a brave, determined, wise and self-respecting woman. This was the Indian womanhood that our ancestors had idolised. For their stubbornness, neither Sita nor Draupadi were decried; instead, they were given a place of honour as great women.

The famous dialogue that Maitreyi had with her husband, sage Yagnavalkya over the nature of *Brahmaan* is a tribute to the scholarship of that great Vedic philosopher and a testimony to the

enormous respect that women enjoyed in the Vedic period. Maitreyi
continued to question Yagnavalkya's arguments until, at one point,
Yagnavalkya warned her that she had come to the end of questions
as 'knowing the Knower' was beyond knowledge.

A similar incident happened much later when Adi Shankara,
the famed proponent of *Advaita Vedanta* from Kerala, reached Kashi
and invited Mandana Mishra, a renowned *Mimamsa* scholar and
staunch ritualist, for a *Shastraartha*—scholarly debate. Mandana
Mishra's wife, Ubhaya Bharati, was also an equally profound scholar
and she presided over the debate between her elderly husband and
the young hermit. The dialogue went on for weeks and at one point,
Ubhaya Bharati, without any hesitation, declared her husband as the
loser. But she insisted that Adi Shankara could not claim ultimate
victory until he defeated her as well in a debate. Her questions were
related to *Kama Vidya*—knowledge of sexual life. Adi Shankara was
forced to retreat because as a hermit he did not have any knowledge
of that science. Through his mystic powers, he entered the dead
body of a Kashmiri king and acquired the knowledge to come back
to answer Ubhaya Bharati.

These were not mere stories. They demonstrate the societal
mores of the times. Renowned Australian feminist Geena
D. Andersen puts it very beautifully: 'Feminism is not about making
women stronger. Women are already strong. It is about changing
the way the world perceives their strength.'[30] We need to teach our
generation respect for women. We need to make them understand
and celebrate the strength and glory of womanhood. It is about
womanhood, not just about sisterhood or motherhood alone. A
woman needs to be respected as an equal human being irrespective
of who she is. No strings attached.

∾

Epilogue

'Philosophers have only interpreted the world in various ways. The point, however, is to change it,' said Karl Marx.[1] Those words were inscribed on his grave later. India's opportunity to change itself and strive to change the world came at the time of its independence. Philosophers like Mahatma Gandhi, Sri Aurobindo and Deen Dayal Upadhyay had not only interpreted India, but had also laid out a roadmap for its future. Like David Ben Gurion in Israel and Mao Tse-tung in China, they too insisted that India chart its own distinct course as a nation and build a future that would not only make it great but also present an example to the rest of the world. Aurobindo went to the extent of calling it India's destiny.

Ben Gurion was clear that Israel would be a Jewish nation from the day of its foundation on 14 May 1948. For him, the Jewish past was 'the very being'. *Eretz Yisrael,* Hebrew for 'Land of Israel', Palestine, was the birthplace of the Jewish people. Their spiritual, religious and political identity was shaped here. It was here that they first attained statehood, created cultural values of national and universal significance, and gave to the world the eternal Book of Books. 'After being forcibly exiled from their land, the people kept faith with it throughout their Dispersion and never ceased to pray and hope for their return to it and for the restoration in it of their political freedom,' reads the Declaration of Independence.[2] Building a model to inspire all of humanity from the 'bare, besieged little land' on the Negev desert was, for him, the 'highest Jewish ideal'.

For Mao, the victory of the People's Liberation Army over the reactionary Kuomintang forces showed that the 'Chinese people have stood up'. Delivering his opening address at the First Plenary Session of the Chinese People's Political Consultative Committee (CPPCC), which is regarded as the Chinese Parliament, on 21 September 1949, Mao proclaimed that the Chinese have always been 'a great, courageous and industrious nation', and it had fallen behind only due to 'oppression and exploitation by foreign imperialism and domestic reactionary governments'. From now on, our nation will work courageously and industriously to foster its own civilization and well-being and, at the same time, to promote world peace and freedom. Ours will no longer be a nation subject to insult and humiliation. We have stood up,' he jubilantly told his countrymen.[3]

Having secured independence in 1947, India too embarked on its reconstruction around the time that Ben Gurion and Mao were engaged in building their newly freed nations into role models of their ancient civilisations. It had built a constitution like no other. In Ambedkar's own words, no other country's constitution 'could be found to be so bulky'.[4] But the point of departure for India's constitution was that India was not a nation, and hence, the constitution's primary responsibility was to build one. It did not take into much confidence its greatest philosophers of the time like Gandhi and Aurobindo. The belief that building a modern Indian nation needed the experience of the West guided the process of constitution making.

The makers of the Indian Constitution had, in their wisdom, decided to depend heavily on the American and the British models, while also trying to draw from constitutions of a few other countries like Canada and Australia. A functional constitution was inaugurated on 26 January 1950, and it has served the country for the last seven decades. Despite more than a hundred amendments, the constitution continues to serve the nation as its greatest unifier. India's successful democracy owes its existence fully to the constitution. The constitution has ensured, expect for the days of Emergency, smooth functioning of India's polity on the principles laid out in it.

Can and should the clock be turned back now? Do the ideas of philosophers like Deen Dayal even seem relevant today? Does Integral Humanism have a role to play in twenty-first century India and the world?

Ideas have a long shelf life. As Keynes observed, they keep shaping history. Marx and Engels had published their *Communist Manifesto* in 1848. The first communist government to implement it was Lenin's Soviet Union in 1917. Lenin did not adopt the Manifesto in toto. His was Leninism. Hundred years after the publication of the manifesto came the communist rule in China under the leadership of Mao. It turned out to be Maoism. Milton Friedman's twentieth-century capitalism is not a mirror image of the ideas of Adam Smith from the eighteenth century.

Ideas articulated by Deen Dayal, in his Integral Humanist philosophy, too can be interpreted, improved and adopted by successive generations. Not everything may be relevant in present times. For example, Deen Dayal's views on English may sound anachronistic today. Speaking about growing influence of English, Deen Dayal had said, 'Those who consider English to be the cause and instrument of Bharat's national consciousness seem to ignore the positive content of our nationalism. It appears that Macaulay's prediction has come true, and the English-educated people of Bharat have remained Bharatiya in name only. These people can neither realise the soul of Bharat, nor can they impel the people to strive for the attainment of any positive ideals. There will always be an unbridgeable gulf between the leaders and the led as long as English continues. It will result either in the people continuing to be inert with a feeling of suppression and subjugation or their rising in revolt against the leadership. Both these situations are not desirable for a peaceful, orderly and democratic development of the country. If we want to avert this catastrophe, we must replace English by Hindi and the regional languages as early as possible.'[5]

In the early years after attaining independence, there was an effort to promote Hindi as a national link language. It faced stiff resistance from some regions. The ruling establishment had developed cold feet and given up on the effort. As a result, English started playing an increasingly greater role in Indian polity. Can that be reversed? Can India develop a national language for itself, or at least a native link language? There do not seem to be any affirmative answers to these questions.

Countries like Turkey and Israel had addressed the question of language at the right moment in history—Turkey, immediately after it emerged from the Ottoman stranglehold in 1920, and Israel, on securing independence in 1948. Mustafa Kemal Ataturk replaced Arabic with Turkish as soon as he became the prime minister in 1920 and zealously implemented the new language policy. In Israel, David Ben Gurion made Hebrew the official language as soon as the new nation was born, and took language proficiency classes for himself.

In the case of both Turkey and Israel, as well as in many other nation-states in the West, language formed the core of the national identity. In India's case, multiplicity of languages had never been an impediment to its national life as all languages reflected the same civilisational and cultural ethos. Sanskrit, as the mother of almost all Indian languages, stood a chance of revival as the national language—*a la* Hebrew—at the time of independence. Efforts by Sanskrit enthusiasts continue to this day, but the road to its revival as India's lingua franca remains distant. Over the decades, English has been sufficiently Indianised with the creation of massive literature in that language. While it fails to reflect fully the nuances of Indian culture and civilisation as Indian languages can, it has nevertheless emerged as an important link language for a large number of Indians today.

Apart from the language question, there are many invaluable ideas in Deen Dayal's thesis that can find relevance and traction in contemporary polity. Integral Humanism broadly stands for decolonised nationalism, economic conservatism, political morality and decentralism, and social liberalism. These themes are as relevant today as they had been when they were articulated.

One significant fallout of those times was the inability of the Indian mind to decolonise itself. Ambedkar had talked about the dilemma of the members of the Drafting Committee of the constitution over whether to choose the American model completely or the British model. They ended up going for a mix of both systems. It led to a 'square peg in a round hole' situation.

Following the American model, India got a president-led executive and a dual polity with the states and centre having different sets of rights. But then, the constitution makers adopted the British parliamentary system for the legislature. There is a fundamental dissonance in governance between the US and British systems. In the American system, the three wings of governance—executive, legislature and judiciary—are independent and autonomous in functioning. The judicial autonomy in the American system is built into its constitution. But no such separation exists in the British parliamentary system. The UK did not have an independent supreme court until 2009. The House of Lords, the upper house of the British Parliament, used to act as the ultimate adjudicating authority. In effect, an independent judiciary did not exist in the UK.

There were a lot of discussions in the Constituent Assembly over the need for protecting judicial independence. Many members had advocated that the Indian Constitution explicitly declare separation of the three wings—legislature, executive and judiciary—on the lines of the US constitution. But the constitution did not talk about any such separation. Although the president appoints judges like in the US, the cabinet mandatorily guides them. As a consolation to members' demands, Ambedkar created 'single judiciary' for the country. The Supreme Court of India emerged as the pinnacle judicial institution with subordinate courts in three tiers.

In the last several decades, the judiciary has meticulously crafted an independent space for itself. It not only created a mechanism of 'in-breeding'—selection of judges through an internal collegium— but also unilaterally acquired powers of scrutiny over legislative and executive actions. There is backlash from the executive wing. Separation of the executive and legislature too does not exist in India. The executive is led by ministers who are elected members of either of the houses.

For the three wings of India's democratic polity to work effectively and autonomously, mature leadership is critical. Like individual morality, Ambedkar talked about constitutional morality. 'Constitutional morality is not a natural sentiment. It has to be cultivated. We must realise that our people have yet to learn it. Democracy in India is only a top-dressing on an Indian soil which is essentially undemocratic,' opined Ambedkar.[6]

Deen Dayal's life itself was a shining example of political morality. Morality and values are increasingly being obscured in politics. Many eminent persons, including those like Machiavelli and Lenin, concluded that morality has no place in politics. In his famous treatise on politics, *The Prince*, Machiavelli declared that 'politics have no relation to morals'.[7] Vladimir Lenin went a step further and stated, 'There are no morals in politics; there is only expedience. A scoundrel may be of use to us just because he is a scoundrel.'[8]

Deen Dayal viewed political decentralism and collective leadership as the basis of an ethical and moral political order. The coronavirus pandemic, that struck in early 2020 and ravaged the world for a couple of years, has led to political leaderships in many countries overcentralising power in the hands of the supreme leader. Democracies will face a challenge due to this.

Deen Dayal's idea of economic conservatism calls for returning the reins of the economy to citizens. Where such economic empowerment of citizens has happened, those countries have achieved good progress. From Antyodaya to Aatmanirbhar Bharat, all steps are in that direction. While fully supporting individual initiatives in the economic sphere, governments have to play a regulatory role to ensure that the fruits of development reach the last human.

GLOBAL GOVERNANCE

The global order created more than seven decades ago is weltering today under the unprecedented stress created by the COVID pandemic. A new world order is taking shape in the post-COVID era.

The challenge to global governance today comes from the decay of the very institutions created for that purpose some 75 years ago. When the charter of the founding of the United Nations was being signed on 26 June 1945, Harry Truman, who had just become the president of the United States of America, proclaimed, 'Oh! what a great day this can be in history!'[9] Like his predecessor of more than 25 years, President Woodrow Wilson, Truman also believed that the countries of the world would overcome differences and come together 'in one unshakable unity of determination—to a way to end wars'.[10]

Speaking at the United Nations General Assembly in 1950, Truman had said, 'The United Nations represents the idea of a universal morality, superior to the interests of individual nations. Its foundation does not rest upon power or privilege; it rests upon faith. They rest upon the faith of men in human values—upon the belief that men in every land hold the same high ideals and strive toward the same goals for peace and justice.'[11]

Those words sound hollow and hubristic today. Existing global institutions have failed to realise those ideas. Global governance needs new ideas and institutions to represent the reality of the twenty-first century. The new, post-COVID world order will put old agenda items like trade, commerce and defence on the backburner. In their place, issues like climate change, holistic healthcare, education for innovation and creativity, managing frontier technologies like artificial intelligence, robotics, blockchain and big data are going to gain centre stage. Securing human dignity and human rights in the newly evolving world order will be critical issues that need concerted deliberation. Deen Dayal's thoughts and ideas can act as lampposts in managing the agenda of the new world order. 'Human-centric' development, the key element of Integral Humanist thought, can become the sacred obligation of both national and global governance institutions.

'21st century world doesn't belong to globalists; it belongs to patriots,' proclaimed President Donald Trump at the United Nations in 2019.[12]

Instead, it should belong to Integral Humanists.

Notes

Preface

1. Krishnamurti, J., 1972, *You are the World*, Krishnamurti Foundation Trust, p. 5.
2. Berman, Morris, 1989, *Coming to Our Senses: Body and Spirit in the Hidden History of the West*, Simon and Schuster, p. 312.

1. Deen Dayal Upadhyay: The Man

1. John Kenneth Galbraith, 1999, *Name Dropping: From FDR On*, Houghton Mifflin Company, p. 132.
2. Bal Ram Nanda, 2008, *The Nehrus: Motilal and Jawaharlal*, Oxford India Paperbacks edition, Oxford University Press, pp. 42–43.
3. Shashi Tharoor, 2017, *Nehru: The Invention of India*, Skyhorse Publishing Inc., p. 365.
4. M.K. Gandhi, 1988, *The Complete Works of Mahatma Gandhi*, Vol. 98: 6 December 1947–30 January 1948, Gandhi Sevagram Ashram, https://www.gandhiashramsevagram.org/gandhi-literature/mahatma-gandhi-collected-works-volume-98.pdf, p. 333, accessed on 12 March 2021.
5. Kandarpa Ramachandra Rao, 1995, *Integral Humanism*, Sahitya Niketan, p. 97.
6. S. Gurumurthy, 2019, 'Modi did what Nehru wanted to, but couldn't, on Article 370', https://www.newindianexpress.com/opinions/columns/s-gurumurthy/2019/aug/07/modi-did-what-nehru-wanted-to-but-couldnt-on-article-370-2015302.html.

7. *Report on the First General Elections in India (1951-52)*, Vol. 1 (General), Election Commission of India, p. 94.

8. Ibid., p. 92.

9. https://deendayalupadhyay.org/jansh.html.

10. Kandarpa Ramachandra Rao, 1995, *Integral Humanism*, Sahitya Niketan, p. 93.

11. 'Annual Session of the Bharatiya Jana Sangh at Bombay—The General Secretary's Report', in Mahesh Chandra Sharma (ed.), 2019, *Complete Works of Pandit Deen Dayal Upadhyay*, Vol. 3, Prabhat Prakashan, p. 80.

12. Dr Mahesh Chandra Sharma, 2015, *Builders of Modern India: Pandit Deendayal Upadhyay*, Publications Division, Ministry of Information and Broadcasting, Government of India, p. 131.

13. Ibid.

14. Ibid., p. 157.

15. *Statistical Report on General Elections 1967 to the Fourth Lok Sabha*, Vol. 1 (National and State Abstracts & Detailed Results), Election Commission of India, p. 84.

16. 'Jansangh President', https://deendayalupadhyay.org/jansh_4.html, accessed on 12 March 2021.

17. Deendayal Upadhyay, Presidential Speech in Calicut on 28 December 1967.

2. Twentieth Century: 100 Years of Political Tumult

1. Isaiah Berlin, 1950, 'Political Ideas in the Twentieth Century', *Foreign Affairs*, Vol. 28, No. 3 (April), p. 351.

2. Gideon Rose, 2012, 'Making Modernity Work: The Reconciliation of Capitalism and Democracy', *Foreign Affairs*, Vol. 91, No. 1 (January/February), pp. 3–6.

3. Jill Lepore, 2019, 'A New Americanism: Why a Nation Needs a National Story', *Foreign Affairs*, March/April, https://www.foreignaffairs.com/articles/united-states/2019-02-05/new-americanism-nationalism-jill-lepore.

4. Michael O'Sullivan, 2019, *The Levelling: What's Next after Globalisation*, Public Affairs Hachette Book Group, p. 234.

5. Frederick Douglass, 1869, 'The Composite Nation', https://www. blackpast.org/african-american-history/1869-frederick-douglass-describes-composite-nation/, accessed on 23 March 2021.

6. Harold J. Laski, 1923, 'Lenin and Mussolini', *Foreign Affairs*, Vol. 2, No. 1 (September), pp. 43–54.

7. Anne Applebaum, 2020, *Twilight of Democracy: The Failure of Politics and the Parting of Friends*, Penguin Random House, p. 24.

8. Francis Fukuyama, 1989, 'The End of History?', *The National Interest*, No. 16 (Summer), pp. 3–18.

9. Kandarpa Ramchandra Rao, 1995, *Integral Humanism*, Sahitya Niketan, p. 62.

10. Sri Aurobindo, 1947, 'Karmayogin', *Complete Works of Sri Aurobino*, Vol. 8, Sri Aurobindo Ashram Trust, p. 245.

11. Theodore L. Shay, 1956, *The Legacy of the Lokmanya: The Political Philosophy of Bal Gangadhar Tilak*, Oxford University Press, p. 193.

12. Arnold Toynbee, 'India's Contribution to World Unity', in S.A. Vasudevan and M. Sathya Babu (eds), 1970, *Perspectives: Selections from Modern English Prose and Fiction*, Orient Longman, p. 23.

13. Kandarpa Ramchandra Rao, 1995, *Integral Humanism*, Sahitya Niketan, p. XXIX.

14. Bryan Teixeira, 1992, *A Gandhian Futurology*, The University of Michigan.

15. G.A. Natesan, 1934, 'Pandit Jawaharlal Nehru, Lahore—1929', *Congress Presidential Addresses: From the Silver to the Golden Jubilee*, G.A. Natesan & Co., p. 884.

16. M.K. Gandhi, 1924, 'My Path', *Young India, 1924–26*, p. 887.

17. R.K. Prabhu and U.R. Rao (eds), 1960, 'The Communist Creed', *Mind of Mahatma Gandhi*, Part IX, Navajivan Mudranalaya.

18. P.N. Chopra and Prabha Chopra, 2001, *Inside Story of Sardar Patel: The Diary of Maniben Patel*, Vision Books.

19. Elise Boulding, 2000, *Cultures of Peace: The Hidden Side of History*, Syracuse University Press, p. 40.

20. Gaurav Datt and Martin Ravallion, 2010, 'Shining for the Poor in India too?', *Economic and Political Weekly*, Vol. XLV, No. 7 (13 February), p. 56, Figs 1 and 2; *Economic Survey of India 1964–65*, Part II, Ministry of Finance, Government of India, p. 1.

21. Lok Sabha Debates, Third Series, Vol. XIX, No. 7, 13–23 August 1963, Lok Sabha Secretariat, New Delhi, p. 1852.

22. Arun Jaitley, 2018, 'On Dr. Syama Prasad Mookerjee's Anniversary—How Pt. Nehru's intolerance towards Dr. Mookerjee's views led to a Constitution Amendment Restricting Free Speech', https://www.arunjaitley.com/on-dr-syama-prasad-mookerjees-anniversary-how-pt-nehrus-intolerance-towards-dr-mookerjees-views-led-to-a-constitution-amendment-restricting-free-speech/.

23. Nayantara Sahgal (ed.), 2000, *Before Freedom: Nehru's Letters to his Sister 1909-1947*, HarperCollins.

24. Jawaharlal Nehru, 1941, *Towards Freedom: The Autobiography of Jawaharlal Nehru*, The John Day Company, p. 128.

25. Tathagata Roy, 2018, *Syama Prasad Mookerjee: Life and Times*, Penguin Viking.

26. Ibid.

27. Bharatiya Jana Sangh, *Bharatiya Jana Sangh 1951–1972: Principles and Policies, Manifestos and Constitution*, p. 49.

28. Deendayal Upadhyaya, 1962, 'Is this Nationalism?', *Political Diary*, 30 April.

29. Deen Dayal Upadhyaya, 1963, 'National Democrats Democratic Socialists & National Socialists', *Organiser*, Diwali issue.

30. Deen Dayal Upadhyaya, 1958, 'The Battle for the Cow Is the Battle for Freedom and Democracy', *Organiser*, 15 December.

31. Dr Mahesh Chandra Sharma (ed.), 2019, *Complete Works of Pandit Deendayal Upadhyaya*, Vol. 12, Prabhat Prakashan, New Delhi, p. 79.

32. 'The Emancipation Proclamation', accessed at National Archives by The U.S. National Archives and Record Administration, https://www.archives.gov/exhibits/featured-documents/emancipation-proclamation.

33. Dr Mahesh Chandra Sharma (ed.), 2019, *Complete Works of Pandit Deendayal Upadhyaya*, Vol. 9, Prabhat Prakashan, p. 166.

34. Deen Dayal Upadhyaya, 1960, 'The Rationale of Jana Sangh', *Organiser*, 23 January.

35. Ibid.

36. Ibid.

3. The Four Lectures

1. Sheri Berman, 2006, *The Primacy of Politics: Social Democracy and the Making of Europe's 20ᵗʰ Century*, Cambridge University Press, pp. 187–189.
2. Gideon Rose, 2012, 'Making Modernity Work: The Reconciliation of Capitalism and Democracy', *Foreign Affairs*, Vol. 91, No. 1 (January/February), pp. 3–6.
3. Daniel Bell, 1990, 'The End of Ideology in the West', in Jeffrey C. Alexander and Steve Seidman (eds), *Culture and Society: Contemporary Debates*, Cambridge University Press, p. 293.
4. Elise Boulding, 2000, *Cultures of Peace: The Hidden Side of History*, Syracuse University Press, p. 32.
5. Ibid., p. 5.
6. Joseph M. de Torre, 2001, 'Maritain's "Integral Humanism" and Catholic Social Teaching', in Timothy Fuller and John P. Hittinger (eds), *Reassessing the Liberal State: Reading Maritain's Man and the State*, American Maritain Association, p. 204.
7. Ibid.
8. Ibid.
9. Pope John Paul II, 1980, 'In the Work of Culture God has made an Alliance with Man, Rio de Janerio, 1 July.
10. N.K. Singh and A.P. Mishra, 2007, *Encyclopaedia of Oriental Philosophy and Religion: Christianity*, Vol. 12, Global Vision Publishing House, p. 402.
11. Deen Dayal Upadhyaya, 1965, 'First Lecture' (22 April), http://www.deendayalupadhyay.org/leacture9.html, accessed on 5 April 2021.
12. Ibid.
13. Ibid.
14. Mahesh Chandra Sharma, 2019, *Complete Works of Pandit Deendayal Upadhyay*, Vol. 12, Prabhat Prakashan.
15. Ibid.
16. Deen Dayal Upadhyaya, 1965, 'First Lecture' (22 April), http://www.deendayalupadhyay.org/leacture9.html, accessed on 5 April 2021.

17. Deen Dayal Upadhyaya, 1965, 'Second Lecture' (23 April), http://www.deendayalupadhyay.org/leacture2.html, accessed on 5 April 2021.

18. Ibid.

19. Ibid.

20. Ibid.

21. Ibid.

22. Ibid.

23. Ibid.

24. Vasant Raj Pandit, 2002, 'Integral Humanism: Lecture 2', Deendayal Research Institute, April, http://www.chitrakoot.org/download/IntegralHumanism.pdf.

25. Ibid.

26. Ibid.

27. Ibid.

28. Deen Dayal Upadhyaya, 1965, 'Third Lecture' (24 April), http://www.deendayalupadhyay.org/leacture3.html, accessed on 5 April 2021.

29. Vasant Raj Pandit, 2002, 'Integral Humanism: Lecture 3', Deendayal Research Institute, April, http://www.chitrakoot.org/download/IntegralHumanism.pdf.

30. Ibid.

31. Deen Dayal Upadhyaya, 1965, 'Third Lecture' (24 April), http://www.deendayalupadhyay.org/leacture3.html, accessed on 5 April 2021.

32. 'Major Theories to Explain: Why the Crowd Behaves in a Particular Way?', https://www.sociologydiscussion.com/theories/major-theories-to-explain-why-the-crowd-behaves-in-a-particular-way/2250.

33. Deen Dayal Upadhyaya, 1965, 'Third Lecture' (24 April), http://www.deendayalupadhyay.org/leacture3.html, accessed on 5 April 2021.

34. Swami Vivekananda, 2001 (Reprint), 'The Common Bases of Hinduism', *Complete Works of Swami Vivekananda*, Vol. III, Advaita Ashram.

35. Deen Dayal Upadhyaya, 1965, 'Third Lecture' (24 April), http://www.deendayalupadhyay.org/leacture3.html, accessed on 5 April 2021.

36. Ibid.

37. Ibid.

38. Ibid.

39. Ibid.

40. Ibid.

41. Ibid.

42. Vasant Raj Pandit, 2002, 'Integral Humanism: Lecture 3', Deendayal Research Institute, April, http://www.chitrakoot.org/download/IntegralHumanism.pdf.

43. Ibid.

44. Ibid.

45. Ibid.

46. Ibid.

47. Ibid.

48. Deen Dayal Upadhyaya, 1965, 'Fourth Lecture' (25 April), http://www.deendayalupadhyay.org/leacture4.html, accessed on 5 April 2021.

49. Ibid.

50. Ibid.

51. Ibid.

52. Ibid.

53. Ibid.

54. Ibid.

55. Ibid.

56. Ibid.

57. Ibid.

58. Vasant Raj Pandit, 2002, 'Integral Humanism: Lecture 4', Deendayal Research Institute, April, http://www.chitrakoot.org/download/IntegralHumanism.pdf.

59. Ibid.

60. Ibid.

61. Ibid.

62. Ibid.

63. Ibid.
64. Ibid.
65. Ibid.
66. Ibid.
67. Ibid.
68. Ibid.

4. Nationalism, Communism and Fascism in Twentieth-century Europe

1. Sudhakar Raje (ed.), 1972, *Pandit Deendayal Upadhyaya: A Profile*, Deendayal Research Institute.

2. Jill Lepore, 2019, *This America: The Case for the Nation*, Liveright Publishing Corporation, p. 11.

3. 'Act of Union 1707', UK Parliament, https://www.parliament.uk/about/living-heritage/evolutionofparliament/legislativescrutiny/act-of-union-1707/.

4. 'Origins of the Scottish Parliament', The Scottish Parliament, https://www.parliament.scot/about/history-of-the-scottish-parliament.

5. 'Scottish Independence Referendum', Government of United Kingdom, https://www.gov.uk/government/topical-events/scottish-independence-referendum/about.

6. Samuel P. Huntington, 2004, *Who Are We? The Challenges to America's National Identity*, Simon & Schuster, p. 4.

7. William R. Bowen Jr, 2021, 'The Rise of the Nation-States', Owlcation, 9 February, https://owlcation.com/humanities/nation-state.

8. Michael Howard, 1978, *War and Nation State*, Clarendon Press, p. 9.

9. Dani Rodrik, 2011, *The Globalisation Paradox: Why Global Markets, States, and Democracy Can't Coexist*, Oxford University Press.

10. Jean-Jacques Rousseau, 1762, *The Social Contract*, Book III.

11. Michel Seymour, 1999, 'On Redefining the Nation', *The Monist*, Vol. 82, No. 3 (July), pp. 411–445.

12. Isaiah Berlin, 1978, 'Nationalism: Past Neglect and Present Power', *Against the Current: Essays in the History of Ideas*, Princeton University Press, p. 431.

13. Ernest Gellner, 1964, *Thought and Change*, The University of Chicago Press, p. 168.

14. Benedict Anderson, 2016, *Imagined Communities: Reflections on the Origin and Spread of Nationalism*, Verso.

15. 'Fundamentals of Democracy', Deendayal Sansar—A Complete Deendayal Reader—A portal created by Dr Syama Prasad Mookerjee Research Foundation, https://deendayalupadhyay.org/demo.html.

16. Karl Marx and Friedrich Engels, *The Communist Manifesto*.

17. Helena Rosenblatt, 2018, *The Lost History of Liberalism: From Ancient Rome to the Twenty First Century*, Princeton University Press, p. 146.

18. Ibid., p. 259

19. The Communards were members and supporters of the short-lived 1871 Paris Commune formed in the wake of the French defeat in the Franco-Prussian War.

20. Harold J. Laski, 1923, 'Lenin and Mussolini', *Foreign Affairs*, Vol. 2, No. 1 (September), p. 50.

21. Ibid., p. 54.

5. *Rashtram*: The Indian Concept of Nationhood

1. Sir John Strachey, 1888, *India*, Kegan Paul, Trench & Co., London, p. 5.

2. 'Report of the Indian Statutory Commission—Volume 1—Survey', His Majesty's Stationary Office, London, p. 31.

3. Constituent Assembly of India Debates (Proceedings), Vol. IX, Parliament of India, 18 September 1949.

4. Constituent Assembly of India Debates (Proceedings), Vol. VII, Parliament of India, 8 November 1948.

5. Constituent Assembly of India Debates (Proceedings), Vol. VII, Parliament of India, 9 November 1948.

6. Constituent Assembly of India Debates (Proceedings), Vol. VII, Parliament of India, 8 November 1948.

7. Constituent Assembly of India Debates (Proceedings), Vol. VII, Parliament of India, 6 November 1948.

8. Constituent Assembly of India Debates (Proceedings), Vol. XI, Parliament of India, 25 November 1949.

9. Ibid.
10. Ibid.
11. Girilal Jain, 1998, *The Hindu Phenomenon*, South Asia Books.
12. Rabindranath Tagore, 1915, *Sadhana: The Realisation of Life*, The Macmillan Company, p. 6.
13. *The Complete Works of Sri Aurobindo: Volume 8, Karmayogin: Political Writings and Speeches, 1909–10*, Sri Aurobindo Ashram, Pondicherry, https://www.aurobindo.ru/workings/sa/02/0016_e.htm.
14. *The Complete Works of Sri Aurobindo: Volume 7, Part IV: Bande Matram under the Editorship of Sri Aurobindo* 28 May–22 December, Sri Aurobindo Ashram, Pondicherry, 2002.
15. Deen Dayal Upadhyaya, 1965, 'Third Lecture' (24 April), http://www.deendayalupadhyay.org/leacture3.html, accessed on 5 April 2021.
16. Dara Lind, 2014, 'Why Are You Supposed to Say "Next Year in Jerusalem"?', *Vox News*, https://www.vox.com/2014/8/5/18002034/why-are-you-supposed-to-say-next-year-in-jerusalem.
17. K. Raja Rao, 2005, *The Meaning of India*, Orient Paperbacks, p. 18.
18. Radhakumud Mookerji, 1914, *The Fundamental Unity of India*, Longmans, Green and Co., p. viii.
19. Deen Dayal Upadhyaya, 1965, 'Fourth Lecture' (25 April), http://www.deendayalupadhyay.org/leacture4.html, accessed on 5 April 2021.
20. 'State of the Union Message: Message from the President of the United States of America', US Government Printing Office, 1998, p. 2.
21. Dr Mahesh Chandra Sharma (ed.), 2019, *Complete Works of Pandit Deendayal Upadhyay*, Vol. 15, Prabhat Prakashan, pp. 16–17.
22. F. Max Müller, 1883, *India: What Can It Teach Us*: A Course of Lectures Delivered before the University of Cambridge, Funk & Wagnalls Publishers.

6. *Chiti*, the National Soul, and *Virat*, the National Life-Force

1. Gilbert Keith Chesterton, 1992, *What I Saw in America,* Kessinger Publishing LLC.

2. Ibid.

3. Ibid.

4. Samuel P. Huntington, 2004, *Who Are We? The Challenges to America's National Identity,* Simon & Schuster, p. 69.

5. John Micklethwait and Adrian Wooldridge, 2004, *The Right Nation: Why America is Different,* Penguin Books, p. 13.

6. *Complete Works of Sri Aurobindo, Volume 25,* 1997, Sri Aurobindo Ashram Trust, p. 35.

7. Corinne McLaughlin and Gordon Davidson, 2002, *The Soul of Nations,* Center for Visionary Leadership, http://www.visionarylead. org/soul-of-nations.html.

8. Sudhakar Raje (ed.), 1972, *Pandit Deendayal Upadhyay: A Profile,* Deendayal Research Institute.

9. Ezra Taft Benson, 1974, *God, Family, Country: Our Three Great Loyalties,* Deseret Book Co., p. 360.

10. Lawrence E. Harrison, 2006, *The Central Liberal Truth: How Politics Can Change a Culture and Save It From Itself,* Oxford University Press.

11. Woodrow Wilson, 1918, 'Woodrow Wilson: Fourteen Point Speech', https://kr.usembassy.gov/education-culture/infopedia-usa/ living-documents-american-history-democracy/woodrow-wilson-fourteen-points-speech-1918/.

12. Third Inaugural Address of Franklin D. Roosevelt, 20 January 1941, http://www.fdrlibrary.marist.edu/_resources/images/msf/ msf01411, accessed on 12 April 2021.

13. '9 Billion World Population by 2050', Population Research Bureau, https://www.prb.org/resources/9-billion-world-population-by-2050/.

14. Lawrence P. Harrison and Samuel P. Huntington (eds), 2000, *Culture Matters: How Values Shape Human Progress,* Basic Books, p. xix.

15. Ibid., p. xiii.
16. Swami Vivekananda, 1893, 'Address at the Parliament of Religions', *The Complete Works of Swami Vivekananda, Vol. 1*, Reprint, Advaita Ashram, 2001, p. 3.
17. Michael Wood, *Legacy: The Origin of Civilisations*, Episode 6, The Barbarian West.
18. Sister Nivedita, 1904, *The Web of Indian Life*, William Heinemann, p. 262.
19. Lionel Giles (tr.), 2009, *Sun Tzu's The Art of War*, Pax Linrorum Publishing House, p. 4.
20. Swami Krishnanda, 'A Study of the Bhagavad Gita: Chapter 2—The Background of the Bhagavad Gita', https://www.swami-krishnananda.org/gita1/bhagavadgita_02.html.
21. Dr Mahesh Chandra Sharma (ed.), 2019, *Complete Works of Deendayal Upadhyay*, Vol. 15, Prabhat Prakashan, p. 25.
22. 'Research—Man as a Social Animal', *The Hindu*, 12 March 2012, https://www.thehindu.com/features/education/research/man-as-a-social-animal/article2988145.ece.
23. Constituent Assembly of India Debate—Proceedings, Vol. VII, 4 November 1948, Parliament of India.
24. 'Speeches of Prime Minister Lal Bahadur Shastri', 9 June 1965, Publications Division, Ministry of Information and Broadcasting, Government of India, p. 9.
25. Winston Churchill, 1940, 'We Shall Fight on the Beaches', 4 June, https://winstonchurchill.org/resources/speeches/1940-the-finest-hour/we-shall-fight-on-the-beaches/.

7. Dharmic vs Semitic: Worldviews at Variance

1. 'Our Nationhood', *Deen Dayal Sansar—A Complete Deendayal Reader*, a portal created by Dr Syama Prasad Mookerjee Research Foundation, https://deendayalupadhyay.org/nationhood.html.
2. Rajiv Malhotra and Satyanarayana Dasa Babaji, 2020, *Sanskrit Non-Translatables: The Importance of Sanskritizing English*, Manjul Publishing House, p. xxxi.
3. Sudhakar Raje (ed.), 1972, *Pandit Deendayal Upadhyay: A Profile*, Deendayal Research Institute.

4. Dr Mahesh Chandra Sharma (ed.), 2019, *Complete Works of Deendayal Upadhyay*, Vol. 15, Prabhat Prakashan, p. 40.

5. R.K. Prabhu and U.R. Rao (comp. and eds), *The Mind of Mahatama Gandhi—Encyclopedia of Gandhi's Thoughts*, Navjivan Mudranalaya, p. 139.

6. *The Foundations of Indian Culture: And The Renaissance in India*, Sri Aurobindo Birth Centenary Library, Vol. 14, Sri Aurobindo Ashram, Pondicherry, 1972, p. 122

7. *Collins Dictionary*, accessed at https://www.collinsdictionary.com/dictionary/english/religion.

8. Lexico, powered by Oxford Dictionary, accessed at https://www.lexico.com/definition/Religion.

9. C.N. Shankar Rao, 2004, *Sociology of Indian Society*, S. Chand Ltd, p. 19.

10. *Manohar Joshi vs Nitin Bhaurao Patil & Anr, Supreme Court of India*, 11 December 1995.

11. *Dr Ramesh Yeshwant Prabhoo vs Shri Prabhakar Kashinath Kunte & ..., Supreme Court of India*, 11 December 1995, pp. 481–482.

12. Ibid., p. 799.

13. Kenan Malik, 2014, *The Quest for a Moral Compass: A Global History of Ethics*, Atlantic Books, p. 337.

14. Shimon Peres, 2017, *No Room for Small Dreams: Courage, Imagination and the Making of Modern Israel*, Weidenfeld & Nicolson, p. 174.

15. Janaki Abhisheki, 2005, *Religion as Knowledge: The Hindu Concept*, Akshaya Prakashan.

16. Ibid., p. 49.

17. Dr Mahesh Chandra Sharma (ed.), 2019, *Complete Works of Pandit Deendayal Upadhyay*, Vol. 12, Prabhat Prakashan, p. 76.

18. Sudhakar Raje (ed.), 1972, *Pandit Deendayal Upadhyay: A Profile*, Deendayal Research Institute.

19. Shloka: 'Shantiparva', *Mahabharata, Adhyaya 109, Shloka 10*; Translation: https://www.hindujagruti.org/hinduism/hindu-dharma/dharma.

20. https://www.hindujagruti.org/hinduism/hindu-dharma/dharma.

21. Valmiki Ramayana, *Aranya Kanda*, 8:26.

22. Swami Krishnananda, 'Isavasya Upanishad for Beginners', https://www.swami-krishnananda.org/isavasya/isavasya_1.html.

23. 'The Tenets and Philosophy of Sanatana Dharma', https://sanatanmission.com/tag/ekam-sat-vipra-bahudha-vadanti/.

24. K.V. Sundaram and Sudesh Nangia, 2010, *Development Concerns in the 21st Century*, Concept Publishing Company, p. 10.

25. S. Radhakrishnan, *The Hindu View of Life*, Unwin Paperbacks, p. 14.

26. Ibid., p. 16.

27. Ibid., p. 91.

28. Ayesha Mujahid, 2017, 'Abu Bakr and Uthman's Role in Preservation of Holy Quran', https://saudigazette.com.sa/article/512795.

29. 'Dharma and Religion', *Vedic Knowledge Online*, http://veda.wikidot.com/dharma-and-religion.

30. Charles Darwin, 1876, *The Origin of Species: By Means of Natural Selection or the Preservation of Favoured Races in the Struggle for Life*, Cambridge University Press, p. 50.

31. Deen Dayal Upadhyaya, 1965, 'Second Lecture' (23 April), http://www.deendayalupadhyay.org/leacture2.html, accessed on 5 April 2021.

32. Herbert Spencer, 1864, *Principles of Biology*, Williams and Norgate, p. 445.

33. 'Rights and Duties', *Comprehensive Gandhi Website* by Bombay Sarvodaya Mandal and Gandhi Research Foundation.

8. Institutions to Sustain Dharmic Social Order

1. Aristotle, 1962, *The Politics*, translated by T.A. Sinclair, Penguin Classics, p. 452, section 1337aI.

2. John Stuart Mill, 2006, *Collected Works of John Stuart Mill: Essays on Some Unsettled Questions of Political Economy*, Liberty Fund Inc., p. 326.

3. Alexander Spirkin, 1983, 'Man and Society', in *Dialectical Materialism*, Progress Publishers.

4. Deen Dayal Upadhyaya, 1965, 'Second Lecture' (23 April), http://www.deendayalupadhyay.org/leacture2.html, accessed on 5 April 2021.

5. Hsu Dau Lin, 1970–71, 'The Myth of the "Five Human Relations" of Confucius', *Monumenta Serica*, Vol. 29, Taylor & Francis Ltd., pp. 27–37.

6. *Svetasvatara Upanishad*, Chapter 2; Verse 5.

7. Kenan Malik, 2014, *The Quest for a Moral Compass: The Global History of Ethics*, Atlantic Books, p. 50.

8. Dr Mahesh Chandra Sharma (ed.), 2019, *Complete Works of Deendayal Upadhyay*, Prabhat Prakashan.

9. Ibid.

10. A.W. Geiger and Gretchen Livingston, 2019, '8 Facts about Love and Marriage in America', Pew Research Center, https://www.pewresearch.org/fact-tank/2019/02/13/8-facts-about-love-and-marriage/.

11. Joseph Dibona (ed.), 1983, *One Teacher, One School: The Adam Reports on Indigenous Education in 19th Century India*, Biblia Impex, p. x.

12. Subramanian Swamy, 2014, 'Freeing Temples from State Control', *The Hindu*, 20 January.

13. Ibid.

14. Ibid.

15. Dr Mahesh Chandra (ed.), 2019, *Complete Works of Deendayal Upadhyay*, Vol. 15, Prabhat Prakashan, p. 62.

16. M.K. Gandhi, 1955, *My Religion*, edited by Bharatan Kumarappa, Navjivan Mudranalaya, Ahmedabad, p. 169.

17. Dr Mahesh Chandra (ed.), 2019, *Complete Works of Deendayal Upadhyay*, Vol. 15, Prabhat Prakashan, 2019, p. 63.

18. Ibid.

19. Ibid., p. 74.

20. M.K. Gandhi, 1955, *My Religion*, edited by Bharatan Kumarappa, Navjivan Mudranalaya, p. 169.

21. Himanshu Roy and M.P. Singh, 2017, *Indian Political Thought: Themes and Thinkers*, Pearson, p. 304.

22. Dhananjay Keer, 1954, *Dr Ambedkar: Life and Mission*, Popular Prakashan, p. 267.

23. B.R. Ambedkar, 2014, *Annihilation of Caste: The Annotated Critical*

Edition, edited and annotated by S. Anand, Navayana Publishing Pvt Ltd, p. 424.

24. Balasaheb Deoras, 1974, 'Social Equality and Hindu Consolidation', *Suruchi Sahitya*, 8 May, http://www.archivesofrss.org/Speeches-and-articles.aspx.

25. M.K. Gandhi, *The Collected Works of Mahatama Gandhi*, Vol. 57: 5 Sep, 1932—15 Nov, 1932, Gandhi Sewagram Ashram, p. 95.

26. Jaithirth Rao, 2019, *The Indian Conservative: A History of Indian Right-Wing Thought*, Juggernaut Books, Chapter 4.

9. Integral Economic Vision and Programme

1. Swapan Dasgupta, 2019, 'How the Indian Right Views the Economy', 8 July, *Livemint*.

2. Ibid.

3. Hindol Sengupta, 2019, 'The Economic Mind of Narendra Modi', ORF Issue Brief No. 318, October, Observer Research Foundation.

4. 'Constitution and Rules', Bharatiya Janata Party, https://www.bjp.org/en/constitution.

5. Dr Hari Desai, 2018, 'Four Decades of BJP and Gandhian Socialism', *Asian Voice*, 2 April, https://www.asian-voice.com/Opinion/Columnists/Four-decades-of-BJP-and-Gandhian-Socialism.

6. Statement by Franklin D. Roosevelt, 29 June 1944, https://www.cvce.eu/content/publication/2003/12/12/051f8720-94b9-4aee-991b-901dd926a578/publishable_en.pdf.

7. Harry S. Truman, 1947, 'Address of the President to Congress, Recommending Assistance to Greece and Turkey', https://www.trumanlibrary.gov/library/research-files/address-president-congress-recommending-assistance-greece-and-turkey?documentid=NA&pagenumber=1.

8. Francis Fukuyama, 2012, 'The Future of History: Can Liberal Democracy Survive the Decline of the Middle Class?', *Foreign Affairs*, Vol. 91, No. 1 (January/February).

9. Ibid.

10. Sri Aurobindo, *Complete Works of Sri Aurobindo*, Vol. vi-vii, Part III, Sri Aurobindo Ashram Trust, pp. 203–204.

11. N.S. Gehlot (ed.), 1991, *The Congress Party in India: Policies, Culture, Performance*, Deep and Deep Publications, p. 102.
12. Sir Valentine Chirol, 1910, *Indian Unrest*, Macmillan and Co. Ltd, p. 88.
13. *Speeches of Bipin Chandra Pal (Delivered at Madras)*, 1907, Ganesh & Co., p. 90.
14. Brahmachari Rewachand Animananda, 1949, *The Blade: Life and Work of Brahmabandhab Upadhyay*, Roy and Son, p. 136.
15. Ibid.
16. M.K. Gandhi, *The Collected Works of Mahatma Gandhi*, Vol. 62: 1958–84, Publications Division, Government of India, Delhi, p. 241.
17. R.K. Prabhu and U.R. Rao (comp. and eds), 1966, *The Mind of Mahatma Gandhi*, Navjivan Mudranalaya, 1966, Ahmedabad, p. 332.
18. M.K. Gandhi, 1942, *Harijan*, Vol. 9, Ahmedabad, p. 238.
19. E.F. Schumacher, 2011, *Small Is Beautiful: A Study of Economics as if People Mattered*, Vintage Books, p. 169.
20. M.N. Srinivas and A.M. Shah, 1960, 'The Myth of Self Sufficiency of the Indian Village', *The Economic and Political Weekly*, 10 September, https://www.epw.in/system/files/pdf/1960_12/37/the_myth_of_selfsufficiency_of_the_indian_village.pdf.
21. Ibid.
22. M.N. Srinivas, 1987, 'The Indian Village: Myth and Reality', in *The Dominant Caste and Other Essays*, Oxford University Press, pp. 20–59.
23. M.K. Gandhi, 1968, *Selected Works of Mahatma Gandhi, Vol. V*, Navjivan Publishing House, p. 277.
24. M.K. Gandhi, 1946, *Harijan*, Vol. 10, No. 30, 1 September, Ahmedabad.
25. E.F. Schumacher, 2011, *Small is Beautiful: A Study of Economics as if People Mattered*, Vintage Books, p. 43.
26. M.K. Gandhi, *Speeches and Writings of MK Gandhi*, Third Edition, G.A. Natesan and Co., p. 273.
27. M.K. Gandhi, 1926, *Young India*, Vol. VIII, No. 24, 17 June, Ahmedabad.

28. M.K. Gandhi, 1940, *Harijan*, Vol. VIII, No. 29, *25* August, Poona.

29. *Complete Works of Swami Vivekananda*, Advaita Ashram, pp. 484–86.

30. Sundar Sarukkai, 2020, *JRD Tata and the Ethics of Philanthropy*, Taylor & Francis.

31. R.P. Mishra, *Rediscovering Gandhi*, Vol. I: Hind Swaraj-Gandhi's Challenges to Modern Civilization, Concept Publishing Company.

32. Ibid.

33. Constituent Assembly of India Debates (Proceedings), Vol. VII., 5 November 1948, Parliament of India.

34. Constituent Assembly of India Debates (Proceedings), Vol. VII., 6 November 1948, Parliament of India.

35. Constituent Assembly of India Debates (Proceedings), Vol. VII., 9 November 1948, Parliament of India.

36. Constituent Assembly of India Debates (Proceedings), Vol. VII., 4 November 1948, Parliament of India.

37. Ibid.

38. M.K. Gandhi, 1945, *The Collected Works of Mahatama Gandhi*, Vol. 88: 30 Aug, 1945–6 Dec, 1945, Gandhi Sewagram Ashram, p. 118.

39. Ibid.

40. Jawaharlal Nehru, 1945, *Selected Works of Mahatma Gandhi: Volume 4*, Section 1: Letters: From Jawaharlal Nehru, Gandhi Sewagram Ashram.

41. Ibid.

42. Gaurav Datt, 1998, 'Poverty in India and Indian States: An Update', *The Indian Journal of Labour Economics*, Vol. 41, No. 2, p. 194.

43. Dr Mahesh Chandra Sharma (ed.), 2019, *Complete Works of Deendayal Upadhyay*, Vol. 12, Prabhat Prakashan, p. 91.

44. Dr Mahesh Chandra Sharma (ed.), 2019, *Complete Works of Deendayal Upadhyay*, Vol. 15, Prabhat Prakashan, p. 57.

45. S.A. Kulkarni, 2014, *Pt. Deendayal Upadhyay Ideology & Perception—Part 4 – Integral Economic Policy*, Suruchi Prakashan, p. 79.

46. Deen Dayal Upadhyaya, 1965, 'Fourth Lecture', 25 April, http://www.deendayalupadhyay.org/leacture4.html, accessed on 5 April 2021.

47. S.A. Kulkarni, 2014, *Pandit Deendayal Upadhyay: Ideology and Perception—Part IV*, Suruchi Prakashan, p. 29.

48. Deendayal Upadhyay, 2014, *Political Diary*, Suruchi Prakashan, p. 49.

49. S.A. Kulkarni, 2014, *Pandit Deendayal Upadhyay: Ideology and Perception—Part IV*, Suruchi Prakashan, pp. 32–33.

50. Narendra Modi, 2020, 'What are the five pillars of a self reliant India?', https://www.narendramodi.in/what-are-the-five-pillars-of-a-self-reliant-india-read-to-find-out-more-549630.

51. Sanjay Baru, 2020, 'Self Reliance: Third Edition', *The Week*, 7 June.

52. Deen Dayal Upadhyay, 1961, 'The Third Plan X-Rayed', *Organiser*, 21 August, https://deendayalupadhyay.org/thirdplan.html, accessed on 24 April 2021.

53. Ibid.

54. https://www.financialexpress.com/archive/good-farm-growth-pulls-gdp-to-8.5-in-0304/122994/.

55. 'Government Has No Business To Be In Business, PM Modi Tells US investors', https://www.ndtv.com/business/government-has-no-business-being-in-business-pm-modi-tells-us-investors-673411.

56. 'English Rendering of Prime Minister Shri Narendra Modi's Address to the Nation on 12.05.2020', https://pib.gov.in/PressReleasePage.aspx?PRID=1623418.

57. Data Source: World Bank Data.

10. Democracy, with Popular Moral Authority

1. James Madison, 1788, 'Federalist No. 51—The Structure of the Government Must Furnish the Proper Checks and Balances between the Different Departments', Library of Congress, 8 February.

2. Mychal Denzel Smith, 2018, 'The Truth about the Moral Arc of Justice', *Huffpost*, 18 January, https://www.huffpost.com/entry/opinion-smith-obama-king_n_5a5903e0e4b04f3c55a252a4.

3. 'Pioneer of Democracy' Deendayal Sansar—A Complete Deendayal Reader, a portal created by Dr Syama Prasad Mookerjee Research Foundation, http://www.deendayalupadhyay.org/democracy.html.

4. Jawaharlal Nehru, 'Democracy', Indian National Congress, https://www.inc.in/our-values/democracy.

5. M.S. Golwalkar, 1966, *Bunch of Thoughts*, Sahitya Sindhu Prakashan, p. 26.

6. Matthew 22:21, https://www.biblegateway.com/passage/?search= Matthew+22%3A21&version=NRSV.

7. Sudhakar Raje (ed.), 1972, *Pandit Deendayal Upadhyay: A Profile*, Deendayal Research Institute.

8. Kandarpa Ramachandra Rao, 1995, *Integral Humanism*, Academy of Integral Humanism, p. 86.

9. 'Pioneer of Democracy' Deendayal Sansar—A Complete Deendayal Reader, a portal created by Dr Syama Prasad Mookerjee Research Foundation, http://www.deendayalupadhyay.org/democracy.html.

10. M.K. Gandhi, 1922, *Young India*, Vol. IV, No. 9, 2 March, p. 129.

11. M.K. Gandhi, 1922, *Young India*, Vol. IV, No. 4, 26 January, p. 54.

12. L.K. Advani, 2013, 'Churchillian Strategy for India, post independence', *Times of India*, 14 November, https://timesofindia. indiatimes.com/blogs/lkadvanis-blog/churchillian-strategy-for-india-post-independence/.

13. Durga Das (ed.), 1973, *Sardar Patel's Correspondence 1945–50— Volume VIII*, Navajivan Trust, p. 7.

14. John H. Kautsky, 1956, *Moscow and the Communist Party of India*, Wiley and MIT Press, New York and Boston, p. 80.

15. Constituent Assembly of India Debates (Proceedings)—Vol. I, 13 December 1946, Parliament of India.

16. Constituent Assembly of India Debates (Proceedings)—Vol. XI, 25 November 1949, Parliament of India.

17. Constituent Assembly of India Debates (Proceedings)—Vol. VII, 9 November 1948, Parliament of India.

18. 'Pioneer of Democracy' Deendayal Sansar—A Complete Deendayal Reader, a portal created by Dr Syama Prasad Mookerjee Research Foundation, http://www.deendayalupadhyay.org/democracy.html.

19. Ibid.

20. B. Shiva Rao, 1968, 'The Framing of India's Constitution—Select Documents Vol II', Advisory Committee Proceedings, Indian Institute of Public Administration, p. 248.

21. Constituent Assembly of India Debates (Proceedings)—Vol. VIII, 16 June 1949, Parliament of India.

22. Constituent Assembly of India Debates (Proceedings)—Vol. VII, 6 January 1949, Parliament of India.

23. Motilal Nehru, 1928, 'Nehru Report', https://www. constitutionofindia.net/historical_constitutions/nehru_report__ motilal_nehru_1928__1st%20January%201928.

24. Constituent Assembly of India Debates (Proceedings)—Vol. XI, 26 November 1949, Parliament of India.

25. M.K. Gandhi, 1937, *Harijan*, Vol. IV, No. 47, 2 January, Poona.

26. Constituent Assembly of India Debates (Proceedings)—Vol. XI, 25 November 1949, Parliament of India.

27. 'Inauguration Day Letter Obama Left for Trump', 2017, *CNN Politics*, Washington, 5 September.

28. Joseph Story, 1833, *Commentaries on the Constitution of the United States*, Vol. III, Hilliard, Gray and Company, p. 759.

29. Ibid.

30. Anne Applebaum, 2020, *The Twilight of Democracy: The Seductive Lure of Authoritarianism*, Penguin Random House, p. 14.

31. Alexander Hamilton, 1788, 'Federalist No. 68', 12 March 1788, https://founders.archives.gov/documents/Hamilton/01-04-02-0218.

32. Anne Applebaum, 2020, *The Twilight of Democracy: The Seductive Lure of Authoritarianism*, Penguin Random House, p. 14.

33. Ibid., p. 15.

34. 'Ronald Reagan Interview with Mike Wallace', available at Ronald Reagan Remembered, https://www.cbsnews.com/news/ronald-reagan-remembered/.

35. 'Pioneer of Democracy' Deendayal Sansar—A Complete Deendayal Reader, a portal created by Dr Syama Prasad Mookerjee Research Foundation, http://www.deendayalupadhyay.org/democracy.html.

36. Mahesh Chandra Sharma, 2017, *Pandit Deendayal Upadhyay: Builders of Modern India*, Publications Division, Ministry of Information and Broadcasting, Government of India, Delhi, 27 September.

37. Ibid., p. 70.

38. 'Pioneer of Democracy' Deendayal Sansar—A Complete Deendayal

Reader, a portal created by Dr Syama Prasad Mookerjee Research Foundation, https://deendayalupadhyay.org/democracy1.html.

39. Ibid.
40. Ibid.
41. Ibid.
42. Ibid.
43. Constituent Assembly of India Debates (Proceedings)—Vol. XI, 25 November 1949, Parliament of India.
44. Sudhakar Raje (ed.), 1972, *Pandit Deendayal Upadhyay—A Profile*, Deendayal Reserach Institute.

11. Identity as Ideology

1. Raje Sudhakar, 1972, *Pandit Deendayal Upadhyaya: A Profile*, Deendayal Research Institute.
2. Balraj Madhok, 1970, *Indianisation*, Hind Pocket Books, p. 33.
3. M.S. Golwalkar, 1966, *Bunch of Thoughts*, Sahitya Sindhu Prakashan, p. 494.
4. 'History of Europe', *Encyclopedia Britannica*, https://www. britannica.com/topic/history-of-Europe/Cultural-nationalism, accessed on 29 April 2021.
5. Deendayal Upadhyaya, 2009, *Integral Humanism: An Analysis of Some Basic Elements*, Prabhat Prakashan.
6. Conrad Hackett, 2017, '5 Facts about the Muslim Population in Europe', Pew Research Center, https://www.pewresearch.org/fact-tank/2017/11/29/5-facts-about-the-muslim-population-in-europe/.
7. Alan Greenblatt, 2011, 'Arab Refugees Finding Harsh Welcome in Europe', National Public Radio, https://www.npr. org/2011/03/18/134622556/arab-refugees-encounter-harsh-welcome-by-some.
8. 'Europe and Right Wing Nationalism: A Country-by-Country Guide', BBC News, https://www.bbc.com/news/world-europe-36130006.
9. Ibid.
10. Ibid.
11. Koen Damhuis, 2019, 'The Biggest Problem in the Netherlands: Understanding the Party for Freedom's Politicization of Islam',

Brookings, 24 July, https://www.brookings.edu/research/the-biggest-problem-in-the-netherlands-understanding-the-party-for-freedoms-politicization-of-islam/.

12. 'Europe and Right Wing Nationalism: A Country-by-Country Guide', BBC News, https://www.bbc.com/news/world-europe- 36130006.

13. Ibid.

14. Riazat Butt, 2008, 'Archbishop Backs Sharia Law for British Muslims', *The Guardian*, 7 February, https://www.theguardian.com/uk/2008/feb/07/religion.world.

15. Rick Noack, 2015, 'Multiculturalism is a Sham, Says Angela Merkel', *The Washington Post*, 14 December, https://www.washingtonpost.com/news/worldviews/wp/2015/12/14/angela-merkel-multiculturalism-is-a-sham/.

16. Ben Smith, 2020, 'The President vs. The American Media', *The New York Times*, 15 November, https://www.nytimes.com/2020/11/15/business/media/macron-france-terrorism-american-islam.html.

17. Ajay Kamalakaran, 2013, 'The Iron Lady and the Iron Curtain', *Russia Beyond*, 9 April, https://www.rbth.com/blogs/2013/04/09/the_iron_lady_and_the_iron_curtain_23667.

18. Swami Vivekananda, 2001, 'The Common Bases of Hinduism', *The Complete Works of Swami Vivekananda, Vol. III*, Reprint edition, Advaita Ashram, Calcutta, p. 371.

19. C.P. Bhishikar, 1991, *Pandit Deendayal Upadhyay—Ideology and Perception—Part V—Concept of Rashtra*, Suruchi Prakashan, p. 121.

20. Max Weber, 1992, *The Protestant Ethic and the Spirit of Capitalism*, translated by Talcott Parsons, Routledge.

21. Devendra Swarup (ed.), 1986, *Politics of Conversion*, Deendayal Research Institute.

22. Justin McCarthy, 1881, *A History of Our Own Times, Volume III*, Chatto & Windus, p. 46.

23. Vinayak Damodar Savarkar, 1909, *The Indian War of Independence 1857*, Karnatak Printing Press, pp. 11, 38, 76, 113.

24. Latif Ahmed Sherwani (compiler and editor), 1977, *Speeches, Writings and Statements of Iqbal*, Iqbal Academy, pp. 3–26.

25. Address by Quaid-i-Azam Mohammad Ali Jinnah at Lahore Session

of Muslim League, Directorate of Films and Publishing, Ministry of Information and Broadcasting, Government of Pakistan, Islamabad, 1983.

26. Constituent Assembly of India Debates (Proceedings)—Vol. IX, 11 August 1949, Parliament of India.

27. Constituent Assembly of India Debates (Proceedings)—Vol. V, 14 August 1947, Parliament of India.

28. Constituent Assembly of India Debates (Proceedings)—Vol. V, 15 August 1947, Parliament of India.

29. M.K. Gandhi, *The Complete Works of Mahatama Gandhi*, Vol. 95: April 30, 1947—July 6, 1947, Gandhi Sevagram Ashram, p. 252, https://www.gandhiashramsevagram.org/gandhi-literature/mahatma-gandhi-collected-works-volume-95.pdf, accessed on 29 April 2021.

30. M.K. Gandhi, *Hind Swaraj or Indian Home Rule*, Navajivan Publishing House.

31. *Independence and After: A Collection of the More Important Speeches of Jawaharlal Nehru from September 1946 to May 1949*, Publications Division, India, p. 121.

32. Dhananjay Keer, 1966, *Veer Savarkar*, Popular Prakashan, p. 313.

33. Subbarao Prabhala, 2015, 'The British PM Who Oversaw India's Independence', *Outlook India*, 24 August, https://www.outlookindia.com/website/story/the-british-pm-who-oversaw-indias-independence/295156.

34. *Dr Syama Prasad Mookerjee: A Selfless Patriot*, Dr Syama Prasad Mookerjee Research Foundation, p. 28.

35. B.R. Ambedkar, 2013, *Pakistan or the Partition of India*, Samayak Prakashan.

36. Aravindan Neelakandan, 2016, 'The Vedic—Harappan Legacy of the Word Hindu', *Swarajya*, https://swarajyamag.com/culture/the-vedic-harappan-legacy-of-the-word-hindu.

37. Ibid.

38. Mohan Bhagwat, 'Bharat of Future—An RSS Perspective (Day 2)', https://www.rss.org//Encyc/2018/9/19/Bharat-of-Future-An-RSS-Perspective-day-2-mohanji-bhagwaat.html, accessed on 29 April 2021.

39. Ibid.
40. Ibid.
41. Ibid.
42. Ibid.
43. S. Radhakrishnan, *The Hindu View of Life*, Unwin Paperbacks, p. 17.
44. Rakesh Sinha, 2020, 'Every Word Masked with "Hindutva" Is Not the View of the RSS', *Indian Express*, 3 November, https://indianexpress.com/article/opinion/columns/hindutva-rss-on-hinduness-vijayadashami-function-mohan-bhagwat-6915391/.
45. Mohan Bhagwat, 'Bharat of Future—An RSS Perspective (Day 2)'.
46. M.K. Gandhi, 1946, *Harijan*, Vol. X, No. 13 (5 May), Ahmedabad.
47. M.K. Gandhi, 1947, *Harijan*, Vol. XI, No. 38 (19 October), Ahmedabad.
48. Constituent Assembly of India Debates (Proceedings)—Vol. VIII, 25 May 1949, Parliament of India.
49. Constituent Assembly of India Debates (Proceedings)—Vol. VII, 27 December 1948, Parliament of India.
50. G.J. Holyoake, *The Origin and Nature of Secularism*, Watts and Co., p. 51.
51. Sanjeev Sanyal, 2015, 'Ashoka, the Not So Great', *Swarajya*, https://swarajyamag.com/culture/ashoka-the-not-so-great.
52. Deendayal Upadhyay, 2016, 'Politics in India', *Kamal Sandesh*, reprinted, 16–29 February, p. 12, http://www.kamalsandesh.org/wp-content/uploads/2016/02/KS-E-Feb-2-2016.pdf.

12. Symbols of Cultural Integration 1: The Ram Janm Bhumi

1. Judgement of the Supreme Court of India in *Bramchari Sidheswar Bhai vs State of West Bengal Etc.*, 2 July 1995, https://indiankanoon.org/doc/967081/, accessed on 30 April 2021.
2. Constituent Assembly of India Debates (Proceedings)—Vol. VII, 4 November 1948, Parliament of India.
3. Ibid.
4. Constituent Assembly of India Debates (Proceedings)—Vol. VII, 5 November 1948, Parliament of India.

5. Ibid.

6. Constituent Assembly of India Debates (Proceedings)—Vol. VII, 9 November 1948, Parliament of India.

7. Ibid.

8. Ibid.

9. Ibid.

10. Constituent Assembly of India Debates (Proceedings)—Vol. VII, 6 November 1948, Parliament of India.

11. Justice Y. Chandrachud, *Mohd. Ahmed Khan vs Shah Bano Begum And Ors*, 23 April 1985, Supreme Court of India, accessed at https://indiankanoon.org/doc/823221/.

12. Judgement of the Supreme Court of India in *M Siddiq (D) Thr Lrs vs Mahant Suresh Das & Ors*, 9 November 2019, https://indiankanoon.org/doc/107745042/, accessed on 30 April 2021.

13. Ibid.

14. Judgement of the Supreme Court of India in *Sastri Yagnapurushad Ji And …. vs Muldas Brudardas Vaishya And ….* , 14 January 1966, https://indiankanoon.org/doc/145565/.

15. V.S. Naipaul's interview to Sadanand Menon, 1998, *The Hindu*, 5 July.

16. Arnold Toynbee, 1960, *One World and India*, Indian Council for Cultural Relations.

17. Durga Das, 1969, *India: From Curzon to Nehru and After*, Collins Clear Type Press, p. 331.

18. *Speeches of President Rajendra Prasad*, Director, The Publications Division, Old Secretariat, Delhi, April 1957, pp. 242–244.

19. Ibid.

20. 'Press Conference Addressed by Sarsanghchalak Ji after Shri Ramjanmabhoomi judgement', https://www.rss.org//Encyc/2019/11/9/RSS-press-conference-after-ramjanmabhoomi-judgement.html.

21. 'Text of Prime Minister Narendra Modi's Speech at Ayodhya', https://www.narendramodi.in/text-of-prime-minister-narendra-modi-s-speech-at-bhoomi-pujan-ceremony-of-shree-ram-janmabhoomi-mandir-in-ayodhya-uttar-pradesh-550821, accessed on 30 April 2021.

22. Swami Chinmayanand's interview to Ram Madhav, July 1993, https://www.rammadhav.in/articles/pujya-swami-chinmayanandas-interview-to-shri-ram-madhav-taken-in-january-1993/, accessed on 30 April 2021.

23. Eugen Weber, 1976, *Peasants into Frenchmen: The Modernisation of Rural France, 1870-1914*, Stanford University Press.

24. Abigail Jacobson, 2011, *From Empire to Empire: Jerusalem between Ottoman and British Rule*, Syracuse University Press, p. 8.

25. Robert P. Goldman (tr.), 1984, *The Ramayana of Valmiki—An Epic of Ancient India—Volume I—Balakanda*, Princeton University Press, p. 3.

26. L.K. Advani, 2008, 'Rama: An Inspiring Symbol of Indian Culture', *The Week*, 23 January.

27. Ibid.

28. Kenan Malik, 2014, *The Quest for a Moral Compass: A Global History of Ethics,* Atlantic Books Ltd, p. 73.

29. Dilip Mandal, 2020, 'Whose Ram Rajya Does Ayodhya—Gandhi's or Modi's? Ambedkar Can Answer', *The Print,* https://theprint.in/opinion/ram-rajya-ayodhya-bhoomi-pujan-temple-gandhi-modi-ambedkar/475024/.

30. B.R. Ambedkar, 2014, *Annihilation of Caste: The Annotated Critical Edition*, edited and annotated by S. Anand, Navayana Publishing Pvt. Ltd, p. 406.

31. B.R. Ambedkar, 2016, *Riddles in Hinduism: The Annotated Critical Edition*, edited and annotated by S. Anand and Shobhna Iyer, Navayana Publishing, p. 226.

32. Friedrich Wilhelm Nietzsche, 1888, *The Antichrist.*

33. M.K. Gandhi, 1937, *Harijan*, Vol. IV, No. 47, 2 January, Poona.

34. B.K. Kelkar, *Pt. Deendayal Upadhyay Ideology and Perception—Part III*, Suruchi Prakashan, p. 4.

35. L.K. Advani, 2008, 'Rama: An Inspiring Symbol of Indian Culture', *The Week*, 23 January.

36. 'An Area of Awakening', V.S Naipaul's interview to Dilip Padgaonkar, 1993, *Times of India*, 18 July.

37. Ibid.

38. Nirad Chaudhari's interview to Dilip Padgaonkar, 1993, *Times of India*, 8 August.

39. William Dalrymple, 2008, 'Masterpiece of Religious Art on Show', *Dawn*, 26 August, https://www.dawn.com/news/416462/a-masterpiece-of-religious-art-on-show.

13. Symbols of Cultural Integration 2: Akhand Bharat, Kashmir

1. Justice P.N. Bhagwati's Judgement in *Dr Pradeep Jain vs Union of India and Ors.*

2. Sudhakar Raje (ed.), 1972, *Pandit Deendayal Upadhyay: A Profile*, Deendayal Research Institute.

3. 'A Declaration by the Mother', 25 April 1954, http://savitri.in/blogs/light-of-supreme/a-declaration-by-the-mother-dated-25-april-1954.

4. M.K. Singh, (ed.), 2009, *Encyclopedia of Indian War of Independence, 1857-1947: Revolutionary Phase: Lala Hardayal, Ajit Singh, Ramprasad Bismil and Ras Bihari Bose*, Anmol Publications, p. 111.

5. Dev Prana, 2010, *Spiritual Quest of a Baby Yogi: Journey Through Islam, Christianity, and Beyond*, iUniverse.

6. Will Durant, 1930, *The Case for India*, Simon and Schuster, p. 4.

7. 'Inaugural Address of the President of the United States on Fourth of March 1861', Senate Exec. Doc No. 1, 8 March 1861, p. 10.

8. 'Akhand Bharat', Deendayal Sansar—A Complete Deendayal Reader, A portal created by Dr Syama Prasad Mookerjee Research Foundation, https://www.deendayalupadhyay.org/bharat.html.

9. Ibid.

10. Ibid.

11. Ibid.

12. M.S. Golwalkar, 1966, *Bunch of Thoughts*, Sahitya Sindhu Prakashan, p. 93.

13. Helmut Josef Michael Kohl, who served as the chancellor of Germany from 1982 to 1998 (West Germany from 1982 to 1990 and reunified Germany from 1990 to 1998).

14. 'Excerpt from the Conversation between Mikhail Gorbachev and

British Prime Minister Margaret Thatcher, September 23, 1989', https://www.margaretthatcher.org/document/112005.

15. Leonard Mosley, 1960, *The Last Days of the British Raj*, Jaico Publishing House, p. 285.

16. Ayesha Jalal, 2013, *The Pity of Partition: Manto's Life, Times and Work across the India-Pakistan Divide*, Princeton University Press, p. 12.

17. Ibid., p. 3.

18. L.K. Advani, 2008, *My Country My Life*, Rupa & Co., p. 147.

19. Abhinavagupta, 1989, *A Trident of Wisdom: Translation of Paratrisika-Vivarama*, translated by Jaidev Singh, State University of New York Press, p. ix.

20. *Vishnu-Purana*, Book II, Chapter 3, Verse 1, p. 151.

21. Constituent Assembly of India Debates (Proceedings)—Vol. V, 20 August 1947, Parliament of India.

22. A.G. Noorani, 2011, *Article 370: A Constitutional History of Jammu and Kashmir*, Oxford University Press.

23. 'Kashmir: A True Story', Ministry of External Affairs, Government of India.

24. Durga Das (ed.), 1973, *Sardar Patel's Correspondence 1945–50, Vol. I*, Navajivan Trust, p. 121.

25. Ibid., p. 304.

26. Hindol Sengupta, 2018, 'No, Sardar Vallabhbhai Patel was Not the Architect of Article 370', https://medium.com/@hindolsengupta/no-sardar-vallabhbhai-patel-was-not-the-architect-of-article-370-975b3c5e0d8a.

27. Durga Das (ed.), 1973, *Sardar Patel's Correspondence 1945–50, Vol. I*, Navajivan Trust, p. 310.

28. V. Shankar, 1974, *My Reminiscences of Sardar Patel—Volume II*, The Macmillan Company of India Ltd, p. 63.

29. Maj. Gen Sheru Thapliyal, 2011, 'Article 370: The Untold Story', *Indian Defence Review*, Vol. 26 (Jan–Mar), http://www.indiandefencereview.com/news/article-370-the-untold-story/.

30. Constituent Assembly of India Debates (Proceedings)—Vol. VIII, 27 May 1949, Parliament of India.

31. Constituent Assembly of India Debates (Proceedings)—Volume X, 17 October 1949, Parliament of India.

32. Ibid.

33. Ibid.

34. B.N. Mullik, 1971, *My Years with Nehru-Kashmir*, Allied Publishers, pp. 29–30.

35. *Lok Sabha Debates*, Third Series, No. 8, 27 November 1963, Parliament of India.

36. 'Article 370 is a Curse on People of Jammu and Kashmir—MP from Jammu Kashmir in Parliament Debate on Article 370 in 1964', https://www.jammukashmirnow.com/Encyc/2019/8/22/Artcile-370-is-Curse-on-people-of-Jammu-kashmir-MP-from-Jammu-kashmir-1964-Parliament-Debate-on-Article-370.amp.html.

37. Ibid.

38. Ibid.

39. Deendayal Upadhyay, 1960, *Organiser Weekly*.

40. Ibid.

41. Ibid.

42. M.K. Gandhi, 1946, *Young India*, Vol. 111, No. 40, 6 October 1921, Ahmedabad.

43. Constituent Assembly of India Debates (Proceedings)—Vol. VII, Statement by Pandit Thakur Das Bhargava, 24 November 1948, Parliament of India.

44. Deen Dayal Upadhyaya, 1958, 'The Battle for the Cow Is the Battle for Freedom and Democracy', *Organiser*, 15 December.

45. Neelkandan Aravindan, 2015, 'Hindutva and the Politics of Beef', *Swarajya*, 30 October.

46. Sudhakar Raje (ed.), 1972, *Pandit Deendayal Upadhyay: A Profile*, Deendayal Research Institute.

47. Ibid.

14. Human Dignity and Human Rights

1. Kenan Malik, 2014, *The Quest for a Moral Compass: A Global History of Ethics*, Atlantic Books Ltd, p. 5.

2. Ibid., p. 22.

3. Ibid., p. 25.
4. Genesis 1:26, https://biblehub.com/genesis/1-26.htm.
5. Voltaire, 1769, *God and Human Beings.*
6. Ben Shapiro, 2019, *The Right Side of History: How Reason and Moral Purpose Made the West Great*, Broadside Books, p. 63.
7. 'Creating the Declaration of Independence', Library of Congress, https://www.loc.gov/exhibits/creating-the-united-states/interactives/declaration-of-independence/pursuit/index.html.
8. Ben Shapiro, 2019, *The Right Side of History: How Reason and Moral Purpose Made the West Great*, Broadside Books, p. 114.
9. George Orwell, 1940, 'Review of *Mein Kampf* by Adolf Hitler'.
10. Isaiah Berlin, 1950, 'Political Ideas in the Twentieth Century', *Foreign Affairs*, Vol. 28, No. 3 (April), p. 365.
11. Frank Dikotter, 'The Great Leap Backward', http://www.frankdikotter.com/start-reading/the-great-leap-backward.html.
12. 'Message to Congress … 1941', Franklin D. Roosevelt Presidential Library and Museum, https://www.fdrlibrary.org/documents/356632/390886/readingcopy.pdf/42234a77-8127-4015-95af-bcf831db311d.
13. Raghav Iyer (ed.), 2000, *The Moral and Political Writings of Mahatama Gandhi Vol. III*, Clarendon Press Oxford, p. 492.
14. Ibid.
15. Miloon Kothari, 'India's Contribution to the Universal Declaration of Human Rights'.
16. 'Rights and Duties', Comprehensive Gandhi Website by Bombay Sarvodaya Mandal and Gandhi Research Foundation, https://www.mkgandhi.org/thiswasbapu/134rightsandduties.htm.
17. Contribution from S.V. Puntambekar, 'The Hindu Concept of Human Freedoms', *The UNESCO Courier*, https://en.unesco.org/courier/2018-4/hindu-concept-human-freedoms.
18. Minoo Masani (1905–1998) was a founder member of the Swatantra Party. He served as a member of the Constituent Assembly of India and later as a member of Parliament between 1963 and 1971. He was India's representative to the UN Sub-Commission on Minorities and also served as India's ambassador to Brazil in 1948, for a year.

19. Lakshmi Menon was an elected Member of the Rajya Sabha in 1952, 1954 and 1960 and also Minister of State for External Affairs (Independent Charge) in the cabinets of Pandit Jawaharlal Nehru and Shri Lal Bahadur Shastri. In 1948 and 1950, she was nominated as a member of the Indian delegation to the UN and nominated to the Committee on Status of Women (CSW) at the UN. She was also the head of the Indian delegation to UNGA.

20. Miloon Kothari, 'India's Contribution to the Universal Declaration of Human Rights'.

21. Debate on 'Draft International Declaration on Human Rights' at Ninety Ninth meeting held at Palais de Chaillot, Paris on Monday, 11 October 1948, https://documents-dds-ny.un.org/doc/UNDOC/GEN/NL4/804/40/PDF/NL480440.pdf?OpenElement.

22. Miloon Kothari, 'India's Contribution to the Universal Declaration of Human Rights'.

23. Judgement of the Supreme Court of India in *Maneka Gandhi vs Union of Bharat*, 25 January 1978, https://indiankanoon.org/doc/1766147/.

24. Swami Vivekananda, 2001, 'Raja Yoga' *The Complete Works of Swami Vivekananda, Vol. 1*, reprint edition, Advaita Ashram, p. 124.

25. Evelyn Beatrice Hall, 1906, *The Friends of Voltaire*, Smith, Elder & Co., p. 199.

26. 'Fundamentals of Democracy', Deendayal Sansar—A Complete Deendayal Reader, A portal created by Dr Syama Prasad Mookerjee Research Foundation, https://deendayalupadhyay.org/demo.html.

27. Swami Madhavananda, *The Brihadaranyaka Upanishad*, Advaita Ashram, pp. 336–337.

28. Sent-ts'an 'Hsin Hsin Ming'.

29. Kenan Malik, 2014, *The Quest for a Moral Compass: A Global History of Ethics*, Atlantic Books Ltd, p. 48.

30. Ibid., p. 45.

31. *Atharva Veda—Samjnana Sukta*.

32. Justice Dr M. Rama Jois, *Human Rights and Bharatiya Values*, Bharatiya Vidya Bhavan.

33. M. Rama Jois, *Guruji and Social Harmony*, Sri Guruji Janm Shatabdi Samiti, Karnataka.

34. Kenan Malik, 2014, *The Quest for a Moral Compass: A Global History of Ethics*, Atlantic Books Ltd, p. 57.
35. Swami Jitatmananda, 1985, *Swami Vivekananda—Prophet and Pathfinder*, Sri Ramakrishna Math.
36. Subhash Kashyap, 2007, *Understanding Bharat—Relevance of Hinduism*.
37. Dharma Kosha, '*Narada Smriti*'.
38. 'Fundamentals of Democracy', Deendayal Sansar—A Complete Deendayal Reader, a portal created by Dr Syama Prasad Mookerjee Research Foundation, https://deendayalupadhyay.org/demo.html.
39. Swami Jitatmananda, *Modern Physics and Vedanta*, Sri Ramakrishna Ashrama, Rajkot.
40. Harbilas Sharda, 'Hindu Superiority'.
41. Deen Dayal Upadhyaya, 1965, 'Second Lecture' (23 April), http://www.deendayalupadhyay.org/leacture2.html, accessed on 5 April 2021.
42. S.D. Sharma, 1988, *Administration of Justice in Ancient Bharat*.
43. *Rig Veda,* Mandala-5, Sukta-60, Mantra-5.
44. Sunil Deshta and Partap Singh, 2004, *Human Rights in India: Enforcement, Protection and Implementation*, Allahabad Law Agency, p. 11.
45. *Rig Veda*, Mandala-10, Sukta-191, Mantra-4.
46. Justice Dr M. Rama Jois, 'Text of Speech at Tenth Durga Das Basu Memorial Lecture on Uniform Law regulating the Constitution and Organisation of High Courts Necessary', The WB National University of Juridical Sciences, Kolkata, https://www.nujs.edu/news/10thddbasumemorial-lecture.pdf.
47. Constituent Assembly of India Debates (Proceedings)—Vol. XI, 25 November 1949, Parliament of India.
48. Kenan Malik, 2014, *The Quest for a Moral Compass: A Global History of Ethics*, Atlantic Books Ltd, p. 25.
49. Harbilas Sharda, 'Hindu Superiority'.
50. Swami Vivekananda, 2001, 'The Future of India', *Complete Works of Swami Vivekananda Vol. III*, reprint edition, Advaita Ashram, p. 294.

51. Swami Vivekananda, 2001, 'Notes Taken Down in Madras', *Complete Works of Swami Vivekananda Vol. VI*, reprint edition, Advaita Ashram, p. 115.

52. 'Social Equality and Hindu Consolidation: A Speech by Shri Balasaheb Deoras', http://www.archivesofrss.org/Speeches-and-articles.aspx, accessed on 18 April 2021.

53. Swami Vivekananda, 2001, 'The Future of India', *Complete Works of Swami Vivekananda Vol. III*, reprint edition, Advaita Ashram, p. 291.

54. Lord Alfred Tennyson, '*Morte d'Arthur*'.

15. Womanhood in Western and Indic Traditions

1. Swami Vivekananda, 2001, 'Epistles—Second Edition', *Complete Works of Swami Vivekananda Vol. VI*, reprint edition, Advaita Ashram, p. 328.

2. Herbert Spencer, 1950, *Social Statistics,* Robert Schalkenbach Foundation.

3. Harbilas Sharda, 1917, *Hindu Superiority*, p. 81.

4. Wang, Robin, 2003, *Images of Women in Chinese Thought and Culture*, Hackett Publishing Company, pp. 2–3.

5. Alfred J. Andrea and James H. Overfield, 1994, *The Human Record: Sources of Global History*, Vol. 1, Houghton Mifflin.

6. Bret Hinsch, 1998, 'Women, Kinship and Property as Seen in a Han Dynasty Will', *T'oung Pao*, Vol. 84, No. 1, https://www.jstor.org/stable/4528735.

7. Bella Vivante, 1999, *Women's Roles in Ancient Civilizations: A Reference Guide*, Greenwood Press, pp 87–88.

8. *The Wisdom of the East—The Instruction of Ptah-Hotep and The Instruction of Ke'Gemini: The Oldest Books in the World*, translated from Egyptian with an introduction by Battiscombe Gunn, London, p. 50.

9. Elizabeth Rose, 2015, *The Pandora Curse*, Book 4, Createspace Independent Pub.

10. Robert Fagles (tr.), 1990, *The Iliad*, Penguin Classics.

11. Pamela Milne, 1989, 'Genesis from Eve's Point of View',

Washington Post, 26 March, https://www.washingtonpost.com/archive/opinions/1989/03/26/genesis-from-eves-point-of-view/dc371184-1f4c-4142-ac2d-d5efee72a0da/.

12. Elizabeth Cady Stanton, 1974, *The Woman's Bible*, Washington, p. 26.

13. M.K. Gandhi, *The Complete Works of Mahatama Gandhi*, Vol. 70: October 21, 1936—February 24, 1937, p. 1, Gandhi Sevagram Ashram, https://www.gandhiashramsevagram.org/gandhi-literature/mahatma-gandhi-collected-works-volume-70.pdf.

14. K.D. Gangrade, 'Gandhi and Empowerment of Women—Miles to Go', https://www.mkgandhi.org/articles/Gangrade.htm.

15. 'Soumya Murder: CM Remark has City Fuming', *The Times of India*, 3 October 2008.

16. Carry P. Meek, 1996, 'Talking Points: To The International Union Of Police Unions (AFL-CIO)', http://gos.sbc.edu/m/meek.html.

17. Annie Karni, 2015, 'Hillary's Hair: She's in on the Joke', *The Politico*, https://www.politico.com/story/2015/05/hillary-clinton-hair-118381.

18. 'Standing Up for Gender Equality this IWD', 6 March 2018, https://sevenwomen.org/blog/2018/03/07/standing-up-for-gender-equality-this-iwd.

19. Kahlil Gibran, 'On Children'.

20. *Manusmriti*, Chapter V, Verse 168.

21. *Manusmriti*, quoted by Madhava and Vidyanatha Dikshita; Parasara; Narada; Yagnavalkya; *Agni Purana*.

22. *Manusmriti*, Chapter IX, Verse 80.

23. *Manusmriti*, quoted by Madhava and several other scholars.

24. *Manusmriti*, Chapter IX, Verse 79.

25. *Manusmriti*, Chapter IX, Verse 76 and several others.

26. Naresh Rout, 2016, 'Role of Women in Ancient India', *Odisha Review*, January, p. 42.

27. Joanna Baillie, 1849, *'Ahalya Baee—A Poem'*, printed for Private Circulation by Spottiswoodes & Shaw, London.

28. Antonia Fraser, 1989, *The Warrior Queens*, Alfred A Knopf, pp. 294–295.

29. V.S. Srinivasa Sastri, 1949, *Lectures on the Ramayana*, Madras Sanskrit Academy, pp. 347–401.

30. https://gdanderson.com.

Epilogue

1. Karl Marx and Frederick Engels, 1969, *Marx and Engels Collected Works*, Vol. 1, Progress Publishers, pp. 13–15.

2. 'Declaration of Independence', Provisional Government of Israel, Official Gazette No. 1, Tel Aviv, https://m.knesset.gov.il/EN/About/Pages/Declaration.aspx.

3. 'The Chinese People Have Stood-up', Opening Address by Mao Zedong, Chairman, Chinese Communist Party, First Plenary Session of the Chinese People's Political Consultative Conference, 21 September 1949, https://china.usc.edu/Mao-declares-founding-of-peoples-republic-of-china-chinese-people-have-stood-up.

4. Constituent Assembly of India Debates (Proceedings), Vol. VII, Parliament of India, 4 November 1948, http://loksabhaph.nic.in/Debates/cadebatefiles/C04111948.html.

5. Deen Dayal Upadhyay, 1961, 'Retention of English Will Lead to a Class between Rulers and Ruled', *Organiser*, 23 October.

6. Constituent Assembly of India Debates (Proceedings), Vol. VII, Parliament of India, 4 November 1948, http://loksabhaph.nic.in/Debates/cadebatefiles/C04111948.html.

7. Niccolo Machiavelli, 1966, *The Prince*, translated by Daniel Donno, Bantam Books, p. 7.

8. Hourly History, 2017, *Vladimir Lenin: A Life from Beginning to End*, Independently published.

9. Roger Butterfield, 1947, *The American Past: A History of the United States from Concord to Hiroshima, 1775–1945*, The University of Virginia, p. 456.

10. Harry Truman, 1945, 'Address in San Francisco at the Closing Session of the United Nations Conference', 26 June, Harry S. Truman Library and Museum, https://www.trumanlibrary.gov/library/public-papers/66/address-san-francisco-closing-session-united-nations-conference.

11. Harry Truman, 1950, 'Address by President Harry S Truman to UN General Assembly', 24 October, US Department of State, https://2009-2017.state.gov/p/io/potusunga/207324.htm.

12. Donald Trump, 2019, 'Remarks by President Trump to the 74th Session of the United Nations General Assembly', 25 September, https://ml.usembassy.gov/remarks-by-president-trump-to-the-74th-session-of-the-united-nations-general-assembly/.

Index